MS. Bodleian 1059 (Laud Misc. 656), f. 2a

The Siege of Jerusalem

EDITED FROM MS. LAUD. MISC. 656
WITH VARIANTS FROM ALL OTHER EXTANT MSS.

BY

E. KÖLBING, Ph.D.

AND

MABEL DAY, D.Lit.

LONDON:
PUBLISHED FOR THE EARLY ENGLISH TEXT SOCIETY
BY HUMPHREY MILFORD, OXFORD UNIVERSITY PRESS
AMEN HOUSE, E.C. 4.
1932.

OXFORD
UNIVERSITY PRESS

Great Clarendon Street, Oxford OX2 6DP
United Kingdom

Oxford University Press is a department of the University of Oxford.
It furthers the University's objective of excellence in research, scholarship,
and education by publishing worldwide. Oxford is a registered trade mark of
Oxford University Press in the UK and in certain other countries

© The Early English Text Society 1932

The moral rights of the authors have been asserted

Database right Oxford University Press (maker)

First Edition published in 1932

All rights reserved. No part of this publication may be reproduced,
stored in a retrieval system, or transmitted, in any form or by any means,
without the prior permission in writing of Oxford University Press,
or as expressly permitted by law, or under terms agreed with the appropriate
reprographics rights organization. Enquiries concerning reproduction
outside the scope of the above should be sent to the Rights Department,
Oxford University Press, at the address above

You must not circulate this book in any other form
and you must impose this same condition on any acquirer

Published in the United States of America by Oxford University Press
198 Madison Avenue, New York, NY 10016, United States of America

British Library Cataloguing in Publication Data
Data available

Library of Congress Cataloging in Publication Data
Data available

Original Series, 188

ISBN 978-0-85-991923-4

PREFATORY NOTE

THIS edition of the *Siege of Jerusalem* was begun by Professor E. Kölbing, for whom the text, with the variant readings, was set up in 1898, when pp. 1–32 were printed off. It has now been completed by Dr. Mabel Day, who has revised the text and provided an Introduction, Notes and Glossary.

A. W. P.

CONTENTS

	PAGE
INTRODUCTION	vii
TEXT	1
APPENDIX I (corrections in ll. 1–580)	79
APPENDIX II (extract from the *Vindicta Salvatoris*)	83
APPENDIX III (extract from the *Polychronicon*)	86
NOTES	91
GLOSSARY	107
INDEX OF PROPER NAMES	133

INTRODUCTION

I. The Manuscripts.

There are seven manuscripts of the *Siege of Jerusalem* :—

(i) Bodleian 1059 (Laud Misc. 656, printed here and denoted by L), ff. 1b–19a, a vellum MS. of the early fifteenth century. It also contains a C text of *Piers Plowman*, and is described (with a facsimile) by Skeat in E.E.T.S. O.S. 54, pp. xxiv–xxx. The size of the page is $8\frac{1}{8}$ in. by $5\frac{5}{8}$ in. The first gathering comprises ff. 0–13, the second ff. 14–25. On the reverse of f. 0 is written, in a fifteenth-century hand :

" Ete, drynke, slepe lasse, loue masse,
Wake, wepe, bid[d]e, faste,
lete lustes passe, be man, noȝt hors noþer asse."

Below this, in a different hand of about the same period, is the following Latin note :

{Mercurius habet iiij^{or}\} regit cum virgine dominatur aque
{condiciones   } loquitur facunde manet cum sole.

The first *condicio* states that the 'exaltation' of Mercury is in Virgo (see Skeat, *Chaucer*, V. p. 310, and *Confessio Amantis*, vii. 1085); the second, Mr. Steele tells me, refers to Mercury as the 'lord of the principle of fluidity'; the others need no explanation. For a further account of the MS. see Skeat, *Piers Plowman* C, E.E.T.S. 54, pp. xxiv–xxx.

(ii) Brit. Mus. Add. 31042 (denoted by A), the Thornton MS., of the mid-fifteenth century, on paper $10\frac{1}{2}$ in. by $7\frac{1}{2}$ in., with about 40 lines to the page. It is divided by the heading 'Passus' before ll. 441, 633, 893 and 1109, and an initial capital. This capital is also found in ll. 25, 49 and 264. Ll. 289–374 are missing. At the foot of the page containing ll. 375–410 is written in a different but contemporary hand, "Vnde versus : Pluribus intentus Minorum est in singula sensus." There is a facsimile, giving the last lines of the *Siege*, with a description of the MS., in E.E.T.S. E.S. 35.

(iii) Brit. Mus. Cotton Vesp. E. xvi (denoted by V), an incomplete vellum MS. of the fifteenth century, 8½ in. by 5¾ in., with about 30 lines to the page, and beginning at l. 962. It has capitals in blue and red at ll. 1021 and 1109, and the heading 'Septim*us* passus' before the latter.

(iv) Brit. Mus. Cotton Calig. A. ii. (denoted by C), a paper MS. of the mid-15th century, 8¼ in. by 5¾ in., with 39–44 lines to the page. The beginning of each quatrain is marked in the left-hand margin, but mechanically, so that the poem is made to end on the third line of a quatrain. Space is left at the beginning for an initial, otherwise the poem runs straight on. The beginnings of Passus III to VII are marked and numbered at ll. 441, 635, 734, 893, 1109,[1] but there is no indication at l. 301. These and the quatrain marks may well be later additions. A page has been lost, containing ll. 163–244. Ll. 110, 484, 742, 1014, 1218, and the line following l. 608 are ticked in the margin, and 'no*ta*' is written against ll. 893, 922, 1171. The MS. is described by Dr. E. Rickert in *Emaré*, E.E.T.S. E.S. 99, p. ix.

(v) Camb. Univ. Mm. 5. 14 (denoted by U), a vellum MS. of the 15th century, 10 in. by 6⅞ in., with about 32 lines to the page. It is divided into a Prologue (not named) and seven Passus, each with its number and beginning with a blue initial at ll. 185, 301, 441, 633, 734, 893, 1109. It is also divided by § marks, alternately blue and red, into 8-line stanzas, some defective through missing lines, *e.g.* ll. 157–63. A four-line stanza occurs in ll. 173–6, in order that a new stanza may begin the first Passus. Since Passus V begins at l. 734, the scribe makes a stanza of ll. 724–32 and omits l. 733. Ll. 741–68, containing the account of the arming of Vespasian in 37 lines, are not divided. After f. 203*b* the § marks cease, and are replaced by a tick in the margin.

(vi) Lambeth Palace 491 (denoted by D), a paper MS. of the first half of the fifteenth century, with the outside and inside leaves of each gathering of 16 ff. in vellum, 8¾ in. by 5¼ in., with about 31 lines to the page. It is divided by § marks into stanzas of various lengths.

(vii) Ashburnham 130, now in the Huntington Library (denoted by E), a vellum MS. of the fifteenth century, 9⅝ in. by 6⅝ in., with 53 to 59 lines to the page. It is divided by red capitals at ll. 185, 441, 633, 734, 893, 949, 1109 and 1173. It is also divided by red § marks into quatrains. These are often defective, where lines have

---

[1] The Passus number is generally written in the right-hand margin of the preceding line, but it follows the line itself in l. 635, which begins a page, and l. 1109, apparently because a correction had been made to the right of l. 1108.

Introduction. ix

been omitted. Many of the single lines added in E rectify irregular quatrains, *e.g.* the lines following ll. 73, 79, 213, 216, and were probably added with this purpose. For a description of the contents of the MS. see Sotheby's Catalogue, May 1st, 1899, p. 44.

From the description of the MSS. it will have been noted that the poem, like *Patience, Cleanness* and *St. Erkenwald,* was originally divided into quatrains,[1] and that this division was recognized by scribes. Though the poet occasionally wrote an irregular group, *e.g.* ll. 729-33, 893-8, 1137-42, he immediately rectified the metre. This is a useful guide in deciding the authenticity of lines not found in all texts. One may, for example, be fairly certain that the six-line group, ll. 1325-30, found in L alone, is a later addition. In the same way, the line following l. 1300 is rejected (see the Note), and ll. 679 and 876 are added.

None of the MSS. is directly descended from any other (though A and V are very closely connected); all have individual omissions. An important indication of their descent, however, is the division of the poem into parts. In L large capitals are placed after ll. 440, 892, and 1108, each of which ends with an invocation, as 'now blesse vs our lorde.' This was evidently the original division. In A each of these divisions is headed by the word 'Passus.' An additional division is made before l. 633. There may also have been one at l. 301, where a passage is omitted. V, a fragment beginning at l. 962, heads l. 1109 'septimus passus.' Of the four MSS. CUDE, which form a group, U shows the whole of this arrangement. It is divided into a Prologue and seven numbered Passus, which begin at ll. 185, 301, 441, 633, 734, 893, 1109. That this is the original division is very unlikely, since at l. 734 it falls at a place where the quatrains have gone wrong; again, the break between ll. 184 and 185 does not seem logical. C is divided almost mechanically into quatrains; as no account is taken of omissions, they are very often wrong. Hence the scribe omits Passus Secundus, which would fall on the third line of a quatrain, and postpones Passus Quartus to l. 635. The fifth

[1] The discovery that the lines of this poem, as well as of some others, are arranged in quatrains, is due to Kaluza (see *Englische Studien,* XVI. 169-80). His further theory, that the quatrains are grouped into twelve-line stanzas, which are again combined in groups of three to form a 36-line stanza, and that the poem itself is divided into three parts, each containing twelve great stanzas, cannot be maintained in face of the MS. evidence now available (see *Englische Studien,* LXVI, 245-8).

Passus he allows to fall on the second line of a quatrain; but at the sixth, which would have fallen on the third line, he starts numbering afresh. The passage containing l. 185 is missing. D has no numbered sections, but is divided into paragraphs of various lengths from 2 to 80 lines. There are none at ll. 301 or 734. E is divided by capital letters at ll. 185, 441, 633, 893 and 1109. There are none at ll. 301 or 734, but they are also found at ll. 949, 1173 (which correspond with paragraph beginnings in D).

The evidence, therefore, points to an original division into four parts, represented by L, and a further splitting up into eight, begun in A by divisions which respect the quatrains, complete in VCU (except that VC may not have had a Prologue), and with vestiges remaining in the capitals in E.

The group CUDE is marked by certain characteristics. All these MSS. omit ll. 209–10 (C has lost a whole page here), 69–70, 83–4, 313–16, 405, 407, 722, 769, 1226. These passages are found in LA, except 313–16 where A is defective, and the last is in V (which only begins at l. 962). All place ll. 39–40 after l. 34, against LA, and have a different line from LA in l. 960. Of the four C is the nearest to LAV in having ll. 853–8 and 987–8, which UDE omit. Also, DE alone omit ll. 82, 608, and change the order in ll. 114–16.

In the group LAV, L alone contains ll. 1232–6,[1] and it also gives better readings in ll. 328, 684, 836 (see Glossary and Notes on these passages). We may, therefore, represent the relationship of the MSS. somewhat as in the following diagram:

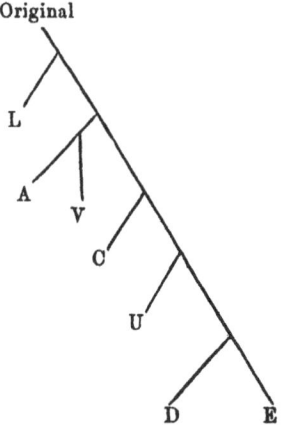

[1] Ll. 1325–30, as stated above, are probably a later addition.

Introduction. xi

There also seems to have been some cross-connection between C and AV. In ll. 1165–6, A's substitution of 'knawen' for 'aspyede' seems to have been the cause of V's omitting 1165*b* and 1166*a*. C follows this, though UD have the lines much as in L. Again, the line following 1223 is in AVC alone, as is 1308. The latter is surely authentic, though it is difficult to see why both L and UDE have lost it; the former I have rejected, mainly because of the quatrains. The omission of ll. 1232–6, or some of them, in all MSS. but L seems to have arisen from an early scribe skipping from 'helde,' l. 1233, to 'hadde,' l. 1236. C omitted l. 1233 also for the sake of the sense. The original of AV omitted ll. 1232–3, considering both sense and quatrain division (having inserted, for the sense, the line following 1228). The C scribe who collated with an AV manuscript, though he took this line, did not omit l. 1232.

A few other passages may be noted. L. 743 is omitted in EU alone. But U has made the mistake through substituting 'wede' for 'clopes' in l. 742; DE have not done this; the joint omission is therefore a coincidence. L. 814 is omitted in AU. But U has paraphrased ll. 813–14 into one line, keeping the word 'syde(s).' He therefore had l. 814 before him, and the omission is again due to coincidence. In ll. 974–5 LDE and AVCU have different orders; the latter is the better, and is adopted here. Possibly in both cases 'tille' attracted 'toured toun' by force of alliteration.

II. THE DIALECT.

(*a*) Facts deduced from the alliteration.[1]

The most important evidence as to the original dialect of the *Siege* is to be found in the alliteration, as this is least affected by scribal alterations. French *h* mute alliterates with vowels, *e.g.* ll. 5, 565, 994, etc., *h* aspirate with English *h*, *e.g.* ll. 19, 510, etc. Neither of these ever alliterate with a vowel. This agrees with the use in *Troy Book, Wars of Alexander* and *Morte Arthure* against *William of Palerne, Piers Plowman* and the *Gawain* group.

The alliteration of *w* and *wh* is found three times only: ll. 197, 348, 465, otherwise they are kept separate; this agrees as above. *Wh* and *qu* alliterate in l. 11, and possibly in ll. 503 and 622. This

---

[1] See K. Schumacher, *Studien über den Stabreim in der mittelenglischen Alliterationsdichtung, Bonner Studien* XI, from which the details concerning the other poems mentioned here are taken.

Introduction.

alliteration is common in *Troy Book*, and is found in *Wars of Alexander*, but only occurs twice in the whole of *Morte Arthure*, twice in the *Parlement of the Thre Ages*, and in no other poems.

Sh and *S* alliterate only in ll. 315, 1329 (the latter perhaps by another hand). This alliteration belongs to the more southern poems, *William of Palerne*, *Piers Plowman* and *Richard the Redeless*. In one point the *Siege* stands apart from all others except the *Alexander Fragments*, it contains no liaison alliteration.

The words *give* and *again* alliterate on either hard or spirant *g*; cp. ll. 274, 343, 948, 1142, 1159, 1215 with 646, 1083. *Get* has hard *g* only: ll. 26, 921, 1176, 1215. *Kirk* is found in ll. 236 and 255, and probably *church* in l. 139. *ʒat* (= gate) always begins with a spirant. Final -*n* in the infinitive is necessary to the metre in ll. 351, 427, 937, 1135, etc. *Hem* (= them) alliterates in l. 1310.

This evidence points to a Midland dialect of a more northerly type than *Piers Plowman* or even the *Gawain* group, a little south of *Troy Book*, and approaching most nearly to *Morte Arthure*.[1] The Northern dialect itself is ruled out by the last two points mentioned, and probably by the discrimination between *qu* and *wh*.

(b) Phonology of L. The phonology of this MS. is exceedingly confused, with characteristic forms from all parts of the West Midlands, and also from the South-east. The principal points are summarized below:

$\bar{a} > \bar{\varrho}$. The only exception is *man*, 166. Probably the scribe took it to be the W.M. spelling of OE. *mann*.

$\bar{æ}$, of whatever origin, is generally shortened to *a*: (OE. $\bar{a} + i$) *lafte(n)*, 185, 302, 437, 568, 603, 632, 983, 1245; *clansed*, 241; *ladde*, 435, 1133, 1156; *sprad*, 486; *brad*, 599; (ON. $\bar{æ}$) *atle*, 366, 379; (PG. $\bar{æ}$) *adradde*, 459; *radde*, 478; *lat*, 495, 509; *brad*, 1090. It is shortened to *e* in *redden*, 591; *lefte*, 595, 928; *ledde*, 892.

ÿ is generally unrounded, but often remains (generally after a labial or before *r*): *bruneys*, 955, 1119, 1238; *brused*, 722; *brutned*, 1235; *burde*, 100; *burie*, *busy*, 568; *churche*, 139; *cupe*, 38; *fur*, 415, 530, etc.; *furst*, 858; *fuste*, 1027, 1140; *gult*, 1159; *kuppe*, 90; *luper*, 149, 946, 1072; *mulle*, 1286; *prudely*, 759; *prute*, 138; *sup*, 13, 334. *Myche(l)* is always unrounded.

y > *e* in *bretnes*, 1128; *crepel*, 1029; *ferste*, 429, 831; *leften*, 279;

---

[1] Cp. S. O. Andrew, *The Dialect of Morte Arthure*, *Review of English Studies*, IV. pp. 418-23, where *Morte Arthure* is assigned to the N. W. Midland.

Introduction. xiii

scherte, 348, 1238; *lestenyþ*, 488; *yþrelled*, 1117. French *u*>*e* in *rede*, 55; *rebies*, 1250.

a before length-groups regularly >*o*; but remains in *þrange*, 17, and the compouhds *hand-whyle*, 168; *hande-darte*, 812; and consequently in *hande*, 347, 444.

a before a nasal remains, but >*o* in *bonke*, 290, 636, 663, 665, 774; *mony*, 431 (but regularly *many*); *blonkes*, 521, 695; *donked*, 624; *dommyn*, 681; *þonkeþ*, 1051, 1209. The forms in -*nk* may be southeastern.

AN. *a* before *n* in a closed syllable >*au* : *auntred*, 147; *daunsyng*, 851; *chaunce*, 883; *chaunge*, 1020; but has been monophthongized again before *m* : *jambers*, 1114; *lampe*, 1256.

ea, *æ* regularly >*a*; but *e* in *wecche*, 382, 732 (cp. *wacche*, 728); *derst*, 1255; and shortened from *ĕa* in *cheffare*, 1314. On the other hand, note *stap*, 601; *waried*, 1076, from Anglian *æ* for mutation *e*; and *fale*, 926, from OE. *feala*. ON. *kasta* generally becomes *kest*, 641, 675, etc., but *kast*, 944.

ēo is generally unrounded, but the following rounded forms occur: *sulf*, 2; *suþ*, 13, 151, etc.; *wolcon*, 53; *ful*, 61; *burne*, 221, etc.; *storte*, 575; note also the French *pople*, 230.

WS. *īe*>*ū̆*, *ī̆* : *hure*, 886, 1097; *rich*, 790.

WS. *sel*->*syl*- *sil*- in *sille*, 1307.

French *ū̆* is written *ew* in *jewes*, 266; *jewyse*, 349.

weor is regularly written *wor*, except *werke*, 986, etc.; also *worke*, 178, 676. *Swerd*, 317, etc. is from *eo* lengthened.

wo + liquid>NWM. *war* in *warpiþ*, 779 (or from ON.*a*).

e>*i* : *kirnels*, 682; *chyuentayn*, 364, 731; *frytted*, 814.

i>*e* : *clef*, 102; *resen*, 899; *reuer*, 887; *schedered*, 558, 1117.

Northern spellings are : *doil*, 248; *deil*, 641, 712, etc.; *doylful*, 159, 222; *steil*, 522.

The following consonantal forms may be noted : *ld*>*lt* in *vnmylt*, 556; *wh* for *w* in *whyʒtly*, 617; *whiʒt*, 348; *ch* for *sh* in *chertes*, 1238; *f* for *v* in *a-fowe*, 199; *sch* for *sk* in *schye*, 633.

The chief forms to be noted in the accidence are :

Noun : gen. s. *fader*, 1025. Gen. pl. -*en, jewen*, 4, 82; *þornen*, 17; *waspen(e)*, 32, 34; wk. pl. *ton*, 840.

Adjective : comp. *spakloker*, 784.

Pronoun : 3rd s. fem. nom. *ʒo*, 101, 104, 1078; pl. nom. *þey*, 15, etc.; *hy*, 1295; gen. *her*, 140, etc.; obj. *hem*, 20, etc., alliterating in 1310.

xiv *Introduction.*

Verb: inf. *-e*, sometimes *-en, clateren,* 54; *seken,* 293; generally for metrical reasons, *e.g.* 351, 427, 701, 937, 1135; *-y, sauy,* 972. Pr. p. *-ande,* sometimes *-ing; growyng,* 40; *wepyng,* 1093; *syngyng,* 1333. Pp. *-e, cloue,* 822; *be,* 834; also *-en, bonden, beten,* 10; *ge-* retained in *yloued,* 145; *ynempned,* 161; *yschot,* 281; *ycasteled,* 286; *yþrelled,* 1117. Ind. pr. 3 s. *-eth,* 51, 53, etc.; *-es, -is,* 78, 537, 565, 794, 866, (?) 862; pl. *-e(n),* 254, 366, 369, 375, etc.; *-eth, beþ,* 365, 796; *willeþ,* 377, (?) *carieþ,* 255; *tyeþ,* 619; *scheweþ,* 863; *-es,* 779, 780. Imp. pl. *-eþ, -iþ,* 368, 769, etc. Mutation form preserved in *dest,* 996.

(c) Phonology of A and V. A is of a distinctly Northern type. OE. *ā* commonly remains: *sarere, draue, rase, thase, maa, twa* (also *two*); before length groups, *byhalde, handis, lande, langede;* also *strong, hondis.* Northern spellings are *whaym, vale* (=veil), *laythe,* adj., *hare* (=hair). *Taulde* (=told) occurs once or twice. OE, ON. *ō* is sometimes written *u; tuke, gude, sture.* OE. *eo, y* are always *e, i.* Unstressed *sc>s* in *sal, solde,* though forms in *sch-* are also found. Pronominal forms are *scho, þay, þaire, þa(i)m.* The verbal endings are all northern.

V is North Midland. OE. *ā>ō; stone, brood, goos; a* before nasals remains: *biganne, thankes, man.* OE. *y* regularly *>i,* but occasionally *u, e: luste, left, ouer-telt.* The pronouns are *she, þei, here, þeire, hem, þem.* The endings of the verb are pr. 3 s. *-es,* pl. *-en,* imp. pl. *-es,* pr. p. *-and.*

(d) Phonology of CUDE. These are for the most part of an East Midland type. In C OE. *y* generally *>i,* but forms in *e* are also found: *bregge, cherche, feest, thresten,* and invariably *leften,* to lift. *Myche* is the regular form, but *moche* and *mykell* also occur. WM. *mony* is occasionally found; *ur* is found regularly for *-er* in *(n)evur, ovur, aftur.* The verbal endings are EM., with pr. p. in *-iry;* southern plurals are *assayleth, seythe, doth.* The change of *ę̄* to *ī* is shown in the forms *behylden* (pt. pl.), *shylde, ʒylde* (imp. s.).

A peculiarity of this MS. is the use of *th* for *d* or *t: unþur, sythes* (sides), *þefende, brothe, þounther, be-tythe* (betide); *betheth* (beateth), *bitheth* (biteth). The reverse spelling is found in *wordy* for *worthy.*

U shows a few North-west Midland traces in terminations. The pr. p. is generally in *-and,* but occasionally in *-ing.* Pr. 2 s. is *-es,* 3rd s. *-eth* and less often *-es;* pl. no ending, except *metes,* 59, and *assaileth,* 798; imp. pl. *-es* or nothing. The vowels are EM., unless *yknawen,* 156 and *clay* (= cloth), 167 are Northern forms.

Introduction. xv

D is East Midland with certain South-eastern characteristics. ǣ is generally shortened to *e*, as *left, ledden*, but *a* is sometimes found: *laften, rad* (pt. s.). *Y* regularly >*i*, as *mych, chirche, thrist* (thrust), but *e* in *festes, left* (≐ lifted). *Wlonk, thonkid* may also be South-eastern forms. *Tul* is the invariable form for 'till.' The pr. 3 s. is *-eth*, and only occasionally *-es*; the pr. p. is always *-ing*.

E is East Midland with several SE. and SW. forms. *Y* generally >*i*, but there are many forms in *e* or *u* : *meche* (regularly), *lether, besy, heued, feer, dude* and often *dode, wommen*. *Weor-* >*wur* : *wurthi, wurld, wurk*; *eo* remains rounded in *wolkyn*; *sigge* and *ʒuldying* are SW. forms; *h* is often added initially and after *w* : *whiʒtly, while, harmes, herthe, hende*, etc., and often omitted in *undred*. The conjugation of the verb is as in Chaucer; the pp. never takes *-n*, and often prefixes *y-*. Lengthening of *i, u* in open syllables appears in *leeue, weele, smeete* (pp.), and the pt. pl. forms *stredyn, resyn, reedyn*; *soone*. *O* is written *u* after *w* : *wurd, wuxe, wusschen*. The frequent spelling *fook* for 'folk' may be noticed.

(*d*) Conclusion. We have seen that the evidence of the alliteration and metre point to the North Midland as the original dialect. The only MS. which shows a Northern dialect is A; probably the original from which V and the CUDE group descend did not. These latter are all East Midland, with some forms from adjoining dialects. L, which stands alone in containing passages omitted from all the others, and preserving the original division into four parts, has a large WM. element and shows certain traces of having passed through a NWM. dialect. It alone has the unvoiced form *vnmylt* and the pronoun ʒo, and its preservation of unrounded OE. *mān* suggests that some scribe has altered *o* before a nasal to *a* through the poem (see p. xii). It seems the more likely, therefore, that the original dialect was the North-west Midland.

III. The Growth of the Legend.

The mediæval legend which combined the story of the siege of Jerusalem by Titus with that of the Holy Vernicle grew up from different sources. These have been fully investigated by Prof. E. von Dobschütz,[1] to whose work the reader is referred; nothing is attempted

---

[1] *Christusbilder*, Gebhart and Harnack, *Texte und untersuchungen zur geschichte der altchristlichen literatur, Neue Folge*, Bd. III, 1899. See also the Introduction to *Titus and Vespasian*, ed. J. A. Herbert, Roxburghe Club, 1905, for a short summary of the forms of the legend which affect that poem.

here beyond an indication of those writings which seem to have formed the basis of our poem. In the Latin prose *Cura Sanitatis Tiberii*[1] the emperor Tiberius, who is gravely ill, sends the chief priest Volusian to Jerusalem in search of Jesus Christ. Volusian, finding that Christ is dead, arrests Pontius Pilate. He then hears that Veronica has a likeness of Christ; he returns to Rome, bringing with him Veronica, the likeness, and Pilate. Pilate is tried and banished, later (according to some MSS.) committing suicide; Tiberius is cured by the portrait, and becomes a Christian. This story is said by Dobschütz to have arisen in the sixth century.

Next comes the Latin prose *Vindicta Salvatoris*,[2] said by Dobschütz to have been probably composed in Aquitaine about the year 700, and translated into Anglo-Saxon about the eleventh century.[3] It tells how in the time of Tiberius Cæsar Titus ruled over Aquitaine at Bordeaux, and suffered from cancer in the face. Nathan the son of Naum, bringing tribute from Jerusalem to Tiberius, was driven by storm to Bordeaux. He was brought before Titus, who asked if he knew any cure for his malady. Nathan knew of none, but told him of the prophet whose name was Jesus Christ, and of his miracles (including the healing of Veronica from an issue of blood) and slaughter by the Jews. When Titus denounced the emperor Tiberius, under whose rule such a crime had been committed, he was suddenly healed. He then vowed vengeance on the enemies of Christ, and sent to his brother Vespasian (whom the Anglo-Saxon calls his 'fyrdgemaca') in Italy for aid. They invaded Judea, whereupon the kings and princes of that land were struck with fear. Archelaus slew himself, and Pilate shut himself up in Jerusalem, where the Jews suffered the last extremities of famine. When the city had fallen, Titus and Vespasian took Pilate, and asked him how he had not feared to slay the Son of God. Pilate replied that the Jews had condemned him, and that he did not dare to release him. One of his disciples sold him for thirty pieces of silver. He was scourged, pierced with the spear, and laid in the sepulchre. Titus and Vespasian said that they would do with the Jews as the Jews had done to Christ. Some they slew by scourging, some by the sword, some by crucifixion. Vespasian said,

---

[1] Ed. Dobschütz, p. 163**. There is an English prose version in Brit. Mus. MS. Harl. 149.

[2] Ed. Tischendorf, *Evangelia Apocrypha*, 1876, pp. 471-86. See Appendix II for the earlier part of the story.

[3] C. W. Goodwin, *The Anglo-Saxon Legends of St. Andrew and St. Veronica*, Cambridge Antiquarian Society, 1851.

Introduction. xvii

"What shall we do with those who remain?" Titus said, "They sold our Lord for thirty silver pieces, and we will give thirty Jews for one silver piece." And so they did. Then they inquired if there were any picture of Christ, heard of one which Veronica possessed, and forced her to give it up. They sent it and Pilate to Tiberius; Veronica went with them. Tiberius was healed by the Vernicle, Pilate was brought before him, and sentenced to imprisonment in Vienne on the Rhone. Tiberius ordered that no one should give him any cooked food,[1] and for many days he was fed on 'arbusta' (possibly an error for 'arbuta'), honey and cheese. After many days' imprisonment, he asked his jailer if he might come into the light. Seeing that his skin was black, like that of one burnt in the fire, he asked for an apple, and then for a knife with which to peel it. When this was given to him, he stabbed himself in the breast and died. The people of Vienne buried him outside the city, but the earth threw up his body. Then they built him a tomb in an old wall, but those who passed by caught chills and trembling fits which brought them to death. They sank his body in the Rhone, with the result that the ships were tempest-tossed and sunk. Then, after three days' prayer and fasting, they extracted his body from the water, enclosed it in a barrel and sent it down the river, where a rock opened and received it.[2]

The preceding account summarises the story as it is told in three British Museum MSS. of the late thirteenth and early fourteenth centuries, Roy. 8 E. xvii, Roy. 9 A. xiv, and Harl. 495, the first part of which is printed in Appendix II. It differs materially from Tischendorf's text, and stands much nearer to our poem. Apart from small points mentioned in the Notes to ll. 41, 56, 88, 164, it agrees with the *Siege* in ignoring the Volusian story of the *Cura*, in its description of the trial of Pilate taking place before Titus, and in the account of his death. In the printed text, Titus and Vespasian, having taken Jerusalem, send for Velosian, who takes Veronica and Pilate to Tiberius. Pilate is imprisoned in Damascus, and there is no mention of his death.

The *Vindicta*, therefore, introduces the healing of Titus, though there is yet no mention of Vespasian as a sufferer.[3] It unites, in

---

[1] Cp. *Cura Sanitatis Tiberii*, 'coctum ab igne et aqua non comedet.'
[2] This account of the fortunes of Pilate's body, which differs from that in the Latin prose *De Pylato*, is followed in *Titus and Vespasian*, 4411–86.
[3] In the printed text Velosian, who does not appear in the MS., is sent to Jerusalem. When he returns to Tiberius he says, "ego servos inveni Titum et Vespasianum timentes dominum, et mundati sunt ab omnibus ulceribus et passionibus suis" (ed. Tischendorf, p. 483). The Anglo-Saxon stops at 'dominum.'

SIEGE OF JERUSALEM.   *b* defiance of history, the miraculous cure by the Vernicle of the emperor Tiberius with the historical story of the siege. The Latin prose, *De Pylato*,[1] assigned by Dobschütz to the middle of the eleventh century, puts Vespasian, who suffers from wasps in the nose,[2] into the place of Titus, and makes him ruler in Galicia. The messenger is now not the bearer of Jewish tribute, but is sent by Pilate to make his excuses to Tiberius for the death of Christ. The embassy of Volusian and the cure of Tiberius then follow. The life-story of Pilate is given in full; on being sentenced to death, he takes a knife and kills himself. There is no account of the siege.

In the lineage of this prose piece are two other versions which concern us: first, the French chanson de geste, *La Destruction de Jerusalem*,[3] and secondly, the *Legenda Aurea*. In the French poem Vespasian is already emperor at Rome; his seneschal goes to Jerusalem to find a remedy for Vespasian's leprosy and cancer, and to demand from Pilate a rich offering. This Pilate refuses to give, and the seneschal returns to Rome, bringing the portrait and Veronica. At Rome the latter meets St. Clement, tells him the story of her healing, promises to live in future by his counsel, and gives him the Vernicle (ll. 291-347). Vespasian is healed, and in gratitude offers Veronica whatever castle or town in his possession she wishes. She asks him rather to give it to St. Clement, for whatever is hers she will give to him (ll. 350-93). Vespasian and Titus then besiege and take Jerusalem. They return to Rome in triumph, and Pilate is punished.

In the *Legenda Aurea* the part of the story which concerns us is found in the story of St. James the Less (Ch. lxvii).[4] The signs which preceded the siege are enumerated; then follows an account, on the lines of that in *De Pylato*, of how Pilate sent a messenger (called Alban) to Tiberius to clear himself of responsibility for the death of Christ, how the messenger was driven by storm to Vespasian in Galatia, how Vespasian was cured of the plague of wasps and, having got leave from Tiberius, began, in the reign of Nero, to besiege Jerusalem; on being called to Rome to be emperor, he left the leadership to Titus. The

---

[1] Mone, *Anzeiger fur kunde der teutschen vorzeit*, vii, p. 526.
[2] This is the first mention of Vespasian's wasps; see J. A. Herbert, *Titus and Vespasian*, Roxburghe Club, p. xv.
[3] Graf, *Roma nella memoria e nelle immaginazioni del medio evo*, 1882, Vol. I. pp. 429-60.
[4] *Legenda Aurea*, ed. Graesse, p. 298. Ch. lxvii is translated in the Scottish *Legends of the Saints*, ed. W. M. Metcalfe, Scottish Text Society, 1896.

Introduction. xix

story of the siege follows Josephus, but there is added, on the authority of 'a certain apocryphal history' from which the *Legenda* had derived the cure of Vespasian, the story of the ailment of Titus and his cure by Josephus. Finally, as in the *Vindicta Salvatoris*, the captive Jews are sold for thirty a penny.

IV. SOURCES OF THE 'SIEGE OF JERUSALEM.'

When we look at the *Siege of Jerusalem*, we see that four-fifths of the poem are devoted to the siege itself. The preliminary 260 lines, including 28 devoted to the picture of a storm, explain the events which led up to it. It is the tumult of battle, whether of men or of the elements, that interests our author; with the metre of the old pre-conquest poets he has inherited much of their spirit. Hence he makes very little use of the stories of Velosian's embassy to Jerusalem, and of Veronica herself.[1] There is also practically no mention of Pontius Pilate, who plays a very important part in the French poem as a defender in the siege. For the first time, both Titus and Vespasian are healed, the former at Bordeaux, the latter (as in the chanson de geste) at Rome. The material seems to be drawn from three main sources : the *Vindicta Salvatoris*, Higden's *Polychronicon*,[2] and the *Legenda Aurea*.

From the first of these, the first part of which is printed in Appendix II, comes the opening of the poem, ll. 1–8. The words 'zelatus a Tiberio' are altered by the poet, who is too good an historian to connect Tiberius with the siege, to 'þey Sesar sakles were þat oft synne hatide.' Titus and his cancer, the visit of Nathan (though not his mission), the interview between him and Titus, and the latter's cure are from the same source; here again the allusion of Titus to Tiberius is carefully brought into agreement with history.[3] Titus's cancer is in the lip and not in the nose; this may be because the author is going to

[1] The only suggestion of the miraculous origin of the picture is l. 224, " Whan he vnclosed þe cloþe þat *Cristes* body touched ; " cp. 11. 161–4. We may probably trace the influence of the chanson de geste in ll. 209–20 (see Note on l. 213). In both poems, an embassy is sent to claim tribute from Pilate, and to bring some object which will heal Vespasian. The embassy succeeds in the latter aim, but not in the former. There is also an allusion in ll. 217–20 to the episode between Veronica and St. Clement (ll. 380 ff.). There may be in the dying words of Nero, ll. 913–14, a recollection of the last speech of Archelaus, son of Herod, before he killed himself, " De ma mort ne seront ia Sarazin vantant," l. 916.
[2] Ed. Babington and Lumby, Rolls Series, 1865–86. See Appendix III.
[3] Cp. p. 84, l. 27–p. 85, l. 4 with ll. 169–84. See also Note on l. 88.

describe Vespasian's malady, and wishes to make a difference. The trial of Pilate before Titus and the manner of his suicide are from the same source,[1] though the latter may come from the *Polychronicon* (Vol. IV. pp. 364, 366).

It is the *Legenda Aurea* which makes Vespasian ruler in Galatia, as is stated in the best MS. of our poem, though the others have corrupted it into Galicia, following the general tradition as given in *De Pylato*. The wasps also, therefore, probably derive from the *Legenda*, not from *De Pylato*. But the most obvious element clearly due to the *Legenda* is the story of Titus's sickness at the siege, and his healing by Josephus.[2] The symptoms of his disease and the manner of its cure in the *Legenda* are as follows: " Titus autem . . . audiens patrem suum in imperium sublimatum, nervorum contractione ex frigiditate corripitur et altero crure debilitatis paralysi torquetur. . . . Quem Titus respiciens molestia conturbatus infremuit et, qui prius gaudio infrigidatus fuerat, accensione furoris incaluit nervosque distendens curatus fuit." This should be compared with ll. 1023-48, especially ll. 1026, 1046-8. Much of the detail of the siege in the *Legenda* is parallel with that of the *Polychronicon*, but the detail that the Jews were reduced to eating the leather of their shoes is omitted by Hidgen (see Note on l. 1071).

According to history, Vespasian himself was never present at the siege of Jerusalem. It is in the *Legenda* that we read how he began the siege himself, and was recalled to Rome to be made emperor (p. 301). From Ch. lxxxix of the *Legenda* our poet took the manner of Nero's death, " Qui videns, quod evadere non posset, fustem dentium morsibus exacuit et se per medium palo transfixit et tali

---

[1] See p. xvii. The apple-knife story is probably an adaptation of the account of Herod's attempted suicide as recorded by Josephus, I. xxxiii. 7. The bare mention of Pilate's suicide is found in Eusebius, *Hist. Eccles.* II. 7. Gregory of Tours (*Hist. Franc.* I) says that Pilate killed himself with his own hands, and similarly by divine vengeance King Herod, the persecutor of the apostles, when struck with disease, took a knife to peel an apple and slew himself. In the fifteenth century Myrc compares the fate of King Herod, who killed himself with a knife as he peeled an apple, with that of Pilate, who smote himself to the heart with a pair of shears that he borrowed to cut his nails with (*Festial*, ed. Erbe, E.E.T.S., E.S. 96, p. 194), and the same object is alleged in a variant reading of *Titus and Vespasian*. In the *Southern Legendary* (Furnivall, *Early English Poems*, Transactions of Philological Society, 1858, p. 117) we find the story as in the *Vindicta*, with the added detail that Pilate, in asking for a knife, said that it was not right for a man of high rank to eat an apple unpared. In MS. Brit. Mus. Add. 37472, an English MS. of the early twelfth century, there is a picture of Herod stabbing himself; an attendant holds the apple, while a devil is carrying off Herod's soul above.

[2] Ll. 1023-48; cp. *Legenda Aurea*, p. 301.

morte vitam finivit" (cp. ll. 909-16), though the detail that he died four miles from Rome is from the *Polychronicon*.

In his Breslau dissertation on this poem, entitled *The Destruction of Jerusalem*, 1887, pp. 31-8, Dr. F. Kopka compared it with the *Bella Judaica* of Josephus and the Christianized paraphrase of this work attributed to Hegesippus, and assigned the latter, together with the *Vindicta*, as our poet's source. But the three passages from Hegesippus on which he relied for proving this point are also found in the *Polychronicon*,[1] and in one of these Higden's version is distinctly nearer. According to Hegesippus, the woman who ate the flesh of her own child said, "reddite matri quod accepistis, redi fili in illut naturale secretum in quo domicilio sumsisti spiritum." Josephus merely says, "Be thou my food." Higden has "Redde vel semel matri quod ab ea sumpsisti. Redi in id secretum a quo existi." Our poet has "ȝeld þat I þe ȝaf & aȝen tourne, & entr per þou cam out," ll. 1083-4. There is no detail of the siege coming ultimately from Josephus which is not found in the short accounts in the *Legenda*, Ch. lxvii, and the *Polychronicon*, IV. x. We may also compare l. 810, 'brente witℏ brennande oyl,' with Higden's 'ardenti olio superjecto . . . exussit' (p. 86, l. 11), against Hegesippus, III. xi. 4, 'ignibus jactis . . . consumsit,' and Josephus, III. vii. 20, 'Quippe arida omni . . . materia accensa.'

The sketch of Roman history from the death of Nero to the election of Vespasian is derived from the *Polychronicon*,[2] with the exception of some details concerning Nero which come from the *Legenda*. The two together account for all his atrocities (ll. 893-8) except the murder of the senators. Possibly here we have a recollection of a line in Metrum VI, Book II of the *Consolation of Philosophy*, 'Urbe flammata, patribusque caesis,' cp. l. 896, 'Senek & þe senatours, & alle þe cite fured.' It is the *Polychronicon* which calls Otho 'Otho Lucius.' I have found no other chronicle which does this, though in the *Historia Miscella*[3] he is called Lucius Salvus Otho. Again, though neither Hegesippus nor Josephus specifically connects Galba's death with Otho, Higden says that Piso and Galba were killed 'insidiis Othonis in medio foro,' and the English translation in MS. Harl. 2261 (printed in the Rolls Series) has, 'thei bothe were sleyne in the markethe place

---

[1] The other two are l. 811, where according to Josephus, Vespasian was wounded 'in planta pedis,' according to Hegesippus and Higden 'in talo'; and l. 1221, where Josephus has 'vacca' and the other two 'vitula.'
[2] Vol. IV. pp. 412-22.
[3] Muratori, *Rerum Italicarum Scriptores*, I. 56.

of Rome by Otho themperour,' pointing to a variant reading represented by l. 926 of our text.¹ The fall of Vitellius, also, is more closely associated with the death of Sabinus than in other accounts: "His Vitellius Vespasianum regnare metuerit, Sabinum fratrem ejus occidit; deinde cum in quandam cellam timide se conclusisset, a ducibus Vespasiani inde protractus," *etc.* The discrepancy in the length of Galba's reign, which is four months in the poem and seven in the *Polychronicon*, may well arise from a scribal error of iij for vij.

In using these sources, our poet's method is of the freest. Though he is a serious historical student, as is seen by his incidental outline of the reigns of Galba, Otho and Vitellius, he sets the truth of poetry above that of history, and manipulates his material at will. In the *Vindicta Salvatoris* he found the vengeance of Christ on the Jews connected with a miracle of the Vernicle displayed on Tiberius, who, in defiance of history, is emperor throughout the siege. In the *Legenda Aurea* Tiberius is healed by the Vernicle; but the siege, in Nero's reign, follows in consequence of the miraculous healing of Vespasian. Our poet combines the two stories by beginning with the healing of Titus as in the *Vindicta*, and then following with the cure of Vespasian through the Vernicle. As this was now preserved as the most precious relic in Rome, it was necessary to make Vespasian's cure take place there. This had already been done in the chanson de geste (see p. xviii), but there Vespasian was already emperor. Our poet invents the detail that Vespasian had left his kingdom of Galatia and come to Rome because of his sickness. Hence he is able to describe the reception of the holy relic in the church, and the falling down of the idols as it passes through the heathen temple, a detail suggested by an incident from the Gospel of the Infancy which he found in the *Alliterative Troy Book*.²

The treatment of the mission of Nathan (called Alban in the *Legenda Aurea*) is worth notice. In the *Legenda* he bears Pilate's excuses to Tiberius for the crucifixion of Christ, an impossible mission in our story, where the reigning emperor is Nero. In the *Vindicta Salvatoris* he is sent with tribute from Jerusalem to Tiberius. This is not consonant with the historical story of the siege which is to follow; but if reversed, it would supply a motive for the Roman expedition. In the *Polychronicon*, just before the story of the siege, our poet read

¹ For other cases in which this MS. most closely resembles our poet's source, see p. xxiv.
² See p. xxvii.

how Cestius, the president (of Syria), wrote to Nero to answer his inquiry as to the number of Jews in Jerusalem.[1] The messenger is therefore sent by Cestius to report that the Jews will not pay tribute. The account of the preparations for the expedition and of the sea-journey to Jaffa is, of course, original. The Syrian campaign is condensed into a lyrically conceived passage. The sign of the emperor, like that of Arthur, is a golden dragon [2] (l. 280), though the Roman eagle appears in l. 326. The incident of the ambassadors is in the same mediæval tradition;[3] the battle in the vale of Jehoshaphat, in which Christ protected his knights from the heathen defenders till compline time (l. 608), fitly stages the beginning of this divine judgment on the Jews in the scene of the last judgment of all. The elephants and dromedaries were probably suggested by the armed elephants with which Antiochus Eupator fought against the Jews (1 *Macc.* vi). In this battle there appears as leader of the third battalion Sir Sabine of Syria,[4] prince of that province (ll. 434-5). He has been evolved from Higden's description of a Roman soldier who was first to scale the wall (see p. 88, ll. 15-21). From this sketch of an 'heroic soul, worthy of eternal praise' is developed the chivalrous leader, friend of Vespasian and first called on to speak at his council of war (l. 971), beloved of Titus and lamented by him in a passage that faintly recalls the fellowship of the Round Table (ll. 1203-4).

The tricks devised by Josephus to frustrate the Romans were used, not at Jerusalem, but at Jotapata. In the course of the Syrian campaign before the siege, Vespasian besieged this town, where Josephus, who was defending Galilee against him, had retired. It was at this siege that Josephus employed the artifices of the wet garments and the sacks of chaff, and here that Vespasian was wounded in the foot. At the end of the siege, Josephus fell into Vespasian's hands, and consequently was with the Roman army outside Jerusalem. Hence he was available to cure Titus of his sickness. But our poet has transferred all these incidents to the siege of Jerusalem. Consequently Josephus is inside the beleaguered town, and we have the

---

[1] See *Polychronicon*, Vol. IV. p. 426.
[2] In the *Alliterative Morte Arthure* also Lucius

'Dresses vp dredfully the dragone of golde
With thegles alouer, enamelede of sable' (ll. 2026-7).

[3] This may have been suggested by 2 *Samuel* x. 4, which accounts for the shaving and stripping, but not for the blackening or the cheeses.
[4] In Josephus, *Bella Judaica*, II, there is much about Sabinus the Procurator of Syria, but he is not mentioned by Hegesippus or Higden.

chivalrous episode of his coming thence to heal the commander of the besieging army (ll. 1031–62).

Two possible reasons may be alleged for this change. It may have been made in the interest of poetic unity, so that the author might describe one siege alone, and yet not waste any material. More probably it is due to a defect in his copy of the *Polychronicon*. For if the name of the town were corrupted or omitted in two places, the whole story would appear to belong to the siege of Jerusalem. Our poet's *Polychronicon* was nearly allied to that from which the translation in MS. Harl. 2261 was made. This has been noted already,[1] and another instance may be seen in the account of Josephus's artifices. In the Latin text, the sacks of chaff were used against the battering-ram, but in the English translation they are used against 'gunnes and ... oþer engynes,' as in our poem against the mangonels. And for the name of the town MS. Harl. 2261 has first 'Ioppen' and secondly 'Ierusalem.' Probably, therefore, our poet had MS. authority for the transference of the incidents. It involves him in difficulty later on; see Note on l. 1153.

V. Connection with 'Titus and Vespasian.'

There remains to be considered the English metrical romance of Titus and Vespasian,[2] the main sources of which its editor considers to be the lost Latin original of the French chanson de geste, the *Legenda Aurea*, the *Gospel of Nicodemus*, and the history of Josephus or Hegesippus. In over 5000 octosyllables it tells first of the Passion and Resurrection of Christ, and of the signs and prophecies of the impending siege. Nathan the Jew, on his way to Rome, is driven to Bordeaux, where Vespasian, sick of both wasps and a cancer, is king. Nathan is brought before his son Titus, and tells him of the miracles of Christ. The steward, Velosian, overhears the account. Nathan goes on to Nero, and presents Pilate's letter of excuse. The poet then tells us the earlier life of Pilate. Velosian goes to Jerusalem, to find a cure for his master, and brings Veronica with the Vernicle to Gascony, where Clement is Pope in St. Peter's stead. Vespasian is healed; he and Titus, with Nero's permission, besiege Rome. The story proceeds much as in the *Siege*, except that Vespasian, after being made emperor as Nero's next-of-kin, returns to Jerusalem. There follows

[1] See pp. xxi–xxii.
[2] Ed. J. A. Herbert, Roxburghe Club, 1905.

Introduction. xxv

the rest of the story of Pilate, with his suicide and all the marvels associated with his body, and the unwieldy romance concludes with the life of Judas Iscariot.

In his Königsberg dissertation on this poem,[1] Dr. F. Bergau says that it seems to him that the *Siege* has derived certain elements from it. The points of contact which he enumerates are the following:

1. Both begin by describing the passion of Christ. This is only natural, considering the subject; the material comes from the Gospels.

2. The punishment of the Jews is delayed for forty years. This comes from the *Legenda Aurea* and the *Polychronicon* (see p. 88, l. 30) and *Legenda* (p. 298).

3. The Nathan story. In *Titus and Vespasian*, Vespasian reigns in Bordeaux as king of Galicia and Gascony; Titus, his son, lives with him, and is not afflicted. Nathan of Judaea, coming with tribute from Pilate to Tiberius, is driven to Bordeaux (ll. 1275–308); the Vernicle is brought there (l. 2152). The only common factor is the arrival of Nathan at Bordeaux, which comes from the *Vindicta Salvatoris*.

4. Various details of the siege. These come from the *Polychronicon*. Generally speaking, they have legendary accretions in *Titus and Vespasian* which are lacking in our poem. For example, Mary shrinks from eating the flesh of her child, whereupon an angel appears and tells her to do so in order to fulfil prophecy (ll. 3459, etc.); the rich Jews do not die of hunger in the siege, because they have ' noble stones of vertu,' which keep them alive (ll. 3483, etc.).

5. The healing of Titus when he fell sick for joy. This we have seen our poet derived from the *Legenda Aurea* (see p. xx). The only detail of the sickness given in *Titus and Vespasian* is that 'hym toke a cardiake For his fader grete honour ' (ll. 3182–3).

6. The Jews swallow their treasure. Here our version follows the *Polychronicon*, which tells this of the deserters who escaped from the city during the siege, and states that their slaughter was ' contra jussum Titi.' But *Titus and Vespasian* connects it with the period after the fall of the city, when Vespasian, who has returned to the siege, sells the Jews for thirty a penny, and gives permission to their buyers to slay them.

7. The signs before the siege. Here the *Siege*, which has only four of the seven signs given by Josephus and Hegesippus, or the six given

---

[1] *Untersuchungen über quelle und verfasser des mittelenglischen reimgedichts, The Vengeance of God's Death*, 1901.

by Higden, keeps almost the same order; *Titus and Vespasian* has quite a different arrangement. The sword, which stands first in Josephus, Hegesippus, Higden, the *Legenda*, and the *Siege*, is seventh in *Titus*, and so on. The last, that of the man on the wall, cannot possibly be derived from *Titus*, as his final words, ' woe to myself also,' l. 1231, are only found in Josephus, Hegesippus and Higden, not in *Titus* or the *Legenda*.

8. The selling of the Jews for thirty a penny. This may come from the *Vindicta Salvatoris*, the *Legenda* or the *Polychronicon*. As we have seen under (6), *Titus* connects this with the gold in a way that the other sources do not.

9. The death of Pilate. In both poems he kills himself with a knife which he has borrowed 'for to paren' a 'pere';[1] cp. *Titus*, ll. 4388–90,

"þat of oon he borwede a knyfe
For to paren a pere—he drogh,
And þerwith hymself he slogh,"

with the *Siege*, ll. 1327–9. In all other versions of this anecdote the fruit is an apple, the story having been adapted from the attempted suicide of Herod the Great recorded by Josephus.[2] It seems a fair inference that the change was due to the exigencies of alliteration— it was not required by the rhyme—and that the author of *Titus* derived the phrase from our poem.

VI. CONNECTION WITH THE 'TROY BOOK.'

Several passages and single lines in our poem are also to be found in the *Alliterative Troy Book*.[3] A comparison with the source of the latter, the *Hystoria Trojana* of Guido delle Colonne, shows that our poet must be the borrower. The longest of these passages is the description of nightfall, ll. 725–33. With this should be compared the *Troy Book*, ll. 7348–55 :

"When the day ouer drogh, & the derk entrid,
The sternes full stithly starond o lofte;
All merknet the mountens & mores aboute;
The ffowles þere fethers foldyn to gedur.

---

[1] In *Titus* the story is referred to the 'Seven Sages' (see Herbert, p. xxv). Is this a mystification of the Lollius type, to disguise borrowing from a contemporary?
[2] *Bella Jud.* I. xxxiii. 7. See footnote on p. xx.
[3] Ed. Panton and Donaldson, E.E.T.S., 39 and 56.

Introduction. xxvii

> Nightwacche for to wake, waites to blow;
> Tore fyres in the tenttes, tendlis olofte;
> All the gret of the grekes gedrit hom somyn.
> Kynges,& knightes clennest of wit."

Our poet has, of course, no original for his quite imaginary account of Vespasian's battles outside Jerusalem, while the *Troy Book* description is evolved from a rather laboured statement in Guido to the effect that, when it grew dark and the stars appeared, the leaders of the Greeks met in Agamemnon's tent.[1] The arid stretches of the *Troy Book* are often diversified by similar passages of nature description, *e.g.* ll. 1051–69, 4029–41, 4583–90, 9636–43, 12463–74, some hint for which is always given in Guido. The opening line of this extract, or some variation of it, is constantly used in the *Troy Book, e.g.* 673, 4664, 4814, 7807–9, etc.

The description of the idols falling as the Vernicle is borne through the heathen temple, l. 235, is found literally in *Troy Book* 4312, ' Bothe Mawhownus & maumettes myrtild in peces,' where it describes the well-known incident in the Gospel of the Infancy when the Holy Family fled to Egypt. It translates *Hystoria Trojana*, III. vi., ' Quo perueniente puero cum matre omnia ydola egipti insimul corruerunt.'

The two final lines of Vespasian's speech to his council, ll. 877–8, are found in *Troy Book* 5170–1 :

> " For þere as failes the fode, faint is the pepull;
> And þere hongur is hote, hertis ben febill."

where they form part of Agamemnon's speech to the Greek leaders, urging that before beginning the siege, they should lay in a store of provisions from Messana. They translate *Hystoria Trojana*, III. x., " Nam sine multo victualium presidio exercitus noster vix posset prodesse." Somewhat similar passages occur in *Troy Book* 9376–7 and 11162, in each case translating Guido.

Vespasian's sleeplessness, ll. 734–6, is reminiscent of Achilles grieving for the disaster to his Myrmidons, *Troy Book* 10096–7 :

> " And lay in his loge, litill he sleppit,
> But wandrit & woke for woo of his buernes."

Cp. *Hystoria Trojana*, VI. ii.

---

[1] *Hyst. Troj.*, IV. iv.

These passages, which all occur in the parts of the *Siege* where our poet is not following any of his historical sources, are enough to show that it was he who borrowed from the *Troy Book*. We may also note ll. 289-90, 532, as compared with *Troy Book* 12489-90, 12496, a description of the departure of the Greek fleet from Troy, following *Hystoria Trojana*, VIII. ii. :

> " Thai past on the pale se, puld vp hor sailes,
> Hadyn bir at þere backe, and the bonke leuyt . . .
> A thoner and a thicke rayne þrublit in the skewes."

Other passages, which might well in both cases derive from the common stock of the alliterative poet, are probably, in view of these more conclusive examples, additional cases of borrowing. They will be found in the Notes on ll. 576, 590, 613, 778, 853-4, 1016, 1288. It will also be noticed that the vocabulary of the two poems is very similar; see in particular the Notes on ll. 54, 65, 804.

In view of this close connection between the two poems, it might be thought that they were by the same hand. This, however, is most unlikely. The metre of both is very regular, but there are certain radical differences. First half-lines of the type $\underline{/}$ x (x) $\underline{/}$ x (x) $\underline{\smallsetminus}$, e.g. *Troy Book*, 1, 'Maistur in mageste,' are very rare in the *Troy Book*; the first 100 lines contain only ll.1, ll. 49, (?) 57. But in the *Siege* they are very frequent, *e.g.* ll. 4, 5, 7, 8, 9, 10, 17, *etc*. Again, in second half-lines of the type (x) $\underline{/}$ x x $/$ x, in the *Siege* the first foot is often filled by a dissyllabic word with final -e (generally omitted by the scribe), *e.g.* l. 65, ' vmbe ragged[e] tourres,' similarly l. 81, ' with certayn leteres,' l. 82, ' of Jewen law,' l. 99, ' þrow preysed dedes.' This never happens in the *Troy Book* (see Luick, *Anglia*, XI, p. 419).

If we examine the alliteration of prefixes, we find that whereas in the *Siege* the prefix de- never alliterates, in the *Troy Book* there are 62 cases. We may specially note the word ' devise,' which is found three times in each poem, alliterating in the *Siege* always on the root (ll. 485, 756, 1231), and in the *Troy Book* always on the prefix (ll. 660, 4018, 4938).

In peculiarities of alliterating letters they generally agree,[1] except that the *Siege* has no liaison alliteration, and only one certain example of the alliteration of *wh* and *qu*, both of which are common in the *Troy Book*. 'Again' alliterates in *Troy Book* only on *g*, while in the *Siege* it

---

[1] See Schumacher, *Studien über den Stabreim in der M. E. Alliterationsdichtung*, Bonner Studien XI.

Introduction. xxix

is found with both *g* and 3. *W* and *wh* alliterate three times in the *Siege*, but not in the *Troy Book*. These peculiarities point to a slightly more southern origin for the *Siege* than for the *Troy Book*.

VII. DATE.

From the dependence of our poem on the *Troy Book*, we can arrive at its approximate date. For in the *Troy Book*, ll. 8053-4, the author, speaking of the grief of Troilus and Cressida, says :

> " Who-so wilnes to wit of þaire wo fir,
> Turne hym to Troilus, & talke þere ynoghe."

Sir Israel Gollancz pointed out that this can only be a reference to Chaucer's poem, which may be dated *c.* 1382-5. The *Siege* must therefore be well later than this. The earliest MS. of *Titus and Vespasian*, Laud Misc. 622, was written *c.* 1400.[1] If I am right in suggesting that it was influenced by the *Siege* (see p. xxvi), we can safely say that the *Siege* belongs to the last decade of the fourteenth century.

VIII. CONNECTION WITH 'PATIENCE.'

The description of the storm in ll. 53-70 should be compared with *Patience*, ll. 893-96 :[2]

> " An-on out of þe norþ est þe noys bigynes,
> When boþe breþes con blowe vpon blo watteres ;
> Ro3 rakkes þer ros wyth rudnyng an-vnder ;
> Þe see son3ed ful sore, gret selly to here ;
>
> Þe wyndes on þe wonne water so wrastel to-geder
> Þat þe wawes ful wode waltered so hi3e,
> & efte busched to þe abyme, þat breed fysches
> Durst nowhere for ro3 arest at þe bothem.
>
> When þe breth & þe brok & þe bote metten,
> Hit wat3 a ioyles gyn þat Jonas wat3 inne,
> For hit reled on roun vpon þe ro3e yþes :
> Þe bur ber to hit baft þat braste alle her gere.
>
> Þen hurled on a hepe þe helme & þe sterne ;
> Furst to-murte mony rop & þe mast after ;
> Þe sayl sweyed on þe see ; þenne suppe bihoued
> Þe coge of þe colde water ; & þenne þe cry ryses,"

and with *Troy Book*, ll. 1983-96 :

[1] See *Titus and Vespasian*, ed. Herbert, p. xxxv.
[2] Ed. Sir I. Gollancz, *Select Early English Poems*, I, Oxford, 1913.

> "There a tempest hem toke on þe torres hegh :—
> A rak and a royde wynde rose in hor saile,
> A myst & a merkenes was meruell to se;
> With a routound rayn ruthe to be holde,
> Thonret full throly with a thicke haile;
> With a leuenying light as a low fyre,
> Blaset all the brode see as it bren wold.
> The flode with a felle cours flowet on hepis,
> Rose vppon rockes as any ranke hylles.
> So wode were the waghes & þe wilde ythes,
> All was like to be lost, þat no lond hade.
> The ship ay shot furth o þe shire waghes,
> As qwo clymbe at a clyffe, or a clent hille,—
> Eft dump in the depe as all drowne wolde."

There is a resemblance between all three passages, which is closer between the *Siege* and the *Troy Book*, or the *Siege* and *Patience*, than between *Troy Book* and *Patience*, e.g. the passages parallel to ll. 55-6. We know that the author of the *Siege* was following the *Troy Book*, and it is most likely that if there is any direct connection with *Patience*, he is also the borrower here. There is a certain parallelism between Jonah and Nathan. Each is going on a sea-journey with a certain object, each is deflected by a storm from that object that he may be the messenger of God. It may be noted that when Nathan hides under the hatches, he is very possibly imitating Jonah, who had Biblical authority for so doing.[1]

IX. CONCLUSION.

As we have seen, the author of the *Siege* overflows with reminiscences of other poets. *Patience*, the *Parlement*, and probably the *Wars of Alexander* have left their impress on him; and especially the *Troy Book*.[2] And yet nothing in the *Troy Book* has anything like the force of his description of the Syrian campaign, or of the open battle in the vale which precedes the siege itself. He writes best when he is free of his sources; compare the triteness of Titus's reported speech in ll. 1151-2, as of all the part which paraphrases Higden, with the vigour

---

[1] If this dependence is accepted, it follows that *Patience* is not likely to have been written after 1390. Sir I. Gollancz, in his edition of *Cleanness*, p. xiii, drew attention to the influence on that poem of the *Book of the Knight of La Tour Landry*, which was written in 1371-2, and *Patience* must have been written shortly before or after *Cleanness*, probably before (see *Purity*, ed. Prof. R. J. Menner, Yale Studies in English, LXI, pp. xxvii-xxxviii).

[2] All these poems belong to the North or North Midlands. I find no influence of the *Piers Plowman* group in this poem.

of the council held by Vespasian when he is summoned to Rome, or of his speech before the walls of Jerusalem.

His kinship with the pre-Conquest poets is manifested in the description of thė storm, suggested by its bare mention in the *Vindicta*. In like manner did the poet of the Anglo-Saxon *Andreas* draw his vivid picture of the ' terror of water ' on the authority of two or three words in his source. Vespasian stands to his men as the Anglo-Saxon heroic leader to his hearth-companions; if he had fallen outside Jerusalem as did Byrhtnoth at Maldon, they would have felt and behaved as did his followers. It may even be that the insignificance of the part played by Veronica (who after all was one of the causes of the siege) is due to the poet's heroic cast of mind.

Yet the poem is thoroughly mediæval, of the true chivalrous school. ' Corteys Crist ' is the poet's rendering of ' Judex meus et rex meus.' The Roman legions behave like ' knights of Logres or of Lyonnesse ' when they dance all night after having fought all day. When beleaguering Jerusalem, they pass their time as does Youth in the *Parlement*, hunting and hawking and jousting. Above all, the ideals of chivalry are voiced in Nero's dying vaunt, that no churl shall boast that he has killed his king. In Hegesippus the poet might have read the traditional ' qualis artifex moritur '; it is safe to say that it would not have appealed to him.

The Siege of Jerusalem.

In Tiberyus tyme, ⁊ þe trewe emperour,
    Sir̛ Sesar̛ hym sulf ⁊ seysed in Rome,
Whyle Pylat was prouost ⁊ vnder̛ þat prince riche
& ȝewen iustice also, ⁊ in Judeus londis.
Herodes vnder his emperie, ⁊ as heritage wolde,
Kyng of Galile ycalled, ⁊ whan þat Crist deyed.
þey Sesar sakles wer̛, ⁊ þat oft synne hatide,
þrow Pylat pyned he was ⁊ & put on þe rode ;
A pyler pyȝt was doun ⁊ vpon þe playn erþe,
His body bonden þer to, ⁊ beten with scourgis ;
Whyppes of quyrboyle ⁊ by-wente his white sides,
Til he al on rede blode ran, ⁊ as rayn [i]n þe strete.
Suþ stoked hym on a stole ⁊ with styf Mannes hondis,
Blyndfelled hym as a be ⁊ & boffetis hym raȝte :

Fol. 1 a.
In the reign of Tiberius

4

8 Christ was tortured by Pilate, and fixed to the cross.

12

Hic Incepit Distruccio Ierarusalem (!), quomodo Titus & Vaspasianus obsederunt & distruxerunt Ierusalem et vi[n]dicarunt mortem Domini Ihū Xp̄i. The Segge of Ierusalem off Tytus and Vaspasyane A ; Here begynneth þe scege of Ierusalem . & how it was destroyed E. Here bygynnith þe sege of Ierusalem D ; Incipit destruccio de Ierusalem per Titum & Vespasianum U ; The Siege of Ierusalem C ; No title in L.
1. Tyberyes ED. þe] that AU.
2. seluyn AE ; was add. A.
3. Whyle] The while þat A.
4. An (!) E. Iewen] I wyn (!) hey (added by a second hand above the line) D. also justece of I[ewen] A. in] of EDUC ; lost in A. Iudees ED ; Iudee U ; lost in A. londe EDUC.
5. And H. AED. Herode AC ; Herowd EDU. vnder] in ED. his] that ED. empyre EDUC. his—wo-] lost in A.
6. calde AEDUC ; was ycalled L. -an—deyed] lost in A.

7. If D. gyltles E. sakles w.] is sakles D ; gyltles were E. that myche E ; he þat C. -ere—hatide] lost in A.
8. ȝitt thurghe A. peyned E. he] has (!) E ; om. C. þrow—was] þan Pylate hym pynid D. pyned—rode] lost in A.
9. was] thare add. A. doun was pyȝt EDU ; was dowun pyght C. appon A ; on EDC. plate A. vpon—erþe] al of grey marble U.
10. body] was add. E. to] and add. AEDUC.
11. Withe whippes A. whirboyl E ; wherebole C. by-w.] abowte A. sythes (!) C.
12. he] om. AEDUC. al] om. DUC. blode] he add. EDUC. rayn] water C. in] so AEDUC ; on L.
13. Sythen ED ; And sythen AUC. stoked hym] strekyn A ; set EDUC. ane A. stole] sete C. mens AU ; mennys EC ; men D.
14. & bl. EDUC. hym] om. AEDUC. &] om. EDUC. hym] he EDUC. cauȝte E.

SIEGE OF JERUSALEM.   B

"ȝif þou be prophete of pris, ꞉ prophecie," þey sayde,
"Whiche [beryn] her' aboute ꞉ bolled þe laste!" 16

A crown of thorns was pressed on his head, and he was put to death.

A þrange þornen croune ꞉ was þraste on his hed,
Vmbe-casten hym with a cry ꞉ & on a croys slowen.
For al þe harme þat he hadde ꞉ hasted he noȝt,
On hem þe vyleny to venge, ꞉ þat his veynys brosten, 20
Bot ay taried ouer þe tyme, ꞉ ȝif þey tourne wolde,
ȝaf hem space þat hym spilide, ꞉ þey hit spedde lyte,

Still the revenge was delayed,

XL wynter, as y fynde, ꞉ & no fewer' ȝyrys,
Or princes presed in hem ꞉ þat hym to pyne wroȝt. 24
Til hit tydde on a tyme, ꞉ þat Tytus of Rome,
þat alle Gascoyne gate ꞉ & Gyan þe noble,
Whyle noye noyet hym ꞉ in Neroes tyme ;

until Titus and his father Vespasianus fell ill.

He hadde a malady vn-meke ꞉ a-myd[dis] þe face : 28
þe lyppe lyþ on a lumpe ꞉ lyuered on þe cheke ;
So a canker vnclene ꞉ hit cloched to gedres.
Also his fader' of flesche ꞉ is ferly bytide,
A biker' of waspen bees ꞉ bredde on his nose, 32

---

15. *pris*] *now add.* A.
16. *beryn*] *so* ADU ; *man* LEC. *here ab.*] *at this borde now* A. *bolled*] *bufete* A ; *buffetid* D ; *bobbyd* EU ; *bobette* C.
17. *A þrange*] *A strong* DUC ; *A scharp* E ; *And sythen a kene* A. *þorn. cr.*] *crown of thorne (thornes* E) AE. *was þr.*] *they thrust* EDUC ; *thay thrange* A. *his*] *hy* (!) E.
18. *Vmbe—a*] *þei cast vp a grete* DUC ; *& made a wel gret* E. *&*] *that hym* EDUC. *a*] *om.* AEDUC. *crosse* AEDUC. *slowen*] *dede* E.
19. *And for* C. *those harmys* A. *hadde*] *ȝit add.* EDUC. *hasted he*] *he hastede hym* A.
20. *On thaym* A ; *om.* E. *þe*] *that* AEDUC. *þat—brosten*] *but mekeliche it suffrede* E.
21. *ay*] *euere* DC. *ouer*] *he* AD ; *om.* EUC. *tourne*] *amende hem* E.
22. *& ȝaf* E ; *And lent* A. *thaym* A. *þat h. sp.*] *of mendement* E. *littill* AEDUC.
23. *wynt.*] *was add.* L. *as*] *om.* DC. *faςre* A. *&—ȝyrys*] *feithfully no lesse* D ; *faithly no lesse* U ; *trewly no lesse* C ; *& neuer a day lasse* E.
24. *Or*] *Our* (!) L. *Or—hem*] *Or he þe* (om. U) *prince (ponyshynge* C) *on hem put* DUC ; *Ar he veniaunce on hem took* E ; *Or he oghte put at that prynce of þat pepill* A. *hym*] *hem* D. *to*] *om.* DUC. *to p.*] *þose paynes* A. *þat—wroȝt*] *for sothe y ȝow telle* E.
25. *betyde*] *one dai tyme* A. *þat*] *oon* EDU ; *þat oon* C.
26. *gate*] *so* AEDUC ; *gaten* (!) L. *Gyen* EDU.
27. *Whyle*] *A* A. *neghede* ADC ; *neght* U. *hym*] *to add.* DUC ; *nere add.* A. *Whyle—hym*] *He was desesed fulsore* E. *in*] *to add.* (!) L.
28. *He*] *þat* DUC. *He h.*] *With* E. *mal.*꞉ L. *vn-mete* AC. *yn myddis* DUC ; *in the myddis* A ; *amyddis* E ; *a-myd* L. *þe*] *his* EDC ; *of his* A.
29. *His* AEDUC. *laye* AEDC ; *lye* U. *lyu. on*] *& cleuyd to* E. *þe*] *his* AEDUC.
30. *As* EDC ; *With* A ; *om.* U. *hit—gedres*] *clotherede to gedir* A ; *enclynid (enclosyd* E) *it (he* UC) *hadde* EDUC.
31. *And also* A ; *And* E ; *om.* DUC. *of fl.*] *Waspasian* E ; *Vaspasiane* C ; *Vaspazian* D ; *Vespasian* U. *is*] *a* AD ; *om.* UC. *is f. b.*] *wurderlyche* (!) *betydde* E.
32. *beke* A ; *byke* UC ; *swarm* E. *waspe bees* A ; *waspis & bees* DU ; *waspes & of bees* E ; *waspes* C. *on*] *in* AEDUC.

Nathan is sent to the Emperor of Rome.

Hyued vpon his hed, ⸵ he hadde hem of ȝouþe,
And Waspasian was caled ⸵ þe waspene bees after.
Was neuer syknes sorer' ⸵ þan þis sir' þoled ;
For in a liter he lay, ⸵ laser at Rome.   36
Out of Galace was gon, ⸵ to glade hym a stounde ;
For in þat cuþe he was kyng, ⸵ þey he car' þolede.
Nas þer no leche vpon lyue, ⸵ þis lordes couþ helpe,
Ne no grace growyng ⸵ to gayne her' grym sores.   40
Now was þer on N[a]than, ⸵ Neymes sone of Grec[e],
þat souȝt oft ouer þe se ⸵ fram cyte to oþer,
Knewe contreys fele, ⸵ kyngdomes manye,
& was a marener myche ⸵ & marchaunt boþe.   44
Sensceus out of Surye ⸵ sent hym to Rome,
To þe athel Emperour ⸵ an eraunde fram þe Jewes,
Caled Nero by name, ⸵ þat hym to noye wroȝt,
Of his tribute to telle, ⸵ þat þey witⱨtake wolde. 48
Nathan toward Nero ⸵ nome on his way
Ouer þe Grekys grounde, ⸵ myd þe grym yþes,

Fol. 2 a.

No physician
was able to
help these
two men.

Senaceus
sends Nathan
out of Syria
to Rome, to
tell the emperor Nero
that the Jews
would no
more pay the
tribute.

33. & were heuyd E. vpon] vp in DUC ; vp heghe in A ; in E. þam A ; them U. of] in his D. ȝouþe] thoght C. he—ȝouþe] while þat he was ȝong E.
34. was] is UC. þe—after] by cause of the (his C) waspes EDUC.
35. Ther (om. D) was no ED. so sor EDUC. þan] þat EDUC. þis] that U ; eny EDU ; euer C. sire] man E. suffrid EC ; folwed U.
36. on EUC. liter] lepir AEDUC. laser at] ȝit þer to in EDUC.
37. For out DUC. Out of] Vn to A. Galice ADUC ; he add. ADUC. was g.] come DUC. This line is omitted in E.
38. For in] Of EDUC. þat c.] Galys E. lord E. suffered C ; hadde E.
39. Nas þ. n.] Ne was there U ; Was there D ; Thare was no (non E) AEC. lechis A. appon A ; on EC. lyue] the loude E. those A. couþ] to DUC. hele EDUC.
40. Ne no] Ne EDU ; Nor C. gras EDUC ; grise (!) A. grow.] appon (on EDUC) grownde add. AEDUC. to g.] þat gaynid DU; þat vayfed C; to graythe A. þaire A. grym] om. DUC. to— sores] that hem helpe myȝte E.
l. 39, 40 follow l. 34 in EDUC.
41. Now] Than AE. Nathan] so EDUC; Natane A; Nothan L. Naym D ; Nayhym A. Grece] so AEDU ; Grecke C ; Grecys L.

42. oft soght DUC ; soghte A ; ofte passyd E. ouer] om. E. þe] salte add. A. fro A. till ADUC.
43. He knewe AEUC. contr.] kyngdomes D ; full add. AD. fele] manye E ; & add. AEDUC. kyndomes C ; kymdomys (!) E ; cuntres D ; full add. A.
44. &] He A. myche] of michte A. &] a add. A. boþe] also E ; in fere UC ; yfere D.
45. Senscyus C ; Senstius EU ; Systynes D ; Syscenis (or Systeius) A. out] om. EDUC. Surye sent] lost in A.
46. Vn to A. þe a.] Nero the (þat C) EDUC. an er.] in message EDUC. -thel—eraun-] lost in A. fro þe A ; of EDUC.
47. Caled] That w[as called] A ; þei (That U) callid hym DUC. hem DUC. Nero—hy- lost in A. to] a U ; om. ADC. This line is lost in E.
48. þey] he hem E ; him add. U. withtake w.] paye (it add. C) noolde EDUC. Of—witht-] lost in A.
49. This Nathan EDUC. toward] vn to A ; to EDUC. nome] took ED. nome on] takyn hase A. on his] þe nexte EDUC.
50. Of D ; On C. grykesche EDU. grounde] see EDUC. with EDUC. grym] grete E. wawes EDUC. myd—yþes] graythande full ȝcrne A.

4 A Storm overtakes the Travellers.

When the ship has left the shore, a very heavy storm rises,

An heye setteþ þe sayl, ⁚ ouer þe [salte] water,
& with a dromound on þe deep ⁚ drof on faste.   52
þe wolco[n] wanned anon ⁚ & þe water skeweþ,
Cloudes clateren gon, ⁚ as þey cleue wolde.
þe racke myd a rede wynde ⁚ roos on þe myddel
& soue sette on þe se ⁚ out of þe souþ syde,   56
Blewe on þe brode se, ⁚ bolned vp harde.

and drives the vessel to the north.

Nathannys naue a-non ⁚ on [þe] norþ dryueþ,
So þe wedour & þe wynd ⁚ on þe water metyn,
þat alle hurtled on an hepe, ⁚ þat þe helm ȝemyd.   60
Nathan flatte for ferde ⁚ & ful vnder hacchys,
Lete þe wedour & þe wynde ⁚ worþe, as hit lyked.
þe schip scher vpon schore, ⁚ schot froward Rome
Toward vncouþ costes, ⁚ keuereþ þe yþes,   64

The travellers are in danger of being drowned.

Rapis vnradly ⁚ vmbe ragged tourres ;
þe brode sail at o brayd ⁚ to-bresteþ a twynne.

Fol. 2 b.

þat on ende of þe sschip ⁚ was ay toward heuen,

---

51. setteþ] sett he AUC ; sette þei D. An h. s.] & sone reysed vp E. þe] his C. ouer] on DC. salte] so EDUC ; wode L. þe s. w.] those salte watirs A.
52. &] om. A. on] in EDUC. þe] om. EUC. he drawe A ; drivyn D ; dryued EU ; drywcth C. on] full add. A. faste] swythe AEDUC.
53. þe] þan D. welken AC ; wolkyn E ; walkyn DU ; wolcom (?) L. wan.] wawis DU. on one U. wan. an.] wexe full wanne A. skeweþ] flowis D ; flowyd E.
54. The clowdes EDUC. clat. g.] alle toclatred EDU ; all to-clateren C ; claterde one the lande A. clyne U ; to-cleue ED.
55. myd] with EDUC ; & A. a] the AEDC. on] in AEDUC. myddis AE DUC.
56. sette] thaym add. A. on] ouer AU. out of] on DUC ; in E. þe] om. E. syde] ende E ; clene A. This line is put after l. 60 in D.
57. It blewe AEDUC. on] & ED ; that U. se] and add. AC. bolmyd (?) E. vp harde] sa faste A.
58. Nath. naue] Natan Naymes sone DUC ; Nathan þo E ; That Nathan A. a-non] on one U ; hym allone A ; om. D. þe] so AEDUC ; om. L.
59. whedirs A. on] and A. metis AU ; metith E ; walkys D.
60. alle] hit add. EDC. hurlede ADC.

an] om. AEDUC. hepis A. solde ȝeme A ; kepte E.
61. And N. DUC. flatte] plate downe A. flatte f. f.] for fer tho E ; for fere D ; aferd tho (þanne C) UC. & f.] flew EDU ; & flodde C. vnder] þe add. DC. hechis A.
62. & leet EUC. wed.] wynd EDUC. wynde] wawes EDU ; weþur C. worþe] wirke AEDUC. hit] thaym A. hit l.] þey wulde EDUC.
63. appon A ; vp a D. scher vp. schore] turned aȝenward E ; and add. AEDUC. schot] om. E. fromward D ; frawardes A ; no thyng toward E.
64. Towardes A ; Vpon EUC. costes vncowthe ADUC ; costes vnknowe E. keu. þe y.] caried hem þe wawes DUC ; þanne caryed hem E ; kayrande full swythe A.
65. Ropis AEUC ; þan ropis D. vnr.] full rathely A ; ful redyly EUC ; ful radly D ; thanne add. EUC. vmbe] om. AED. ragged] raschede A ; rasyd E ; racyd D ; reyked C ; railed U. tourres] in peces A ; in sondur EUC ; on sundre D.
66. sayles C. to-br.] brystis A ; brestyth E ; brast D ; brekyn C ; in sundre brast U. a tw.] in tweyne E ; a twey U ; in two A ; yn sundur D.
67. The tone ADU ; The on E. ay] euere D. of—tow.] fro þan vp to warde þe A.

Nathan lands at Bordeaux and sees Titus.

þat oþer doun in þe deep, ⋮ as alle drenche wolde.	68
Ouer wilde wawes he wende, ⋮ as alle walte scholde,	
St[a]rke stremes þrow yn, ⋮ stormes & wyndes;	
With mychel langour atte laste, ⋮ as our lord wolde,	
Alle was born at a by[rre] ⋮ to Burdewes hauene.	72 The vessel is driven to the harbour of Bordeaux.
By þat wer' bernes atte banke, ⋮ barouns & knyȝtes,	
& [citezeins], of þe syȝt ⋮ selcouþ [hem] þoȝt,	
þat euer barge oþer bot ⋮ or berne vpon lyue	
Vnpersched passed hadde : ⋮ þe peryles wer' so many.	76
Þey token hym to Titus, ⋮ for he þe tonge couþe ;	Nathan is introduced to Titus,
& he [hem] fraynes, how fer ⋮ þe flode hadde yferked.	
"Sir', out of Surre," ⋮ he seide, "y am come,	
To Nero sondis-man sent, ⋮ þe [seygnour] of Rome,	80
Ffram Senseeus, his seriant ⋮ with certayn leteres,	
þat is iustise & iuge ⋮ of Jewen lawe.	and reveals to him the aim of his travel.
Me wer' leuer, at þat londe ⋮ le[ngede] þat y wer',	
Þan alle þe gold oþer good ⋮ þat euer god made."	84
Þe kyng in to conseyl ⋮ calleþ hym sone	

68. *The toþer* ADU ; *The oþer* E. *donward* E ; *ende* U. *in*] *to* E. *as a. d.*] *drenche as it* ED ; *droune as hit* C ; *drenche as she* U. *solde* AED.
69. *Ouer*] *these* add. A. *thay went* A. *wolte* A.
70. *Starke*] so A ; *Stroke* (!) L. *þrow yn*] *and stronge* A.
l. 69 f. are omitted in EDUC.
71. *meche* EDUC. *anger* UC ; *desese* E. *at þe* EDC ; *at* U. *lord*] *it* add. C.
72. *was*] *is* UC. *at*] *one* A. *byrre*] so AC ; *breyd* ED ; *birth* U ; *by* L ; *in* add. D. *Burdieux* A ; *Burdeux* EDU.
73. *By þ. w.*] *Bot by that the* A ; *Thanne were there* EDUC. *beryns* A ; *folke* C ; om. ED. *atte*] *one the* AC ; *on a* E ; *on* D ; *vpon* U. *bankes* AU ; *bothe* add. A. *knyȝtes*] *meny oþer biernes* D. *Walkyng up on strounde . as þey ywunt were* add. E.
74. *& Cetaȝens* A ; *The citeȝeins* DUC ; *The peple* E ; *& suþ* L. *þe*] *þat* AUC. *syȝt*] *cyte* ED ; *full* add. A. *hem*] so DUC ; *thaym* A ; om. L. *selc. h. þ.*] *wunder they hadde* E.
75. *oþer*] *or* AEDC. *berne*] *beerd* U ; *body* D ; *man* EC. *appon* A.
76. *Vnperischede hade passede* A ; *Passed hadde (hath* D) *vnperschid* EDU. *Unp.—per.*] *Passed hadde þo perelles vnperysched, þey* C. *were*] om. D. *many*]

thikke ED ; *fele* UC.
77. *Till þay* A. *him*] *thaym* A ; *hem* DUC ; *tho* add. E. *þe*] *that* E ; *thaire* A ; *her* U. *tonges* A. *knewe* AU.
78. *hem*] so DUC ; *thaym* A ; *hym* E ; om. L. *fraynede* AEDUC. *flodes* C ; *hem* add. U. *hadde*] *hem* add. DC ; *þam* add. A ; *hym* add. E. *yf.*] *drevyn* A ; *bore* EDUC.
That spake Nathan anone, for noycde was he mekill add. A.
79. *Out of Surry, sere* E. *he*] *þei* D. *y am c.*] *yscyled haue y* E ; *saylid haue we* DUC ; *I ame sent to Nero* A ; *swithe* add. ED ; *now* add. UC.
& meche wo in þe water . þe wynd hath me wrought add. E.
80. ⋮ *sent* L. *sond. sent*] *ysent am y now* EDUC. *To—sent*] *Sandis by me aren sente to* A. *þe*] om. D. *seygnour*] so EDUC ; *Senyȝoures* A ; *senatour* L.
81. *Fro* AEC. *seruaunt* EDUC. *cert.*] *many straunye* U.
82. *of*] *the* add. UC. *of J. l.*] *ouer the Jewes alle* A. l. 82 om. ED.
83. *were*] *hade* A. *londe*] *lorde* A. *lengede*] so A ; *leue* L.
84. *oþer*] *& the* A. *god m.*] *gome aughte* A.
l. 83, 84. om. EDUC.
85. *in*] *vn* AU. *to*] *his* add. E. *cons.*] *þanne* add. EDUC. *callyd* EDUC.

6 Nathan speaks of Veronica and Christ.

Asked for a remedy against Titus's disease,

& saide : " Canste þou any cur' ⸱ or craft vpon erþe
To softe þe grete sore, ⸱ þat sitteþ on my cheke ?
& y schal þe redly rewarde, ⸱ & to Rome sende." 88
Nathan nyckes hym with nay, ⸱ sayde, he non couþe :

he refers him to a woman that lives in Judæa,

" Bot wer' þou, kyng, in þat kuþþe ⸱ þer.þat Crist deyed,
þer is a worlich wif, ⸱ a womman ful clene,
þat haþ softyng & salue ⸱ for eche sore out." 92
" Telle me tyt," quoþ Titus, ⸱ " & þe schal tyde better,
What medecyn is most, ⸱ þat þat may vseþ,
Wheþer gommes, oþer graces, ⸱ or any goode drenches,
Oþer chauntementes, or charmes ? ⸱ y charge þe to say." 96
" Nay, non of þo," quoþ Nathan, ⸱ " bot now wole y [telle] :
þer was a lede in our londe, ⸱ while he lif hadde,
Preued for a prophete ⸱ þrow preysed dedes,
& born in Bethleem, one by, ⸱ of a burde schene, 100
& 30 a mayde vnmarred, ⸱ þat neuer man touched,

Fol. 3 a.

As clene as clef, ⸱ þer cristalle sprynges.

where Christ was born by a pure virgin.

Without hosebondes helpe, ⸱ saue þe holy goste,
A kyng & a knaue child ⸱ 30 conceyued at ere ; 104

---

86 Canste] couthe A. &—þou] Canstow, quod he EDU ; Kennest þou, quod he AC. cure] craft EDUC. or] of D. craft] cures EDU ; cure C. appon A ; on EDU.
87. That myghte soften A. softe] ese C. þe] þy E ; this ADUC. grete] grym EUC ; ginly (!) D ; om. A.
88. &] om. DUC. schal] solde A ; wil DUC. þe r.] richely the A ; redely UC ; þe E. rew.] þe add. UC.
89. nykkede ADUC. nyck.—naj] seyde tho E ; and add. A. sayde] þat EDUC.
90. kyng] kydde A ; knowe EDUC. kuþþe] court D ; lond EC. in þ. k.] for a knyghte A. þat] als A ; as DUC.
91. For þere E. worthly U ; wurthi EDC ; wirchipfull A ; worldlich L. wif] wenche and A.
92. soft. &] softyngnynge (!) and A ; a soft thing and UC ; a softyng D ; a softnyng E. eche] euery EDUC ; alle A. out] hurtis A ; on erþe D.
To softe þis grymly sore that sittiþ on my cheke add. D.
93. Now tell thou A. titely D ; om. AEC. þe] thou EU. schalt E. tyde] fare E ; þe add. AEDUC.
94. medecyns A. most is DUC ; moste A. What is þe mooste medicyne E. þat þat] þat þe EC. mayden C.

95. or AEDUC. grassis E ; grissys A ; grasse DC ; grees U. any] ells A. drynkes AEDUC.
96. Enchauntementys EDUC. Charmes or enchantemetis (!) A. y—say] or what maner salues E.
97. Nay] om. EDUC. non] Noght one DUC. þo] thase A ; these EUC. wole y] y wele þe EDUC. telle] so AEDUC ; sey L.
98. lede] lord D ; man E. lond] lawe UC. while] whiles U ; þat add. A. lif hadde] leeue (lyve D) myght ED.
99. þrow pr. d.] in d. wele praysid D ; & in dedes preysed E ; in dedes wele to preise UC.
100. &] om. EDC. ⸱ one L. one] vs AEDUC ; faste add. E. burde sch.] clene mayde E.
101. a m.] mayden A. vnmarrid a mayde DUC. This line is omitted in E.
102. But as DUC ; And as E. cleer E. as] þe add. AEDUC. clyfe AEDUC. þer] þere þat E ; þat AC. crist.] of add. A ; in add. UC.
Or as þe sunne on þe morwe . whanne it furst schyneth add. E.
103. With owtlyn AU. saue] bot AE DUC ; of add. D ; be add. E.
104. knaue] man C. 30] om. AEDUC. at] the add. A ; here add. DUC. at ere] be her here E.

Christ performed many miraculous Works.

A touche of þe trinyte ⁚ touched hir' hadde,
Þre persones in o place ⁚ preued to godres,
Eche grayn is o god, ⁚ & o god bot alle,   *Nathan explains to Titus the idea of the Trinity,*
& alle þre ben bot one, ⁚ as eldres vs tellen.   108
Þe first is þe fader', ⁚ þat fourmed was neuer,
Þe secunde is þe sone, ⁚ of his sede growyn,
Þe þridde in heuen myd hem ⁚ is þe holy goste,
Neþer merked ne made, ⁚ bot mene fram hem passyþ.   112
Alle ben þey endeles, ⁚ & euer of o myȝt
& weren endeles euer, ⁚ [er] þe world was bygonne.
As sone was þe sone ⁚ as þe self fader',
Þe holy goste with hem ⁚ hadde þey euer.   116
Þe secunde persone, þe sone, ⁚ sent was to erþe,
To take careynes kynde ⁚ of a clene mayde,
& so vnknowen he came ⁚ caytifes to helpe,
& wroȝt wondres ynowe ay, ⁚ tille he wo driede.   120 *and tells of the miracles of Christ.*
Wyne he wroȝt of water ⁚ at o word ene,
Ten lasares at a logge ⁚ he leched at enys,
Pyned myd p[ar]il[sye] ⁚ he putte to hele
& ded men fro þe deþ ⁚ eche day rered.   124
Croked & cancred, ⁚ he keuered hem alle,

---

105. *A*] *The* A. *touche*] *trothe* AEDUC. þe] om. E.
106. *The* (!) E. *togydre* EUC.
107. *And ilke a gr.* AU ; *& eche a gr.* EDC. *o—bot*] *bot a god erc* A ; *o god been* E ; *o god is* D ; *on is* C ; *on greyne is* U.
108. þre] om. D. ben] ere A ; are D ; is C ; nis U. *bot one*] *o god* D. *&—one*] *This is my beleeue* E. *eldres*] *clerkys* EUC. vs] me E. tel.] *teche* EU.
109. þe] om. A.
110. þe (*His* C) *sone is þe seconde* DUC. *his syde* EDU ; *hym* C. *gr.*] *sawen* A.
111. þridde] *is* add. EDUC. *in h.*] þe *holy goost* E. myd] *with* AEDUC. *thaym* A ; *þat* add. C. *is*] om. EDU. þe h. g.] *euere dwellyng* E.
112. *That nowþer m. es* A. *markid ne makid* D. *nor* U. *mene*] *euyn* ED. *fro* AEUC. þam A. *passid* D.
113. *are* AEDC ; *erc* U. *end.*] *a god* A. *euer*] *evyn* AEC ; *al* DU.
114. &] *Alle* A. *cnd. e.*] om. EDUC. *er*] so EDUC ; *byforc* L. *end.—was*] *inwardly endlcs, was neuer nane* A ; *euer* add. EDUC. This line is put after l. 117 in ED.

115. *Also* E. *as*] *was* add. A.
116. *& þe* EDUC; *hye* add. ED. *goste*] om. (!) A ; *also* add. A. *thayn* A.
117. *pers.*] *es* add. A. *sone*] *that* add. A. *till* A.
118. *take*] *cacche* D ; *carefull* add. A. *car.*] *mannys* EDUC ; *manes* A. *kynde*] *here* add. UC. *a*] *that* E. *clene mayden* AD ; *mayden clene* C.
119. &] om. DUC. *came*] *was comen* vs A. *hele* ED.
120. *ay*] om. EDUC. *wo*] *deth* C. *dricde*] *suffryd* EDUC.
121. *of water he wroghte* (*made* E) AE DUC; *al* add. U. *ene*] *one* A ; *euen* EDC ; om. U.
122. *at*] *wiþ* D. *logge*] *luke* AEDUC. *lech.*] *helid* DC.
123. *Pyned m.*] *Thase þat pynede ware in* A ; *Peyning in* E ; *þe pyned* (*payned* C) *in þe* DUC. *parilsye*] so A ; *palseye* EDUC ; *piles* (!) L. *putte*] *þam* add. A ; *in* add. EDUC.
124. *from* U. *eche*] *euer ilke* A ; *a* add. C. *rered*] *he raysede* ADUC ; *areysed* E.
125. *keu.*] *cured* EDUC. *hem*] *also* E. *Kankirde and krokede he couerde thaym full clene* A.

His Disciples and Apostles.

Boþ þe dombe & þe deue, ⁝ myd his der' wordes,
Dide myracles mo ⁝ þan y in mynde haue;
Nis no clerk with countours ⁝ couþe aluendel rekene. 128
Fyf þousand of folke, ⁝ is ferr' to here,
With two fisches he fedde ⁝ & fif ber' loues,
þat eche freke hadde his fulle, ⁝ & ȝit ferre leued
Of brede & of broken mete ⁝ bascketes twelue. 132

Seventy-two men follow Him as His disciples, which He sends out to preach.
þer suwed hym out of an cite ⁝ [seuenty] & twey,
To do what he dempte, ⁝ disciples wer' hoten.
Hem to citees he sende, ⁝ his sawes to preche,
Ay by two & by two, ⁝ til hy wer' a-twynne. 136
Hym suwed of an-oþer cite ⁝ semeliche twelue,

Fol. 3 b.
From another place He chooses twelve men, which are called apostles.
Pore men & noȝt prute, ⁝ aposteles wer' hoten,
þat of cay[ti]fes he ches, ⁝ holy churche to encresche,
þe out-wale of þis worlde; ⁝ þis wer' her names: 140
Peter, James & Jon, ⁝ & Jacob þe ferþe,
& þe fifþe of his felawys ⁝ Phelip was hoten,
þe sixte Symond was caled, ⁝ & þe seueþ eke

---

126. *The deef & þe doumbe* EDUC; *men* add. U. *with* AEDUC. *worde* C.
127. *ȝitt did he* A; *He dede* EUC; *And did* D; *of* add. DUC. *mir.*] *many* add. L. *haue in mynde* UC.
128. *Nis no*] *Es nowþer* A; *Ther is no* DC; *There nis* U; *Ther is* E. *clerk w. c.*] *counter ne* (*nor* UC) *clerke* AEDUC; *that* add. AE. *can* EDC. *alu.*] *the halfe* A. *alu. rek.*] *rykene hem alle* E; *hem rekyn alle* DUC.
129. *thowsynd* E; *thowsandes* A. *is ferre*] *es ferly* AD; *ferly is* U; *ferly it is* E; *it is meruayle* C. *here*] *telle* A; *lere* D.
130. *two*] *thre* A. *he*] *þam* add. A. *bere*] *barly* AEDUC.
131. *So þat* E; *And* C. *eche*] *ilke* AU; *a* add. AUC. *freke*] *man* EC. *the fulle* U; *ynowgh* C. *ȝit f.*] *forthir* ADUC; *more* E. *leued*] *was lefte* A; *ouer leuyd* EDUC.
132. *brede*] *battes* EDU; *bettes* C. *of*] om. D. *basck.*] *lepys* E; *full* add. AEDC.
133. *þer s. h.*] *Sone hym sewede* A. *out*] om. AEDUC. *an*] written on an erasure, L. *cite*] *sekte* A; *soort* E; *suyte* D; *sute* U; *assent* C. *seuenty*] so AED UC; *sixty* L. *twa* AE; *tweyne* DUC.
134. *what*] *alle that* A; *as* EDUC.

were h.] *whare* (!) *chosen* A; *ychosyn* DC; *echone* EU.
135. *Hem*] *That he* EDUC. *That to the* A. *he*] om. EDUC.
136. *Euer ED. hy w. a-tw.*] *alle departyd* E; (*alle were* (*þei were all* D) *disseueryd* DUC; *thay ware twelue makede* A.
137. *suw.*] *out* add. L. *cite*] *soyte* A; *sute* U; *soort* ED; *sent* C. *sem.*] *fulliche* E.
138. *&*] om. EDUC. *nogh* (!) C. *were h.*] *they hiȝten* EDUC.
139. *þat*] *he* add. AU. *caytifes*] so AEDU; *cayftes* (!) L; *pore kynreden* C. *he*] om. AU. *holy—encr.*] *fro holy kirke to fell synn* A; *his chirche to fulfill* (*rule* E) EDUC.
140. *þe—þis*] *That* (*These* E) *wyde walked in þe* (om. U) EDUC. *worlde*] *&* add. A. *þis*] *thus* C. *were*] *ben* E. *thaire* A; *þere* E; *he* (!) C.
141. *Iames*] *Iacob* U. *Iacob*] *Iamys* EU. *ferþe*] *lasse* E.
142. *&*] om. AEDUC. *fifþe*] *firste* A; *fyst* (?) U. *his*] *her* D; *þat* E; *þe* UC. *felaschipe* EC; *felawrede* DU. *was h.*] *he hyȝte* EDUC.
143. *S. is callid* DUC; *hiȝte S.* E; *man was Symonde* A. *seuent* AU: *seuenthe* EDC. *eke*] *than* A; *after* EDUC.

Pilate puts Christ to death. 9

Bertholomewe, þat his bone ʄ neuer breke nolde ; 144
þe cyȝt man was Mathu, ʄ þat is myche ylouod,
Tadde & Tomas ; ʄ her' ben ten euen,
& Andreu þe elleueþ, ʄ þat auntred hym myche
Byfor princes to preche, ʄ was Petrus broþer. 148
þe laste man was vnlele ʄ & luþer of his dedis,   The twelfth is Judas, the traitor.
Judas, þat Jesu Crist ʄ to þe Jewes solde ;
Suþ hymsulf he slowe ʄ for sorow of þat dede,
His body on a balwe tree ʄ to-breste on þe myddel. 152
Whan Crist hadde heried helle ʄ & was [to] heuen passed,
For þat mansed man ʄ Mathie þey chossyn.
Ȝit vnbaptized wer' boþe, ʄ Barnabe & Poule,
& noȝt knewen of Crist, ʄ bot comen sone after. 156
þe princes & þe prelates, ʄ aȝen þe paske tyme
Alle þei hadde hym in hate ʄ for his holy werkes ;
Hit was a doylful dede, ʄ whan þey his deþ caste.
þrow Pilat pyned he was, ʄ þe prouost of Rome, 160 Christ is tortured by Pilate.
& þat worliche wif, ʄ þat arst was ynempned,
Haþ his visage in hir' veil, ʄ Veronyk ȝo hatte,   Veronica has His visage in her veil.
Peynted priuely & playn, ʄ þat no poynt wanteþ ;

144. *Bartholomew* DUC ; *Bathillmewe* A ; *Barthemew* (!) E. *þat*] added above the line in L. *bone*] *bown* (!) A ; *bode* E ; *heste* U. *wulde* EUC. *breke wolde neuer* A.
145. *aghtten* (!) A. *was*] *is* UC ; *hyȝte* ED. *mekill es luffede* A ; *Crist meche* (*michul* U) *louede* EUC ; *miche Crist folwid* D.
146. *Thadde and Thomas* A ; *Thomas & Thadde* (*Thadee* D ; *Taddye* C) EDUC. *ben*] *are* A ; *ere* U ; *is* DC.
147. *&*] om. E. *þe*] om. U. *enlefthe* E ; *ellcwynyt* A ; *elleucnt* U ; *ellevenethe* DC. *myche*] *ofte* AEDUC.
148. *Afore* ED ; *Aforne* U. *was*] *seynt* E ; om. DUC.
149. *man*] om. EDUC. *vnl.*] *a tretour* E. *luþer*] *vntrewe* C. *dedis*] *tunge* U.
150. *And that was Iudas* A. *Crist*] om. ADUC. *vn to* A.
151. *Suþ—he*] *And sen him self* U ; *Afterward hym sylf* E ; *Aftur he hym self* C. *And sythyn slewe he hym selfe* A.
152. *body*] *hynge* add. C. *a*] om. EDC. *balghe tre* A ; *bale tre* D ; *baltre* U ; *alther* C ; a lacuna in E. *brast* EDU ; *he braste* C. *on*] in AEDUC. *middis* ADUC.
153. *þan* DUC. *hadde*] om. DUC. *was*] om. DUC. *to*] so DUC ; *till* A ; om. (!) L. *pas.*] *turnyd* DUC. *Tho þe*

oþer apostelys. *tokyn hem togydre* E.
154. *And for* DUC. *mased* A ; *cursed* UC. *For—man*] *& in the stede of Iudas* E. *þey*] *he* DU ; *was* A. *chese* DUC.
155. *And ȝitt* AEDUC. *are* D ; *ere* U ; *were* C. *vnb. w. b.*] *were not cristenyd* E. *&*] *ne* E.
156. *&*] om. DUC. *noȝt*] *Now* (!) D ; *ne* add. A. *&—Crist*] *Ne ychose for postelys* E.
157. *prince* DU. *agaynes* ADU. *þe paske*] *hym spake þat* ED.
158. *Alle þei*] *& alle* E. *hadde—hate*] *hatede hym in herte* A.
159. *doylf.*] *dolerous* DUC ; *wel fowl* E. *dede*] *deth* (!) U.
160. *By* EDUC. *pyned*] *dampned* E. *þe*] *that* A ; om. DU. *prou.*] *was* add. A.
161. *&*] om. A ; *ȝit hath* add. E ; *þan* add. DUC. *þat*] *þis* EDUC ; *ilke* add. A. *worl.*] *wurthi* ED ; *wordy* C ; *worthily* A ; *worthly* U. *wif*] *woman* C ; *þat—yn.*] *that I firste neuymnede* A ; *of whom y ferst* (*arst* E) *tolde* EDUC.
162. *Haþ*] om. E. *vys* D. *hire*] *a* AEDUC. *veil*] *and* add. A. *Veronyke* AU ; *Veronica* EDC. *highte* AEDUC.
163. *Enpryntede* A ; *Prented* U. *priu.*] *opely* (!) E. *& pl.*] *in pleyne* DU ; *þer on* E. *no*] *neuer a* EDU. *poynt*] *ne* add. A. *wantid* D ; *fayleth* E ; *lakketh* U.

For loue he left hit hir' ⁑ til hir' lyues ende. 164

This veil cures of every illness.
þer is no gome [o]n þis [grounde] ⁑ þat is grym wou*n*ded,
Meselry ne meschef, ⁑ ne man vpon erþe,
þat kneleþ doun to þat cloþ ⁑ & on Crist leueþ,
Bot alle hapneþ to hele ⁑ in [ane] hand whyle." 168

Titus grieves at the damnation of Christ, and regains his health.
" At Rome reyned þe emp*er*our," quoþ þe kyng riche þa*n*,
" Cesar, sy*n*ful wrecche, ⁑ þat sent hy*m* fra*m* Rome:
Why nadde þy lycam be leyd ⁑ low vnder erþe,

Fol. 4 a.
Whan Pilat prouost was made, ⁑ suche a prince to jugge?" 172
& or þis wordes wer' [wel] ⁑ wonne to þe ende,
þe canker þat þe kyng hadde, ⁑ clenly was heled,
With out faute þe face, ⁑ of flesche & of hyde,
As newe as þe nebbe, ⁑ þat neuer was we*m*myd." 176

He implores the Son of God
" A, corteys Crist!" ⁑ seide þe kyng riche þa*n*,
" Was neuer worke þat y wroȝt, ⁑ worþy þe to telle,
Ne dede þat y haue don, ⁑ bot þy deþ mened,
Ne neuer sey þe in siȝt, ⁑ goddis sone der'; 180
Bot now [be] bayne [to] my bone, ⁑ blessed lord,

---

164. *hit] his* (!) D; *with* add. ED. *hire] with* add. A. *vn till* A; *in to* D; *to* E. This line is omitted in U.
165. *is no] nis* U. *gome] withc* (!) E; *grefe* A. *on] so* AD; *in* LU. *grounde] so* AD; *wurld* E; *erþe* (!) LU. *þat is] ne gome* A; *so* add. AED. *grym] sore* E.
166. *With m.* E. *ne] nor* U; *or* E. *ne] on* D. *ne m. vp.] that mane hase on* A; *nor sekenes on* U. *ne—crþe] siknesse or sowre* E.
167. *þat cl.] the clay* U. *on] in* A. *byleues* AE.
168. *to hele] thaym the hele with* A; *to helle* (!) L. *alle—hele] þat he be fulliche hool* E. *þat he ne happith be hole* DU. *ane] so* AEDUC; *&* (!) L.
169. *At] A* A; *regnith* D; *renayede* A. *þe emp.] quod the kynge* ADU; *quod Tytus* E. *qu. þe] þe* D; *a* U; *thou* A; om. E. *þe] þat* E. *kyng r.] riche Emperour* AEDU. *þan] om.* AEDU.
170. *Thou Cesare* A; *hym self* add. D; *thou* add. A; *þe* add. EDU. *wrecche] om.* EDU. *fro* A; *to* EU; *sent h. f.] sette is in* D.
171. *Why ne hadde* EU; *A a whyen hade* A; *Why nere* D. *þy] his* D; *þis* E. *leghame* A; *Cesar* E. *be leyd] be lokyn* E; *helid or he be lokyn* D. *low] om.* EDU.
172. *was] he* E. *made] þat* add. AE DU. *a] om.* D. *prince] lord* E. *to j.]*

jugede A; *slow* EDU.
173. *&] om.* EDU. *or] vnnethes ware* A. *those* A. *were] om.* A. *wel] om.* LE. *wonne] wele wonnen* A; *wele warpyn* D; *al worþen* U; *yseyd fulliche* E.
174. *When the* A. *þat] om.* U. *þe k.] Tytus* E. *clene* EU. *was clene* D.
175. *owtten* A. *defawte* AE; *in* add. A; *on* add. D; *was* add. U. *þe] his* EU. *face] was* add. E. *&] or* AED. *hyde] hewe* E; *hewe* (struck out) *hyde* A. *of— hyde] and his flessh als* D.
176. *& as* E. *newe] clenc* U. *þe] a* ED. *as þe] and als* A. *nebbe] nedle* D; *nobill* AE. *þat n. w.] als newer hade bene* A. *wem.] wymmede* A; *apeyred* E; *hurte* DU.
177. *A] comly* add. A. *seide] quode* ADU. *þe k.] Tytus* E. *riche] om.* AEDU. *þan] anon* E.
178. *worþy] wurth* E; *neuer* (!) U. *þe to t.] to thi wille* EDU; *þe till* A.
179. *Nor* U; *neuer* add. A. *don haue* EDU; *dide* A. *bot] onlicke* add. E. *men.] rewyde* EU; *royd* D.
180. *Nor* U. *sawe* ADU; *I* add. AD. *god* U. *dere] of heuen* A.
181. *be] so* A; om. L. *to] so* A; *me* L. *be.—bone] y boune me to be bysy* D; *mun me be boun* U. *blessed] thou blyssed— full* A. *be—lord] blessyd lord, graunte me my boone* E.

Titus leaves for Rome with Nathan.

To stire Nero with noye ⁖ & newen his sorowe ;
& y schal buske me boun, ⁖ hem bale to wyrche,   *to allow him*
To do þe deucles of dawe, ⁖ & þy deþ venge.   184 *to take revenge for His death.*
Telle me tit," quoþ Titus, ⁖ " what tokne he lafte
To hem þat knew hym for Crist ⁖ & his crafte leued !"
"Nempne þe trinyte by name," ⁖ quoþ Nathan, "at þries,
& þer myd baptemed be ⁖ in blessed water !"   188
Forþ þey fetten a font ⁖ & foulled hym þer,   *He is baptized,*
Made hym cristen kyng, ⁖ þat for Crist werred.
Corrours in to eche coste ⁖ þan þe cours nomen
& alle his baronage broȝt ⁖ to Burdewes hauen.   192
Suþ with þe sondes-man ⁖ he [s]ouȝt to Rome,   *and sets out for Rome*
þe ferly & þe fair' cure ⁖ his fader' to schewe ;   *with Nathan to see his*
& he gronnand glad ⁖ grete god þanked   *father,*
& loude criande on Crist ⁖ carped & saide :   196
" Worþy, wemlese God, ⁖ in whom y byleue,   *who thanks God and*
[Als] þou in Bethleem was born ⁖ of a bryȝt mayde,   *prays for the restoration*
Sende me hele of my hurt, ⁖ & heyly y a-fowe   *of his own health.*
To be ded for þy deþ, ⁖ bot hit be der' ȝolden."   200

---

182. *stire*] *note* D. *To st.*] *Stirre thou* A. *&*] *to* ADU. *his*] *her* U ; *thaym with* A.
183. *schal*] *wele* ED. *buske*] *bese* E. *me*] *and* A ; *be* add. AD. *boun*] *what y may* E. *thaym* A. *bale*] *for* add. A. *hem—wyrche*] *here bales to brewe* EDU.
184. *þe*] *tho* U ; *those* A ; *þes* D. *of*] *a* D ; *on* (!) U. *To—dawe*] *That dede the this sorwe* E. *thine* U. *auenge* ED. *Primus Passus* add. U.
185. *Telle me tit*] *Now telle me* AEDU. *tok.*] *þat* add. AE.
186. *To*] *With* E. *thaym* A. *knawes* A. *knew—Crist*] *hym knowe* E. *&*] *on* add. EU ; *in* add. A. *lewyn* D ; *lewys* A. *his cr. l.*] *hym byleeue* E.
187. *Newyn* A. *quoþ*] *seyde* E. *at*] *a* U ; om. ED.
188. *with* AEDU. *baptized* ED ; *baptist* U. *bapt. be*] *alle be baptizede* A. *in*] *wiþ* D; *clene* add. E. *water yblessed* EDU.
189. *fechede* A ; *þere* add. D. *font*] *fat* EDU ; *þo* add. E. *foul. h. p.*] *fylde it ful of water* E: *baptizede þat beryn* A.
190. *And made* AE. *hym cr.*] *cristyn* E ; *cristenyde that* A. *for*] *efter* A ; *aftir* DU. *Crist after* E. *wer.*] *seruede* AEDU.
191. *Than currous* (!) A. *into*] *in till* A ; *in* EDU. *cche*] *euery* ED ; *ilke* U ; *ilk a* A. *þan þe c.*] *here cours* EDU ; *thaire curses* A ; *thanne* add. ED ; *thay* add. AU. *nom.*] *made* AEDU.
192. *&*] om. A. *bar.*] *þei* add. D. *broȝt*] *to brynge* A. *Burdeux* EDU ; *Buredieux* A. *hauen*] *anone* A ; *in hast* EDU.
193. *Suþ—man*] *And sythen sone on with the sondis* A ; *And afterward his sondes* E ; *And sen after his sonde* U ; *And sithin sondis* D. *he*] om. AE. *souȝt to*] *soghte to warde* A ; *pouȝt* (!) *to* L ; *sente* (*vn* add. U) *to* EU ; *sente a-none vn to* D.
194. *That* AU. *&*] om. U. *þe*] *that* A. *& þe*] om. ED. *fad.*] *for* add. A.
195. *he*] *alle* A. *gronyng* DU. *glad*] *with gladnes* A ; *þe* add. DU. *god*] *lord* U ; *he* add. A. *&—god*] *Tho was his fadur wundur glad . & Iesu Crist* E.
196. *&*] om. A. *cryde* EDU. *vpon* EU. *Crist* ⁖ *he* add. U. *carpande* (!) A. *Crist* ⁖ *carp. &*] *hym . & these wurdes* E.
197. *Worþy w.*] *Now thou gracious* A. *Worþy w. G.*] *Mercy, lord myȝtful* EDU. *y*] *now* add. D.
198. *Als*] *so* AEDU ; *& L. bryȝt*] *clene* AE. *mayden* A.
199. *hele*] *helpe* AED. *myn* U. *hurt*] *desese* E. *hally* A ; *holy* U. *heyly y*] *y to þe* E.
200. *be d. ȝ.*] *yuengyt be* E.

12   *Veronica is sent for.*

þat tyme Peter was pope ⁖ & preched i*n* Rome
þe lawe & þe lore, ⁖ þat our byleue askeþ,
Folowed faste on þe folke ⁖ & to þe fayþ tou*r*ned,
& Crist wroȝt for þ*at* wye ⁖ wondres ynow.   204

Vespasianus sends for Peter the pope, who tells him the true story of Veronica and the veil.
þ*er* of Waspasian was war', ⁖ þ*at* þe waspys hadde,
Sone sendeþ hym to ⁖ & þe soþe tolde
Of Crist & þe kerchef, ⁖ þ*at* keuered þe sike,
As Nathan, Neymes sone, seide, ⁖ þ*at* to Nero was come. 208

Fol. 4 b.
þa*n* to consayl was called ⁖ þe knyȝtes of Rome,
& assenteden sone ⁖ to sende messages.

Twenty knights are deputed to fetch her.
XX^{ti} knyȝtes wer' cud, ⁖ þe ker[ch]yf to fecche,
& asked trewes of þe empero*ur*, ⁖ þ*at* crand to done. . . . 212
Ac w*ith* out tri*b*ute or trewes ⁖ tenfulle wyes,
þe knyȝtes w*ith* þe kerchef ⁖ come*n* ful blyue.

þe pope ȝaf p*ar*doun to hem, ⁖ þ*at* passed þ*er* aȝens
W*ith* p*ro*cessioun & pres, ⁖ princes & dukes ;   216

She kneels before St. Peter, and commits the veil and herself to his charge.
& whan þe womman was war', ⁖ þ*at* þe wede owede,
[Of] seint Peter þe pope ⁖ ȝo platte to þe grou*n*de,
Vmbe-felde his fete ⁖ & to þe freke saide :
" Of þis kerchef & my cors ⁖ þe kepyng y. þe take." 220

---

202. *Of the* ADU. *lawe*] lord D. *lore*] *lawe* D.
203. *He folowede* A ; *Fullid* D ; *Cristnede* E. *on*] *of* D ; om. E. *þe*] om. E.
204. *wye*] *wight* D. *for* þ. *w.*] *al day for hym* E.
205. *is Vesp. ware* U.
206. *Sone*] *& anon* E ; *he* add. DU. *sendis*] *sente* E ; *shewed* U ; *he* add. A. *to hym* E. *&*] *he* add. AED.
207. *þe kerch.*] *of þe cloth* E. *þat*] *and* D. *keu.*] *curyd* EDU.
208. *Nayhym* A. *seids*] *had saide* A. *Neymes s. s.*] *hadde byfore* (*a-for* DU) *seyd* EDU. *was to Nero* A. *was*] om. DU. *kam* U. *þat—come*] *as y to ȝow toolde* E.
209. *to*] *sone* (!) A. *knyghthede* A.
210. *&*] *thay* add. A. *to s. mess.*] *messangers forthe to sende* A.
ll. 209, 210 om. EDU.
211. *xx^{ti}*] *Anon* E. *knyȝtes*] *that* add. A. *were*] *ere* U. *cud*] *ycald* E. *þe*] *that* A. *kerch.*] *kergyf* (!) L ; *clooth forto* E.
212. *asked—emp.*] *aske* (*hadde* E) *of Nero a trewe* EDU. *þat—done*] *to gon & to come* E ; *answer þei abydyn* D ; *an answere thei herken* U.
This line is omitted in A.
213. *Ac*] om. AEDU. *With owttyn* A.

or trewe A ; *or trowe* D ; *or payment* E ; *to be* U ; *by* add. AEDU. *wyes*] *wayes* AU ; *dayes* D. *tenf. w.*] *be eny maner woeye* E.
So þat þey myȝte . go with owte lettyng add. E.
214. *kerch.*] *vernycle* E. *comen*] *thay come* A. *ful*] *as* EU ; *agayne* A. *blyue*] *sone* A ; *swythe* ED.
215. *to hem*] *to them þat*, struck out, add. D ; *thare to* AU ; om. E. *þat*] *and* AEDU. *passed*] *wente* E. *þer*] *it* EDU. *ayen* D.
216. *presynge* A ; *of* add. AEDU. *princes*] *lordes* U.
& with al þe solempnyte . þat he make myȝte add. E
217. *&*] om. AE. *was*] *is* U. *ywar* E ; *comen* A. *wede aughte* ADU ; *clooth hadde* E.
218. *Of*] *so* EDU ; *By fore* A ; *To* L. *grounde*] *erthe* D.
219. *Scho umbyfaldide* A ; *&* (om. D) *fyl down to* EDU. *his fete*] *the erthe* U. *þe fr.*] *hym* E.
220. *Of þis*] *This haly* A. *cors*] *body* A. *þe kep.*] *to kepe* A. *Of—y þe*] *This clooth to thy* (*my* D) *kepyng. & my corps* (*body* E) *y* EDU. *bytake* ADU.

Veronica and the Veil are brought to Vespasianus. 13

Þan bygan þe burne ⁝ biterly to wepe
For þe doylful deþ ⁝ of his der' mayster,
& longe stode in þe stede, ⁝ or he stynte myȝt,
Whan he vnclosed þe cloþe, ⁝ þat Cristes body touched.   224   The pope receives the veil with reverence.
Þe wede fram þe womman, ⁝ [he] warpe atte laste,
Receyued hit myd reuerence ⁝ & rennande teris.
Out of þe place myd pres ⁝ þey passed on swyþe
& ay held hit on hey, ⁝ þat alle byhold myȝt.   228
Þan XII barouns bolde ⁝ þe emperour bade wende,   Veronica and the kerchief are brought to Vespasianus.
& þe pope departe ⁝ fram þe pople faste ;
Veronyk & þe vail ⁝ Waspasian þey broȝt,
& seint Peter þe pope ⁝ presented boþe.   232
Bot a ferly byfelle ⁝ forþ myd hem alle :
In her' temple bytidde ⁝ tenful þynges,
Þe mahound & þe mametes, ⁝ to-mortled to peces
& al to-crased, as þe cloþ ⁝ þroȝ þe kirke passed.   236
In to þe palice with þe printe ⁝ þan þe pope ȝede,
Knyȝtes kepten þe cloþe ⁝ & on knees fallen.
A flauour flambeþ þer fro, ⁝ þey felleden hit alle,

---

221. *Bot than* A ; *Tho* U. *gan* DU. *þe] that* AU ; *blessid* add. DU. *beryn* A ; *beerd* U. *þe b. b.*] *Petur* E ; *full* add. A.
222. *doylf.*] *dolerous* DU ; *dispytful* E.
223. *stude lange* A. *þe] þat* EDU ; *a* A. *myȝte stynte* E.
224. *Whan*] *Bot when that* A ; om. DU. *he] scho* A. *Than vnclosed he* E. *Cristes] his* A. *body] face* AE.
225. *þe] That* DU. *wede] clooth* E. *fro* AEU. *þe] that* U. *he warpe*] so A ; *he warpid* DU ; *þey warpen* L. *atte l.*] *atonys* DU. *he—laste*] *thanne mekelich he took* E.
226. *& rec.* E ; *Rescheyuede* A. *with* ADU. *&] with* add. D. *rennyng* ED.
227. *Out of] To warde* A ; *To* EDU. *place] palese* AEDU. *with* AEDU. *pres] pees* U. *they—swyþe*] *he passed sone* (*þere* D) *after* EDU.
228. *ay] euer* ED. *hey] height* D ; *lofte* A. *alle] men* U.
229. *þan] om.* AEDU. *XII] Ten* ED. *bar.] that were* add. A. *bolde] to* add. A. *emp.] kyng* AEDU. *bade] om.* A ; *to* add. EDU. *went* A.
230. *&] so* add. U. *departede* A ; *parted* U. *fro* A. *faste] swithe* AU.

To fecche (fette D) *þe womman with þe wede (clooth* E). *þat þe wundres wroughte* add. ED.
ll. 229—32 are placed after l. 236 in A.
231. *The veyle (clooth* E) *with Veronica* EDU ; *to* add. EDU. *þey] is* U.
232. *&] to* add. D. *sayne* A. *þe p.*] *þei* add. D ; *and* add. U. *pres. boþe*] *there present ware they bothe* A ; *also in feere* E.
233. *Bot] þanne* add. EDU. *byf.] thare* add. A. *forth with* U ; *anon with* E ; *byfore* AD. *þam* A.
234. *For in* E. *thaire* A ; *þe* ED. *bet.] full* add. A.
235. *þe] Thaire* A ; *Her* E. *þe] thaire* A ; *her* E. *mamentis* E ; *mauments* U ; *Mawmetries* A. *to-mortled] mourlede* A ; *hurtlid* DU ; *al to-brast* E. *to] in* A ; *on* E. *to p.] togidris* ED.
236. *to-cr.] to-thruschede* A ; *to-clateryd* ED. *þroȝ] to* EDU. *kirkc] kyng* ED. *passed] ȝede* EDU.
237. *to] om.* A. *printe] prynce* A. *with þe pr.] þe pope* EDU. *þan] als* A. *þan— ȝede] fro (from* D) *þe peple wente* ED ; *went fro the puple* U.
238. *&] þei* add. D. *on] her* add. U. *fyllen* EU ; *sette* A.
239. *fla. fl.] A sauoure flowe* A ; *Then fley a flauour* EDU. *alle] ilkone* A.

The veil exhales a sweet fragrance, and glitters so that nobody is able to look at it.	Was neuer odour ne eyr' ⁖ vpon erþe swetter;	240
	þe kerchef clansed hit self ⁖ & so cler' wexed,	
	My3t no lede on hit loke ⁖ for li3t þat hit schewed.	
	As hit a-proched to þe prince, ⁖ he put vp his hed,	
	For comfort of þe cloþ ⁖ he cried wel loude :	244
The prince prays for his	"Lo, lordlynges, her', ⁖ þe lyknesse of Crist,	
Fol. 5 a.	Of whom my botnyng y bidde ⁖ for his bitter woundis."	
healing.	þan was wepyng & wo, ⁖ & wryngyng of hondis,	
	With loude dyn & dit ⁖ for doil of hym one.	248
The pope touches his visage with the veil, and the waspe vanish.	þe pope availed þe vaile ⁖ & his visage touched,	
	þe body suþ al aboute, ⁖ blessed hit þrye.	
	þe waspys wenten away, ⁖ & alle þe wo after;	
	þat er lasar was longe, ⁖ ly3tter was neuere :	252
	þan was pypyng & play, ⁖ his pyne was awey,	
	þey 3elden grace to god, ⁖ þis two grete lordes,	
The kerchief puts up itself in the church.	þe kerchef carieþ fram alle ⁖ & in þe [kirke] hangyþ,	
	þat þe symple my3t hit se, ⁖ in to soper tyme.	256
	þe veronycle after Veronyk ⁖ Waspasian hit called,	

240. *Was n.*] *Ther nas* EDU. *ne*] *nor* U. *appon* A; *on þe* D. *vpon erþe*] *vnder heuene* EU.
241. *Te* (!) E. *kerch.*] *clooth* EDU. *clans.*] *cleryd* EDU; *vnclosede* A. *clere*] *it* add. E. *wexe* A; *wax* ED.
242. *There myghte* A. *no lad* D; *nonbody* E. *schewed*] 3*af* DU; *hadde* E.
243. *apr.*] *apperide* A. *þe*] *that* A. *put*] *heeld* E. *vp*] *forth* D.
244. *& for* EDU; *And alle for* A. *he*] om. E. *wel*] *ful* DU; *on* A.
l. 163—l. 244 are missing in C.
245. *Lo*] *And seyde* E. *lordynges* EDUC. *lord. h.*] *here, lordynges, he sayde* A.
246. *whayme* A. *my*] *y* ED. *bote* A; *help* C; *nowe* add. A. *y bidde*] *I praye* C; *abyde* ED.
l. 246 is omitted in U.
247. *was*] *is* U; *bot* add. A.
248. *loude*] *grete* AE. *dyn*] *dremyng* D; *lowe dremyng* U; *lamentacyon* E; *wepynge* C. *& dit*] *and dym* (!) D; *& noyse* C; *all that daye* A; om. EU. *doil*] *sorwe* EC; *drede* U. *hym alone* D; *þe kyng* E.
249. *Te* (!) E. *valid* D; *with* add. A. *the*] *his* UC. *av. þe v.*] *took doun þe clooth* E. *his*] *the* U. *vice* U; *vysage*, corrected from *vys*, D; *face* C; *nose* E.

250. *þe*] *Sythen the* A; *& his* E. *sethen* U; *after* C; om. AE. *ob.*] *and* add. A. *hit*] *hym* A; *he* EDUC. *thryse* AEDUC.
251. *wenten*] *alle* add. EDUC. *þe wasp. went.*] *Than went the waspes* A. *alle*] om. EU. *þe*] *his* E.
252. *er*] *arst* ED; *byfore* C. *was lazar* EDU; *ful* add. U. *longe*] *laythe* A; *lich* EDC; *leke* U. *ly3tter*] *so ly3t* EDC; *so faire* U. *was*] *he* add. AEDUC.
253. *þan*] *There* EDUC. *was*] *with* A. *his—awey*] *thay partede at the laste* A; *and* (om. UC) *partyng at þe laste* EDUC.
254. *þay 3. gr.*] *And gaffe grace* A; *Yeld graces* DU; *Graces 3uldyng* E; 3*olden thankynge* C. *vn-to* A. *þis two*] *alle these* A; *all* þe DUC. *þis—lordes*] *of alle þat pere were* E.
255. *Than the* A. *car. fr. a.*] *wente fro thayrn alle* A. *þe—alle*] *The clooth caught was* (*was takyn* E) *hem fro* EDUC. *chirche* EDUC; *eyr* LA. *hyngede* A; *honged* EDUC.
256. *þat þe*] *That* A; *For þe* EDUC. *symple*] *somple* (!) C; *synful* ED; *pople* add. LA. *my3t hit*] *schulde it* E; *shold* D; *it to* UC. *in to*] *tyl* þe EC; *tul* (!) D; *to the* AU.
257. *vernacle* A; *vernycle* EDU; *vernache* (!) C.

Vespasianus and Titus are sent to Judæa. 15

Garde hit gayly agysen ⁚ in gold & in seluere.
ʒit is þe visage in þe vail, ⁚ as Veronyk hym broʒt,
þe Romaynes at Rome, ⁚ for a relyk hit holden. 260
þis whyle Nero hadde noye, ⁚ & non nyʒtes reste,   *Nero is very ill pleased with the loss of the tribute.*
For his tribute was [tynt], ⁚ as Nathan told hadde.
He commaundiþ knyʒtes to come, ⁚ consail to holde,
Erles & alle men ⁚ þe emperour aboute. 264
Assembled þe senatours, ⁚ sone vpon haste,   *A council is held,*
To iugge, who jewes myʒt best ⁚ vpon þe Jewys take;
& alle demeden by dome, ⁚ þo dukes to wende,
þat wer' cured þrow Crist, ⁚ þat þey on croys slowen. 268
þat on Waspasian was ⁚ of þe wyes twey,   *and it is determined that Vespasianus and Titus shall go to Judæa.*
þat þe trauail vndertoke, ⁚ & Titus an oþer,
A bold burne on a blonke ⁚ & of his body comyn,
No ferþer sib to hym-self ⁚ bot his sone der', 272
Crouned kynges boþe, ⁚ & mychel Crist loued,
þat hadde hem ʒeuen of his grace, ⁚ & her' grem stroyed.

---

258. *Garde hit*] *And garte* ADU; *& made it* EC. *gayly*] *greithely* DU; *worschipfully* C. *ag.*] *it gyse* A; *been arayt* E; *arayde* C; *hit greithe* DU.
259. *þe*] om. (!) D. *vis.*] *vys* DU; *face* EC. *in*] *on:* A. *the v.*] *clooth* E. *hyn*] *it* AEDUC.
260. *þe*] *That* UC; *Alle þe* E. *Rom.*] *rively* add. DUC; *telles þus* add. A; *hit holdeþ* add. L. *Rome*] *&* add. LA. *for*] om. EDUC. *a*] om. A. *haldis* A.
261. *hadde*] *hase* A. *no* AED. *nyʒtes r.*] *rest myght haue* U.
262. *was*] *is* U. *tynt*] *so* DU; *nat payd* E; *loste* C; *with-hold* L. *was t.*] *to tell* (!) A. *had tolde* A; *hym toolde* EDUC.
263. *He*] *Tho he* E; *The kyng* C. *comaundid* DC; *somund* U; *bad* E. *knyʒtes*] *kynges* EU; *þe kyng* D. *to c.*] om. D; *a* add. C. *to*] *take*, expuncted, add. L. l. 263 om. A.
264. *Erles*] *Now than the emperour and his erlis* A. *men*] *of* add. E. *þe empyre* EDUC; om. A.
265. *Ass.*] *He callyl* (!) *also* E. *appon* A. *sone vp. h.*] *in Rome al abowte* E.
266. *Tho to* A. *iugge*] *ordeyne* E. *jewes myʒt best*] *solde the journaye* A. *appon* A. *who—take*] *what iuggement (iuggementz* D). *þe Iewes (iugges* D) *schulde haue* EDUC.
267. *alle*] *thay* add. AEDUC. *dem.*] *it* add. A. *þo*] *those* A; *þe* DU; om. C.

dukes] *princes* E; *for* add. U. *to*] *sholde* C.
268. *couerde* A. *þrow*] *in* DUC; *be* E. *þat*] *whom* E. *crosse* ADUC. *& destroye hem vtterly . for þat wykkyd dede* add. E.
269. *The tone* A. *was Waspasyan* AEDC. *þe*] *those* A. *wyes*] *wyghtis* AD; *lordes* E; *dukes* C. *two* AEDC. This line is omitted in U.
270. *That*] om. U. *þe*] *þat* DU; *this* E. *trau.*] *iorneye* E. *vndert.*] *to vndertake* U. *an*] *þat* ED. *the toþer* A. *That oþer was Tytus . þat þe trauayle vndertoke* C.
271. *bool* (!) E. *burne*] *knyʒtc* C; *man* E. *beern bold:* U. *blonke*] *hors* C. *on a bl.*] *for þe nonys* E. *&*] om. DUC. *his b.*] *his blood* ED; *hye blode* G; *hye kyn* U; *hyn selfe* A.
272. *forther* UC; *ferrere* A. *sib*] *kyn* C. *to*] *fro* A. *bot*] *than* U. *sone d.*] *owne sune* EDUC.
273. *kynges*] *ware thay* add. A. *Crouned k. b.*] *Bothe kynges vnder (with* C) *crowne* UC; *Bothe were they kynges* ED; *wiþ crowne* add. D. *&*] *that* AED. *Crist mychel (meche* EDC) AEDUC.
274. *hadde*] *hase* A; om. C. *thaym* A. *ʒeuen of*] *grauntid* DUC. *þat—his* For *he graunted hem* E. *&*] om. E. *grame* DUC; *game* E. *destroyed* DU; *to destroye* E. *here gr. str.*] *owte of grefe broghte* A.

Moste þei hadde hit in hert, ⁑ her' hostes to kepe
& her' forwardis to fulfille, ⁑ þat þei byfor made. 276
þan was rotlyng in Rome, ⁑ robbyng of brynnyes,
Schewyng of scharpe, ⁑ scheldes ydressed.
Lauȝte leue at þat lord, ⁑ leften his sygne,
A grete dragoun of gold, ⁑ & alle þe [g]yng folwed. 280

The fleet is fitted out; Fol. 5 b.
By þat schippis wer' schred, ⁑ yschot on þe depe,
Takled & atired ⁑ on talterande ypes,
Ffresch water & wyn ⁑ wounden yn faste,
& stof of alle maner store, ⁑ þat hem strengþe scholde. 284
þer' wer' floynes a flot, ⁑ farcostes many,
Cogges & crayers, ⁑ y-casteled alle.
Galees of grete streyngþe ⁑ with golden fanes,
[þe brede] on þe brod se ⁑ aboute four' myle. 288

It leaves Italy, and reaches port Jaffa.
þey tyȝten vp tal-sail, ⁑ whan þe tide asked,
Hadde byr at þe bake ⁑ & þe bonke lefte,
Souȝte ouer þe se ⁑ with soudeours manye,
& [ioyned in to] port Jaf ⁑ in Judeis londys. 292

---

275. *For moost* E. *holde* A. *hit*] om.
EC. *thaire* A; *his* ED. *highttis* A.
276. *&*] om. DUC. *here*] *the* A. *for-
warde* ADUC; *auowes* E. *fulf.*] *hold* D.
afore E; *aforne* UC.
277. *Sone was there* A. *was*] *is* U.
rotl.] *ruschynge* A; *rightyng* D; *rumer*
E. *Rome*] *and* add. ADUC. *rob.*] *roll-
ynge* A. *bryn.*] *harneys* E; *helmes* C;
rust D.
278. *Shiueryng* D; *Shimering* UC;
Grydyng E. *scharpe*] *stele* add. AEC;
shelde add. U; *and* add. AEU. *scharpe
scholdes*] *sheldis of sharp stele* D. *y-
dressed*] *to drysse* A; *arayed* E.
279. *Toke* D; *To* (!) U; *Thay tuke*
AEC; *her* add. DUC; *he* (!) add. E;
thaire add. A. *at*] *of* E. *þat*] *her* ED;
thaire A; *the* UC. *lord*] *londe* C; *and*
add. AEUC. *lyftys* A; *lifte vp* DUC;
reysed up E. *his*] *here* ED; *a* C.
280. *A grete*] *Which was a* E. *þe*]
om. D. *gyng (genge* UC)] so DUC;
gentills A; *kyng* (!) L. *folwed*] *after*
ADUC. *alle—folwed*] *forth wente yfeere*
E.
281. *þat*] *the* add. AC. *schred*] *shrowde*
D; *yshrud* U; *arayed* E; *redy* A; *gon*
C; *and* add. AEDUC. *schotte* A; *put*
E; *shift* DU; *rowed* C. *appon* A; *in*
EDUC.
282. *Trussyd & tyred* EDUC. *on*] *for*

E. *talt.*] *toterynge* EDU; *towrynge* C.
ypes] *wawes* AEDUC.
283. *wyn*] *thay* add. AC. *wynde* AC.
faste] *full swythe* A; *soone* EDUC.
284. *man.*] om. C; *of* add. A. *thaym
strenghe* A; *strenghen hem* UC.
285. *floygnes* UC; *schippes* ED; *flew-
ande* A. *on* DUC; *in the* A. *flete* A;
and add. EDUC. *fercostes* A; *farstes* (!)
C; *full* add. A.
286. *Cokkes & karekkes* C. *encastelled
ylkone* A.
287. *And g.* AEDUC. *of*] *full* add.
A. *strenghe* A; *myȝt* EDUC. *gilden* A.
288. *þe brede*] so DUC; *They spredde
abrod* E; *Sprad* L; *Alle abowote* A. *on*]
in EC; *of* DU. *brod*] om. E. *fyve* AE
DC; *seuen* U.
289. *tyen* DC; *teisen* U; *gan drawe*
E. *topsaill* DUC; *her seyl* E. *askis*
DU; *wulde* E.
290. *þei had þe* DUC. *byr*] *piry* U;
pyre C. *at*] *on* DUC. *bonke*] *londe* C.
& drowyn in to deep water . *þat þey
myȝte scyle* E.
291. *Souȝte*] *þei sailid* DC; *& thanne
þey scyled* E; *Thei saiden* (!) *and sailed*
U. *þe*] *salt* add. DC. *ouer þe se*] om. U.
292. *& ioynyd in* (om. C) *to*] so DC;
& tooke londe at E; *Right vnto* U; *&
ryued vp at* L. *Iudee* U; *Iudeus* C.
londe EDUC.

The Roman Army ravages Syria with Fire and Sword. 17

Suree, Cesaris londe, ' þou may seken eu*er*,
Ful mychel wo m[o]n be wroȝte ' in þy [w]lonk tounes,   *An ill fate is*
Cytees vnder S[yon], ' now is ȝo*ur* sorow uppe :   *imminent to Judæa.*
þe deþ of þe dereworþ Crist ' der' schal be ȝolden.   296
Now is, Bethleem, þy bost ' y-broȝt to an ende ;
Jer*usa*lem & Ierico, ' for-juggyd wrecchys,
Schal neu*er* kyng of ȝo*ur* kynde ' wi*th* croune be ynoyntid,
Ne Jewe for Jesu sake ' [i]ouke in ȝou more.   300
þey setten vp-on eche side ' Surrie wi*th*-yn,   *Syria is*
Brente ay at þe bak ' & [all] bar' laften ;   *devastated and ruined by fire.*
Was noȝt bot roryng & r[ut]h ' in alle þe riche toun*n*es,
& red laschyng lye ' alle þe londe ouer' ;   304
Token toun & tour', ' teldes ful fele,
Brosten ȝates of brass ' & many borwe won*n*en ;
Holy þe heþen here ' hewyn to grounde,   *The heathen*
Boþ in bent & in borwe, ' þat abide wolde.   308 *army is destroyed.*
þe Jewes to Ier*usa*lem, ' þ[ere] Josephus dwelde,   *The Jews flee*
Flowen, as þe foule doþ, ' þat faucou*n* wolde strike.   *to Jerusalem.*
A cite vnder' Syon ' sett was ful noble
Wi*th* many toret & tour', ' þat toun to defende.   312

293. *Now Surry* E ; *Dymuer* (?) C. *mayst* DC ; *mythe* (!) E. *sekcn*] *sorwe* EDUC.
294. *Ful*] *For* E ; *Now* DUC. *meche* ED. *mon*] *men* L ; *worþe* DUC. *bewroȝte*] *bewroȝte* L ; *þe wroght* D ; *wroght* þe C. *mon—wroȝte*] *wurgh ywrough* (!) E. *in*] *on* D ; *thurgh* U. *wlonk*] so DU ; *blonk* L ; *fayre* E ; *welthy* C.
295. *& cytees* E. *vnder*] *in* E. *Syon*] so EDUC ; *sene* (!) L.
296. þe] om. EDUC. *derworthi* U ; *derwurgh* (!) E. *Crist*] *ful* add. U. *schal be*] *schul ȝe* EDUC ; *hit* add. C. *ȝolden*] *bye* DUC ; *abye* E.
297. *Betheem* (!) *is* C. *brough* (!) C. *an*] þe ED.
299. *Schal*] *That* D. *of*] *in* D. *ȝow* (!) E. *kyn* EDUC. *anoynted* EDC ; *enoynted* U.
300. *Nor* UC ; *Ne no* E. *iouke*] so DU ; *joke* C ; *dwelle* E ; *ronke* (!) L. *ȝou*] so EDUC ; *ȝour* (!) L.
Passus secundus add. U.
301. *eche*] *ilk* U. *eche s.*] þe *cheef* E. *Surrie*] *sorwe* C.
302. *And brend* EDUC. *ay*] *euere* EDC. *all*] so DUC ; *ful* L. *at—laften*] *as they wente . cytees & townes* E.
303. *þere was* EC. *ruthe*] DUC ; *weep-ing* E ; *rich* (!) L. *in—tounnes*] *aboute* E.
304. &] *For* C ; *wiþ* add. D. *red*] *liȝt* EDUC. *lastyng* U. *leye* EDU ; *flame* C ; *in* add. E. *londes* E ; *cuntre* U ; *about* add. D. *ouere*] *abowte* E.
305. *They tooke* EDU ; *The* (!) C. *townes and touris* DUC ; *towres & townes* E ; & add. EDUC. *teldes*] *holdes* C ; *castelles* E. *ful*] om. U. *fele*] *many* U ; *ryche* EDC.
306. *& brast* E ; *They brasten* UC ; þe add. C. *borwe*] *townes* U. *borwe w.*] *queynte gynnes* E.
307. *Holy*] *All* DUC ; *& alle* E. þe] om. EU. *here*] *folk* (*fook* (!) E) EUC. *heþen h.*] *faitheles* D ; þey add. EDUC. *hewyn*] *felde* E ; *drowe* U ; *fill* D. *grounde*] þe *dethe* DUC ; *foote* E.
308. *Boþ*] om. E. *in*] *on* DUC. *benche* DUC ; *halle* E. *boure* EDU.
309. *þere*] so EDUC ; *þat* (!) L. *dwelleth* U.
310. *Fledde* EDUC. *as* þe] *faste &* (!) E. *foule*] *folk* ED. *fauc. w. str.*] *fomen assayleth* EDUC.
311. *ful*] *wol* E. *noble*] *riche* EDUC.
312. *many*] *a* add. C. *many—toure*] *torettys & towres* E. *þat*] þe EDUC.

18 *Jerusalem is besieged by the Romans.*

    Pri̇nces & prelates ⁑ & poreil of þe londe,
    Clerkes & comens ⁑ of contrees aboute,
    Wer' schacked to þat cite, ⁑ sacrifice to make
    At paske tyme, as preched hem ⁑ prestes of þe lawe.   316

Many Jews are killed.   Many swykel at þe sweng ⁑ to þe swerd ȝede ;
    For penyes passed non, ⁑ þoȝ he pay wolde,
    Bot diden alle to þe deþe ⁑ & drowen hem after
    With engynes to Jerusalem ⁑ þer' Jewes wer' þykke.   320

Fol. 6 a.   Þey sette sadly a sege ⁑ þe cite alle aboute,
A siege is laid to Jerusalem, and costly tents are raised.   Piȝten pauelouns doun ⁑ of pallen webbes,
    With ropis of riche silk, ⁑ raysen vp swyþe
    Grete tentis as a toun, ⁑ of torke[is] cloþys,   324

Especially the tent of the chieftains is fitted up most splendidly.   Choppyn ouer þe cheuentayns ⁑ with charboklis four'
    A gay egle of gold ⁑ on a gilde appul,
    With grete dragouns grym, ⁑ alle in gold wroȝte,
    & [þer] to lyouns two, ⁑ lyande þer vnder'.   328
    Paled & paynted ⁑ þe paueloun was vmbe,
    Stoked ful of storijs, ⁑ strayned myd armys
    Of quaynte colour to know, ⁑ kerneld a-lofte,
    An hundred stondyng on stage ⁑ in þat stede one.   332

---

ll. 313—16 om. EDUC.
317. *swykel—sweng*] *a swykyll swayne* þen C ; *swykeful swayn* D ; *a orpyd man* E. *swerd* ȝ.] *deth wente* E. l. 317 om. U.
318. *For*] no add. E. *peny* EDUC ; *nor pownd* add. C. *passeth* U. *non*] *not one* DUC. þoȝ] þat EDUC. *he*] þei E ; þat D. *peyne* (!) E. *wolde*] *myȝte* EDUC.
319. *Bot diden*] *They dude hem* EDU ; *That þey deden hem* C. *alle*] om. C. *&—after*] *that thei catche myght* U ; *with dyntys of swerd (swerdys* E) EDC.
320. *With gynnys* DC ; *& thanne* E. þere J. *were*] þei *chasyn (chased* C) *ful* DC. þere—þykke] *they priked wel faste* E. This line is omitted in U.
321. þey] *And* DUC. þey *s. s.*] *Than sette thei* E. *alle*] om. E.
322. *Piȝten*] þei *pight down* DUC ; *& pyȝt vp* E. *pavel. d.*] *a pauyloun* ED ; *her pauilons* UC. *pallen*] *arras* E ; *silken* C.
323. *With*] *The* U. *riche*] *clene* E. *silk*] *thei* add. UC. *reiled* U ; *reysed* EDC ; *hem* add. C ; *it* add. E. *vp*] *ful* U. *swyþe*] *heyȝe* EUC ; *on hy* D.
324. *& grete* E. *as a t.*] *as townes* U. *torkeis*] *turkeyes* EDC ; *turky* U ; *torken* (!) L.

325. *Chopt* U ; *They chopped* C. *ouer*] on D. *chivsteyn* DUC. *Chop.—cheu.*] *They settyn vp on þe cheef* E. *with*] om. EDUC. *charbuncles* EDU ; *charboukeles* C.
326. *A gay*] *With an* E. *egle*] *al* add. EC. *gold*] *stode* add. C.
327. *drag.*] *&* add. EDUC. *in*] *of* D. *alle—wroȝte*] *grysly on to loke* E.
328. *þer*] so EDUC ; *lyk* L. *two*] so EDU ; *tweyne* C ; *also* L. *liggyng* EDU. þer] *her* D.
329. *Paled*] *& paued* add. C. *was*] om. UC. *Puled—was*] *Pale and pavilon peyntid al* D ; *The paale and þe pauylun . was peynted* E. *vmbe*] *abowte* EUC ; *al a-bout* D.
330. *Stoked—storijs*] *Ful of stories (stonys* D) *stikid (ystilled* U) DUC ; and add. UC. *steynyd with* DUC. *Stoked—myd*] *With storyes of knyȝthod & of diverse* E.
331. *quaynte*] *diuers* DUC ; *wunderful* E. *coloures* EDUC. *kerneld*] *& coueryd* DC ; *and keuerd* U. *vpon lofte* C. *kern. al.*] *ho hem outhe* (!) E.
332. *An*] *And* C. *on*] *on a* D ; *in* UC. *stag* (!) D. *in—one*] *in þat place alone* C ; *on stedis about* D. *Y trowe nat in þis wurld . were swiche oþer* E.

Vespasianus deputes twelve Messengers to the Jews, 19

Toured with torettes ⁑ was þe tente þanne,
Suþ britaged a-boute, ⁑ briȝt to byholde.
Er alle þe sege was sette, ⁑ ȝit of þe cite comyn   *The masters*
Messengeres, wer' made ⁑ fram maistres of þe lawe;   336 *of the law send messengers to the*
To þe chef cheuentayn ⁑ þey chosen her' wey,   *Romans to inquire after*
Deden mekly by mouþe ⁑ her' message attonys,   *the reason of their coming.*
Sayen : "þe cite haþ [vs] sent ⁑ to serche ȝour wille,
To here þe cause of ȝour comyng, ⁑ [& what] ȝe coueyte wolde."
Waspasian no word ⁑ to þe wyes schewed,   341 *Vespasianus*
Bot sendeþ sondismen aȝen, ⁑ xii siker' knyȝtes,   *gives no reply, but deputes twelve*
ȝaf hem charge to go, ⁑ & þe gomes telle,   *knights, to tell that they*
þat alle þe cause of her com[e] ⁑ was Crist forto venge. 344 *intend to take revenge for*
"Sayþ, y bidde hem be boun, ⁑ bishopes & oþer,   *the death of Christ.*
To morow or [mydday] ⁑ [modur nakyd] alle,
Vp her' ȝates to ȝelde, ⁑ with ȝerdes an hande,
Eche whiȝt in a white scherte, ⁑ & no wede ellys,   348
Jewyse for Iesu Crist ⁑ by juggement to take,
& make hem come, þat Iesu Crist ⁑ þroȝ conseil bytrayede ;

---

333. was] ȝit were E. tent] tentys E ; toun U. þanne] om. E.
334. And seth D ; And sethen U; And aftur C ; & E. brit.] bright gold U. briȝt] light U.
335. & ar E. alle] om. EU. was] were C ; al add. E. ȝit] out add. ED.
336. were m.] ymaad EDUC. fram] of EDC ; om. U. maistres of þe] Moyses ED.
337. cheuyntcyn cheef EC ; chefteyn chefe DU. chosen thei U.
338. Deden] & made EDUC. mek.] meche E. by] with her ED. here m. at.] & to hym seyde E.
339. They seyþe C ; om. EDU. cytesens han EUC ; citezeins D. vs] so EDUC ; ȝou (!) L. serche] wetyn E.
340. To here] To knowe D ; & E. come DU. & what] so EDUC ; ȝif (!) L. ȝe—wolde] þat (om. U) ȝe (ye now U) cleypne EDUC.
341. Wulde W. ED; Now wold W. C; The while V. U. wyes] wiȝhts D ; men C ; messagerys E. shewe DC ; telle E ; said U.
342. sente EDUC. sondes UC ; sodeynliche E. sikere] wurthi E.
343. ȝaf h. ch.] Gert (Made U) hem greithely DU ; & bad hem faste E ; They made hem redy C. &] om. ED ; to add. UC. gomes] lordes C ; cytescyns E ; to
add. ED. telle] seye E.
344. alle] om. EDUC. her] his UC. come] so DU ; comyng EC ; coms (!) L. was] is UC. forto v.] to auenge EDUC.
345. Sey EUC ; þat add. C ; hem add. D ; hem þat add. E. y b. h.] þey make hem E. boun] redy EC. bisshope EDC ; the bisshop U. oþer] alle EDC ; thei all U.
346. morn U. or] before E ; þe add. UC. mydday] so EDUC ; vndren of þe day L. al modur nakyd DUC ; to be clene nakyd E ; open-heded alle L.
347. And vp C. here] þe D. Up here] At þe E. to ȝ.] hem to opene E. an] in D ; in her EUC. hondes EU.
348. Ilk U ; a add. EDU. whiȝt] bierne D ; body E ; wye U ; mon C. a white] his EDUC. scherte] breech ED. & no—ellys] with owte (oþer wede (oþur cloth C ; gere more U) EDUC.
349. þe Iewis DUC. Crist] om. DUC ; sake add. D. ; to take add. (!) L. by] þe D ; her U ; om. C. Iuggement for to take . for Crist whom they slowyn E.
350. &] om. E. make hem come] bring Cayphas DUC ; Bryngge also Cayphas E. Iesu] om. DC. þroȝ] by D. cons.] iuggement D. þat—cons.] thurgh conseil that Iesu U. bytr.] cursidly slow D. þat—betr.] þe cursyd schrewe E.

	Or y to þe walles schal wende ⸭ & walten alle ouere ;	
	Schal no ston vpon ston ⸭ stonde, by y passe."	352
	þis sondismen sadly ⸭ to þe cite ȝede,	
	Þer þe lordes of þe londe ⸭ lent weren alle,	
They deliver the message,	Tit tolden her' tale, ⸭ & wonder' towe made,	
	Of Crist & of Cayphas, ⸭ & how þey come scholde.	356
	& when þe knyȝtes of Crist ⸭ carpyn bygonn,	
	Þe Jewes token alle xii, ⸭ with-out tale mor',	
	Her' hondis bounden at her' bak ⸭ with borden stauys,	
Fol. 6 b.	And of flocken her' fa[x], ⸭ & her' fair' berdis,	360
but the Jews send them back after having disfigured them in the most scandalous way,	Made hem naked as a nedel ⸭ to þe neþer houe,	
	Her' visages blecken with bleche, ⸭ & al þe body after,	
	Suþ knyt with a corde ⸭ to eche knyȝtes swer'	
	A chese, & charged hem ⸭ her' chyuentayn to ber' :	364
and bid them tell the prince that they refuse to surrender the town.	" Sayþ, vnbuxum we beþ, ⸭ his biddyng to ȝete,	
	Ne noȝt dreden his dom, ⸭ his deþ haue we atled ;	
	He schal vs fynde in þe felde, ⸭ ne no ferr' seke,	
	To morowe pryme or hit passe, ⸭ & so ȝour prince telliþ."	368
	Þe burnes busken out of burwe, ⸭ bounden alle twelf,	

---

351. *wall* DUC. *schal to þe walles* E. *walten alle ouere*] *warpe (caste* C) *hit* (om. U) *to þe erþe* DUC ; *falle* (!) *hem doun to grounde* E.

352. *Schal—vpon*] *þat (For* U) *þer ne* (om. C) *shal stik ne (nor* U) DUC. *stonde*] *ligge* E. *by y p.*] *ere I hens go* U ; *whan y go* DC ; *whan I weende* E.

353. *þis*] *The* E. *sond.*] *messagers* EC ; *soudeours* U ; *were* add. E. *sadly*] *foorth sent* ED ; *sent forth* UC. *to þe*] *& to* E. *ȝede*] *went* ED.

354. *lent w.*] *lengedyn hem* D ; *linggenen* (!) U ; *dwelleden* C. *lent w. a.*] *iloggyd were* E.

355. *A lstite* U ; *Anone* D ; *As sone as þey* C. *tolden*] *þei* add. DU. *here*] *this* DUC. *&—made*] *in truþe as þei shold* DUC. *& þis tale toolde . riȝt as þey were bode* E.

356. *Of Cayphas and of Crist* DC. *how*] *þat* ED.
This line is omitted in U.

357. *& when þe*] *Whan these* EDUC. *Cristes* C. *carpyng* EU ; *spekynge* C. *byginne* D.

358. *alle XII*] *hem as tyte (sone* C) DUC. *token alle XII*] *wentyn anon* E. *tale*] *talkynge* C ; *any* E.

359. *And here* C. *& bounde her hondes* E. *with borden stauys*] *wol (ful* UC ; om. D) *beterly þanne* EDUC.

360. *fax*] *face* (!) L. *of—fax*] *of (fluen þei þe (flewen her* U) *faxe* DU ; *And schoven of her fax* C ; *& kytte of þe fayr her* E. *&*] *of* ED ; *all* add. C. *her*] *þo* D. *faire*] *longe* E. *bernes* D.

361. *Made hem*] *As* EDUC. *nele* U ; *heel* E ; *in* add. EDUC. *þe*] *her* EDU. *houe*] *hyue* U ; *coyfe* E.

362. *vis.—bleche*] *face enbawmyd with (in* C) *blood* EDUC. *al þe*] *her* EU.

363. *And seth* D ; *And sen* U ; *And thanne* E ; *And aftur þis* C. *eche*] *ilk a* U ; *euery* E. *knyȝt.*] *knyght* ADU. *swere*] *nekke* E ; *corps* D. *with—swere*] *to eche a knyȝte . with a gret corde* C.

364. *chefteyns* E.

365. *Seyȝt* (!) E. *And sey* DUC. *ȝete*] *kepe* EDUC.

366. *Ne n. d.*] *We (& ED) drede (no thyng (noght* U) EDUC. *we*] om. (!) E. *atled*] *ordeynid* DUC ; *cast* E.

367. *ne no f.*] *no furthere to* EDUC.

368. *morn* U. *or*] *at* (!) E.

369. *þe*] *þes* DUC. *burnes*] *knyȝtes* E ; *men* C. *busked* DUC ; *hem* add. DUC. *of*] *þe* add. DU. *busken—burwe*] *turnyd aȝen* E. *bounden*] om. U.

The Knights deliver the Message of the Jews.

Aȝen message to make ⁞ fram þe maister Jewes.
Was neuer Waspasian so wroþe, ⁞ as whan þe wyes come,
þat wer' scorned & schende ⁞ vpon schame wyse.   372
þis knyȝtes byfor þe kyng ⁞ vpon knees fallen
& tolden þe tale, ⁞ as hit tid hadde:
"Of þy manace ne þy myȝt ⁞ þey make bot lyte:
þus ben we tourned of our' tyre, ⁞ in tokne of þe soþe,   376
& bounden for our bolde speche; ⁞ þe batail þey willeþ
To morowe prime or hit passe, ⁞ þey put hit no ferre.
Hit schal be satled on þy-self, ⁞ þe same þat þou atlest,
þus han þey certifiet þe, ⁞ & sende þe þis cheses."   380
Wode wedande wroþ ⁞ Waspasian was þanne,
Layde wecche to þe walle ⁞ & warned in haste,
þat alle maner of men ⁞ in þe morowe scholde
Be sone after þe sonne ⁞ assembled in þe felde.   384
He streyȝt up a standard ⁞ in a stour' wyse,
Bild as a belfray, ⁞ bretful of wepne;
Whan oȝt fauted in þe folke, ⁞ þat to þe feld longed,
Atte þe belfray to be, ⁞ botnyng to fynde.   388

The messengers come back,

and inform Vespasianus of the euger desire of the Jews to fight.

Vespasianus erects a standard in form of a belfry full of weapons.

---

370. *Message for to* E. *fro* DUC. *fram—Iewes*] *as þey were chaargyd* E.
371. *Waspasian neuer* EC. *wroþe*] *wo* EDUC. *wyes*] *knyȝtys* EDUC.
372. *scorned &*] *shamed and* UC; *y-schaue & * E; *shamefully* D. *vpon sch.*] *on (in* D) *such a foul* EDUC.
373. *The* EDUC. *byfor*] *come to* ED UC. *vpon*] *& * (om. U) *on* (*vpon* C) *her* EDUC. *fyllyn* EUC.
374. *&*] *thei* add. U; *alle þey* add. EDC. *þe*] *by* U. *as hit*] *that thei* U. *tid*] *byfalle* C.
ll. 289—374 are lost in A.
375. *Of*] *By* E. *ne*] *& * EDUC. *þi mynt* D; *thretnyng* E. *make*] *sette* EC; *recche* U. *bot*] *a* add. DUC. *lytel* ED UC. *Ne noghte drede thay thy domes, thy dede hafe thaye ettyllede* A.
376. *And thus* A. *ben*] *are* ADUC. *of oure*] *in* DUC. *þus—tyre*] *Loo how we been arayed* E. *takynnynge* A.
377. *our*] om. E. *for our*] *hem by* C. *þe*] *to* AUC; *for to* D. *wille* ADU; *wyllen* C. *þe—willeþ*] *as theues we were* E.
378. *putte* C. *forthire* AEC; *ferþere* DU.
379. *be satl.*] *sattille* ADU; *falle* E. *Hit—satled*] *And seyn it shall lyȝte* C.

þat] þa (!) A; om. DU. *you* A. *ettillede* A; *hem mentist* EDU; *hem demes* C.
380. *þe*] *you* A. *han þey cert.*] *thei certifie* UC; *they sent* ED. *þe*] *ȝow* A; om. U; *to saye* add. AEDU; *& seyn* add. C. *sendis* AE; *sent* DC. *þe*] *ȝow* A. *chese* UC.
381. *wed.*] *wepyng* EDC; *wepand* U. *Wode wed.*] *Full wode, wylde and* A.
382. *He leyde* EU. *wecche*] *waytes* A. *walles* AE.
383. *Till* A. *of*] om. D. *men*] *that* add. A. *in*] *one* AEDUC. *morne* AU; *thay* add. A.
384. *By* UC. *semblyd* EDU; *gedered* C.
385. *streyȝt*] *sette* C. *He str. vp*] *Than thay strake* A. *in*] *appone* A. *stoure*] *steerne* EDU; *angry* C.
386. *Byggid* DU; *Ytymbryd* E. *a*] om. D. *berfray* DUC. *bretful*] *euen full* C.
387. *That when* C. *fayled* EDUC. *in*] om. A. *folke*] *feeld* EDUC. *þe*] om. EC. *feld*] *fighte* ADUC; *werre* E. *longeth* U.
388. *þe*] om. U. *berfraye* ADUC. *Atte—to*] *Men schulde to þe belfrey renne . & there it redy* E. *fynde*] *haue* DUC. *botnyng to f.*] *baynly botede alsone* A.

22 *A golden Dragon is placed on the top of the belfry.*

On the top of it they dress a golden dragon supplied with arrows in its mouth, and a falchion with four blades under its feet.

A dragou*n* was dressed, ⁙ drawyn a lofte,
Wyde gapande, of gold, ⁙ gomes to swelwe,
W*ith* arwes armed i*n* þe mouþe, ⁙ & also he hadde
A fauch[ou]n vnde*r* h*is* feet, ⁙ w*ith* four' kene bladdys, 392
þer of þe poyntes wer' pi3t ⁙ in p*a*rtyis four'
Of þ*is* wlonfulle wor[l]de, ⁙ þer þei werr' fondyn.
In forbesyn to þe folke ⁙ þ*is* fauchoun hengeþ,
þ*at* þey hadde wonnen w*ith* [werre] ⁙ al þe world riche. 396
A bal of bre*n*nande gold ⁙ þe beste was on sette,

Fol. 7 a. This dragon is fastened on a golden ball.

H*is* taille tr*a*yled þer a-boute, ⁙ þ*at* tou*r*ne scholde he neue*r*e,
Wha*n* he was lifte vp-on lofte, ⁙ þer þe lord werred,
Bot ay lokande on þe londe, ⁙ tille þ*at* al lau3te wer', 400
þer by þe cite my3t se, ⁙ no setlyng wolde rise
Ne no trete of no trewes, ⁙ bot þe tou*n* 3elde,
Or ride on þe Romayns, ⁙ for þey han her rede take,
þer britned to be ⁙ or þe [burghe] wy*n*ne. 404
H*is* wynges sprad wer' abrode, ⁙ bou*n* forto flee,

---

389. *was*] *is* DUC; *thare* add. A. *dryssede* A; *and* add. AEDUC. *vp a loft* D; *vpon (appon* A) *lofte* AEUC.
390. *gapyng* EDC. *of gold*] *with his mouth* E. *þe gomes* D; *þe lordes* C; *þe Iewes* E. *of g.—to*] *the gomes of gold* U. *to swelwe*] *for (vn* C, om. ED) *to schewe* EDUC.
391. *arwes*] *arghely* add. A. *armed*] *& armour* C. *þe*] *his* AD; om. UC. *&*] om. D. *in—hadde*] *on eche syde* E.
392. *& a* EC. *fauchyn* (!) L. *fawkone* AED. *fote* UC. *kyn* D. *foure k.*] *many maner* E. *blad.*] *fetheres* EDU; *fedcres* C.
393. *There with* A. *were p.*] *y-pight* DUC.
394. *And of* DUC. *þis*] þ*at* D. *wlonf. worlde*] *wankille werlde* A; *wantoun worme* DUC. *words* (!) L. *þer*] *that* A. *werre*] *hade were* A. *þer—fondyn*] *is wondur to here* DUC.
395. *forb. to*] *schewynge of* A; *rebukynge of* C. *þe*] om. D. *þis*] þe ADUC. *fauchoun*] DU; *fawkon* AC; *fauchouns* (!) L. *heng.*] *thay hangede* A; *he held* DUC.
396. *werre*] *swerd* LA. *hadde—werre*] *had wiþ werre* D; *wonne with werre* U; *with werre wonne* C.
ll. 393—6 are omitted in E.
397. *On a* EDUC. *byrnande* A; *brent* EDUC. *þe b.*] *þe brest* D; *þis worm* E. *on sette*] *yfastnet* E; *assisid* DUC.
398. *þer ab.*] *adoun* ED; *ther doune* U; *doun* C. *trayl. þer ab.*] *takynede to be* A. *he*] *þay* A.
399. *Whan*] þ*at* add. E. *lyftede* AUC. *vp-*] om. ADUC. *lifte—lofte*] *reysed* E. *þer—werred*] *thare lordis werrayde* A; *þe lordis aforn* DUC; *þe Iewes my3te it se* E.
400. *Bot ay*] *Moost* DUC. *lokande*] *to luke* A; *þei lokyd* DU; *þey looke* C. *on*] *to* DC. *londe*] *lane* C. *one the l.*] *therto* U. *þat*] om. A. *þat al*] *hit* DUC. *Al þe day longe to feryn hem more* E.
401. *my3te þe cyte* C. *se*] *þat* add. ED. *non saughetillyng* AD; *saulyng* U; *pece* C; *acord* E. *schulde* EDC; *shul* U.
402. *Ne no*] *Ne* ED; *Nor* UC. *entrete* DU; *entre* C. *of*] om. E. *no*] *ne* E; om. AUC. *trewe* D; *truwe* E; *trewe lowe* UC. *bot*] *tyl* EDUC. *toun*] *cite* DU. *wynne*] *be 3oldyn* DUC; *were 3olde* E; *3oldyn* A.
403. *Or*] *But* E. *on*] *ouer* C. *Or—þe*] *And now the riche* A. *for þey*] om. A. *her*] *to* A; om. DUC. *for—take*] *spede what thei my3te* D.
404. *þer*] *At thay there wolde* A. *to*] om. A. *br. to be*] *bykere to abyde* C. *or*] *ells* add. A. *burghe*] so ADUC; *toun* L. *Or be kyld as caytyfes . & cowardes be hoolde* E.
405. *sprad*] *brighte* A. *abr.*] *& brade and* A. *flye* A. This line is omitted in EDUC.

The Investment of the Town begins.

W*ith* belles bordored a-boute, ⁆ al of bri3t seluer*e*,
Redy, whan ou3te ru*n*nen ⁆ to rynge ful loude
W*ith* eche [wap] of a [wynde], ⁆ þat to þe wy*n*ges sprongyn.
Ibrytaged aboute ⁆ þe belfray was þa*n*ne   409 *The belfry is fortified with a tower.*
W*ith* a tenful tour', ⁆ þat ouer þe tou*n* gawged.
þe b[est] by þe bri3tnesse ⁆ burnes my3t knowe
Four' myle þer fro, ⁆ so þe feldes schonen;   412
& on eche pomel wer' py3t ⁆ penseles hy3e
Of selke & sendel, ⁆ w*ith* seluere ybetyn.
H*it* glitered as gled fur', ⁆ ful of gold riche,   *The dragon glitters far*
Ouer al þe cite to se, ⁆ as þe so*n*ne bemys.   416 *off.*
Byfor þe four' 3ates ⁆ he formes to lenge
Sixtene þousand by somme, ⁆ while þe sege lasteþ,
Sette ward [to] þe walles, ⁆ þat no3t awey scaped,
Sixe þousand i*n* sercle ⁆ þe cite alle a-boute.   420 *The town is blockaded round about.*
Was no3t, while þe ny3t laste, ⁆ bot nehy*n*g of stedis,
Strogelyng i*n* stele wede ⁆ & stuffyng of helmes.

---

406. *With*] *Braydyn* D; *Brouden* U; *They* (!) *honged* C. *bord.*] om. DUC. *of*] *in* A. *al—seluere*] *þat boldly (bysyly* C) *rongyn* DUC. This line is omitted in E.
407. *runnen*] *range* A. *ful*] *appon* A. l. 407 is omitted in EDUC.
408. *At* UC. *eche*] *yche a* C; *a eche* (!) D; *ilke a* AU. *wape (weef* D; *waif* U; *blaste* C) *of the wynde* ADUC; *wynde of a wap* (!) L. *to þe*] þe DC; *his* A. *wynge* DU. *spr.*] *touchede* ADC; *touches* U. l. 408 is omitted in E. ll. 406 and 408 are put after l. 414 in DUC.
409. *Ibr.*] *Bigly brestede* A; *bigly* add. DUC. *berfra* A; *berfray* DUC. *was*] *is* UC. *The berfrey was britagyd strongliche abowte* E.
410. *a*] om. D. *tenful*] *dredefull* C; *wounder strong* E. *touris* D. *ouer*] *to* A. *toun*] *cite* D. *gaggede* A; *goggid* D; *gogges* U; *lokyd* E; *hangedde* C.
411. *best*] so ADUC; *dragun* E; *batail* (!) L. *þe*] *his* ADUC. *burnes*] *berynns* A; *þe bernes* D; *men* EC. *burnes m.*] *best myght thei* U. *kenne* EDUC.
412. *felde* A. *schone* A. *so—schonen*] *forsothe at þe leest (beste* C) DUC; *for soþe & no lasse* E.
413. *&*] om. AEDUC. *eche*] *cche a* DC; *ilk a* U; *euery* E; *a* A. *pomel* ⁆ L. *were*] *was* A; *is* DUC. *py3t* L. *pesalls* A; *full* add. A. *hye*] *many* D.

414. *Of*] *With* A. *&*] *of* add. EDUC; *with* add. A. *sendel*] *syluer* EDC; *selcouthe werke* A. *with*] *of* A. *enbetyn* A. *with s. yb.*] *seemliche arayed* EDUC.
415. *gled f.*] þe *glede of fyer* C; *gledis of fyre* A; *red feer* E. *ful of*] *or of* A; *in* þe DUC. *ful—riche*] þe *gold was so fyn* E.
416. *al*] om. A. þe] om. C. *to—bemys*] *whan þe sonne schyned* E.
417. *Than by fore* A; *A-fore* EDC; *A-forn* U. 3*ates*] þoo add. C. *thay fourmede* AU; *formede þey* C; *fourmyd þan* D. *lenge*] *lye* DUC. *þey—lenge*] *ordeyned were* E.
418. *Sixty* EDUC. *thowsandes* A. *while*] *till* A. *laste* E; *lastede* ADC.
419. *Thay sett* A; *And sette* DUC; 3*it was* E. *ward*] *wacche* EDUC; *sadly* A. *to*] *so* ADUC; *abowte* E; *on* L. *wal* DUC. *noght*] *none* DC; *on* (!) U. *scaped*] *went* DUC. *þat—scaped*] *of strong ordynaunce* E.
420. *And sex* UC. *thowsandes* A. *in sercles* A; *to serche* UC. *þat no wy3th my3th awey . in no maner wyse* E. l. 420 is omitted in D.
421. *Was*] *ther* add. C. *whils* AU. *ny3t*] *sege* C. *lastede* ADC.
422. *Stowryng* E; *Steryng* DUC. *in*] *with* A; *of* EDUC. *wedis* D; *werke* A. *&*] om. DC. *Ri3t so in þe cite . þey schapte hem perfore* add. L.

Both parties make preparations for a battle.	With armyng of olyfauntes ⁝ & oþer arwe bestes, A3en þe cristen to come ⁝ with castels on bake. Waspasya[n] in stele wede ⁝ & his wyes alle,	424
The army of Vespasianus marches to the vale of Josaphet.	Weren di3t forþ by day, ⁝ & drowen to þe vale Of Josophat, þer Jesu Crist ⁝ schal juggen alle þinges, Bigly batayled hym þer, ⁝ to abide his oþer.	428
The vanguard is led by Titus, the middle part by Vespasianus, the third by Sabyn of Syria.	Þe fauward Titus toke, ⁝ to telle vpon ferste, With six þousand soudiours, ⁝ assyned for þe nones, & mony in þe myd-ward ⁝ wer' merked to lenge, Þer Waspasian was ⁝ with princes & dukes ; & sixtene þousand in þe þridde ⁝ with a þryuande kny3t,	432
Fol. 7 b.	Sir' Sabyn of Surrie, ⁝ a siker man of armes, Þat prince was of Prouynce ⁝ & michel peple ladde, Fourty hundred in helmes ⁝ & harnays to schewe,	436
The rest is left behind for the protection of the tents.	& ten þousand atte tail ⁝ at· þe tentis lafte, Hors & harnays ⁝ fram harmyng to kepe. By þat bemys on þe burwe ⁝ blowen ful loude, & baners beden hem forþ. ⁝ Now blesse vs our lorde!	440

423. *With*] om. AEDUC. *elefauntes* A. *arwe*] *stronge* EDC ; *grete* U.
424. *Agaynes* AU. *cast.*] *strenght* U. *on*] *her* add. AEU. *bakkes* AED.
425. *Waspasial* (!) L. *in st. w.*] *yarmed* C. *wyes*] *wightis* D ; *knythes* E ; *meyne* C. *alle*] *keene* E.
426. *Weren*] om. DC. *Were d.*] *He dight him* U ; *Arayed hem* E. *forþ*] om. E. *by*] *with the* ADUC ; *to the* U ; *a3ens* E. *&*] om. ED. *drawyng* E. *dale* D.
427. *Josephat* E ; *Josaphat* AUC ; *Josaphath* D. *Crist*] om. AEDUC. *juggen*] *deme* UC. *alle þ.*] *man kynde* E.
428. *And bygly* A ; *And boldely* D ; *And* EUC. *enbatelde* AEU. *hym*] *thaym* A ; *hem* EDU. *hem enbatelede* C. *bydyn* ADC. *þis*] *thise* UC ; *that* A ; *þe* E.
429. *Tytus (anon* add. E) *took þe vaward (vale* ED) EDUC ; *for* add. C. *appon firste* A ; *þe sothe* EDUC.
430. *sexty* AD ; *sixtene* EUC. *thowshandes* A. *soud.*] om. EDUC. *assignede* AEDUC.
431. *&*] add. A. *medillwarde* A. *mony—myd.*] *in þe myddelwaard als many* EDUC. *were*] *was* A. *were—lenge*] *markid to be* DC ; *assigned to bene* U ; *arayed to be* E.
432. *þer*] *The* (!) E ; *als* add. A.

433. *sixt.*] *seuyntene* A. *in*] *on* A. *prid.*] *syde* add. A. *sixt.—prid.*] *in þe reerwarde as manye (fele* U ; *fell* C) EDUC. *þryuande*] *wurthi* E ; *fayre* C. *with—kny3t*] *with dukes and knyghtes* U ; *so semely of sight* D.
435. *Þare (He* E) *was a prince* EDUC. *&*] *þat* DUC. *meche* EDUC.
436. *in*] *on* EDUC. *helmes*] *an here* A ; *an heep* EDUC. *& harn.*] *with helmes* AEDUC. *to sch.*] *yty3ed* E ; *& scheldis* A.
437. *atte*] *of þe* A ; *in þe* DUC. *atte t.*] *were yleeft* E ; *was* add. A. *atte* U ; *at thaire* A. *tentis*] *were* add. UC. *atlafte*] *be hynde al in tentes* E ; *to kepe her tentis* D.
438. *Thaire horse* A ; *Her hors* EDUC. *&*] *thaire* add. A ; *her* add. EDUC. *hanayse* (!) A. *fro* AE. *harmes* AEDC ; *harme* U. *kepe*] *loke* DC.
439. *By þat*] *Sone after* E. *biernes* D ; *trumpours* E ; *trumpes* C. *on*] *in* AED UC. *burwe*] *town* E. *ful*] *wol* ED ; *appon* (!) U.
440. *baners*] *beryns* A. *beden*] *b* written on erasure, L ; *bode* E ; *benten* U ; *benden* C. *thaym* A. *Now*] *þer* A ; *&* EUC ; om. D. *blys* DU. *our l.*] *betyde* DU ; *þe tyde* C. *blesse—lorde*] *penselys manye* E.

The Army of the Jews marches out.   25

Þe Jewes assembled wer' sone, ⸴ & of þe cite come   The army of
   An hundred þousand on hors, ⸴ with hamberkes a-tired,   the Jews
                                                                     leaves the
With-out folke vpon fot, ⸴ at þe four' ȝates,   town,
þat preset to þe place, ⸴ with pauyes on hande.   444
Fyf & twenti olyfauntes, ⸴ defensable bestes,   with many
                                                                     elephants,
With brode castels on bak ⸴ out of burwe come;
& on eche olyfaunte ⸴ armed men manye,
Ay an hundred an hey, ⸴ an hundred with-yn.   448
Þo drowen dromedarius doun, ⸴ deuelich þicke,   dromedaries
                                                                     and camels,
[An] hundred þousand, & yheled ⸴ with harnays of mayle,
Eche beste with a big tour, ⸴ þer bold men wer' ynne,
Twenty, told by tale, ⸴ in eche tour euene.   452
Cameles closed in stele ⸴ comen out þanne
Ffaste toward þe feld, ⸴ a ferlich nonbr',
Busked to batail, ⸴ & on bak hadde   bearing
                                                                     castles on
Echon a toret of tre, ⸴ with ten men of armes.   456   their backs.
Chares ful of chosen, ⸴ charged with wepne
A wonder' nonbr' þer was, ⸴ who so wite lyste.
Many douȝti þat day, ⸴ þat was adradde neuer',

Passus add. A; *Passus tercius* add. U as superscription to the following part.
441. *semblyd* ED; *gadered* C. *were sembled* U. *&*] *owt* add. ADU. *of*]*fro* E. *þe*] om. U.
442. *An h.* þ.] *Thousyndes* E. *appon* A. *with*] *in* AEDUC. *haweberkes* AED; *hauberk* U; *armour* C. *ytired* U.
443. *-owten* AU. *appon* A.
444. *þat*] *&* E. *pressed* A; *presed* EDU; *precedde* (!) C; *forthe* add. AE; *out* add. DUC. *to*] *in* D. *playn* EDUC. *to þe pl.*] *with pryde* A. *paveys* D; *paneschis* A; *panys* EU; *panyce* C. *on*] *in* ADU. *on h.*] *ynowe* E.
445. *And fyf* DUC. *twenty*] *fourty* ED. *fensable* ED; *fusabull* C.
446. *brode*] *brothe* (!) C; om. E. *appon* A; *here* add. EU. *bakkes* AE. *of*] *þe* add. EDUC. *burwe*] *town* E.
447. *eche an* C; *ilke ane* AU. *manye*] *were* E.
448. *Ay*] *Hase* A; *Nyghe* UC. *Ay an*] *Nyne* D. *highte* A. *an h.*] *and hurdeschede* A; *wiþ hurdys* D; *& hurdes* C; *and hurdist* U. *To fyȝte in hurdys . anoward on here bakkes* E.
449. *Thay* A; *There* UC; *Than* E. *drewe drewmondaryes* A; *dromedaryes drowyn* EUC. *doun*] *owte* AE. *deu.*] *dulfully* A. *pickc*]*fele* U; *manye* C.

450. *An*] so EA; *And* UC. *& yhcled*] *& alle helyd (hyled* C) EC; *ȝarmed* U; *hosede and hillide* A. *with*] *in* AEC. *armes* UC; *helmys* A.
451. *& eche* EC; *Ilke a* A; *And ilk* U. *beste*] om. EUC. *with*] *baar* E. *þer*] *&* EC; om. U. *were*] *ther* EUC. *in ware* A.
ll. 449—451 are omitted in D.
452. *ytool* (!) E; *telled* C. *ilke* AU; *a* add. AEUC.
453. *Cameles*] *a* corrected from ? L. *closed*] *ycloþed* E.
454. *þe f.*] *that fyghte* A. *a*] om. D. *ferly* U; *full felle* A; *full grett* C; *wonderful* E; *deflich many* D.
455. *Thay buskede* A; *Busk* U; *hem* add. UC. *to*] *warde the* add. A. *&*] om. DU. *on*] *vpon* C; *here* add. EDUC. *bakkes* AEDC. *hadde*] *leddyn* DUC; *beere* E.
456. *Ilkane* A; *Eche* EDC; *Ilk* U.
457. *Chayers* A; *Charyettys* ED. *choys* DU; *men* add. AUC; *folk* add. ED. *charged*] *þo com* E. *wapyns* A.
458. *wondere*] *gret* E. *wite*] *se* D; *wolde* A. *lyste*] *myght* DUC. *so w. l.*] *wiste þe sothe* E.
459. *And many* A; *For many* EDUC; *a* add. C. *was*] *were* ED. *drede was* A. *was neuur a-dradde* C.

26 An Elephant bears Caiaphas and his Scribes.

Wer' fond fey in þe feld, ⸵ er þat fiȝt endid. 460

An armed elephaunt comes out of the town, with a tow-ered castle.
An olyfaunt yarmed ⸵ came out at þe laste,
Keuered myd a castel, ⸵ was craftily ywroȝt,
A tabernacle in þe tour ⸵ atyred was riche,
Piȝt as a paueloun, ⸵ on pileres of seluere, 464

A tabernacle is established in the tower,
A which of white seluere ⸵ wal[w]ynde þer-ynne
On four' goions of gold, ⸵ þat hit from grounde bar',
A c[h]osen chayr' þer-by ⸵ on charbokeles twelfe,
Betyn al with barn[d] gold, ⸵ with brennande sergis. 468
Þe chekes of þe chayr' ⸵ wer' cha[r]bokles fyue,

where Cai-aphas and his scribes are sitting.
Couered myd a riche cloþe, ⸵ þer Cayphas was sette.
A plate of pulsched gold ⸵ was piȝt on his breste,
With many preciose perle ⸵ & pured stones. 472

Fol. 8a.
Lered men of þe lawe, ⸵ þat loude couþe synge,
With sawters seten hym by ⸵ & þe psalmys tolde
Of douȝty David þe kyng, ⸵ & oþer der' storijs
Of Joseph, þe noble Jewe, ⸵ & Judas þe knyȝt. 476
Cayphas of þe kyst ⸵ kyppid a rolle
& radde, how þe folke ran ⸵ þroȝ þe re[d]e wa[ters],

---

460. *Was* AUC. *fey fownden* A; *fownþen feynte* C; *feld* E. *þe] that* A. *er] by þat* ADUC. *þat] þe* ADUC.
461. *enarmedde* C; *vnarmyd* EU.
462. *myd]* added above the line, L. *Couerde with* AEDUC. *cast.] þat* add. AUC. *craftily was (is* UC) AUC. *was]* om. ED.
463. *tab.] n* added above the line, L; *wiþ* add. D. *in þe] and a* A. *at.] arayed* E. *tired is* UC. *riche] hyȝe* C.
464. *as] vp als* A; *vp on* DC; *on* U. *With a pauylun pyȝt* E. *on] of* DU. *pil.] postes* EDUC.
465. *An hucche* E; *An owche* C; *A kyste* A; *And an arke* U. *white] fyn* E; om. AUC. *sel.] full schene* add. A. *walowid* DUC; *hanged* E; *was sett* A; *walynde* (!) L. *þer] with* add. A.
466. *goionys* E; *gownes* C; *gargons* A; *gcauntis* D. *fro (from* D; *þe* add. C) *ground þat hit* DUC. *bere* U. *þat—bare] to bere it fro þe grounde* E; *with birnande serges* A.
467. *chosen]* so EDUC; *closen* (!) L. *chariot* U. *on charb.] & (wiþ* D) *chaundelers* EDUC.
468. *al] &* (!) E. *with] of* DUC. *brend* ED; *bright* UC; *barne* (!) L. *with] and* U. *brennyng* EDC. *sergis]* *tapers* C.
l. 467 and 468 are omitted in A.
469. *On þe* C. *checke* AU. *was* A. *charbuncles* ED; *charbuncle* U; *charbokeles* C; *chabocles* (!) L; *charbocle* A. *fyue] four* DC; *stonys* EU; *full fyn* A.
470. *with* AEDUC. *a]* om. ED. *riche] clene* U. *clothe] &* add. C. *þer] in which* E. *is set* DU; *saat* E; *solde sytt* A.
471. *polischid* DC; *polest* AU. *was]* om. A. *piȝt] put* EDU; *sette* C.
472. *many] a* add. C. *perles* U. *pured] full proude* A; *oþer (eke* U) *ryche* EU.
473. *Leernyd* ED; *And lernede* C. *couþe] myȝte* E; *gan* U. *synge] spcke* E.
474. *psalters* C. *satt* E; *sitten* U. *&]* om. EDC. *þe]* om. U. *salmes* E. *tolde] þei redde* DUC; *to reede* E.
475. *kyng] duke* DUC. *oþer] of his* ED; *of þe* C; *of* U.
476. *Ioseph] Iosue* AEDU. *&] of* add. D. *þe kynge* C; *Machabeus* E.
477. *Cayph.] owte* add. AEDUC. *þe] a* DC. *kyst] hucche* E. *kyp.] cawghte vp* EDUC; *clekis* A.
478. *folke] childrym of Irael* E. *þroȝ] ouer* U. *rede waters]* so A; *rede watir* DU; *rede se* EC; *rerewarde* (!) L.

Whan Pharao & his ferde ! wer' in þe floode drouned ;
& myche of Moyses lawe ! he mynned þat tyme.   480
Whan þis faiþles folke ! to þe feld comen,
& batayled after þe bent ! with many burne kene,
For baneres þat blased ! & bestes y-armed,
Myȝt no man se þrow þe sonne, ! ne þe cite knowe.   484
Waspasian dyuyseþ ! þe [vale] alle a-boute,
þat was with baneres ouer-sprad ! to þe borwe wallis,
To barouns & bold men, ! þat hym a-boute wer',
Seiþ : "Lordlynges," a-loude, ! "lestenyþ my speche : 488
Her' nys king noþer knyȝt ! comen to þis place,
Baroun, ne burges, ! ne burne, þat me folweþ,
þat þe cause of his come ! nys Crist forto venge
Vpon þe faiþles folke ! þat hym fayntly slowen.   492
Byholdeþ þe heþyng ! & þe harde woundes,
þe betyng & þe byndyng, ! þat þe body hadde :
Lat neuer þis lawles ledis ! lauȝ at his harmys,
þat bouȝt vs fram bale ! with blod of his herte.   496

Caiaphas reads aloud the story of Pharaoh's drowning in the Red Sea.

Vespasianus addresses his generals.

Their only purpose is to avenge Christ,

---

479. ferde] feris AD ; fook EUC. floode] see C. were—floode] there in were U. were] om. EDC. drenchyd ED. in—drouned] dronkynede in the flode A.
480. mekill A. he] thay A. myn.] mewyde AEDUC ; in add. E.
481. Bot when A. þis] those (!) A ; þe EDUC. faiþl.] hethen C. folke] were add. AED ; was add. UC. komen to þe feelde C.
482. &] þere were add. E. embatelde AE. after] by A ; byfore D ; a-fore C ; a-forne U. þe] þat A. bent] oste C. after þe b.] om. E. beryns A. burne k.] brith wepene ED ; (a add. C) bigge wepyn UC.
483. With EDUC. þat bl.] and beme wode A ; and bemewede U ; and bright wede D ; & trumpes C ; & pensellis E. enarmede AD.
484. þrow] om. EDUC. sonne] some (!) A. ne] nor UC ; vneþ add. L.
485. Than Wasp. A. douysede AED UC. vale] so AEDUC ; feld L.
486. þat was] om. EDUC. ban.] al add. DU ; & add. (!) E. ouerspr.] brode A ; vn- add. AD. borwe] town E ; cyte C. walles] walle C ; ȝatis AEDU.
487. Til U. bar.] beryns A. &] to add. A. abowte hym C.

l. 487 is wanting in D.
488. He sayde AEDUC. Lordyngs AED ; lordes UC ; all add. C. one lowde A. lest.] herkeneth C ; to add. AE.
489. There A. nys] ne es AE ; is nother C. kynȝt (!) L. noþer] nor UC ; ne AED.
490. ne] nor UC. burges] bachillere AEDUC. ne] nor C. burne] man EC.
491. But þat C ; But E ; ne add. (!) A. come] so ADU ; comyngge EC ; comes (!) L. nys] es AEC ; but add. DU. forto v.] to auenge EDUC.
492. Appon A. þe] þese EC ; þes DU ; ȝone A. hym f.] falsely hym AEDUC.
493. Byholde U ; Loketh vp E ; to add. AEDC ; vnto add. U. þe heþ.] hewynward EU ; his passyon C. &] to add. ADUC. þe h.] þenkyth on his E.
494. þe] Of E. bet.] bynddyng EDUC ; buffettynge A. &] om. AEUC. þe] of E ; om. D. bynd.] betynge AEDUC. þe] he one AEDUC ; his add. E. hadde] bode D.
495. & lat EC. neuer] nat E. þis] ȝone A. led.] men C. lawl. l.] helle houndes E. his] hir A.
496. That] dere add. AU ; so dere EC. fra A ; of DU ; out of C. fram b.] om. E.

whom the Jews have tormented to death.
[I] quycke clayme þe querels ⸴ of alle quyk burnes,
& clayme of euereche kyng, ⸴ saue of Crist one,
þat þis peple to pyne ⸴ no pite ne hadde :
þat preueþ his passioun, ⸴ who so þe paas redeþ.   500
Hit nediþ noȝt at þis note ⸴ of Nero to mynde,
Ne to trete of no trewe ⸴ for tribute þat he askeþ ;
þat querel y quik cleyme, ⸴ [qweþer] he ne wilneþ
Of þis rebel to Rome, ⸴ bot resoun to haue.   504

The government of the world belongs to Rome.
Bot mor' þing in our mynde ⸴ myneþ [vs] to-day,
þat by resoun to Rome ⸴ þe regnance fallyþ,
Boþe þe myȝt & þe mayn, ⸴ [&] maist[rie] o[n] e[rþe],
& lord[chipe] of eche londe, ⸴ þat liþe vnder heuen.   508
Lat neuer þis faiþles folke ⸴ with fiȝt [of] vs wynne

Fol. 8 *b.*
Don't allow these Jews to win anything from us by fight.
Hors ne harnays, ⸴ bot þey hit hard byen,
Plate ne pesan ⸴ ne pendauntes ende,
While any lyme may laste ; ⸴ or we þe lif haue,   512
For þei ben feyn[t] at þe fiȝt, ⸴ fals of byleue,
& wel wenen at a wap ⸴ alle þe wo[r]ld quelle,

---

497. *I qwytte* ADU. *I qu. cl.* þe] *I voyde awey all cleymes & C. I*] om. L. *querel* U. *alle] the* add. A. *bur.*] *men* C.
498. *claymes* A ; om. C. *euery* DUC ; *a* add. AU ; *crowned* add. C. *saue] but* DUC. *alone* DC.
499. þat] *The whyche* C. *peyne* D ; *hym of hym* add. A. *pite] pay* add. AC. *ne*] om. A.
500. *Alls* A ; *As* DUC. þe *p.*] *at paske* A. *who—paas] the pase (pask* D ; *gospell* C) *who so (it* U) DUC.
501. *at* þis]*to our* D. *note] tyrn* AC. *mynne* DU ; *mene* A ; *mynge* C.
502. *Nor* C ; *for* add. U. *of] for* U. *trewes* C. This line is omitted in D.
503. *His* ADU. *quercl] here* add. A. *quik] qwite* ADU. þat—*cleyme] The quarell of Nero clene I avoyde* C. *qweþer] qwedir* A ; *queþe hit* D ; *byqwede it* C ; *quite it* U ; *for oþer* L ; *where* add. DUC. *ne*] om. C. *will* AC. *he ne w.*] *hym likiþ* DU.
504. þis] *his* DUC. *rebelles* C ; *robberie* D. *bot*] om. C. *to*] *it wolde* U. *bot—haue] of realte fallith* D.
505. *more þing] murnyng* UC. *mynde] mode* UC. *vs mynnes* U ; *vs mynges* C ; *mene we* A. *vs*] om, L. *to*] *this* A.
506. *regn.] rygalite* A ; *rialte* UC. *fal.] longeth* C.

ll. 505 and 506 are omitted in D.
507. *mayn] maystrie* A. *&* (þe add. C) *maistrie on (of* U) *erþe*] so DUC ; *maister or ellys* L ; *of all oþer londis* A.
508. *&*] *the* add. A. *lordchipe*] so ADUC ; *lord sub* L. *of*] om. D. *euery* DC ; *ilk* U ; *ilke a* A.
ll. 497—508 om. E.
509. *Lat] And lete hem* E. þis] ȝone A. þis *f. f.*] *be no wey* E. *of*] so AEDU ; om. L. This line is omitted in C.
510. *Neyþer hors* E. *ne*] *nouther* U ; *ny* (!) C. *hard] dere* AU. *abigge* E.
511. *Plate*] so ADCU ; *Pate* E ; *Prelate* (!) L. *ne*] *nor* U. *pysan* EU ; *puseyne* D ; *besaunte* C. *ne*] *nor* UC. *pendande* A. *endes* U.
512. *Till* A. *lime*] *l* corrected from *h*, L. *lyf* ED. *any l.*] *we* C. *may*] *vs* add. A. *we*] om. C. *or—haue*] *in eny of oure hertis* E. This line is omitted in U.
513. *thei are* EDUC ; *thaire* (!) A. *feynt*] so AEDUC ; *feyn* (!) L. *at*] *in* C. þe] om. ED. *fiȝt*] *&* add. AEUC.
514. *wel*] *wol* DC ; *wolde* U. *& wel*] *But ȝit þey* E. *at*] *with* A. *wap*] *wecf* ED ; *wayf* U ; *lefte* C. þe *world*] so EDUC ; þey *wold* L ; *to* add. EDC. *kylle* C ; *wynne* E. *alle—quelle*] *to wyn alle this werlde* A.

The Battle begins.

Noþer grounded on god, ⋮ ne on no grace tristen,
Bot alle in st[erynne]s of stour' ⋮ & in strengþ one ;   516   *May this faithless people sustain a total defeat!*
& we ben di3t to day ⋮ dri3ten to serue :
Hey heuen kyng ⋮ [take] hede to his owne ! "
þe ledes louten hym alle ⋮ & a-loude sayde :
" To day, þat fleþe any fote, ⋮ þe fende haue his soule ! "   520
Bemes blowen anon, ⋮ blonkes to ne3e,
Stedis stampen in þe felde ⋮ stif steil vnder',
Stiþe men in stiropys ⋮ striden alofte ;
Kny3tes croysen hem-self, ⋮ cacchen her' helmys   524
With loude clarioun cry ⋮ & alle kyn pypys ;   *The Jews are frightened by the clang of the musical instruments of the Romans.*
Tymbris & tabourris, ⋮ tonelande loude,
3euen a schillande schout, ⋮ schrynken þe Jewes,
As womman schal in a swem, ⋮ whan hir' þe water ne3eþ.   528
Lacchen launces a-non, ⋮ lepyn to gedris,

---

515. *Neyther* ED; *Nor* C; *Thay ne are noghte* A. *on*] in AEDUC. *ne*] nor U. *on*] in AEDUC. *no*] his EDUC. *no grace tr.*] *god traystis* A.
516. *alle*] om. EC. *ster.*] so ADC; *sternenysse* E; *storijs* (!) L. *of stoure*] *of hem self* E. *in*] *her* add. E. *strenghe* AE. *alone* DC. This line is omitted in U.
517. *ben*] *are* EDUC. *dighten* (= *dight in* ?) U; *in* add. EDC. *to*] *this* AEDUC. *dere dryghttyn* A; *Crist for* E; *allmy3ty god* C.
518. *Hey*] *Now you* A. *heuens* A. *take*] so A; om. L. *hede*] *kepe* A. *his*] *thyn* A. [*To do* (*brynge* C) *þes develis on dawe* (*out of lyfe* C) [*& þese deuelys to distreye* E] *& his deth* (*to* add. C) *avenge* (*venge* UC) DEUC.
519. *Those* A; *His* DUC. *ledes*] *meyne* C. *lowttede* A; *loued* C; *leued* U; *left* (!) D. *alle*] om. C. *one lowde* AC. *sayde*] *crydyn* D. *Þan seyde his lordes & his peple abowte* E.
520. *To*] *This* A. *day*] *he* add. A. *He þat þis day* C. *any*] *a* A. *fende*] *deuyl* EU. *haue*] *feche* A.
521. *Beryns* A; *Clariouns* C. *Bemes bl.*] *Trumpores trumped* E; *þan* add. D. *anone*] *on hy* DUC; *vp on heygh* E; *and* add. AEDUC. *blonkes*] *horses* UC; *begonne* add. C. *bl. to n.*] *& blewyn vp faste* E; *baners vp brayde* D.
522. *stampid* DUC; *staunped* E. *in*] *one* A. *þe*] *þat* EC; om. U. *felde*] *stede* EDU; *place* C. *stif*] *stuffede* A. *stif st. v.*] *vndur steel wedes* EU; *vndur þe stele aray* C.
523. *Stiff* EDUC; *And styffe* A. *men*] om. C. *in*] *þe* add. C. *in st.*] *vpon stedes* U. *studen* U. *al.*] *one lofte* A; *vp on lofte* EDUC.
524. *crossyn* DUC; *crossede* AE. *thayn selfe* A; *and* add. AEUC. *cac.*] *cawthen* E; *kaste one* A. *thaire* A; *hem* E.
525. *claryons* A. *With—cry*] *Clarions cryed faste* EDUC. *alle kyn*] *cormous* A; *cornmuse* D; *coryous* EC; *curiouses* (!) U.
526. *Tymberers* D; *Trompis* A. *&*] om. C. *tabres* E; *taboreres* AD. *tonel. loude*] *tyndillede one harde* A; *& trompers* (*trumpes* U) (*ful trie* (*crye* D) DUC; *& mynstracye ynowe* E.
527. *They yaf* DUC; *With* A. *schakande* A; *shrike in* (*& C) a DUC. *shoure* U. *3euen—schout*] *Whan þis noyse was ymaad* E; *thane* add. A; *þo* add. EU. *schrenked* AU; *for to shrynke* C; *tremblyd* E; *to shame wiþ* D.
528. *And* UC. *wommen* AEUC. *schal—swem*] *weltir solde in swounn* A; *wepeth an hey* EC; *shrillen on hye* U; *wepith & waylith* D. *hire þe w.*] *water hire* D; *water hem* (*thaym* A) AU; *watur he* C; *þat sorwe hem* E.
529. *þay* add. AEDUC. *laughte* AD; *lawgthen* EU; *kaw3te* C. *anon*] *and* add. AEDUC. *gedcr* UC.

The Description of the Battle.

<small>A murderous battle begins.</small>

As fur' out of flynt ston ꞉ ferde hem bytwene,
Doust drof vpon lofte, ꞉ dymedyn alle aboute,
As þonder & þicke rayn, ꞉ þrowolande in skyes. 532
[þei] beren burnes þrow, ꞉ brosten launces,
Knyȝtes crosschen doun ꞉ to þe cold erþe,
Ffouȝt faste in þe felde, ꞉ & ay þe fals vnder',
Doun swowande to swelt ꞉ with out swar more. 536

<small>Especially Titus excels in deeds of arms.</small>

Tytus tourneþ hym to, ꞉ tolles of þe beste,
For-justes þe jolieste ꞉ with joyn[yng] of werr'.
Suþ with a briȝt bronde ꞉ he betiþ on harde,
Tille þe brayn & þe blod ꞉ on þe bent ornen ; 540
Souȝt þroȝ an oþer side ꞉ with a sore wepne
Bet on þe broun stele, ꞉ while þe bladde laste,
An hey breydeþ þe brond, ꞉ & as a bore lokeþ,
How hetterly doun, ꞉ hente who so wolde. 544
Alle briȝtned þe bent, ꞉ as bemys of sonne,
Of þe gilden ger' ꞉ & þe goode stones.

---

530. *As*] *the* add. A. *ston*] *it* add. ED ; *thus* add. C. *faredde* C. *thaym* A. *ferde h. byt.*] *thei hewen on harde* U.
531. *The duste* A. *appon* A ; *vpa* D. *dym. alle*] *& dryued* EU ; *drivyng* DC. *dyn.*] *the dale* A.
532. *&*] *in* EDUC. *þrow.*] *threpande* A ; *hurleth* E ; *þirlid* D ; *thrilles* U ; *persheth* C. *in*] om. DUC ; *þe* add. EDUC. *skewes* A.
533. *þei*] so AEDU ; *The* EUC ; om. L. *bare* ED ; *bolde* U ; *berne* (!) C. *barnes* EC. *þrow*] *thorw owt* ED ; *there aboute* UC ; *&* add. E. *brost.*] *with* add. A. *launces*] *her sperys* EDUC.
534. *cros.*] *thruschen* A ; *knelyd a-* EDUC. *doun*] *thraly vn-* add. A.
535. *And fowȝten* C ; *Fightyn* DU ; *Thay fyghte* A. *in þe f.*] *on fote* U. *ay*] *euer* C ; *fals*] *Iewes* E.
536. *sw. to*] *sweyande one* A. *wttyn* A. *þere was non mercy at al . but alle to deth wente* E. This line is omitted in DUC.
537. *turnyd* EC. *hym*] om. D. *to* ꞉] ꞉ *to* L ; *anon* EDC ; *on one* U ; *and* add. AEDC. *tollith* D ; *telles* (L)U ; *kylleth* E. *beste*] so AEDUC ; *bestes* (!) L.
538. *Forth* (!) *justeth* C ; *Foriustid* D. *Iusters of* A. *jol.*] *joly knyȝte* C. *with*] *in* U. *ioynyng* EDUC ; *pynynge* A ; *joyned* (!) L.

539. *&* AEDUC. *sythyn* AD ; *sen* U ꞉ *after* C ; *also* E. *bronde*] *swerde* C. *he*] om. AEDUC. *bet.*] *brittynes* A. *faste* C.
540. *Tille*] *That* AEDUC. *brayn*] *blode* A. *blod*] *brayne* A. *appon* A ; *vp on* C. *bent*] *brond* EDU ; *swerde* C. *ornen*] *lefte* AEUC ; *laft* D.
541. *He soghte* A ; *And sythen (seth* D ; *sen* U) EDU ; *And after* C. *þroȝ*] *one* AUC ; *in* ED. *an oþer*] *that other* UC ; *þe same* ED. *side*] *stede* ED. *sore*] *sade* A.
542. *And betis* A ; *Smoot* E. *on*] *vpon* EDUC ; *appon* A. *þe*] om. AEDUC. *whils* AU ; *þat* add. A. *lastid* DC ; *lastis* AU.
543. *An*] *& hye* E. *breydis* D ; *arcysed vp* E ; *he lefte* C ; *he* add. ADU. *þe*] *his* AC. *brond*] *swerde* C. *bore*] *he* add. C. *lokyd* E.
544. *& hewyd* E ; *He hewedde* C ; *Hewys* ADU. *heuyly* A. *hett. doun*] *on hertlych* EDC ; *on ful hertly* U. *hente*] *cacche* C. *wolde*] *hapyns* A.
545. *brightnes* D ; *bretned* U ; *shryned* (!) C. *bent*] *feelde* C. *þe b.*] *on þe bentis* D. *of*] *the* add. AUC. *briȝt.—bent*] *glisteryd his gere* E. *as þe sunne bemys* E ; *hew who so wold* D.
546. *For* A. *gilten* (!) A ; *golden* UC. *gild. g.*] *prys perre* E. *&*] *of* add. EDUC.

The Description of the Battle. 31

Ffor schyueryng of sche[l]des, ⸲ & schynyng of helmes	Fol. 9a.
H*it* ferde, as alle þe fi*r*mament ⸲ vp-on a fur' wer'. 548	
Waspasian in þe vale ⸲ þe fanward byholdeþ,	Vespasianus inspects the vanguard.
How þe heþyn her' ⸲ heldiþ to g*r*ounde,	
Cam w*ith* a fair' ferde ⸲ þe fals me*n* to mete.	
As greued griffou*n*s ⸲ girden in samen, 552	
Spakly her' speres, ⸲ on sprotes þey ȝeden,	A horrible massacre takes place.
Scheldes as schidwod, ⸲ on scholdres to-cleuen,	
Schoken o*u*t of scheþes, ⸲ þ*a*t scharpe w[ere] ygrou*n*de,	
& mallen metel, . þroȝ vn-mylt hertes, 556	
Hewen on þe heþen, ⸲ hurtlen to-gedr'	
For-schorne gild schroud, ⸲ sch[o]dered burne[s].	
Baches woxen ablode ⸲ a-boute in þe vale,	
& goutes fr*a*m gold wede ⸲ as goteres þey ru*n*ne. 560	
Sir' Sabyn setteþ hy*m* vp, ⸲ whan hit so ȝede,	Sabyn with the rearguard
Rideþ myd þe rereward, ⸲ & alle þe route folweþ.	

547. *For*] *Of* ED. *schymeryng* EDU; *schemerynge* A. *of*] om. E. *scheldes*] so AEDUC; *schendes* (!) L. *of*] om. EUC.
548. *alle*] om. AEDUC. *firm.*] *al* add. U. *appon* A; *on* EDUC. *a*] om. AU.
549. *vawmwarde* AD; *vaunwarde* E; *vannward* D; *vaward* UC.
550. *And howe* U. *here h.*] *hoppedyn* (*hepid* D) *heuydles* EDUC. *to*] þe add. AUC.
551. *He come* AU; *& com* ED; *And he come* C. *a*] *meche* E. *ferde*] *folke* AE. *a fair f.*] *his feris* D. þe] *those* A. *men*] *folk* U; om. AEC; *for* add. AD; *vn-* add. C.
552. *As*] *And als* AE; *Right as* DUC. *greued*] om. AEDUC. *griff.*] *with granne* add. ED; *one grounde* add. A; *on grene* UC; *þei* add. AEDUC. *in*] *all* A. *in samen*] *to gydre* EDUC.
553. *Full spakly* A; *Speedly* EDUC. *thayre* A. *on*] *in* A. *spr.*] *sprates* U; *spildirs* A; *peces* C; *men* E. ȝ*eden*] *sprungyn* D. þey ȝ.] *gunne* (*to* add. E) *sprynge* EUC.
554. *schold.*] *sounder* C. *to-*] þey ED; *dede* C. *cleue* C.
555. *Than thay schoke* A; *Swerdis shokyn* DC; *Schottyn* E; *And shoten* U. *shede* C. *of sch.*] *arwes* E. *schrape* (!) A. *were*] so AEDUC; *was* L.
556. *melyn* A; *mallede* C; *malle* U; *mette* D; *smete* E; *with* þ*a*t add. EUC;
wiþ þe add. D. *vn*m.] *maltyn* A; *mennys* DUC; *many mennys* E. *herte*] E.
557. *They* add. AEDUC. *on* þe *h.*] *appone harde stele* A; *and* add. AEDUC. *hurtlyd* E; *fowȝten* C.
558. *Forshore* D; *For schire* A; *For-shere* U. *gyltyn* A; om. DU. *shroudis* DU. *For—schroud*] *They hewen* þe *armour* C; *ful shene* add. DUC. *schodires* A; *on shidring* D; *on shiderand* U; *on shynynge* C; *schedered* L; *those* add. A. *barnes* C; *burnee* (!) L. This line is omitted in E.
559. *Bankis* DC; *Bank* U; *Hors* E; *Alle* A. *one blode* A; *al blody* E. *woxen abl.*] *blowyn on* (*with* U) *blode* DU; *flowen of floode* C. *abouten* U. *in* þe] *all that brode* A. *ab.—vale*] *so thei were ywoundyd* E.
560. *guttis* A; om. DUC. *fram*] *out of* ADUC. *gold*] *gilten* A; *gay goldyn* D; (þe add. C) *gay golde* UC. *wede*] *gere* D; om. C. *as*] om. DUC. *&—*þey] *Manye stremes in* þe *vale . of blood faste* E. þey *r.*] þere *yedy̆m* DUC. *For there was meche more ysched . þan eny man can telle* add. E.
561. *sette* C; *sees* A. *vp*] *selfe* A. *hit*] added above the line in L. *hit so* ȝ.] *he sey tyme* EDUC.
562. *And rydis* A; *& rood* EDUC. *with* AEDUC. *folweþ*] *after* EDUC.

attacks the castles.   Kenély þe castels ⋮ came to assayle,
　　　　　　　þat þe bestes on her' bake ⋮ out of burwe ladden,　564
All the elephants, Atles on þe olyfauntes, ⋮ þat orible wer',
camels and dromedaries Girdiþ out þe guttes ⋮ with grounden speres.
full, and the garrison are killed, R[o]ppis rispen forþ, ⋮ þat redles an hundred
　　　　　　　Scholde be busy to burie ⋮ þat on a bent lafte.　568
　　　　　　　Castels clateren doun, ⋮ cameles brosten,
　　　　　　　Dromedaries to þe deþ ⋮ drowen ful swyþe.
　　　　　　　þe blode fomed hem fro ⋮ in þe flasches aboute,
　　　　　　　þ[at] kne-depe in þe dale ⋮ dascheden stedes.　572
　　　　　　　þe burnes in þe bretages, ⋮ þat a-boue wer',
　　　　　　　For þe doust & þe dyn, ⋮ as alle doun ȝede,
　　　　　　　Al for-stoppette in stele, ⋮ storte-blynde wexen,
　　　　　　　Whan hurdiȝs & hard erþe ⋮ hurtled to gedre,　576
　　　　　　　& vnder dromedaries doun ⋮ diȝten hem sone.
except that one elephant which Caiaphas is riding. Was non left vpon lyue, ⋮ þat a lofte standeþ,
　　　　　　　Saue [ane] o-lepy olyfaunt ⋮ at þe grete ȝate,
　　　　　　　þer as Cayphas þe clerke ⋮ in castel rideþ ;　580

563. *And full kenly* A ; *& kenely* EC. *þe*] *her* D. *cast.*] *þey* add. DUC. *came*] *yan* C ; *he caste hym* E. *thay come the castels* A.
564. *on her b.*] *one bakke* C ; *one bakkes* AD. *of b.*] *of þe cyte* C ; *fro towne* E. *ledith* D ; *beryn* E.
565. *Atl. on þe*] *Thay eghtillede to those* A ; *Than þe* EU ; *Vp-on þe* DC. *olyf.*] *thei hitte* add. E ; *he hit* add. DUC.
566. *And* add. AEDUC. *gird* DC ; *gurt* EU. *þe*] *thayre* A ; *here* E. *with*] *scharpe* add. A.
567. *Roppes* A ; *Ropis* DU ; *& ropes* E ; *Here ropes* C ; *Rappis* L. *risp.*] *broken* C ; *alto* (!) *burste* E. *forþ*] *owte* A ; *a right* DU ; *down ryght* C. *redles*] *redily* DUC ; *rydders* A. *forþ—hund.*] *& rente on smale peeces* E.
568. *burie*] *bere* (!) A. *Scholde—bur.*] *þer myȝt non hors bere* E. *on*] *in* E. *a*] *the* AED. *bent*] *feeld* E ; *bank* DUC. *leuyde* A.
569. *clatered* A. *Cast. cl. d.*] (þere add. D) *claterid castellis adoun* EDUC ; *& * add. ED ; *þe* add. UC. *cam.*] *thay* add. A ; *to-* add. ED.
570. *And drom.* DUC ; *Dromondaryes* A. *drivyn* D. *ful*] *wol* E ; *wel* U ; *als* A ; om. D. *sw.*] *fast* DC.
571. *Tha* (!) *the* A. *thaym from* A.

in] om. A. *þe*] om. AEDUC. *flattis* A ; *feeldes* E ; *flodis* DUC ; *al* add. U.
572. *þat*] so AEDUC ; *þe* L. *dale*] *vale* EC. *dasschyne* A ; *stopen* E ; *þe* add. EUC ; *thaire* add. A.
573. *burnes*] *men* E ; *mayne* C. *bretage* U ; *bretace* A ; *bastyles* C. *abowne* A ; *abouen* UC ; *about* D.
574. *doust*] *dyntes* ED. *&*] *of* E. *as*] om. EDUC. *adoun* EDUC.
575. *for-stoppede* ADUC ; *for-stuffyd* E. *in st.*] *for hete* E. *storte, o* changed from *r*, L ; *stane-* A ; *stark-* EDUC. *þey wuxe* E.
576. *Thenne* C ; *þe* add. D. *hurdesche* A. *hurtlyn* D ; *justed* C. *togedirs* A ; *op hepe* E.
ll. 575 and 576 are transposed in AEDUC.
577. *& vnder*] *An hundrid of* DUC ; *And vndred of* E. *dromondaries* A. *: doun* L ; om. AEDUC. *diȝten hem*] *dyede* AEDUC. *sone*] *full sone* A ; *in a (that* U) *stounde* EDU ; *in a whyle* C.
578. *Was non*] *Thare was no beste* A. *appon* A ; *on* D. *lofte*] *grounde* U ; *foot* E. *stude* AEDUC.
579. *But* ED. *ane*] so A ; *on* EDUC om. L. *anlepy* A ; om. EDUC. *ol.*] *alone* add. EUC. *grete* ȝ.] *brode ȝatis* A.
580. *as*] *þat* E. *in*] *a* add. DUC ; *þe* add. E. *rid.*] *howyd* E.

Caiaphas and the Scribes are seized. 33

He say þe wrake on hem wende, ⸝ & away tourneþ
With twelf maystres made ⸝ of Moyses lawe.
An hundred helmed men ⸝ hien hem after,   *Fol. 9 b.*
Er þey of castel myȝt come, ⸝ cauȝten hem alle,   584 *Caiaphas and his clerks are taken prisoners.*
Bounden þe bischup ⸝ on bycchyd wyse,
þat þe blode out barst ⸝ eche band vnder',
& broȝten [to] þe [berfraye] ⸝ alle [þo] bew clerkes
þer þe standard stode, ⸝ & stadded hem þer.   588
þe beste & þe britage ⸝ & alle þe briȝt ger',
Chair' & chaundelers ⸝ & charbokel stones,   *Their treasures are carried off as booty.*
þe rolles, þat þey redden [on], ⸝ & alle þe riche bokes
þey broȝte myd þe bischup, ⸝ þou hym bale þouȝte.   592
Anon þe feyþles folke ⸝ fayleden herte,
Tourned toward þe toun ⸝ & Tytus hem after ;
Ffel[d]e of þe fals ferde ⸝ in þe felde lefte,
An hundred in her' helmes, ⸝ myd his honde one.   596
þe fals Jewes in þe felde ⸝ fallen so þicke   *The Jews fall in masses.*
As hail froward heuen, ⸝ hepe ouer oþer ;

---

581. *wrake*] *werke* C. *thaym* A. *away*] *aȝeyn* C. *turned* EU.
582. *twelf maystres made*] *alle þe grete maystres* E.
583. *And an* C ; *And than an* A. *hund.*] *of* add. C. *hyede* AEDUC. *hym* A.
584. *And or þat* A. *of*] *to* AD ; *þe* add. AC ; *her* add. D. *may* U. *come*] *&* add. C. *cauȝ.*] *to cacch* D. *thaym* A. *& toke hem alle ar thei myȝte* . *out* (!) *þe castel come* E.
585. *Thaye bonde* A ; *And b.* E. *þe b.*] *þis Cayfas* E ; *besyly* add. A. *on*] *in* ED ; *a* add. EUC ; *ane* add. A ; *þe* add. D. *bych.*] *byter* E ; *sory* C.
586. *ylke* A ; *a* add. AEC. *band*] *bone* C. *band vndere*] *veyne aboue other* U.
587. *&*] *þei* DUC. *br.*] *ledde* E. *to* (*vn-to* A) *þe berfraye*] *so* AEDU ; *to þe bastyle* C ; *þe bischup*⸝ & L. *þo*] *those* A ; *þe* EDUC ; *his* L. *bew*] *bone* A ; *grete* E ; *sorye* C ; *benche* DU.
588. *Where* EDUC ; *þat* add. E. *stedde* A ; *stokkyd* EUC ; *stowid* D. *thaym* A ; *alle* add. A.
589. *&*] *of* C. *bretace* A ; *castell* C.
590. *Cheyers* D. *chaund.*] *þe candelstykkes* C. *&*] *with* E. *charbuncle* EDUC.
591. *And þe* C. *rolle* AEDUC. *thay rede* A ; *he radde* EDUC. *on*] *so* EDUCA ; om. L. *þe*] *those* A. *riche*] *fayre* E.

592. *with* AEDUC. *þou*] *þat* add. A. *he* U. *bale*] *heuy* C.
593. *On one* U ; *Than on none* A. *faylid* DC ; *the* add. A ; *her* add. C. *hertes* EDUC.
594. *Thay tournede* A ; *& turned* AE. *tow.*] *homward to* E. *thaym* A ; *sone* U ; *faste* E.
595. *Ffelde*] *He felde* A ; *And felde* C ; *Ffele* L ; *Feld* U. *þe*] *those* A. *fals*] *faithles* U. *ferde*] *folke* ADUC. *in*] *on* D ; *and thei* UC ; *whils that* A. *lafte* DU ; *laste* A ; *fledde* C.
596. *And* (!) C. *in here h.*] *of hethyn* DUC ; *of those haythyn men* A. *with* ADUC. *his*] *owene* add. C. *handis* AD. *allone* DUC. *He britnyd with his bronde & broght to þe deþe* add. D.
595 f. differ considerably in E :
 & chasyd hem abowte . as houndes
  doþ þe hare,
 & felde an vndryd hym self alone .
  ar þat he stynte.
597. *Iewes*] *folk* EDUC. *in*] *on* A. *ware fallyn* A ; *fellen* C ; *flowyn* D. *fyllyn in þe feeld* EU.
598. *hagille* A ; *doth* add. E ; *þat cometh* add. C. *frow.*] *from* EDU ; *fro* C ; *fro the* A. *heuynward* EDUC. *hepe*] *in hepis* A ; *eche hepid* D ; *eche* E ; *ilkone* U. *ouer*] *vp-on* E ; *on* U ; *from* D. *hepe ouer o.*] *hoppeth vp & vndur* C.

SIEGE OF JERUSALEM.   D

34 The Jews retire to Jerusalem.

So was þe bent ouer-brad, ⁏ blody by-runne,
With ded bodies aboute ⁏ alle þe brod vale.   600
My3t no stede doun stap ⁏ bot on stele wede,
Or on burne, oþer on beste, ⁏ or on bri3t scheldes;
So myche was þe multitude, ⁏ þat on þe molde lafte,
þer so many wer' mar[red]; ⁏ mereuail wer' ellis.   604

But the Romans are as fresh as when they came from Rome.
3it wer' þe Romayns as rest, ⁏ as þey fram Rome come,
[Vnrevyn] eche a renk, ⁏ & no3t a ryng brosten;
Was no poynt perschid ⁏ of alle her' pris armur',
So Crist his kny3tes gan kepe, ⁏ tille complyn tyme.   608
An hundred þousand helmes ⁏ of þe heþen syde
Wer' fey fallen in þe felde, ⁏ [þat no freke skapide,]

The rest of the Jews flee to the town and shut the gates.
Saue seuen þousand of þe somme, ⁏ þat to þe cite flowen,
& wy[nn]en with mychel wo ⁏ þe walles with-ynne.   612
Ledes lepen to a-non, ⁏ louken þe 3ates,
Barren hem bigly ⁏ with boltes of yren,
Brayden vp brigges ⁏ with brouden chaynes

---

599. *were* D. *bent*] *banke* UC; *bankis* D; *vale* E. *ouer alle* A; *al about* DUC; om. E. *blody b.*] *ybawmyd* (*baumed al* U) *with blood* EU.
600. *With*] *those* add. A. *bod.*] *al* add. UC. *alle*] *by* U; om. C. *þe*] *that* A. *alle—vale*] *ywis on euery syde* E. This line is omitted in D.
601. *There myghte* AEC; *Ne myght* U. *no*] om. U. *down stepe* A; *steppe doun* EDUC. *but*] *all* add. C. *vpon* C. *stele*] *schene* A. *wedis* D; om. C.
602. *Othir* AE. *burne*] *brene* A; *beestes* EDUC. *or* AEDUC. *beste*] *breste* A; *men* EC; *biernes* DU. *or*] *ells* add. A. *scheldes*] *heuedis* A.
603. *So—mult.*] *þe multitude was (is* U) *so mekill* (*meche* EDUC) AEDUC. *on*] *thare on* A. *þe*] om. AU. *molde*] *mosse* ED; *grownde* C.
604. *marred*] *so* EDUC; *merrede* A; *martred* (*red* added above the line by later hand) L; *full* add. A. *merv.*] *veruayl* (!) E. *were*] *hadde be* E.
605. *þe Romaynes were* EU. *also* A; om. DUC. *ristede* A; *sound* DUC; *hool* E. *as*] *whan* add. EDUC. *fro R.* A; *ferst* EDUC.
606. *Vnrevyn*] *so* A; *Weel arayed* EDUC; *Ronnen ouer* (!) L. *eueryche* AE; *ilk* U. *a*] om. ED. *renk*] *man* EC. *&*] om. DUC. *no3t a*] *no* A. *renge* U; *ryengne* A; *thing* D.
607. *My3t* (*May* U) *no bierne* (*body* E) *on hem breke . so booldly* (*bigly* U) *þei stood* (*stonde* U) EDU. This line is omitted in AC.
608. *Thus* A. *gan his men* UC. *tille*] *to* U. *complens* C; *complynes* U. [*For* (*there* add. U) *nas segge* [*So nas þer man* E] *of þe sege, þat of sore wist* DE; add. U. *Ther was no bone broken . better were þey neuer* add. C.
609. *þous.*] *of* add. A. *of*] *on* EDUC. *þe*] om. A. *syde*] *Iewes* A.
610. *fey founden* A; *found fey* DU; *founden faynte* C; *feld* E. *þat—sk.*] *so* A; *&* (om. DC) *not oo man* (*freek* ED; om. U) *skaped* (*lasse* E; *yskaped* U) CEDU.
611. *of þe s.*] om. EDUC. *þe c.*] *toun* E. *flewe* U; *flede* AC. *wynnen*] *wane* AC; *wymē* L; om. EDU. *mekill* A; *mich* DUC; *wunder meche* E. *wo*] *wan* add. DU; *kepten* add. E. *with ynne*] om. E.
613. *Ledes*] *Men* EC. *lopyn* EU; *leppis* A. *to*] *vp* E; om. D. *anon*] *and* add. AEUC. *loukes* A; *lokkyd* EDUC; *to* add. A.
614. *Barrede* ADUC; *& barryd* E. *thaym* A; *full* add. A. *bolt.*] *barres* C.
615. *Thay brayde* A; *And brayde* C. *vp*] *on* add. D; *þe* add. AEDUC. *brygge* A. *with*] *þe* add. DUC; *her* add. E. *broud.*] *brode* D; *bygly* A; *bolde* U; *bownden* C; *stronge* E.

The Jews defend Jerusalem. 35

& portecolis wi*th* pile ⁑ picchen to g*r*ounde. 616
þei wy*n*nen vp why3tly ⁑ þe walles to kepe,   *The Jews defend the town from the walls*
Fr[e]sche vnfonded † folke, ⁑ & g*r*ete defence made,
Tyeþ in-to tou*r*res ⁑ tonnes ful manye
Wi*th* grete stones of gret ⁑ & of gray marble, 620 *Fol. 10 a.*
Kepten kenly wi*th* caste ⁑ þe kernels alofte,
Quar[r]en qu[a]rels out ⁑ with quart[ote]s attonys.
þ*at* oþ*er* folke at þe fote ⁑ freshly assayled,
Tille eche dale wi*th* dewe ⁑ was donked aboute. 624
Wi*th*-drowen he*m* fro þe diche, ⁑ dukes & oþ*er*,
[For] þe caste was so kene, ⁑ þ*at* come fra*m* þe walles;
Come*n* forþe wi*th* þe kyng, ⁑ clene as þey 3ede,
W[ant]ed no3t o wye, ⁑ ne no*n* þ*at* wem hadde. 628
P*r*inces to her' pauelou*n*s ⁑ passen on swyþe,   *The Roman princes retire to their pavilions.*
Vnarmen he*m* as tyt ⁑ & alle þe ny3t resten
Wi*th* wacche vmbe þe walles ⁑ to many wyes sorowe;
þey wolle no3t þe heþen her' ⁑ so harmeles be lafte. 632

616. *&*] *the* add. A.   *pile*] *pyne* AEUC; *pynne* D; *thay* add. A.   *pight* DUC; *putt* AE; *it* add. A.   *to*] *þe* add. AEDUC.   *gr.*] *erthe* U.
617. *wanne* A; *wentyn* EDUC.   *vp*] *full* add. A.   *wy3thy* C.
618. *Fresche*] so AUC; *Fell* D; *Frasche* (!) L; *and* add. A.   *Fresche vnf. f.*] *Brougth forth fressch men* E. *vnf.*] *vnfandide* A; *vnwonded* C; *vnfounded* LUD.   *&*] *þat* A; *aUC*; om. D.
619. *Tyeþ*] *Token* UED; *Thay tuke* AC. *in to*] *to the* U. *torettis* A. *ful*] *wol* E. *many*] *thikke* AEDUC.
620. *Wiþ*] *Ful of* E. *of greke* A; om. ED.   *&*] *all* D. *&—marble*] *of marbel & oþer* E.
621. *Thei kepte* EC; *Thay kepe* A. *kenly*] *sharpely* C. *kern.*] *corners* EDUC. *on lofte* C; *abowte* EU.
622. *Quattid* D; *& quattyd* E; *Warppis* A; *They shette* C; *Quarten* L. *quarells*] so AEDC; *querels* L. *owte quarells* AEDC. *with*] *by* AC; om. ED. *quarters* ACDE.
623. *The toþer* A; *The oþer* ED. *att foot* D; *vpon fote* C; *with oute* E. *freshly*] *bysyly* E. *assayles* A; *assaylyn* D.
624. *ilke* A; *a* add. AED. *dale*] *dich* ED. *with*] *the* add. AC. *with—aboute*] *wereful . of dede mennys bodyes* E.
ll. 622—624 are omitted in U.
625. *Tho w.* EDUC. *hem*] *þei* D;
om. EUC. *With-dr. hem*] *Than thay drewe thaym* A. *dikes* A; *bothe* add. U.
626. *For*] so AEDUC; om. L. *caste*] *schot* E. *kene*] *scharp* EC. *fro* AEDUC. *wall* C.
627. *Thay come* AC; *& comyn* E. *forþe*] om. C. *with*] *to* E. *kynge*] *forth a3eyn* add. C. *þey*] *þe* C.
628. *Wantted*] so ADU; *They wanted* C: *Lakkyd* E; *Wounded* L; *hem* add. DU; *hym* add. E. *no3t*] *neuer* EC. *wye*] *wyghte* AD; *man* EC. *ne no* A; *nor no* C; *not one* D; om. U. *þat*] om. AEC. *wem*] *wounde* A; *a wounde* U; *woundes* C; *harm* ED.
629. *Thanne pr.* C. *thaire* A; om. ED. *passyde* EDU; *presede* AC. *on*] *forth* U; *full* C; om. ED. *swyþe*] *harde* U; *thykke* C.
630. *Vnarmede* A; *And vnarayde* C; *& arayed* EDU. *thaym* A. *as t.*] *rathe* U; *sone* AC; *there* ED. *ryste* A; *restyd* EDUC.
631. *waches* A; *gode wayte* U. *vmbe*] *aboute* AEDUC. *walle* DUC. *to—vyes*] *many wyghtis* (*wye* U; *wight* D; *a man* C) *to* ADUC. *þe—vyes*] *with oute þe wal. many on to* E.
632. *þey*] *Bot* A; *For thei* U. *wulde* E; *nolde* U. *þe*] *this* A; *þese* C. *here*] *houndes* C; om. DU. *heþ. h.*] *false* E. *so*] *thus* AEDUC. *be l.*] *passed* E; *passe* DC; *shuld passe* U.

An Assault is made on Jerusalem.

        Sone as þe rede day ⁝ ros [o]n þe schye,
        Bemes blowen anon, ⁝ burnes to aryse.
        þe kyng comaundeþ a cry, ⁝ þat comsed was sone,

On the next day the Romans plunder the dead Jews,
        þe ded bodies on þe bonke ⁝ bar' forto make ;   636
        To spoyle þe spilt folke, ⁝ spar' scholde none.
        Geten girdeles & ger' ⁝ gold & goode stones,
        Byes, broches bryȝt, ⁝ besauntes riche,
        Helmes hewen of gold, ⁝ hamberkes manye.   640
        Kesten ded vpon ded, ⁝ was deil to byholde,
        Made wide weyes ⁝ & to þe walles comen,

and begin to assail the town.
        Assembleden at þe cite, ⁝ saut to bygynne,
        Ffolke ferlich þycke, ⁝ at þe four' ȝates.   644
        þey broȝten toures of tre, ⁝ þat þey taken hadde,
        A-ȝen euereche ȝate, ⁝ ȝarken hem hey ;
        By-gonnen at þe grettist ⁝ a garrite to rer',
        Groded vp fro þe grounde ⁝ on xij grete postes.   648
        [It] was wonderlich wide, ⁝ wroȝt vpon hyȝte,

Passus add. A ; *Quartus passus* add. U.

633. *As sone as* EC ; *Alsone as* U ; *Sone after* A ; *As rathe as* D. *day*] *rawede and* add. A. *rase one* AEC ; *gan rise on* U ; *rosen* (!) L ; *rosyn* D. *schye*] *skye* AC ; *skyes* EDU.

634. *Bemes*] *Claryones* C ; *Trumpores* E ; *Beerns* U. *blewen* ADUC ; *trumped* E. *anon*] *one brode* AD ; *abrode* C ; *vp* E ; *her bemes* U ; & add. D ; *þe* add. EUC. *bur.*] *lordes* C ; *hoost* EU. *forto* EU ; *gan* DC. *ryse* AD ; *reyse* EU. This line is added on the margin in L. *Passus IIIJ*ᵘˢ add. C.

635. *comaundid* DC ; *comaunde* U ; *hase comandide* A ; *anoon made* E. *conscent* (!) A ; *knowyn* EDUC.

636. *That þe* C. *on*] *in* E. *þe*] om. U. *bonke*] *bent* A ; *feeld* E. *forto*] *vnto* C.

637. *To dispoyle* D ; *And dispoyle* E. *þe*] *that* A. *spilt*] *sleyne* C. *none*] *no man* A. *spare sch. none*] & *spare (hem* add. E) *no lengere* EDUC.

638. *Thay gatt* A ; *Grete* D ; *They geette* C. & *gere*] om. EDUC ; *of* add. AEDUC. *and*] *with* E ; *many* add. EDUC.

639. *Byes*] *Ryngis* A ; *Bedes* & EDUC ; *broch.*] *full* add. A. *bryȝt*] om. EDUC ; *and* add. AEDUC. *bes.*] *full* add. A.

640. *hewyd* D ; *helyd* E.. *of*] *with* AED. *gold*] *and* add. AEUC. *haburgones* C ; *perre* E ; *full* add. A ; *wol* add. E. *many*] *noble* DUCA ; *riche* E.

641. *Thay keste* AC ; *And caste* E. *appon* A. *was deil*] *ruthe* D ; *þat dool was* E ; *þat heuy hit was* C. *byh.*] *se* CE. This line is omitted in U.

642. *They made* C. *wide w.*] *wayes full wyde* ADUC. *Made wide weyes*] *Thanne þey tooke hem to gidre* E. *wal* U ; *town* E. *come*] *wente* C.

643. *And ass.* C. *at*] *to* AEDUC. *cite*] *walles* E ; *in* add. D ; & add. E. *assawte* AEDU ; *a saute* C. *to byg.*] *bygunne* D ; *made* E.

644. *Folke f.*] *Fresche folke full* AC ; *Folk fresshely* D. *pycke*] *fele* D ; *felle* U. *Folk f. þ.*] & *faste felde doun þe folk* E *at þe*] *atte* U ; *byfore the* A.

645. *þey*] *And* E ; om. DU. *torettis* A. *takyn þei* DC.

646. *Aȝaynes* AEU ; *And aȝens* C. *eu.*] *eche* C ; *ilke* A ; *a* add. AU. *yarkyd* DU ; *ȝerkede* A ; *reysed* C ; & *reysed* E. *thaym* A ; *þem* C ; *full* add. A.

647. *Bygan* DU ; *Thay bygan* AC. *at þe*] *atte* U. *gret.*] *ȝate* add. C. *arere* ED.

648. *Graythid* D ; *Ygraithed* U ; *Getyn* AC. *Groded vp fro*] *Deepe ypyȝt in* E. *on*] *wiþ* D. *grete*] *stronge* E ; *sykur* C.

649. *It*] so AEDUC ; *He* L. *wyed* E ; & add. AUC. *ywrought* U. *appon* A ; *on* U. *hyethe* C ; *hy* EDU.

The Assault is continued.

Ffyue hundred in frounte, ⸵ to fiʒten at þe walles.
Hardy men vp-on haste ⸵ hyen at þe grecys
& bygonnen with bir ⸵ þe borow to assayle.   652
Quarels, flambande of fur' ⸵ flowen out harde,
& arwes [vn]arwely ⸵ with attyr enuenymyd ;
Taysen at þe toures, ⸵ tachen on þe Jewes ;
þroʒ kernels cacchen her' deþ ⸵ many kene burnes.   656
brenten & beten doun ⸵ þat bilde was wel þycke,   Fol. 10 b.
Brosten þe britages ⸵ & þe brode toures.
By þat was many bold burne ⸵ þe burwe to assayle,
þe hole batail boun, ⸵ a-boute þe brode walles,   660
þat wer' byg & brode ⸵ & bycchet to wynne,   It is a difficult task to win the town.
Wonder' heye to byholde, ⸵ with holwe diches vnder',
Heye bonked a-bou[t]e, ⸵ vpon boþe sydes,
Riʒt wicked to wynne, : bot ʒif wyles helpe.   664
Bow-men atte bonke ⸵ benden her' ger',   The Romans do their best.
Schoten vp scharply ⸵ to þe schene walles
With arwes & arblastes ⸵ & alle þat harme myʒt,
To affray þe folke ⸵ þat defence made.   668

650. in] on a AEC ; on U ; a D. at] on UC.
651. Armed U. appon A. haste] hiʒhte A ; hy EDU. -on h.] hyed C. hyen] hewyd EU ; hewyn DC. at þe] atte U ; to the A.
652. bygan DU ; bygynnes A ; tho add. UC. with] a add. A. bir] birth (!) U ; myʒt E ; strengthe C. the] to (!) E. bor.] cyte EC.
653. flamb.] flawmynge AC ; flammyd D. of] one A ; in DC. flow.] flappid D. out] in ADC. harde] faste A ; full þykke C.
654. &] om. A. arwes] full add. DC. vn-arwely] so A ; hastely D ; smertelye C ; arwely L. with a.] attirly A.
655. They tachen C ; Thay schotte A. torettis A ; and add. ADC. tachede A ; chasen C. on] om. DC.
656. þroʒ k.] With care DC. cachede A ; kawʒte C. thaire A. kene b.] bolde beryn A ; a sharpe baroune C.
657. þey brynte ADC. þat b. w.] beldis AD ; byggynges C. wel] full A ; so DC. þycke] stronge C.
658. Thay braste A ; They brake C ; of add. A. þe] thaire A. bretace A ; bastyle C. þe] of thaire A. brode] stronge C. toures] wallis D.
659. were C. bu.] menne C. burwe cyte C.
l. 653—659 are omitted in U.
660. The h.] Thei held the U. bat.] full add. A. þe] those A.
l. 659 and 660 are omitted in D.
661. were] was AU. byg] bitter U. & br.] and bare A ; al þe (a C) birre DC ; os a bir U. byc.] bitter DC ; bygge U. forto U.
662. Wonder] Right D. with] and AU. holle A. diche U.
663. And hyʒe bankedde C ; Heye bankis D ; Ybanked U. aboute] so ADC ; abouten U ; aboue L. appon A. sydes] haluys ADC. vpon b. s.] alle the brode walles U.
664. Riʒt] And wondir ADCU. ʒif] om. U. wyles] hem myght add. U. helpede A ; helpen U.
l. 653—664 are omitted in E.
665. Than bowmen A. at þe b. DUC ; at the bankes A ; be nethe E ; thay add. A. bentyn EDU ; vp add. C. thaire A. gere] bowys E.
666. & schotyn (schottyn ED) EDUC. vp] full add. A. to] vnto U ; at ADC. schene] brode U. þe sch.] folk on þe E.
667. arblast DC ; alblastirs (!) A. þat] þat add. C.
668. For to A. þat] the add. A ; hem add. C.

38 *A strong Pale is built about the Walls.*

<small>Burning lead and brimstone are poured from above on the assailants.</small>

þe Jewes werien þe walles ⸘ with wyles ynowe,
Hote [p]l[ay]ande picche ⸘ a-monge þe peple ȝeten,
Brenn[a]n[d] leed & brynston, ⸘ barels fulle,
Schoten schynande doun ⸘ riȝt as schyrˀ water.   672
Waspasian wendeþ fram þe walles, ⸘ wariande hem alle ;
Oþer busked werˀ boun, ⸘ benden engynes,
Kesten at þe kernels ⸘ & clustred toures,
& monye der daies worke ⸘ dongen to grounde.   676

<small>A pale is erected round about the walls,</small>

By þat wriȝtes han wroȝt ⸘ a wonder stronge pale
Alle aboute þe burwe, ⸘ with bastiles manye,
þat [no freke in myȝt fonde with-owttyn fethyrhames,]
[Ne] no segge vnderˀ sonne ⸘ myȝt fram þe cite passe.   680

<small>and the rampart ditches are filled with the dead bodies.</small>

Suþ dommyn þe diches ⸘ with þe ded corses,
Crammen hit myd karayn ⸘ þe kirnels vnder,
þat þe stynk of þe steem ⸘ myȝt strike ouer þe walles,
To coþe þe corsed folke ⸘ þat hem kepe scholde.   684

---

669. *weryde* ADU ; *kepten* E ; *wroȝte on* C. *wall* D. *wyles*] *gynnys* E. *with w.*] *whyles* C.
670. *& hoot* E ; om. U. *playande*] so A ; *blowande* L ; *Boyland* U ; *boylyng* DC ; om. E. *pic.*] *& tar (ter* U) add. EU. *amanges* A ; *ouer* U. *peple*] *wal* U. *ȝett* A ; *caste* EDC ; *thei throwe* U.
671. *Birnande* A ; *Brennyng* EDUC ; *Brennen* L. *leed*] *pyk* A ; *brynston* ED UC. *bromstane* A ; *leed* EDUC ; *meny* add. DU ; *many a* add. C. *barel* DUC. *staffulle* A. *barels f.*] *hoot ymolte* E.
672. *Thay schotte* A. *schyn.*] *shelmyng* D ; *sheluyng* U. *Schoten sch.*] *They shoofedde hit* C ; *Faste threwyn* E. *adown* EDU. *riȝt as sch.*] *as it hadde be* E.
673. *Than Wasp.* A. *went* DUC ; om. E. *fro* ADUC. *wall* DUC. *war.*] *& wericd* DU ; *& cursed* C. *thaym* A. *alle*] *harde* AD. *war. h. a.*] *wente a lytel while* E.
674. *Bot oþer* AEDU ; *And oþer* C ; þan add. D. *were*] *are* D ; *hem* C ; *and* add. A. *boun*] *redy* C. *were boun*] *her bowes* U. *busked w. boun*] *were wunder bysy* E. *bend.*] *and bendide* A ; *& bentyn* DU ; *to beende* EC ; *her* add. U.
675. *Thay keste* AUC ; *To caste* ED ; *faste* add. C. *at*] *to* C. *kern.*] *corners* EDU ; *towun* C. *&*] *þey* C. *clustred*] *clatred* AUC ; *clatere* E ; þe add. AEU ; *her* add. C. *&—toures*] þe *cursid caitifs to quelle* D.
676. *& m.*] *Many a* C. *der*] om. A.

daye AEDU ; *worke*] *thay* add. AEUC. *dongen*] *casten* C. *to*] *the* add. AEUC.
677. þat] *thenne* C ; þe add. DUC. *wretches* (!) U ; *with inne* add. U. *had* AEC. *ywrought* E. *a*] *meny* D. *wonder*] om. DU.
678. *burglit* (!) E. *bast.*] *full* add. A.
679. *freke*] *manne* C. *in*] so U ; om. AEDC. *myȝt fonde*] so ED ; *vnfongede* (!) A ; *out wente* C ; *myght* U. *oute* EDUC. *fethyrhames*] so A ; *fressh harmes* EDUC. This line is omitted in L.
680. *Ne*] so ADU ; *Nor* C ; þat L. *segge*] *manne* C. *myȝt*] om. DU. *fro* AC. *cite*] *toune* U.
Thorw þe seege passe . for auȝt þat he cowde E.
681. *Suþ*] *Sythyn* D ; *And sen* U ; *And thanne* E ; *Aftyr* C ; om. A ; *thay* add. AEC. *demmede* A ; *fil* DU ; *fylled* EC ; *they* add. DU. *dich* EDU. *corses*] *bodies* DUC.
682. *Crammyd* D ; *And kramede* AEC ; *Fillen* U. *hit*] þam A ; *hem* U ; om. ED. *with* AEDUC. *caryons* A. *kirn.*] *corners* EDUC ; *alle* add. U.
683. þe] *stythe* add. A. *stynk*] *steem* ED. *of*] *and* AEDUC. *steem*] *stench* ED ; *stewe* AC. *may* U. *str.*] *stynk* D ; *carie* U.
684. *coþe*] *core* DU ; *poysen* E. *corsed*] *fals* E. *To—folke*] *The cursede folke for* (vn C) *to care (greue* C) AC. *thaym* A. þat—*scholde*] *& so her deth cacche* E ; *to (and* U) *kecche her bane* DU.

Caiphas is condemned to Death. 39

Þe cors of þe condit ⁝ þat comen to [þe] toun,
Stoppen, euereche a streem, ⁝ þer any str[ande] ȝede,
W*ith* stockes & stones ⁝ & stynkande bestes,
þ*at* þey no water myȝt wynne, ⁝ þ*at* weren enclosed. 688
Waspasian tourneþ to h*is* tente ⁝ w*ith* Tit*us* & oþer,   Vespasianus convokes a
Commaundeþ consail ano*n* ⁝ on Cayphas to sitte,   council to pass sentence
W[hat] deþ by dome ⁝ þ*at* he dey scholde,   on Caiphas and the
W*ith* þe lettered ledes ⁝ þ*at* þey lauȝte hadde. 692 scribes.
Domes-me*n* vpon de[y]s ⁝ demeden swyþe
þ*at* ech freke wer' quyk fleyn, ⁝ þe felles of clene,
þe*n* to be on a bent ⁝ w*ith* blonkes to-drawe,
& suþ honget on an hep ⁝ vpon heye galwes, 696
þe feet to þe f*ir*mament, ⁝ alle folke to byholden,   Fol. 11 a.
W*ith* hony vpon ech [halfe] ⁝ þe hydeles anoynted ;   They are condemned to a
Corres & cattes ⁝ w*ith* claures ful scharpe   most painful death.
Ffour' kagge[d] & knyt ⁝ to Cayphases þeyes, 700
Twey apys at h*is* armes ⁝ to angren hy*m* mor',

---

685. *curses* A. *þe*] om. UC. *condites* AC. *comen*] *come* AEDUC. *to*] *fro* DU ; *þe*] *so* AEDUC; om. L. *toun*] *wellis* D.
686. *And stoppede* A ; *Thei stopped* EDUC. *cuer ylke* A ; *euery* DUC. *a*] om. DC. *eu. a. str.*] *on euery syde* E. *þer*] *wher* E. *strande*] so A ; *spryng* EDC; *cours* U ; *strem* (!) L. *ȝede*] *was* E ; *were* D.
687. *stakis* AC. *stynkyngge* EDC. *bes.*] *bodyes* E.
688. *may* U. *þat—wynne*] *They myȝte to no watur come* C. *encl.*] *with in closede* AC. *þat—enclos.*] *in to* (om. U) *þe toun yclosid* DU ; *þat in þe town were* E.
689. *Wasp.*] *þan* add. D. *turned* C ; om. E. *tentis* A. *& o.*] *hym turned* E.
690. *Commaundid* D ; *& comaundyd* EC ; *a* add. DUC ; *his* add. E. *anon*] om. EDUC.
691. *What*] so EDUC ; *Whatekyns* A ; *With* (!) L. *by*] *her* add. EDUC ; *dey*] *haue* E.
692. *And also with* C ; *And* D. *þe*] *þo* DU ; *those* A. *ledes*] *menne* C. *þe l.*] *alle his grete clerkys* E. *loght* D ; *cawȝt* E. *þei l. h.*] *þe lawes ledde* C.
693. *The d.* C ; *Than d.* A. *appon* A. *deys* E; *dayes* U ; *desse* A ; *dees* D ; *deþes* (!) L. *vp. d.*] *her dethes* C. *demeden*] *full* add. AUC. *swyþe*] *sone* C.
694. *Whils* A ; *Whyll* C. *ilk* AU ; *euery* C ; *a* add. AE. *freke were*] *man*

was C. *quyk*] om. EDU. *fleyn*] om. C. *fell* U ; *skynnes* C ; *flesche* A. *of*] om. A ; *ful* add. U. *clene*] *to be flayne* C.
695. *þen*] *Firste* ADC ; *But ferst* E. *a*] *the* AC. *bent*] *erþe* C. *to—bent*] *on tentys to be* ED. *blonkes*] *horses* C ; *houndis* D ; *ropes* E. *þen—blonkes*] *And than with bondes ybounden and with hors* U. *to-dr.*] *ydrawen* AEDUC.
696. *&*] om. D. *sythen* AD ; *sen* U ; *thanne* EU ; *after* C. *Ihonged* C. *hongen* U. *on an hep*] *appone heghte* A ; *on hye* DC ; *hye* U ; *in haste* E. *appone* A. *gawes* (!) E.
697. *fote* U. *to*] *towarde* C. *alle*] *þat* E ; *þe* DUC. *to*] *myȝte* E.
698. *appon* A ; *on* EDUC. *ilk* AU ; *euery* E ; *a* add. AC. *halfe*] so ADU ; *parte* C ; *side* LE. *þe*] *her* C. *hiddills* A ; *bodyes* DUC ; *body* E. *enoyntede* AE ; *to enoynt* U.
699. *With curris & * DU ; *And currys with* C ; *& dogges & * E : *And clauerand* (!) A. *with*] *and* D. *clawes* EDU ; *clowes* A. *with cl.*] *þat clawes hadde* C.
700. *Fourty* D. *kagged*] *kagges* L ; *cacchid* DU ; *chachede* A ; *were kawȝte* C. *Foure c.*] *To be bounde* E. *& yknyt* E ; *with a corde* A. *to*] *till* A ; om. DC. *thees* A ; *sydes* U. *Cay. þ.*] *Cayphas abowte* EDC.
701. *Two* A ; *And two* EUC ; *And xx* D. *at*] *to* A. *at his a.*] *also* EDUC. *hym*] *þe* add. C.

Caiphas and his Clerks die.

    þat renten þe rawe flesche ! vpon rede peces.
    So was he pyned fram prime ! with persched sides,
    Tille þe sonne doun souȝt ! in sommere-tyme.   704

They are tor-
mented to
death to the
utmost
sorrow of the
Jews.
    þe lered men of þe lawe ! a litel bynyþe
    Weren tourmented on a tre, ! topsail walten,
    Knyt to euerech clerke ! kene corres twey,
    þat alle þe cite myȝt se ! þe sorow þat þey dryuen.   708
    þe Jewes walten ouer þe walles ! for wo at þat tyme,
    Seuen hundred slow hem-self ! for sorow of her' clerkes,
    Somme hent her' heer' ! & fram þe hed pulled,
    & somme [down] for deil ! dasch[e]de to grounde.   712
    þe kyng lete drawen hem a-doun, ! whan þey dede wer',

and their
bodies are
burnt to
ashes.
    Bade a bole-fur' betyn, ! to brennen þe corses ;
    Kesten Cayphas þer-yn ! & his clerkes twelf,
    & brenten euereche bon ! in-to þe browne askes.   716
    Suþ went to þe walle ! on þe wynde syde,
    & alle a-brod on þe burwe ! blewen þe powder' :

---

702. þat] To EDU ; For to C. rendyn EUC; rente D ; ryve scholde A. þe] his AE. appon A ; all on C. rede p.] euery syde E ; bothe sydes U.
703. So] & thus E. peyned E. fro A ; þe add. A. prime] tyme add. C. fram pr.] om. E. percede AD. sypes C. with p. s.] þat cursyd schrewe E. This line is omitted in U.
704. sonne] was add. C ; a- add. U. souȝt] sett AUC ; syed D. in] the add. ADUC. somers UC. tyde ACU. Al þe longe somer day • fro morwe tyl euyn E.
705. leerned EDC. men] ledis DU. þe] om. E. by nethen U ; be syde E.
706. Thay were A ; Are D ; Ere U. tourment AU ; turned C. tourm—tre] also yhongyd E ; & add. DU. walte A ; waltur C ; ylurnyd D ; tumbled U ; y wene E.
707. knyt] And knytte AC; were add. C. euerech] a add. AU. kene c.] curredoggis DUC ; cattis A. twayne AC ; two DU. With dogges & cattys also ybounde E.
708. Til D. þe c.] men E. may U. yse E. sorow] wo U. þat] om. E. dry.] hade AEDC ; fele U.
709. þe] Manye E. welte A ; waltrid D ; tombledde C ; om. E. þe] om. AD. wal DC. wo] sorough U ; sorwe C. at] in DC ; om. U. at þat t.] þan þei fyllyn E.
710. hund.] score EDU. thaym selfe A sor.] wo C. thaire cl. A ; þat syȝte E.

711. Somme] Thei EDU. hente] toke C. her] thaim A ; hem seelf EDUC ; by þe add. AEDUC. fro AUC. fram—pulled] pullyd it of faste E.
712. som.] come A. down] so AED UC ; om. L. dole AEDU ; sorowe C. daschede] so AEDUC ; daschande L. to] the add. AEDC.
713. lete] garte A ; bad EUC ; hem hete þan D. hem] thaym A ; om. D. drawen h.] hem hem (!) be drawe E. a-] om. AEDUC. whan—were] for þay were sone dede A.
714. He badde C ; And bad U ; And AED. a] om. U. bale A ; gret E ; om. DUC. betyn] to be fet DU ; be maad E ; to make C ; faste add. EC. brennen] in add. C ; with add. D ; alle add. U. þe] thaire E ; þese C. cors.] clerkis DUC. to—corses] be þe galwys E.
715. Keste A ; And cast D ; Thei casten UC ; & þanne E. &] al add. D. his] cursid add. D. twelf] alle AUC ; caste E ; om. D.
716. &] þer þey add. C. & brynte A ; To be brent E ; vp add. D. euery EUC ; eche D ; a add. AU. in] al E ; om. U. þe] om. AEC. browne] smale E.
717. And seth D ; & sythen AU ; And thanne E ; & aftur C ; þey add. E. walles E.
718. &] om. C. alle] om. EDU. one brode A. on] in AD ; in to C. burwe] burgth (!) E ; cyte C ; þey add. C. blew.] thay add. AU.

" þer is doust [to] ȝour drynke!" ! a du[ke] to hem crieþ,
& bade hem bible of þat broþ ! for þe bischopes soule.   720
Þus ended coursed Cayphas ! & his clerkes alle,   *This is the end of the traitors who killed Christ.*
Al to-brused myd bestes, ! brent at þe laste,
In tokne of tresoun ! & trey þat he wroȝt,
Whan Crist þrow his conseil ! was cacched to deþ.   724
By þat was þe day don, ! dym[m]ed þe skyes,   *The night is coming on.*
Merked [þe] montayns ! & mores a-boute,
Foules fallen to fote ! & her' feþres r[y]s[t]en,
Þe nyȝt-wacche to þe walle ! & waytes to blowe;   728
Bryȝt fures a-boute betyn ! a-brode in þe oste,
Þe kyng & his consail ! carpen to-gedr',
Chosen chyuentayns out ! & chiden no mor',   *The king and his counsellors post the checkwatch*
Bot charged þe chek-wecche ! & to chambr' wenten,   732 *and lie down.*
Kynges & knyȝtes ! to cacchen hem reste.
Waspasian lyþ in his logge, ! litel he slepiþ,   *Vespasianus cannot sleep.*
Bot walwyþ & wyndiþ ! & waltreþ a-boute,

---

719. *to*] so AEDUC; *for* L. *duke*] so AEDUC; *doun* (!) L. *to*] *on* U. *to thaym* A; *þo* C. *crieþ*] *sayde* AEC.
720. *&*] *He* C. *thaym* A. *byb* D; *bebe* A; *drynke* EC. *of þat*] *þat* D; *it in* UC. *broþ*] *beuerache* D. *of þ. br.*] *alle abowte* E. *byschoppe* AU.
721. *And thus* U. *endeth* U. *coursed*] om. EDU. *alle*] *twelue* EDUC.
722. *Alto brused* L. *Those gylefull bestis with bale were one thaire bodyes hangede* A. This line is omitted in EDUC.
723. *In the tokynnynge* A. *of*] *the* add. AE; *her* add. UC. *he*] *þey* EDU. *&—he*] *þat þey to Iesu* C. *&—wroȝt*] *that thay brewede hade* A.
724. *Whan*] *þat* add. A. *þrow*] *in* E; *by* C; *at* DU. *his*] *here* EDUC; *thaire* A. *cac.*] *kawȝte* C; *demyd* E; *& put* add. C. *to*] *the* add. AD.
725. *þat*] *þen* C. *don*] *and* add. AU; *& þenne* add. C. *dymmyd* DUC; *dynnede* A; *dymned* (!) L. *skye* AC.
& so þe day be þat tyme. was brought to þe hende E.
726. *Markyd* DU; *And mirkenede* A; *Then wax dirke* C; *þe* add. ADUC. *&*] *þe* add. C. *marreis* U; *al* add. D.
727. *And fowles* C. *fellen* UC. *fote*] *the grownde* A. *&*] om. DUC. *thaire* A. *rysten*] *so* A; *rusken* L; *to reste* DUC.
728. *nyȝt*] om. C. *waches* A; *wente*

add. C. *to*] *on* DU. *wallis* AC. *&*] *þe* C. *to*] *ganne* C; *gun* U.
729. *fyre* U. *aboute b.* ! *a-br.*] *one brode bett* A; *al o brode is brent* U; *and brood ar bette* D; *& brode were made* C. *oste*] *cite* A.
ll. 726—729 are omitted in E.
730. *carpis* A; *carped* E; *speken* C. *togedirs* A.
731. *& chosyn* E; *They chosen* C. *out chifteynes* EDUC. *Chosen — out*] *Full gude cheftans þay chese owte* A. *&*] om. D. *chidden* UC; *þay* add. A. *&—more*] *manly men of harmes* E.
732. *charged*] *g* written on an erasure in L; *chargen* A. *chek*] *chief* UC. *chek w.*] *chefteins* D. *to*] *her* add. DC. *chambirs* A. *wente*] *ȝoden* A. *To kepe þe wacche al þe nyȝt ouer* E.
733. *Bothe kynges* C. *knyȝtes*] *princes* C. *to*] om. A. *cac.*] *taken* C. *hem*] *her* D; *thaire* A; *somme* add. C.
& tho he took his reeste . as reysoun wolde E.
This line is omitted in U.
Quintus passus added over l. 734 in U; *Passus V*ᵘˢ add. C.
734. *lyþ*] *lyȝte* (!) C; om. E. *his*] om. EDU. *logge*] *and* add. AC.
735. *walowedde* C. *wyndiþ*] *wendith* D; *wrythis* A; *walkeph* (!) E; *turned* C. *&*] *vmwhile* add. U. *waltr.*] *walkith* DU; *turyȝt* (!) E; *meued* C.

At Dawn Vespasianus dresses himself.

At daybreak

Fol. 11 b.

Vespasianus puts on his harness.

Ofte tourneþ for tene ͻ & on þe toun þynkeþ. 736
Whan schadewes & schir' day ͻ scheden attwynne,
Leuerockes vpon lofte ͻ lyften † her' steuenes,
Burnes busken hem *out* of bedde ͻ *with* bemes loude,
Boþe blowyng on bent ͻ & on þe burwe walles. 740
Waspasian bounys of bedde, ͻ busked hym fayr'
Fram þe fote to þe fourche ͻ *in* fyne gold cloþes.
Suþ putteþ þe pr*i*nce ͻ oue*r* h*is* pal[l]e[n] wedes
A brynye, browded þicke, ͻ *with* a brest-plate, 744
[þe] gra[te was] of g*ra*y steel ͻ & of gold riche ;
þe*r*-ouer he casteþ a cote, ͻ colou*r*[ede] of h*is* armys ;
A grete girdel of gold ͻ *with*-out ger' oþer'
Layþ vmbe h*is* lendis, ͻ *with* lacchetes ynow. 748
A bry3t burnesched swerd ͻ he belteþ alofte,

---

736. *Ofte*] *& ofte* E ; *And oft tyme* DU ;
And euer more C. *tourn.*] om. EDUC ;
hym add. A. *for*] *in a* D ; *in grct* E.
for t.] *by-twene* U ; *bytwene tymes* C.
&] om. EDUC. *toun*] *he* add. C.
*How he my3t it wynne . with cny
maner while* add. E.
737. *Whan*] *Till* AC. *schadowe* AEDU.
sch.—d.] þ*e daye & þe ny3te* C. *scheddyn*
AD ; *schewed* U ; *departyd* EC. *in
twyne* AC.
738. *And l.* AU ; *Then larkes* C. *vpon*]
on E ; *lepis one* A. *lyften*] so EDU ; *sone
leften* C ; *to newen* A ; *vp* add. DC ;
lyfteneþ L. *thaire* A. *steuen* AE ; *steuys*
D ; *voys* C.
739. *And beryns* A ; *Barnes* E ; *And
lordes* C. *buskes* A ; *buskyd* D ; *dressede*
C. *hem*] om. ADU. *out of*] *fro* E.
bemes] *one* add. A ; *ful* add. DU. *with b.*]
& claryones blew vp C. *with b. l.*] *& in
to feeld 3ede* E.
740. *Bothe*] þ*an* add. D. *blawande* A ;
blew DUC ; þ*ey* add. C. *on*] *in* DUC ;
the add. ADUC. *bent*] *felde* C. *burwe*]
cyte C. *wal* U.
*Trumpyng & claryonyng . & meche
noyse made* E.
741. *bounys*] *buskes* AU ; *busked* ED ;
dressede 'C ; *hym* add. EC ; *owt* add.
EDU. *of*] *fro* EC ; *his* add. AC. *bedde*]
and add. AUC. *busked*] *bownnes* A ;
bownyd D ; *arayde* C ; *raies* U. *hym*]
ful add. U. *fayre*] *to ryse* A. *busked h.
f.*] *blyue* E.
742. *Fro* EDUC ; *And fro* A. *fote*]
fourche A. *fourche*] *fote* A ; *heed* E ; *for-*

hedde C ; *fronte* DU. *fync*] *fyve* (!) D.
cloþes] *hym clothis* A ; *wede* U. *gold cl.*]
cloth of golde C. *in—cloþes*] *arayed hym
thanne* E.
743. *Sythen* A ; *And seth* D ; *And
aftur* C. *put* D ; *on* add. D. þe] *that*
ADC. *ouer*] *aboue* DC. *pallen w.*] so
ADC ; *pale w.* L ; *gay aray* C. This
line is omitted in EU.
744. *A brene* A ; *An haburionne* C ; *A
bright bye* D. *broudyd* D ; *browdirde*
AC ; *braiden* U ; *full* add. AD ; *al* add.
U. þ*icke*] *wele* A. *A—*þ*icke*] *In fyn
gold weede* E.
745. þ*e grate*] so ADUC ; *Grayþrd* L ;
With a grate E. *was*] so A ; om. LDUCE.
of] *on* DC ; þ*e* add. DUC. *&*] *was* DUC.
&—riche] *ygrounde wol scharpe* E.
746. *ouer*] *on* UC. *keste he* ADU ; *cast-
ede he* C. þ*er—cast.*] *And thanne dode* (!)
on E. *cote*] *of* add. DUC ; *with* add. E.
colourede] so A ; *colours* E ; *colour* L.
þ*e whiche were riche . & dredful on
to looke* add. E.
747. *And a* C. *with owttyn* AU. *oþer*]
more ADUC.
þ*anne gurt hym with a gurdyl . ful
of riche stones* E.
748. *vmbe*] *abowte* A. *Layþ v.*] *He
leyd on* DUC. *latches* U. *ynow*] *many*
DU ; *full monye* C.
*With dyamaundes & perre . richelich
arayed* E.
749. *With a* A. *brond* DA. *he*] *& A.
belteþ*] *girdis* AC ; *gird* DU ; *putte* E ;
hym add. ADUC ; *on* add. E. *one lofte*
A ; *aboue* E ; *about* DUC.

Vespasianus defies the Jews.

Of pur' purged gold ⁝ þe pomel & þe hulte ;
A brod schynande scheld ⁝ on scholdir' he hongiþ,
Bocklyd myd briȝt gold, ⁝ abou[t]e at þe necke. 752
Þe glowes of gray steel, ⁝ þat wer' with gold hemmyd,
Hauleþ [ouer] harnays ⁝ & his hors askeþ ;
Þe gold hewen helme ⁝ haspeþ he blyue,
With viser & with a-vental ⁝ deuysed for þe nones. 756
A croune of clene gold ⁝ was closed vpon lofte,
Rybaunde vmbe þe rounde helm, ⁝ ful of riche stones,
Pyȝt prudely with perles ⁝ in-to þe pur' corners,
& so with saphyres sett ⁝ þe sydes a-boute. 760
He strideþ on a stif stede ⁝ & strikeþ ouer þe bente,
Liȝt as a lyoun, ⁝ wer' loused out of cheyne.
His segges se[y]en hym alle, ⁝ & echon sayþ to oþer :
"Þis is a comlich kyng, ⁝ knyȝtes to lede !" 764
He boweþ to þe barres, ⁝ or he bide wolde,
Betynge on with þe brond ⁝ on þe bras rynges :

Vespasianus mounts a strong horse and challenges the enemies.

---

750. *purged*] *polisched* AEDUC. *þe*]
bothe C. *þe*] om. C. *hiltes* EC. *þe h.*]
alle D. *þe—hulte*] om. A.
751. *schynyng* EDC. *on*] *his* add. ED
UC. *he*] om. EDU. *honged* EC.
This line is omitted in A.
752. *Ybocled* U ; *And bokeled* C. *myd*]
with DUC. *briȝt*] *fyne* DU. *Bockl.–gold*]
om. A. *gold*] *cast* add. D ; *al* add. U.
abou[t]e]so ADU ; *aboue* LC. *at þe*] *his* DU.
Al yclosyd in steel . hard for þe nonys E.
753. *þe*] *His* E ; *With* A. *of*] *the* add.
U. *gray st.*] *plate* E. *was* A. *þat—gold*]
with gold were EDUC. *yhemmed* EU.
754. *ouer*]om. L. *Hauleþ o. h.*] *Thanne
(And then* U ; *And* D) *he hyed hynn in
hast* EDU ; *When he was arayde thus* C ;
Than hendely I ȝowe hete A. *&*] *he* A ;
om. C. *hors*] om. (!) E ; *sone he* add. C.
asked EDUC.
755. *And the* A. *haspeþ he bl.*] *one
his hede hespis* A ; *he askyd (in hye (also
U) DU ; *hym was browȝte þenne aftur* C.
& leep vp lyȝtliche . as a knyȝt schulde E.
756. *with*] om. AEDUC. *a v.*] *aventalle*
AU ; *ventayle* EDC. *auysed* EDUC.
757 *And u* C. *crowne*] *al* add. ED.
of] *full* add. A ; *the* add. U. *vpon*] *one*
A. *vpon l.*] *abouen* C.
758. *Ryb.—rounde*] *Rayed (Rayled* C ;
Ynailed U) *round on (aboute* C) *þe* DUC ;
& set vpon his E. *Ryb.-helm*] *Enverownde
all one rownde* A. *ful of*] *with full* A.

759. *And pyghte* A. *prudely*] om.
EDU. *perle* A ; *of prys* add. EDU.
vnto A. *pure*] *prowde* A. *in to—corners*]
þe helme rounde abowte C ; *& proudly
arayed* EDU.
760. *so*] *also* A ; *þan* E ; om. C. *yset*
DU ; om. A. *syde* E ; *sypes* (!) C ; *all*
add. AEU. *ab.*] *to & fro* C.
761. *on*] *of* (!) D. *stif*] *stythe* A. *strik*]
strekis A ; *styred* C. *ouer*] *on* ADUC.
bente] *ground* DUC.
*Thanne prikeþ he forþ . stefly on his
steede* E.
762. *Lightly* DU ; *As lyȝtly* E. *loused*]
launcid D ; *lete* E. *out of*] *from his* U ;
of his C. *Righte als any* (!) *were owte of
chene lowsede* A.
763. *segges*] *lordes* E ; *menne* C. *se[y]en*]
so D ; *seese* A ; *seen* E ; *syen* U ; *syȝe* C ;
sewen L. *alle*] *eche oone* C. *ilkone* AU ;
eche ED ; *euery manne* C. *seyd* DUC.
till AU. *to oþer seyde* E.
*And boldly may þay byde þat swylke
a beryn folowes* add. A.
765. *Than he* A. *boweþ*] *rood* E ; *pryked* C ; *hies hym* A. *barrers* ADU. *or*]
there U. *abyde* EDC.
766. *Bet.*] *And bet (beteth* C) DUC ; *& bette* E ; *Owte braydis he* A. *on with*] om.
A. *þe*] *his* AEDC. *brond*] *swerd* EC. *on*]
þat DUC. *ringeth* U ; *ryngid* DC. *on—
rynges*] *and bett appone harde* A ; *& seyde
to þe false* E.

Vespasianus addresses the Jews.

"Comeþ, caytifes, forþ, ' ȝe þat Crist slowen,
Knoweþ hym for ȝour kyng, ' or ȝe cacche mor'.   768
Wayteþ doun fro þe walle, ' what wo ist on hande;
May ȝe fecche ȝou no fode, ' þoȝ ȝe fey worþe,
& þoȝ ȝe waterles wede, ' wynne ȝe noȝt o droppe,
þoȝ ȝe deþ scholde dey, ' daies in ȝour lyue.   772
þe pale þat I piȝt haue, ' passe hit who myȝt,
þat is so byg on þe bonke ' & haþ þe burowe closed,

Fol. 12 a. Ffourty to fyȝten ' aȝens fyue hundred,
þoȝ ȝe wer' etnes echon ' in scholde [ȝ]e [tourne].   776

Vespasianus advises the Jews to sue for mercy. & more manschyp wer' hit ' ȝit mercy by-seche,
þan metles marr' ' þer' no myȝt helpys."
Was non þat warpiþ a word, ' bot waytes her' poyntes,

As he gets no reply, he turns round most angrily. ȝif [any] stertis on st[r]ay, ' with stones hem to kylle.   780
þan wroþ as a wode bore ' he wendeþ his bridul:
"ȝif ȝe as dogges wol dey, ' þe deuel haue þat recche,
& or I wende fro þis walle, ' ȝe schul wordes schewe

---

767. *Sayde, commys* A. *forþ*] *owt* A. *cayt. forþ*] *out (ȝe* add. C) *keitifs* UC; *he seyde* add. C; *he crieþ* add. D. *ȝe*] *þe* D; om. C.
768. *And kn.* AEDUC. *kyng*] *god* C.
769. *wallis* A. *is*] *his* L; *es* A. This line is omitted in EDUC.
770. *ȝe may* AEDUC. *fette* EDC. þoȝ] ȝif þat A. *fey w.*] *dye shulde* C. þoȝ— *worþe*] *wulde ȝe neuer so fawe* E.
771. þoȝ] ȝif A. þoȝ ȝe] *also* EC. *wede*] *wone* D; *ben* U; ȝe *be* E. *wat. w.*] *to ȝour watyr* C; ȝit add. A. ȝe *noȝt o dr.*] ȝe *it neuer* A; *shul ȝe neuere* DU; ȝe *maye neuer* C. *wynne—droppe*] *how wulde ȝe leeue* E.
772. *A drope (dope (!) A) þogh (ȝife A) ȝe dye shold* DUCA; *For o drope ne gete ȝe* E; *the* add. A. *in*] *of* AED. *For y haue stroyed alle þe stremys . þat to þe town runne* add. E.
773. *I hafe pighte* AE; *here pyght is* C; *down* add. A. *hit*] om. C. *who*] *to* add. AUC. *may* C. *hit—myȝt*] ȝe *ne mowe* D; ȝe *neuere* E.
774. *þat*] *It* AC. *so*] *full* AC; om. U. *appon þe* A; *at þe* DC; *atte* U. *byg— bonke*] *long & so brood* E. *haþ*] þ written on erasure in L. þe] ȝoure AC. *bur.*] *town* E; *cyte* C. *enclosyd* E.
775. *For fowrty* C; *Twenty* E; *menne* add. C. *fyȝten*] *fende off* ADU; *defende* E. *aȝens fyue*] *& holde of sixe* E.
776. *For thow* E; *If* A. *etnes*] *gyauntes*

A; *deuelles* C. *ilkone* A. *in*] *agayne* AC; *out* E. *schul* EDU. ȝe] *so* AEDU; *we* written above the line in L. *tourne*] so ADU; *neuere* E; *wende* L. *scholde we w.*] *turne ȝe shull* C.
777. *&*] ȝette add. C; om. E. *mansch.*] *menske* A; *wirship* UC; *wysdom* E. *it were* EC; *it is* DU. ȝit] om. EDUC. *mercy*] *to* add. AEDUC. *by-s.*] *seche* D; *craus* A; *crye* E.
778. *metles marre*] *for the mette maren* A; *for to marre (deye* E) *meteles* DUCE. *þere—helpys*] *beestes as ȝe were* E.
779. *Bot was there none* A; *Ther were none* C. *warpen* U; *warpede* AD; *spak* E. *þat w.*] *to speke* C; *agayne* add. A. *wayten* U; *wayted* EDC. *þair* A; *his* E. *poynt* AU; *tyme* EDC.
780. *any*] so ADUC; om. L. *stirrede* A; *styrte* C; *out* add. C. *on*] *a* DC. *stray*] so DUCA; *stay* (!) L. ȝif—*stray*] *How he myȝt prynyly* E. *hem*] *eny* E; *for* U; om. ADC. *to*] om. E. *quelle* D.
781. þan] om. C. *a*] *the* AE. *wode*] *wylde* ADUC. *wode b.*] *wynd* E. *he— bridul*] *Waspasyan seyde* E.
782. *Thogh* C. *as—dey*] *dye as dogges* C; *he sayd* add. AD. þat] *wo* A. *rekketh* C.
783. *or*] *þogh* DUC; om. A. *wende*] *fonde* U. þis] *the* ADUC. *word. sch.*] *wone stille* D; *abyde (there (me here* C) UC. *For ȝif y leeue & y may . fayn schal schal* (!) *y ȝow make* E.

The Stratagem of Josephus is useless.

& efte spakloker' speke, ˹ or y ʒour speche owene." 784
By þat a Jewe Josophus, ˹ þe gentyl clerke,
Hadde wroʒt a wonder' wyle, ˹ whan hem water fayled;
Made wedes of wolle ˹ in wete for to plunge,
Water-waschen as þey wer', ˹ & on þe walle hengen. 788
þe wedes dropeden doun, ˹ d[r]yed ʒerne,
Rich rises hem fro; ˹ þe Romayns byholden,
Wenden wel, her' wedes ˹ hadde wasschyng so ryue,
þat no wye in þe wone ˹ water schold fayle. 792
Waspasian þe wile ˹ wel ynow knewe,
Loude lawʒ[eþ] þer-at ˹ & lordlynges byddis :
"No burne abasched be, ˹ þoʒ þey þis bost make :
Hit beþ bot wyles of werr', ˹ for water hem fayleþ." 796
þan was no-þyng bot a newe ˹ note to bygynne,
Assaylen on eche a side ˹ þe cite by halues,
Merken myd manglouns ˹ ful vn-mete dyntes,

Josephus tries to make the Romans believe that the Jews have plenty of water.

Vespasianus declares this to be a mere stratagem, and continues assailing the town.

---

784. *And oft* DUC; om. E. *spaklyere* A; *speedloker* ED; *spedlier* UC; *for to* add. E. *ʒour*] om. A. *owene*] *profire* A; *here* EDUC.
785. *a*] *the* A. *Josaphus* A. *a. J. J.*] *Josephus þe Jew* EDUC. þe] *a* A; þat *was a* C. *þe g. cl.*] þat *gentyl (gynful* DU) *was euere* EDU.
786. *Hadde ywrought* E; *Wrought had* U; *Wroght* D. *wondirfull* A. *whan*] þat add. A. *thaym* A. *water hem* U. *fayled*] *wantid* DU.
Whenne þat þey water fayledde . wroght a wondur wyle C.
787. *He made* AC. *wete for*] *water* AD. *in—plunge*] *in þe reyn leet legge hem* E.
788. *With water ywasshe* E. *on*] *ouer* U. *wallis* AEDC; *hem* add. E. *hongyn* D; *hongyth* EU; *hangede* AC.
789. *droppyn* D. ˹*doun* L. *adown* EDC; *and* add. AEDUC. *dryede*] so AUC; *dryen* D; *deyed* (!) L; *full* add. A. ʒerne] *anone* C. *dr. ʒ.*] *gunne faste to drye* E.
790. *Reek* E; *Reke* DU; *The reke* AC. *rose* AC; *aryseth* E. *thaym* A; þer DU. *from* D. *byholdis* A; *behylden* C.
791. *Wenden—wedes*] (*þei wende weel (And hadde wonder* C) *in here wyt* EDUC. *hadde—ryue*](þat om. U) *no wantyng they hadde* EU; *no watir hem wantyd* D; *how þat þey were wete* C.
And wele wende thay that those wedis . waschen hade bene A.
792. þat] *Ne* DU; *And* C. *no wight* U; *no manne* C; *noght* D. þe] þat DU. *in þe w.*] *wente þat þer were* C; *that* add.

U. *schold f.*] *with inne* C.
But greet plente of water . eche of hem alle E.
This line is omitted in A.
793. *Bot* W. AEDUC. þe] *that* A. *wel ynow*] *of þe werre* AUC; *of þe werres* E; *of werre wele* D.
794. *And lowde* AE; *he* add.C. *lawʒþe* L; *laghith* D; *laught* U; *lawʒed* E; *lawʒede* C; *to laughe he bygane* A; *he* add. DU. þer-at] om. A. þer *of* EDU. *lordl. b.*] *ledis he badde* A; *to his lordes seyde* EDUC.
795. *Nor* U. *burne*] *body* E. *ab. be*] *basshen nor bowe* U. *No—be*] (*And saide: om. C): Beryns (Syres* C), *beese noghte abasshed* AC. þoʒ] *gif* A. þis] þus E.
796. *beþ*] *bene* AUDC; *be* E. *bot*] om. C. *thaym* A. *fayl.*] *wanteth* EDU.
797. þan] *Tho* EDU. *nas* DU; *there* add. AC. *no þyng* ˹ L; *noghte ells anone* A; *non* C; om. EDU. *bot*] om. E. *a*] om. AEDUC. *note*] *werk* E; *anon* add. ED; *on one* add. U; *aʒeyn* add. C.
798. *To assaile* DC; *He* (om. U) *assayled* EU; *Assemblede* A. *on*] *by* D. *ilke* AU. *a*] om. DUC. *by h.*] *to byholde* U. *on—halues*] þe *cyte . faste on eche a syde* E.
799. *Thay merken* A; *Markid* DUC. *with* ADUC. *manglouns*] *mangonells* A; *magnels* U; *mangynels* C; *machenelles* D. *ful*] om. AD.
& brak doun with engynes . & sparyd nere a place E.

Vespasianus is wounded.

Another stratagem of Josephus is likewise frustrated.

& myche of masou$n$s note ⸲ þey marden þat tyme. 800
þer-of was Josophus war', ⸲ þat myche of werr' couþe,
& sette on þe walle side ⸲ sakkes myd chaf,
A3ens þe streyngþe of þe stroke, ⸲ þer þe stones hytte,
þat alle dered no3t a dy3s, ⸲ bot grete dy[n] made. 804
þe Romayns ru$n$ne to a-no$n$ ⸲ & on roddes knytte
Siþes for þe sackes, ⸲ þat selly wer' kene,
Ra3ten to þe ropis, ⸲ rent hem in sonder',
þat alle dasschande dou$n$ ⸲ in-to þe diche flatten. 808

Still he succeeds in destroying the battering engines by fire.

Bot Josophus þe gynful ⸲ her' engynes alle
Brente † wi*th* bre$n$nande oyle ⸲ & myche bale wro3t.
Waspasian wou$n$ded was þer ⸲ wonderlich sore

Vespasianus is wounded in the heel by a dart.

þrow þe hard of þe hele ⸲ wi*th* an hande-darte, 812
þ*at* boot þrow þe bote ⸲ & þe bone nayled

Fol. 12 b.

Of þe frytted fote ⸲ in þe folis syde.
Sone assembled hy$m$ to ⸲ many sadde hundred,

---

800. *mekill* AC. *of*] om. DU; *the* add. A. *note*] *notte* A; *werke* C. þey] *thaire* (!) A; om. U. *merrede* A. þ*at* t.] *by tymes* U.
þ*at masones & many men wrought in many yeres* E.
801. *Ios. was* AEDC; *Ios. is* U. *mekill* A.
802. *&*] *He* AC. *sett to* A; *hengede on* C. *walle s.*] *walle* C; *wallis* A. *myd*] *of* A; *full of* C. *& fylde sakkes ful of chaaf . & on þe walles hem hongyd* E; *Set sakkis with chaf on (vpon* U) *the walle sydes* DU.
803. *Agayne* AED. *strenghe* AEC. *stone* AU; *gonnes* C. *hittyn* D; *hittes* U.
804. *dy3s*] *dyce* A; *dys* D; *dyte* C; *dissh* U; *del* E. *dyn*] so ADUC; *noyse* E; *dyt* L.
805. *ramaynes* (!) A. *rane* AU; *ren* D; *per* add. C. *on*]*vpon* UC. *roddes kn.*] *poles fastnyd* E.
806. *selly*] *ferly* A. *selly w.*] *sharp were and* D; *were bothe fell &* C. *Sythes þat scharp were . þe ropes for* (!) *kytte* E.
807. *And raughte* AE; *They raw3te* C. *to*] *þe sakkes &* E. *þe*] added above the line in L. *ropis*] *and* add. AEDUC. *thaym* A. *in s.*] *asunder* E.
808. *alle*] *pei* add. DUC. *daschede* AEDC; *dasshen* U. *adown* EDUC; *and* add. AEDUC. *to*] om. AEDUC. *dykes* A. *flat.*]*flowe* A; *fyllen* ED; *fellen* C;

fallen U.
809. *Bot*] *Than* EC. *gynf.*]*gentill* AE; *Iewe* C. *thaire* A. *her eng. a.*] *þese* (þe D) *gynnes aspyed* EDU; *ordeynede wyles moo* C.
810. *Brente*] *Brynte* A; *Brenten* (!) L. *with*] *a* add. A. *birnande* A. *Brente— oyle*] *With (boylyng* DC) *brennyng oyle (men he (he hem* C) *brent* DUC. *mekill* A. *bale*] *thaym* add. A.
& hoot boylyng oyle . on hem he leet caste E.
811. *And Vasp.* C; *þanne* add. E; *there* add. U. *was wondyde* A; *was yw.* E. *þer*] om. AEU. *wonderl.*] om. E.
812. *hard*] *myddel* E; *hert* (!) U. *the*] *his* E. *an hande*] *a scharp* E.
813. *þat*] *It* A. *boot*] *the (he* D) *bitte* DU; *þe poynte* C. *þe*] om. DUC. *&— nayled*] *rennyng bothe sydes* U.
So þat his boote & his heele · *were nayled togydre* E.
814. *Of þe fr. f.*] *And þer to fastnyd (fetered* C) *þe foot* DC; *& also yfastnyd* E. *in*] *to* EDC. *þe*] *his* E. *folis*] *steedes* E; *hors* C.
This line is omitted in AU.
815. *Bot sone* A. *ass.*] *þer kome* C. *ass. h. to*] *to hym semblyd* D; *him sembled to* U. *many*] *a* add. C. *sadde*] *bolde* U. *hund.*] *seggis* D; *segge* U.
Tho were besy wounder sone . many wurthi kny3tes E.

Many Men and Women are killed. 47

þat wolden wrecken þe wounde, ꞏ oþer wo habben. 816
þey bowyn to þe barres, ꞏ bekered ȝerne, *The Roman*
Fouȝt riȝt felly, ꞏ foyned with speres, *engines have a horrible effect,*
Jo[k]ken Jewes proȝ ; ꞏ engynes by þanne
Wer' manye bent at þe bonke ꞏ & to þe burwe þrewen. 820
þer wer' selcouþes sen, ꞏ as segges mowe here :
A burne with a balwe-ston ꞏ was þe brayn cloue,
þe gretter pese of þe panne ꞏ þe pyble forþ strikeþ,
þat hit flow in-to þe feld, ꞏ a forlong or more. 824
A womman, bounden with a barn, ꞏ was on þe body hytte
With þe ston o[f] a staf[-slyng], ꞏ as þe storyj telleþ,
þat þe barn out brayde ꞏ fram þe body clene
& was born vp as a bal ꞏ ouer þe burwe walles. 828
Burnes wer' brayned ꞏ & brosed to deþ,
Wymmen wide open ꞏ walte vnder' stones,
Frosletes fro þe ferst ꞏ to þe flor þrylled,

816. *wreke wolde* A ; *wolde avenge* C. *þat wolde wr.*] *To awreke* E. *þe*] *þat* AEDUC. *oþer*] *or ells* AEC ; *or myche* DU. *wo*] *sorowe* C ; *ioye* U. *habben*] *habyde* AEDUC.
817. *bow.*] *brayde* EDUC ; *brayddede* A. *to*] *on* D. *the barers* AEDU ; *baryers* C ; *and* add. AEDUC. *bek.*] *b* corrected from *k*, L ; *fowȝten* C ; *full* add. AU ; *wol* add. E ; *well* add. C. *ȝerne*] *ofte* C ; *yn iryn* D.
818. *riȝt f.*] *with felonye* A. *Fellich* (*Felonsly* U) *þei foughtyn* EDU ; *With foynynge right felly* C ; *and* add. AEDUC. *funyde* A. *foyned w.*] *spendeden her* C.
819. *Jolken* L ; *Jollid* D ; *Thay jusken at these* A ; *Ther they jolledde* C ; *& beryn* E ; *And the* U. *þroȝ*] *thourght owt* ED ; *throwen out* U ; *&* add. C ; *with* add. D. *by þ.*] *bydene* U. *eng. by þ.*] *in to þe harde walles* E.
820. *That were* A. *manye*] om. DUC. *ybent* U. *atte*] U ; *one the* A. *to*] *in to* C ; *at* A. *burwe*] *cyte* C. *thrawen* A ; *throwen* U ; *drewenn* C.
So angry þey were thanne . for hirt of here kynge E.
821. *For there* A. *selc. ysene* D ; *meruayles mony* C. *seg.*] *men* C. *may* AC ; *myght* D. *here*] *sene* D. *selc.—here*] *segges many . sey selkouthe thinges* U.
822. *burne*] *barne* A ; *manne* C. *balwe*] *balghe* A ; *rounde* UC. *was*] *to* add. DC. *brayn*] *hed* A. *clevid* DC. *was—cloue*] *ythrowen was to grounde* U.
823. *þe gr.*] *A grete* AC ; *The grete* U.

panne] *with* add. C. *pyble*] *pomel* D ; *polel* (!) U ; *stone* A ; *brayne* C. *forth*] *owte* AC. *strake* A ; *started* C.
824. *þat into þe feld it* (om. U) *flye* (*flewe* U) DU. *or*] *and* ADU. This line is omitted in C.
ll. 821-24 are omitted in E.
825. *wom.*] *bierd* D ; *beern* U. *bund.*] *grette* C ; om. E. *a*] om. AEUC. *barn*] *chylde* EC. *on*] *in* D. *body*] *bely* UC. *on—hytte*] *smeete on her woombe* E.
826. *þe*] *a* AEDUC. *of*] *on* ACL. *staf-slyng*] *stayre* AC ; *staf* L. *on a st.*] *in þat* (*a* D) *stounde* ED ; *out of a toure* U.
827. *barn*] *chyld* EC. *brayde*] *wente* EU. *fro* U ; *of* ED. *out—clene*] *fro þe body fell out clene* C.
This line is omitted in A.
828. *& was*] om. EDU. *was*] om. AC. *vp*] om. A. *burwe*] *town* EC.
829. *Bernys w.* A ; *Chyldryn w.* E ; *Ther wer menne* C. *ybrayned* EU. *bros.*] *birssede* A ; *brised* U. *to*] *the* add. DUC. *&—deþ*] *pleyȝyng in þe strctes* E.
830. *And women* AC. *welte* A ; *went* DU ; *fell* C ; *laye* E. *vnder*] *þe* add. DUC.
831. *Forcilettes* D ; *That fylettes* C. *þe f.*] *þe front* D ; *her forhedes* C. *Frosl.—to*] *Thorowe forsoure and forcelett was* A. *thirlede* A. *to—þryl.*] *all abowte flowen* C.
With childryn in here wombes . brosyd to þe grounde E.
This line is omitted in U.

The Jews defend themselves most bravely.

and the town would have been taken if the defenders had not made such valiant efforts.

& many toret dou*n* tilte ⁑ þe temple a-boute. 832
þe cite had ben seised ⁑ myd saut at þat tyme,
Nad þe folke be so fers, ⁑ þat þe fende serued,
þat kilden on þe c*r*isten, ⁑ & kepte*n* þe walles
W*ith* arwes & arblastes ⁑ & archers manye, 836
W*ith* speres & spryngoldes ⁑ spo*n*nen ou*t* hard,
Dryue*n* dartes a-dou*n*, ⁑ ȝeuen depe wou*n*des,

Many Romans are wounded and want physicians.

þat manye renke ou*t* of Rome ⁑ [by] rest[ing] of þ[e] s[o]*n*ne
Was mychel leuer' a leche ⁑ þa*n* layke myd h*is* ton. 840
Waspasian stynteþ of þe stour', ⁑ steweþ h*is* burnes,
þat wer' for-beten & bled ⁑ vnder' bryȝt yren;
Tye*n* to her' tentis ⁑ myd tene þat þey hadde,
Al wery of þat werk ⁑ & wou*n*ded ful sore. 844
Helmes & hamberkes ⁑ hadden of sone,
Leches by torche-liȝt ⁑ loke*n* her' hurtes,
Wasche*n* woundes w*ith* wyn ⁑ & w*ith* wolle stoppen,
W*ith* oyle & orisou*n* ⁑ ordeyned in charme. 848

---

832. *torettes* C. *tirlede* A; *fell* C. *temple*] *town* A; *cyte* C. *down—temple*] *of the toun tilt* U; *al* add. ADUC. *þat gret dool was to se . in many dyuers place.* E.
833. *So* þe C. *þe c. h.*] *Thay had sothely* A. *ben s.*] *takyn* (!) E. *myd*] *with* DC; *by* AU; *at* E; *þat* add. E. *assawte* AD; *than* U. *tyme*] *assaute* U. *at þat t.*] *thanne* ED.
834. *Ne had* AEDU; *Hadde noght* C. *fers*] *stronge* C. *fende*] *deuyl* EC.
835. *Wich* (!) E; *Thay* A. *on*] *of* ED UC; om. A. *crist.*] *men* add. A. *&*] *that* U.
836. *alblasters* A; *arblast* DC. *arch.*] *achillers* A; *asschelers* C. *man.*] *grete* A. *arch. m.*] *many maner schottys* E.
837. *With*] om. EDUC. *&*] *out of* EUC. *With sp. &*] *And with gud* A. *spryngoltes* E; *spryngalles* C. *spynnen* A; *sprongen* EDU. *out*] *wol* E; *full* C.
838. *Driued* U; *Thay dreuen* AC; *owte* add. A. *Daartys dryuen* E. *down* A; *and* add. AEDUC. *gyffen* A; *delyd* EU; *dele* D; *made* C. *depe*] *grete* AC; *many* U. *woundes*] *dyntes* U.
839. *renkes* A; *a manne* C; *on* E. *out*] om. EC. *by resting of þe* (om. D) *sonne*] so AEUC; *reste of þat synne* (!) L.
840. *Were* AC. *mekill* A; *myche* ED UC. *with his toose* A. *layke—ton*] *eny layke* (*pley* E; *thing* U; *body* C) *ellis*

DEUC.
841. *stynt* DU; *stynted* EC. *of*] om. C. *þe*] *that* UC. *of þe st.*] *þanne* E; *and* add. AEDUC. *stowyd* DU; *bestowyd* E; *stemmys* A; *kome to* C. *burnes*] *knyghtis* AC; *peple* E.
842. *betyn* AEDC. *by-bled* E; *brent* D. *vnder*] *thorowe thayre* A; *þe* add. C. *iryns* A; *jrenne* C.
This line is lost in U.
843. *Turnyd* DU; *Thay tournede* AC; *& turned* E. *toward* D. *thaire* A; *his* E. *with* AEDUC; *the* add. A.
844. *Al*] *Wunder* EDUC; *And were* A. *þat*] *þe* D; *thaire* A; om. EU. *werk*] *werre* ED. *ful*] *wol* E. *wounded f.*] *wonderly* A.
845. *Here helmes* C; *Than helmys* A. *haweberkis* AED; *hauberke* U; *here armour* C; *thay* add. AEDUC. *had.*] *dodyn* E; *kaste* C. *of*] *full* add. ADC.
846. *And leches* AC; *Thanne leches* E. *by*] *with* A. *light torches* D; *torches* EU. *lukis* A; *lokyd* EDUC; *to* add. UC. *thaire* A. *hurt.*] *woundes* C.
847. *Wusschen* E; *Thay wesche* A; *They wasshedde* C; *her* add. EUC; *þe* add. D. *wolle*] *hem* add. E. *stoppis* A; *stopped* EC.
848. *þanne with* E. *&*] *with* add. AD UC. *orysons* AEDUC; *þei* add. E. *in*] om. DU. *ord. in*] *& with other* C. *charmes* AEDUC.

Vespasianus calls a Council. 49

Suþ euereche a segge ᛫ to þe soper ȝede ;
þoȝ þey wounded wer' ᛫ was no wo nempned
Bot daunsyng & no deil ᛫ with dynnyng of pipis
& þe nakerer noyse ᛫ alle þe nyȝt-tyme.   852
Whan þe derk was doun ᛫ & þe day spr[o]ngen,
Sone after þe sonne sembled þe grete,
Comen forþ-with þe kyng ᛫ conseil to her',
Alle þe knyȝthod clene ᛫ þat for Crist werred.   856
Waspasian waiteþ a-wide, ᛫ his wyes byholdeþ,
þat wer' frescher' to fiȝt ᛫ þan at þe furst tyme,
Prayeþ princes on ernest ᛫ & alle þe peple after
þat eche wye of þat werr' ᛫ schold his wille specke.   860
" For or þis toun be tak ᛫ & þis toures heye
Michel tor[fere] & tene ᛫ vs tides on hande."
þay tourned alle to Titus ᛫ & hym þe tale scheweþ
Of þe cite & þe sege ᛫ to seyn for hem alle.   864
þan Titus tourneþ hem to ᛫ & talkyng bygynneþ ;

In the evening they feast.
Fol. 13 a.
Next day Vespasianus calls a council.
He asks each man to give his opinion.
Titus takes the word,

---

849. *And* add. ACUD.   *suþ] sythen* A ; *sen* U ; *after þat* C ; *Thenne* E. *euereche] ilke* A. *a segge] manne* C ; om. E ; *vn* add. A. *ȝede] wente* C ; *eche man wente* E.

850. *þey—wer] þe woundes were (be* U) *sore* OUD ; *her woundes sore were* E ; *there* add. ACU. *no] none þat* (om. U ; *of* add. C) CUDE. *menede* CD ; *meneth* U ; *made* E.

851. *deil] sorow* C. *daun.—deil] daunsed delles* UD ; *daunsyd & sunge* E. *dynnyng] noyse* C.

852. *þe] with* CUDE. *nakirrers* AD ; *nakeres* CU. *noyse] nysely* C. *noyse of nakers* E. *nyȝt] nyghtis* ADE. *tyme] tyde* A.

853. *derk]* om. C. *sprongen] so* AC ; *spryngen* L.

854. *sonne] rysynge* add. A. *assemblede* A ; *were gedered* C.

855. *Thay* add. AC. *forþ-with] byfore* A. *her] holde* C.

856. *clene] full clene* A ; *keene* C.

857. *Than* add. A ; *a-wide] abowte* C ; *and* add. A. *wyes byholdeþ] mayne to byholde* C.

858. *wer frescher] fresschere were þanne* C. *at—tyme] þay by-fore were* A ; *euer þey were* C.

SIEGE OF JERUSALEM.

11. 853–58 are omitted in UDE.

859. *He* add. AC ; *Vespasian* add. UDE. *prayde* CDE ; *the* add. AUD. *prynce* A. *on ernest] in haste* A ; *fyrste* C ; om. UD. *alle]* om. D. *princes—after] his his lordes al abowte* E.

860. *eche] ilke a* AU ; *eueru* C. *wye] wight* UD ; *manne* CE. *þat] the* UD. *of þat werr] one his beste wiese* A. *wille] wytte* C ; *avyce* A. *specke] schewe* AUDC. *of . . . specke] schulde schewe his wille of þe werre* E.

861. *or]* om. U. *be] to be* U. *&] or* A ; *with alle* E ; *all* add. CD. *this] thire* A ; *thus* U ; *þe* E. *hye towres* CDE ; *many toures* U ; *towris ȝoldyn* A.

862. *torfere] so* A ; *torment* C ; *tray* UD ; *schame he seyde* E ; *torsom* L. *tene] angur* C. *tides] falleth* C. *on hande] to haue* C ; *to* (om. D) *abyde* UD. *vs —hande] we moste abyde* E.

863. *Than* add. AUDE. *þay]* om. DE. *tourne* A ; *he* add. DE. *scheweþ] grantis* A ; *graunted* CUDE.

864. *&] of* add. CE. *thaym* A.

865. *And* A. *thaym* A. *Titus—to] turnyd* T. DC ; *turned him* T. U ; *answeryd* T. E. *& t.] talke he* A. *& t. b.] wyslyche, y weene* E.

E

Titus will starve the Garrison into surrender.

"þus to layke with þis les[e folke] ⸝ vs lympis þe worse,
For þey ben fel[l]e of defence, ⸝ ferce men & noble,
& þis toured toun ⸝ is tenful to wynne. 868
þe worst wrecche in þe wone ⸝ may on walle lygge,
Strike doun with a ston ⸝ & stuny many knyȝtes,
Whan we schul houe & byholde ⸝ & litel harme wirche,
& ay þe loþe of þe layk ⸝ liȝt on vs-selue. 872
Now mowe þey ferke no ferr' ⸝ her' fode forto wynne;
Wolde we stynt of our strif, ⸝ whyle þëy her' stor' ma[r]den

and proposes to subdue the garrison of the town by hunger.

We scholde with [hunger] hem honte, ⸝ to hoke out of toun,
[With-owttyn weme or wounde ⸝ or any wo ells;] 876
For þer as fayleþ þe fode ⸝ þer is feynt strengþe,
& þer as hunger is hote, ⸝ hertes ben feble."

This plan is generally accepted.

Alle assenteden to þe sawe, ⸝ þat to þe [sege] longed,
Apaied as þe prince ⸝ & þe peple wolde. 880

---

866. *Sayse thus* A. *layke*] *byker* C.
þis] *thise* U; ȝone A; þe D. *lese folke*]
so A; *folk* C; *losse* D; *ledes* U; *lesne* L.
lymp.] *falleth* C; *lent is* D; *ay* add. A.
werre C.
   It is good wurche be auys. who schal dele with schrewys E.
867. *ben*] *are* AUC. *felle*] so ACUE;
fele L. *of*] *at* E. *def.*] *and* add. U. *&
boolde* E; *at nede* U. This line is omitted in D.
868. *is*] *full* A; om. E. *tenf.*] *trowbelous* C.
869. *wrecche*] *wight* U; om. D. *in*] *of*
AUC. þe] ȝone A; *her* D. *wonys* D;
town C. *worst—wone*] *leeste boy among
hem* E. *one*] *in* D; ȝone add. A; *her*
add. D; þe add. UC. *wallis* D. *lygge*]
stonde U. *ligge on þe walles* E.
870. *& stryke* E; *And kaste* C. *with*]
om. C. *a st.*] *stonys* A. &] om. D.
stuny m. kn.] *many men stonye* E.
871. *Whyle* C. *sall* AEUC. *hovere*
D. *litel h. w.*] *no stroke smyte* C.
872. *And euur* C; *Euere* D; *Bot all* A.
loþe] *losse* D; *lesse* U. *loþ—layk*] *hurte
& þe losse* C. *layk*] *shal* add. DC; *to* add.
A. *us*] *owre* AUC. *on our self light* D.
*& þe wo on vs seelf. euyr more schal
reste* E.
873. *And now* D. þey *may* C. *freke*
U; *fare* A. þey *f.*] þe *fook* E. *ferther*
EDU; *forthire* A. *ferke no f.*] *no ferther*

goo C. *thaire* A; *hem* E; om. D. *fode*]
mete C. *forto*] *to* D.
874. *Bot walde* AE. *we*] ȝe EU; *now*
add. A. ȝowre EU. *whils* U; *to* A;
tyll C. þey *h.*] *thaire* A. *store*] *vitailes*
U: om. (!) E. *merride* A; *spendid* D;
spende EU. *haue spended* C; *maden* (!) L.
875. *schal* EC; *shul* D. *hunger*] so
AEDC; om. (!) L. *thaym* A. *hente*
EDC; *hurte* A. *to*] *and* AEDC. *holk*
A; *hunte* E; *hurle* C. *hoke—toun*] *holy
hem shende* D. This line is omitted in U.
876. *With owte* EDC. *weme or w.*]
wound oþer (or U) *werke* DU; *wounde or
eny hurt* E. *or—ells*] *with wantyng (want*
U) *of (her* add. U) *foode* EDU. *With—
ells*] so A; this line is omitted in L.
877. þer *as*] *where* E. *fayl.*] *fawtis* A;
lakketh C. þe] om. EC. *fode*] *mete* C.
faynt] *littill* A. *strenghe* A; *herte* E.
878. *as*] þat E. *hote*] þe add. D. *hurtis*
A; *strenght* E. *are* ADUC; *is* E; *ful*
add. U; *but* add. E.
879. *And alle* A. *assent* U. þe] þat
DU; *his* AC. *sawe*] *segge* ADU. þe *s.*]
hym E. *sege*] so EDUC; *segge* A; *cite*
L. *longed*] *lasten* U.
880. *Apaied—prince*] *The kynge was
(is* DU) *payede (plesed* C) *& (as* DU;
with EC) þe *(his* EU) *prynce (wurdes* E)
AEDUC. *&*] *if* A; *as* add. U. þe] *his*
EU. *pep.*] *princes* E. *wolde*] *alle* EC.
l. 879 is put after l. 880 in A.

The Romans hunt and hawk. 51

To þe kyng wer' called ⸭ constables þanne,   *Vespasianus*
Marchals, maser[s ⸭] me*n* þat he to tristiþ ;   *appoints*
    some to
He chargeþ he*m* che[f]ly ⸭ for chau*n*ce þat may falle,   *watch the town,*
W*ith* wacche of waled me*n* ⸭ þe walles to kepe : 884
" For we wol hu*n*ten at þe hart : þ*is* heþes aboute,   *while the*
    others hunt
& hur' racches re*n*ne ⸭ a-monge þ*is* rowe bonkes,   *and hawk.*
Ride to þe reu*er* ⸭ & rer' vp þe foules,
Se faucou*n*s fle, ⸭ fole of þe beste, 888
Ech segge to þe solas, ⸭ þ*at* hy*m*-self lyked."
Pr*i*nces o*ut* of pauelou*n*s ⸭ p*r*esen on stedes,
Torn[ei]en, trifflyn ⸭ & on þe † toun wayten,   Fol. 13 *b.*
Þ*is* lyf þey ledde longe, ⸭ & [lord] ȝyue vs g*r*ace ! 892
I n Rome Nero haþ now ⸭ mychel noye wroȝt,   *Nero does*
    much evil in
  To deþ pyned þe pope ⸭ & mychel peple quelled,   *Rome.*
Petr' apostlen pr*i*nce ⸭ & seint Poule [also],

---

881. *To—called*] *than the kyng callede hym to* A ; *the kynge kallede to hym his.* C. *þanne*] *tene* A.
    & lcet calle cunstaples . & kepers of þe peple E.
This line is omitted in U.
882. *Mar.*] *&* add. AEUDC. *men macers* AU ; *marcers* D ; *masons* E ; *bedelles* C ; *maser* L ; *&* add. AUC. *men* ⸭ þ*at* L. *to*] om. AUC. *traystis* A ; *troisteth* U ; *trystedde* C. þ*at—tristiþ*] *for chau*n*ce (myȝte befalle (þat may happe* D) ED.
883. *He*] *And* A ; om. U. *thaym* A ; *charged* AUC. *ful* add. U. *chefty*] so A ; *styfly* UC ; *chersly* (!) L. *chances* A ; *charge* U. *myghte* A. *falle*] *happe* U. l. 883 is omitted in ED.
884. *wacches* EDU. *waled*] *waker* C. *With—waled*] *To make þe watches with witty* A. *of w. m.*] *& with* (om. DU) *whiles* (*wylis* DU) EDU. *to k.*] *abowte* A.
885. *we*] *y* E. *þe h.*] *thir hertis* A. þ*is*] þe C. *haithes* U. *heghes* A.
886. *& heere* E ; *Here thire* A ; *And se þe* DU. *&—am.*] *With racches amonge hem in* C. þ*es*] þe ECUD. *bowys* E.
887. *Ride*] *& ryden* E ; *They ridyn pen* D ; *And penne to ryde* C. *to*] on E. þ*e*] inserted above line, *thiese* A. *reuers* AC. *rer*] *rayse* ACU. *& r.*] *reysid* D. þ*r*] om. CDU. *rer—foules*] *foules vp reyse* E.
888. *To se* C. þe add. ADU. *flie* AU. *fole*] *and felle* A ; *& sle* C. *fole—beste*] *and falle on her prayes* DU. This line is omitted in E.

889. *Ech*] *Ilk* U ; *Than ilke* A ; *And eche* C ; *a* add. AEDU. *segge*] *man* C ; *frek* E. þe] *his* C. *to þe s.*] *be hym seelf* EDU. þ*at*] *as* EU. *self*] *best* ECDU. *lyked*] *pleseth* C ; *semyd* D ; *wolde* A ; *semeth* U.
890. *And prynces* A ; *thenne princes* C. *presid* DU ; *precedde* C ; *prikyd* E ; *owt* add. A. *on*] *her* add. EDU. *on st.*] *full thykke* C.
891. *Torneien*] *Tornen* L ; *And turnyd* DU ; *& wente* E. *trifflyn*] *with owte* (om. DU) *taryȝyng* EDU. *T. tr.*]. *Wit tournaye and truffelynge* A ; *With sterne menne & stronge* C. *&*] þ*at* C. *on*] *to* C ; om. AEDU. þe] þe þe (!) L. *waytedde* C ; *kepte* E. *&—wayten*] þe *touris to waytyn* D.
892. *And this lyfe* A. *ledde þey* AC DU. *full* add. A. *&*] *oure* AC. *lord*] so ADUC ; *god* L. ȝ*yue*] *grante* A ; *he* C ; *grace*] *ioye* DU ; *heuen* A ; *blesse* C. þ*at non of þe fals foolk . fle awey myȝte* E. *Sextus passus* UC.
893. *Nero h. n.*] *hath Nero be (by* U ; om. D) *now* EDU ; *nowe hase Nero* A ⸭ *Nero was* C. *mekill* A ; *& mykell* C ; *myche* DU ; *& mcche* E. *noye*] *woo* EC.
894. *dede* A ; *pyned*] *putt* AE ; *he* add. CE ; *Petir the* add. A. *mekill* A ; *myche* ECDU. *kylledde* C.
895. *Petre*] þe add. D. *postelyn* EUD. *ap. pr.*] *prince of posteles* C. *seint*] om. EDU. *also*] so C ; om. L ; *eek* (*yet* DU) þ*er to* EDU. This line is omitted in A.

The Crimes and Death of Nero.

  Senek & þe senatours, ⸝ & alle þe cite fured,   896
His modir' & his my[l]de wif ⸝ murdred to deþe,
Combred Cristen fele, ⸝ þat on Crist leued.

The Romans rise against him. þe Romayns resen a-non, ⸝ whan þey þ[i]s rewþe seyen,
To quelle þe emperour quyk, ⸝ þat hem vnquemed hadde.
þey pressed to his paleys, ⸝ porayle & oþer,   901
To br[it]ten þe bold kyng ⸝ in his burwe riche;
þe cite & þe senatours ⸝ assented hem boþe,
Non oþer dede was to doun, ⸝ þey han his dome ʒolden. 904
He flees from Rome. þan flowe þat freke ⸝ frendles alone,
Out at a pore posterne, ⸝ & alle þe peple folwed,
With a tronchoun of tre, ⸝ toke he no more
Of alle þe glowande gold ⸝ þat he on grounde hadde. 908
On þat tronchoun with his teþ ⸝ he toggeþ & byteþ,
Tille hit was piked at þe poynt ⸝ as a pokes ende.
þan abideþ þat burne ⸝ & biterlych spekeþ
To alle þe wyes þat þer wer' ⸝ wordes aloude :   912
  "Tourneþ, traytours, aʒen : ⸝ schal neuer þe tale rise

---

896. *Seneca* C. *alle*] om. CD. *fured*] *payrid* DU.
897. *mylde*] so ACD; *myde* LEU. *wif*] *he* add. AC. *morthirrede* AD; *mordered* CU; *motheryd* (!) E. *to*] þe add. D.
898. *And combrede* CDU. *full* add. A. *cristen f.*] *many cristen* C. *beleuyd* E.
899. *þe*] *Than thiese* A; om. EDU. *resen*] om. A. *whan*] *fro* A. *this*] so ACED; *þus* L; *the* U. *seyen*] *herde* AD.
900. *Tuke to* A. *kylle* CD. *þe emp.*] *hym* E; *all* add. AE. *hem*] *þam* A; *vn-qwyete* A; *desesyd* E; *quelled* U. *hadde desesed* C.
901. *presse* A; *presyd* E; *preced* C; *presen* U. *his*] *the* ACU. *paleys*] *wardes* add. A. *por.*] *pore peple* C; *pore* A. *&*] *alle* add. A. This line is omitted in D.
902. *britten*] *brittyn* D; *birttyne* AU; *brenten* (!) L. *murder* C; *cacche* E. *þe b.*] *þis cursyd* E. *in*] *and all* U. *his the* D. *in—riche*] ʒif *þat they myʒte* E.
903. *cite*] *comyns* E. *hem*] *hade* A. *ass. h. b.*] *of on assent were* ECDU.
904. *No nothir* A. *was*] *is* D; *for* E. *his*] *the* A. *his d. 3.*] *him demed* U. *þey—ʒoldyn*] *his deth þey haue dyʒte* C; *but deme hym to dethe* E.

905. *flowe*] *fled* AECD. *fledden* (!) U. *þat*] þe ED; *this* U; *frendles* add. A. *freke*] *wrecche* C. *frendles*] om. ED; *frekly* A; *hym self all* add. C. *anone* A. *fr. a.*] *as ferly is to telle* E; *is ferly to here* UD.
906. *Out*] om. E. *pore*]*preue* AECDU. þe] om. E. *folwed*] *sewes* A; *after* ECDU.
907. *With*] *Safe* C; *him* add. U. *of*] *a* add. AC. *toke—more*] *þat he tugges and byttis* A.
908. *glowyng* ED; *glytrynge* C. *grounde*] *erthe* C.
909. *þat*] *this* EDU. *tog.*] *gnawyd* E. *& b.*] *ful fast* U. *bytyd* E.
ll. 908 and 909 are omitted in A.
910. *was*] *is* DU; *were* E. *prykked* CU; *pytte* D; *scharp* E. *poynt*] *ende* E. *pokes*] *prikes* ADU; *prikke* C. *as—ende*] *ryʒt as prykke* E.
911. *ab.*] *byddis* A. *he* add. ACE. *þat*] þe CDU. *burne*] *barones* C. *þat b.*] *those beryns* A; *a while* E. *bit.*] *he* add. AD. *spekeþ*] *seyde* EDU.
912. *And to* C. *wyes*] *wyse* U; *wightis* D; *folk* E; *comens* C. *þat*] om. U. *were*] *was* E; *þese* add. C. *aloude*] *on hye* D. This line is omitted in A.
913. *Turns* C. *schal n.*] *þer shall no* C. þe] om. ECDU. *aryse* ECDU.

The Reigns of Galba and Otho. 53

Of no karl by þe coppe, ⸓ how he his kyng quelde."
Hym-self he strykeþ myd þat staf : streȝt to þe hert,   *Nero kills himself.*
þat þe colke to-clef ⸓ & þe kyng deyed.   916
Six monþe after & no morᵉ ⸓ þis myschef bytydde,
þat Waspasian was went ⸓ to werry on þe Jewes ;
Fourᵉ mettyn myle out of Rome, ⸓ to mynde for euere,
þat erst was emperour of alle, ⸓ þus ended in sorow.   920
þe grete to-gedres þan ⸓ [gete] hem an-oþer,
On Gabba, a gome ⸓ þat mychel grem hadde   *Galba is made emperor,*
þroȝ Othis L[ucy]us, a lord ⸓ þat hym longe hated,
& at þe last þat lord ⸓ out of lyf hym broȝt.   924
Amydde þe market of Rome ⸓ þe[y] mette to-gedres,   Fol. 14 *a.*
Othis falliþ hym fey ; ⸓ ȝaf hym fale woundes,   *and is slain by Otho, who*
þat fourᵉ monþes & [no] morᵉ ⸓ hadde mayntened þe croune ;   *takes his place.*
& þo deyed þe duke ⸓ & þe diademe lefte.   928
& whan þat Gabba was gon ⸓ & to grounde broȝt,
Othis entriþ on ernest ⸓ & emperour was made ;

---

914. *no*] *cursyd* add. E ; *coyfid* add. D ; *capped* U. *by*] *at* A. *Of no*] *That any* C. *by þe c.*] *of ȝour kynde* C ; om. EUD. *how*] *þat* EDU. *how he*] *hath* C. *kyllede* CD ; *slewe* A.
915. *strike* U ; *strikyd* C. *stikyd* D. *He stekyde* (*smote* C) *hym selfe* AC. *with* ACDU. *þat*] *the* ACU. *stake* AC. *streȝt to*] *rith vnto* U ; *thorowe owte* A. *Hym—streȝt*] *With þe trunchun þanne hym seelf . he smoot* E.
916. *þe c.*] *hit* CDU. *all* add. A ; *vnclenly* add. DU. *to-cl.*] *a sounder* add. C. *þat—to-cl.*] *& atwo cleuyd it* E. *&*] so add. ECDU. *kyng*] *schrewe* C.
917. *Seuene* C. *monethes* AECDU. *after*] om. AU. *&*] om. EUD. *mor*] *þat* add. D. *no mor*] om. E. *myschef*] *turn* E. *bytydde*] *bifell* CD.
918. *þat.*] om. E. *was*] *is* U. *went*] *gone* C. *was w.*] *wente* E. *werre* AEDC ; *weren* U.
919. *mettyn*] om. EDU. *myn* DU ; *menyn* A. *to—euere*] *þe sothe for to telle* E.
920. *He þat* A. *erst*] om. AEDU. *alle*] *þat* (!) D ; *Rome* add. A. *þus*] om. D. *endeth* U ; *he* add. D.
11. 919 and 920 are omitted in C.
921. *to g. þ.*] *gadirde þam* (om. C) *to gedire* AC. *gan to gydre gon* ED ; *to geder gan gone* U ; *and* add. AEC. *gete*] *gat* A ; *gette* C ; *to geten* DU ; *chossen* (!) LE.
922. *Gabaa* C ; *Gabaoo* A. *a*] *gode* add. U. *grome* U ; *werche* C. *a g.*] *be name* E. *myche* AECDU. *grame h.*] *sorowe wrowȝte* C.
923. *þroȝ*] *To* CDU ; *Of* E ; *sir* add. C. *Othus* UD ; *Otus* AC ; *on* E. *Lucyus*] so AECDU ; *lyous* (!) L. *a l.*] om. C. *þat*] *had* add. D. *hym l.*] *lange tym had hym* A ; *hadde* add. C.
924. *&*] om. C. *þe*] om. D. *þat*] *þis* E ; *þe* D. *lord*] *lede* U. *at—out*] *that lede at the laste hym* A. *hym*] om. AU. *broughe* (!) E. Catchword *amydde*.
925. *A myddes* U ; *In myddis* AC. *merkett* A. *þey*] so AECDU ; *þe* L. *mettyn* ACDU. *togydre* ECDU ; *in fere* A.
926. *Ther* (*sir* add. C) *Othus* (*Otus* C) ECDU. *felide* A ; *fellede* CU ; *felde* DE. *hym*] *in* add. EC. *fey*] *and* add. AECDU. *felle* A ; *fele* ED ; *many* C ; *ded* U.
927. *&*] om. U. *no*] so ACU ; om. LDE *hadde*] *he* D. *maynt.*] *bore* E.
928. *& þo*] *Thare* A ; *And þer* DU ; *Thus* C ; *& þan* E. *þe*] *þat* AECD. *prince* C. *&*] om. D. *þe*] *his* U ; om. AE. *diad.*] *lyfe* C.
929. *&*] om. AECDU. *þat*] om. C. *Than when* A. *to*] *in* E ; *þe* add. CD. *grounde*] *erthe* C.
930. *enterde* C. *on ern.*] *in areste* A ; *aftur* C. *Ot.—ern.*] *þanne* (*In ernest* DU) *entrid Othus* EDU ; *was*] *is* DU.

The Reign of Vitellius.

Otho kills himself, and the Romans chose Vitellius, who has slain Vespasianus' brother.

þe man in his maieste ⸳ was monþes bot þre,
þan he ȝeldeþ Sathanas þe soule ⸳ & hym-self quelled.   932
þe Romayns risen vp a renk, ⸳ Rome for to kepe,
A knyȝt þat Vitel was calde, ⸳ & hym þe croune rauȝte.
Bot for sir' Sabyns sake, ⸳ a segge þat was noble,
Waspasian broþer of blode, ⸳ [þat] he brytned hadde,   936

Instigated by Vespasianus, the Romans murder him.

Waspasian vpon Vitel ⸳ to vengen his broþer,
S[en]t out of Surrie ⸳ segges to Rome,
þat [a]s naked as an nedul ⸳ þe newe emperour,
For sir' Sabyns sake ⸳ alle þe cite drowe hym ;   940
Suþ gored þe gome, ⸳ þat his guttes alle
As a bowe[l]ed beste ⸳ in-to his breche felle ;
Doun ȝer[m]ande he ȝede, ⸳ & ȝeldeþ þe soule,
& [þey] kayȝt þe cors, ⸳ & kast in-to Tybre.   944
Seuen monþes þis [segge] ⸳ hadde septre on hande,
& þus loste he þe lyf ⸳ for his luþer dedes ;
An oþer segge was to seke ⸳ þat septre schold haue,

---

931. þat ACDU. þe m.] & he E; leuede add. A. was] nys U; om. A. but monethes thre U; but thre monthes E.
932. & ȝalde AEDU; He ȝalde C. þe] his AC. Sath. þe s.] his (þe D) sowle to Sathanas EDU. &] for he CE.
933. Than the A. reisyn DU; rayssede AC. vp] om. AECDU. a renk] a lorde C; þo anon E. for to] vnto U.
934. Vitale AC; Vitall D; Vytayle EU. was] is DU. Vitel w. c.] hyȝt Vytayle E. &] þanne E; þey C; þat D. hym] om. EDU. raughte] cawȝte E; ȝafe C; yemyd D.
935. for] that U; om. D. Sabyn ACDU; sake] sye U; hit sees D. segge] knyȝt C; þat] so ACDU ; om. L. was] is U. was n.] than was A. for—noble] Sabyn of Surry. þerwith was displesyd E.
936. of bl.] om. EDU. brytned] blenkede A; yhurt E; murthered C.
937. Wasp.] roose add. C. on ECDU. broþ.] brotheres deth CU. This line is omitted in A.
938. Sent] so EDU ; He sente C; Sendis A ; Souȝt L. segges] knyȝtes C ; meche folk E.
939. þat] & they E; They C. as] so ED ; al U; is L; made A; made hym C. neel U. þe] þat A.
940. sire S.] Sabyne C. sake] in add. E. drowe h.] drowyn ED; drawen C; drowe U. And his bolde beryns one the bent brittenede to dede A.

941. And add. AECDU. sythen AD; sen U; aftur C. þe] þat C; gome] prince C. gored þe g.] þe gorel gorryd E ; the gome hym selfe A.
942. boweled] so C; bowewed (!) L ; bolnede A. As—beste] Brothely (Hastly U ; Gurd out E) at a breyd EDU ; & add. E. to] om. EDU. in-to his br.] (out add. C) of his body AC. fallyn D.
943. All downe C; Dawe U; þanne E. ȝarande A ; yemerand U ; gronynge C ; stumblyng E; ȝernande L. And þus þere he died D. &] om. C. ȝeld DU ; ȝalde E ; ȝolde C ; ȝaldide A ; vp add. EDU ; out add. C. þe] his E. soule] guste A.
944. &] Thenne C ; And þan DU ; & þo E. þey] so AEDU: om. (!) L. thei catchen vp U ; thei tookyn E. toke þey C. corpse ADU ; body C. into] it in ACDE.
945. þis] þat C; þe DU. segge] so DU ; Vitayl E ; man LC. hadde s.] þe septre had DEU. on] in CDU. þis—hande] and no more the septre he hade A.
946. þus] so CDUE ; than A. loste] lefte ACU. þe] his D. luþer] euell C. dede U. Þo (And then U) alle (the add. U) grete of þe town (besid hem faste (to gedir gun gone U) add. EU.
947. segge] prince C. was] is D ; om. C. An—was] For other segges U. to s.] þey sowȝte C. þat] om. DU ; þe add. ACDU. schold h.] for (om. U) to have DU. segge—haue] emperour to haue . whan þey myȝt hym fynde E.

The Romans choose Vespasianus. 55

For alle þis grete ben gon ⁋ & neuer agayn tournen. 948
Now of þe cite & of þe sege ⁋ wolle y sey mor',
How þis comelich kyng, ⁋ þat for Crist werreþ,
Haþ holden yn þe heþen men ⁋ þis oþer half wynter,
þat neuer burne was so bold, ⁋ þe burwe for to passe. 952
As he to dyner on a day ⁋ with dukes was sette,   *The imperial*
Comen renkes fram Rome, ⁋ rapande swyþe,   *crown is offered to Vespasianus.*
In bruneys & in bryȝt wede, ⁋ with bodeworde newe,
Louten alle to þe lord, ⁋ letres hym rauȝten ; 956
Sayn : " Comelich kyng ! ⁋ þe knyȝthod of Rome,
þroȝ þe senatours assent ⁋ & alle þe cite ellis,
Han chosen þe her chyuentayn, ⁋ her' chef lord to worþe,
And riche emperour of Rome : ⁋ þus redeþ þis letres." 960
þe lord vnlappeþ þe lef, ⁋ þis letres byholdeþ,
Ouer-lokeþ ech a lyne ⁋ to þe last ende ;   *Fol. 14 b.*
Bordes born wer' doun, ⁋ & þe burne riseþ,
Calleþ consail a-non ⁋ & kyþeþ þis speche :   964 *He consults his council.*

---

948. *For*] *Thus* AC. *ar* CD. *neuer*] *non* U. *turneth* V ; *turnede* AC. This line is omitted in E.
949. *þe*] *þis* D. *cite*] *sege* EU ; *segge* D ; *kynge* C. *of*] om. A. *& of the sege*] *of (in* U) *Surry* CDU ; *of Ierusalem* E. *y*] *we* D. *sey*] *talke* E.
950. *And how* A. *weris* A ; *werredde* CD ; *wered* U ; *werre* (!) E.
951. *yn*] *on* EDU ; om. C. *þe*] *thire* A. *men*] om. DE. *þis*] *now* E ; om. DU. *wynter*] ȝere EDU.
952. *neuer*] *no* AC. *burne*] *manne* C ; *boy* E ; om. D. *þe—forto*] *out of þe town* E. *was—forto*] *(oute* add. C) *of the* (om. U) *burghe (cyte* C) *so bold was (is* DU) *to* ACDU.
953. *to*] *the* add. A. *dukes*] *lordes* E ; *renkes* U.
954. *There kome* C. *renkes*] *knyȝtes* C ; *messagers* E. *fro* AECU ; *out of* D. *rap.*] *rydande* AC ; *respyng* DU ; *rennyng* E ; *full* add. A. *swyþe*] *on faste* C.
955. *In*] *With* U. *brun. &*] *breme* D. *in*] om. ADU. *wedis* A. *In — wede*] *Woundeliche* (!) *weel arayed* E ; *All armed in clene stecle* C. *with*] *& broghte* AC. *bodew.*] *tydynges* EC. *newe*] *goode* C.
956. *Thay knete* A ; *& lowtyd* E ; *They kneled* C. *lord*] *&* add. AECDU. *let.*] *þey* add. C. *rauȝten*] *toke* C ; *schewyd* E ; *brought* U.

957. *And seyn* D ; *And sayde* AE ; *They seyde* C ; *Seying* U. *Com. k.*] *semliche* A.
958. *þroȝ*] *With* ECDU. *þe*] om. D. *þe*] om. E. *ellis*] *aftur* C.
959. *Hase* A. *her*] *for* ACU. *cheftayne* AECD ; *chief* U ; *to be* add. ACD. *thaire* A ; *& E. chef l.*] *emperour* EC ; *chiuetaigne* U. *worþe*] *be* EU. *to w.*] om. ACD.
960. *And*] *Thou* A. *þus r.*] *now reden* A. *As* (ȝe *may (þow mayst* E) *se be þe (þis* E) *seel . assay* ȝif *(howe* C) ȝe (ȝow D) ; *þe* E) *lyketh* ECDU.
961. *Than the* A. *vnl.*] *liftes* U ; *lefte* CD ; *vp* add. CDU. *lefe*] *&* add. AC. *þis*] *þe* ACDU. *letter* C. *byh.*] *to byholde* D.
He took þe lettres in his hond . & on hem he loketh E.
962. *He loketh* C ; *And lokith* D ; *He loked* U ; *& radde ouer* E. *ech*] *euery* ECVDU ; *euer ilke* A. *a*] om. EVCD ; *to*] *vn to* V ; *til* D.
963. *Than boordes (burdes* (A) AE. *were borne* AVC ; *were take* E. *adowne* V. *burne*] *kynge* C ; *lord* U. *þe b.*] *beryns* A. *aryseth* EU ; *to rysse* (!) E.
964. *& calleth* E ; *callid* D ; *He kalled his* C. *&*] om. VD. *kythid* D ; *chaunged* C. *þis*] *the* A ; *his* VCDU. *kyþeþ þ. sp.*] *þis mateer mewyth* E.

Vespasianus consults his Council.

"3e ben burnes of my blod, ⁝ þat y best wolde,
My sone is next to my-self, ⁝ & oþer sib manye,
Sir' Sabyn of Surrie, ⁝ a segge þat y triste,
& oþer frendes fele, ⁝ þat me fayþ owen : 968

Can he return to Rome, and yet keep his vow to take Jerusalem?
Now is me bodeword of blys ⁝ bro3t froward Rome,
To be lord ouer þat lond ⁝ as þis letres spekeþ.
Sir' Sabyn of Surrie, ⁝ sey þe by-houyþ,
How y my3t sauy my-self, ⁝ & I so wro3t ; 972
Ffor y haue heylych hey3t ⁝ her' forto lenge,
[Tille] me þe 3ates ben 3et ⁝ & 3olden þe keyes,
[And] I þis toured [t]oun ⁝ ha[ue] taken at wille,
& suþ houshed on hem ⁝ þat þis hold kepyn, 976
Brosten & betyn doun ⁝ þis britages heye,
þat neuer ston in þat stede ⁝ stond vpon oþer'.
Kyþe þ[i] consail, sir' kny3t," ⁝ þis kyng to hym sayde,
"For y wol worche by þy witt, ⁝ 3if worschip may folowe!"

---

965. *burnes*] *barnes* E; *borin* V. *ben b.*] *lordes* AC. *þat*] *and that* U; *þe whyche* C. *y*] *me* V. *best*] *most* C. *y b.*] *my blysse* A. *wolde*] *truste* C; *love* DU.
966. *is*] om. E. *next*] *syb* ED. *to*] om. V. *sone — self*] *nemys and myn sonnys* A. *sib*] *of you* E. *oþer s. m.*] *our seggisman* (!) D.
967. *segge*] *manne* C; *kny3t* E. *þat*] *in whom* E. *trayste* A.
968. *frend.*] *full* add. AV; *here* add. E; *ere* add. U. *fele*] *many* C; *here* add. U. *me f. o.*] *feithe owen to me* V.
969. *me*] om. A. *broght of blisse* V; *me* add. A. *Now—bro3t*] *Here ben tydynges brought to me . ry3t now* E; *Ioyfull worde is me brow3te fro senatours* C. *frow.*] *frome* V: *fro* AE; *of* C; *out of* U.
970. *For to be* A; *þat y schal be* E. *ouer*] *of* AEVCU. *þat*] *the* U. *lond*] *lede* AV. *as*] om. VCU. *þis*] *the* EV; *pines* U. *letres*] *it* add. U; *þus* add. C. *spekeþ*] *sygge* E; *seyn* CU; *tellis* A.
971. *Surrie*] *to* add. CU. *sey þe b.*] *y preye þe to seye* E.
ll. 968—971 are omitted in D.
972. *my3t y* ECDU; *I may* V; *may I* A. *my self sauo* D. *&*] *3if* ECD. *wro3t*] *were* E.
973. *heylych*] *holly* AVDU; *fully* C. *byhight* EU. *forto*] *to* C. *lenge*] *ligge* E; *lende* V; *ahyde* C.
974. *Tyll*] so VCU ; *To* A: & LDE. *me*] om. EVCD. *þe*] *thir* A; *thise* VU.

gates V. *be*] om. E. *gate* V; *yevyn* D; *yolden* U; *openyd* EC. *3oldyn*] *yewen* U. *3olden þe k.*] *the* (om. E) *keys* (*town* C; *to me* add. E) *3olden* AEC.
975. *And*] so A; *tyll*] LDU; *Sithen* VE; *And for to haue* C. *toun*] so AEVCDU. *doun* (!) L. *haue*] *ri3t* C; om. AV *han* L. *taken*] om. EC. *at*] *my* add. AEVCDU.
l. 974 is put after l. 975 in LDE.
976. *suþ h.*] *sithyn* (*also* E) *honged* ED; *sen hongen* U; *vengede be* A; *venge me* V; *for to venge god* C. *on*] *of* AC. *hem*] *hy* EDU; *thies heythen* AVC; *men* add. A. *þat*] *haue* add. U. *þis*] *þe* EDU. *hold*] *towne* EC. *kepte* EU.
977. *Brosten*] *brend* E. *Betyn & brosten* AV; *And beten & broken* C; *Brent and brusten* U; *Brent & broke* D. *þis*] *the* E; *thaire* A; *bretage* U; *bretannyes* A.; *torrettes* C. *so* add. U. *heye*] *alle* A.; *aboute* E.
978. *Tyll þat* C. *neuer*] *no* AVC; *neiþer* ED; *nouther* U. *þat*] *þis* V. *in þ. st.*] *appon* (*vp on* C) *stone* AC; *nor styk ne* U; *ne s'ikke* E. *ston—stede*] *stik nor stone shal* D. *appon* A. *oþere*] *lofte* A; *erthe* U. *stond vp. o.*] *vp on oþer ligge* E; *in þat place be lafte* C.
979 *Now kythe* A. *þi*] so AVDU ; *þe* L. *þis*] *þe* AVDU.
& *perfore tel me þy wyt . y preye þe blywe* C.
980. *witt*] *wille* VED. *may*] *it* EDU.
ll. 979, 980 are omitted in C.

Sir Sabyn advises him to go to Rome.

Þan seiþ sir' Sabyn a-non ꞉ " Semelich lord, 981
We ben wyes þe with, ꞉ þy worschup to furþer,
Of longe tyme bylafte, ꞉ & ledes þyn owen ;
þat we doun is þy dede, ꞉ may no man demen elles. 984
Þe dom demed was þer, ꞉ who so doþ by anoþer,
Schal be soferayn hym-self, ꞉ sein† in þe werke,
For as fers is þe freke ꞉ atte ferr' ende,
þat oft† fleis þe fel ꞉ as he þat foot holdeþ. 988
Bytake Tytus, þy sone, ꞉ þis toun for to kepe,
& to þe douȝti duke ꞉ Domyssian, his broþer ;
Her' I holde vp myn honde, ꞉ myd hem for to lenge
with alle þe here þat I haue, ꞉ while my herte lasteþ ; 992
& þou schalt ride to Rome, ꞉ & receyue þe croune,
In honour emperour to be ꞉ as þyn eure schapiþ ;
So may þy couenaunt be kept, ꞉ þat þou to Crist made,
þy-self dest, þat þy soudiours ꞉ by þyn assent worchen." 996
Þan with a liouns lote ꞉ he lifte vp þe eyen,

Sir Sabyn says that what is done by Vespasianus' own soldiers is done by himself.

Let him leave the conduct of the siege to Titus and Domitian.

---

981. *seiþ*] *said* V. *sir Sabyn sayde* A.
þan—*Sabyn*] *The knyȝt knelyd* ECDU.
anon] *adown* EC ; om. V ; *to that* A.
sem. l.] & *to þe kyng seyde* ECDU.
982. *wyes*] *wightis* D. *wyes þe w.*]
alle þyn owne E. *We—with*] *Here are
meyne with þe þat* C. *furþer*] *saue* E ;
willyn D ; *folwen* U. *to f.*] *wolde* C.
983. *Of*] *a* add. A. *byl.*] *with þe lafte*
C &—*owen*] *þy lege menne echon (ilkone*
U) CDU.
  *þy leege men & sogettys . euyr at þi
wille* E.
984. *don*] AEVCD ; *deme* U. *dede*]
þer add. VC. *elles*] *other* ECDU.
985. *þer*] *þat* add. D. *so*] om. AV.
986. *He sall* AV. *sein*] *sen* AVU ;
seint L ; om. C. *sen in*] *set by* D. *þe*]
þis V ; *þat* U ; *þat same* C. *werke*] *dede*
CDU.
987. *also* C ; *fers*] *foule* A ; *ferfurthe*
V ; *ferforth* C. *þe fr.*] *he* C. *ferrere* A ;
fire V ; *ferther* C.
988. *of*] *so* AC ; *ofte* (!) L ; om. V.
flaes A. *fel*] *skynne* C. *he*] om. V. *þat*]
the add. AC.
l. 987 and l. 988 are omitted in DU.
Instead of l. 985—l. 988 E offers the
following line—*Therfore my leege lord .
telle the oure wille* E.
989. *Betakes* V ; *To take* E. *þy*] *youre*

V. *for*] *now* CDU.
990. *þe*] *that* U. *douȝti*] om. A. *Domyanys* (!) E ; *that es* add. A. *his*] om. E ;
dere add. A.
  *For they beth best wurthi . after þe in
sothe* add. E.
991. & add. AVECDU. *with* AVEC
DU. *theym* A ; ȝow D. *lenge*] *lende*
AV ; *abyde* EC.
992. *here*] *help* ECDU ; *herte* V. *while*]
þer whilles A. *herte*] *lyfe* AVECDU.
993. *vn to* ACU. &] *to* ECU. &—
croune] *thi crown to rescheyue* A.
994. *In*] *With* C. *In h.*] *And* D ; &
there E ; *An* U. *emp.*] *new* add. U. *to*]
om. E. *be*] *maad* add. EU. *as*] *now*
add. A. *þyn*] *the* A. *eure*] *tym* A ;
kynde C ; om. (!) V. *þyn s.*] *þe is* EDU ;
now add. U. *schap.*] *shaped* U ; *askes*
AC ; *happid* D ; *behote* E.
995. *For so* C. *þy*] *the* AVCDU. *commaunt* E ; *conande* A. *kep* (!) E. *to*]
with A ; om. (!) V. *madest* VEU.
996. *self*] *hit* add. V. *dose* AV. *sowd.*]
doon add. V. *þy s.*] *þyne doth* CDU.
by] & DU. *by—worchen*] *yf þy wyll assente* C.
  & *be holde a trewe kyng . for ellys
were gret schame* E.
997. *lote*] *late* A ; *loke* VEUDC. *þe*]
his AVECDU.

Titus is made Commander of the Siege.

Titus promises to take the town or die.
To Titus tourneþ a-non, ⁊ & hym þe tale schewed,
& as sir' Sabyn hadde seid ⁊ he hym sone granteþ,
With his broþer & þe burne[s], ⁊ as he hym blesse wolde:
"& I wol tarie at þis toun, ⁊ til I hit taken haue,   1001
Made weys þrow [þe walles] ⁊ for wenes & cartes,

Fol. 15 a.
Our' boþere heste to holde, ⁊ ȝif me þe happ † tydiþ,
Or her' be to-hewen, ⁊ or I hennes passe."   1004

All swear allegiance to him.
A boke on a brode scheld ⁊ was broȝt on to swer',
Alle burnes boden [to] þe honde ⁊ & barouns hit kyssen,
To be leel to þat lord, ⁊ þat hem lede scholde,
Sir' Titus, þe trewe kyng ⁊ tille þey, þe toun hadde.   1008
Fayn as þe foul of day ⁊ was þe freke þanne,

Vespasianus takes leave of them.
Kysseþ knyȝtes a-non ⁊ with carful wordes:
" My wele & my worschup ⁊ ȝe weldeþ to kepe,
For þe tresour of my treuþ ⁊ vpon þis toun hengyþ: 1012
I nold, þis toun wer vn-take, ⁊ ne þis toures heye,

---

998. *onone turnes* U. *To — a-non*] *Tornes* (*Turned* V ; *hym* add. A) *to Titus an none* AV ; *& (He* C) *turnyd* (*hym to (toward* C) *Tytus* EC. *talc*] *staut* E; om. (!) A. *schewes* ADU ; *tolde* AC; *grauntyd* E.
999. *has* ADU. *he hym sone*] *onone he it* U. *graunted* C.
1000. *þe*] om. DU. *burnes*] so DU ; *burne* (!) L. *With--burnes*] *For to byde* (*To byden* V ; *To abyde* C) *with his brothir* AVC. *as he*] *that* ADU. *blesse*] *blisse* AUD. *wolden* UD. *as—wolde*] *what so be tythe wolde* C ; *till þe burgh be yolden* V. Instead of these two lines E reads—
*Thanne answered Tytus . & be auysement seyde
þese wurdes þat folwyn . & avow maade.*
1001. *&*] *For* C ; om. AVEDU. *wol*] *weele* E ; *sall* AVCDU. *tarie*] *abyde* E. *at*] *on* V. *hit t. h.*] *haue it take* E.
1002. *Made*] *And maad* V ; *And þenne made he* C. *Made w.*] *Weyes made* DU ; *& weyes make* E. *þought* E. *þe walles*] so AE; *þe wall* VCD; *wal* U ; om. (!) L. *waynes* AVECDU.
1003. *bothe* U ; *other* D ; om. VC. *our b.*] *my fader* E. *heestes* VDU ; *hightis* A; *hostes* (!) C ; *for* add. E. *me*] *vs* V. *þe*]om. AVEU. *happe*]so AVEU ; *happis* L. *tyde* AU ; *betyde* E. *me—tydiþ*]*y hele haue* D. *ȝif—tydiþ*]*þat we to Criste made* C.
1004. *Or*] *elles* add. CD. *her* . . .

hewen] *hewen* (*decd* E ; *britned* D ; *for* add. AE) *to* (om. V) *be* AVECUD. *or*] *if* D. *hennes*] *hethyn* A.
1005. *on*] & EU. *was*] *were* E. *on*] *for* AV. *broght was to swere on* D.
1006. *Alle*] *þe* EC ; om. AVDU. *Barnes* V ; *peple* E ; *dukes* AC. *bedyn* ADU ; *putte* C; *leyde* E. *to*] so AVC DU ; *on* E; om. (!) L. *þe*] *her* ECDU ; *thaire* A. *hondes* AVECDU. *&*] om. D. *bar.*] *lordes* C. *bar. hit*] *þe* (!) E. *hit kysten* V ; *hit kyssedde* C ; *to kysse* DU.
1007. *leel*] *trewe* EC. *þat*] *þe* VECDU ; *thaire* A. *thaym* A.
1008. *Sire*] *To* CD ; *Anon* E. *trewe*] om. E. *kyng*] *knyȝte* C. *tille—toun*] *to þe town þei* E.
1009. *þe*] om. AVCDU. *foul*] *folowe* (!) C. *of*] *þe* add. AVCDU. *freke*] *kyng* VC. This line is omitted in E.
1010. *He kyssede* CDU ; *his* add. AVC ; *þe* add. D. *anon*] *sone* C ; *and saies* add. V. *carf.*] *comely* CDU.
& his knyȝtes to gydre . gadrid & seyde C.
1011. *Sayse my* A. *worschup*] *welfare* C. *weld.*] *haue* C. *to*] *and* AV. *to k.*] *in ȝowre hondes* ECDU.
1012. *tres.*] *trust* U. *appon* A; *on* VE CD. *þis*] *ȝondur* C. *hynges* A ; *honges* VECDU.
1013. *nold*] *wolde not* C ; *but* add. CU. *tane* CU. *ne*] & AVCDU ; *with* E; *al* add. D. *þis*] *his* E. *hye touris* D ; *grete toures* E.

Vespasianus is made Emperor. 59

For alle þe glowande golde ⸳ vpon grounde riche,
[N]e no ston in þe stede ⸳ stond[i]n[g] alofte,
Bot alle ouer-tourned & tilt, ⸳ temple & oþer." 1016
þus laccheþ [he] his leeue ⸳ at his ledes alle,
Wende wepande a-way ⸳ & on þe walles lokeþ,
Praieþ [god], as he gooþ, ⸳ hem grace to sende,
To hold þat þey byhot han, ⸳ & neuer her' herte chaunge.
Now is Waspasian went ⸳ ouer wale stremys 1021 *Vespasianus is made emperor at Rome, and Titus falls ill for joy.*
Euen entred in-to Rome ⸳ & emperour maked,
& Titus for þe tydyng ⸳ ha[þ] take [so] mychel joye
þat in his synwys soudeynly ⸳ a syknesse is fallen. 1024
þe freke for þe fayndom ⸳ of þe fader' blysse,
With a cramp & a colde ⸳ cauȝt was so hard
þat þe fyngres & feet, ⸳ fustes & joyntes
Was lyþy as a leke ⸳ & lost han her' strengþe. 1028
[He] croked aȝens kynde ⸳ & as a crepel woxe †,
& whan þey sey hym so, ⸳ many segge wepyþ ;

1014. *glowyng* D; *schynyng* EC. *vpon gr.*] *vndir god* AVC; *vndir þe cope* EU. *riche*] *of heuene* ECDU.
1015. *ne*] so AEVDU; *Nor* C; *Be* (!) L. *no*] om. U. þe] þat C; *þat ilk* U; *this* A; *no* ED. *stede*] *place* C. *stondyng*] so CDU; *standande* AV; *laft* E; *stonden* L. *on loft* DU; *were lefte* AV; *vp on oþer* EC.
1016. *alle*] *þei were* E; om. CDU; *tilt*] *tild* D; *tumbled* C. *ouer-t. & t*] *ouertirlede* A; *ouer-tyld* E. *temple*] *the temples* U. *temple & o.*] *& partyd atwynne* E.
1017. *þus*] *Thenne* C; *Tho* E. *laughte* A; *laughten* (!) V; *lacchid* D; *taketh* C; *took* E. *he*] so AVC; *Wasperyan* E; *þe kyng* DU; om. L. *his*] om. VEUD. *at*] *of* E. *ledes*] *lordis* AECU. *alle*] om. E. *Tho took Waspasyan. leue of his lordes* E.
1018. *& wente* E; *He wente* C. *Wepand awey went* U. *on*] om. E. *walle* V. *lukede* AECU; *waytid* D.
1019. *& preyde* E; *And he prayde* C. *god*] so VECDU; *to god* A; om. L. *gooþ*] *ȝede* E. *as he ȝ.*] *of his godenesse* C; *þat he* add. E. *hem*] om. A. *grace*] *for* add. AU. *to*] om. E.
1020. *hold*] *help* D. *byhot*] *highte* AV ECU; *hit* D. *han*] om. V. *&*] *þat* C. *neuer*] om. A. *thaire &* ; om. U. *hertis* AVECD ; *noghte to* add. A. *chaunge*] *turne* C.
1021. *Now* V. *went*] *igone* C. *anon*
yȝt he wente forth E. *ouer*] *þe* add. AV ECDU. *wale*] *wane* A; *wylde* ED; *wyde* U; *bygge* C. *stremys*] *wawys* E.
1022. *Euen*] & E. *entirs* A. *in*] om. D. *emp.*] *es* add.. A; *was* add. EC.
1023. *for*] *of* EDU. *þe*] *that* UD; om. (!) E. *tithing* U; *tithandes* V; *tyȝandes* (!) A. *haþ*] so AVCDU; om. E. *han* (!) L. *take*] *made* V; *took* E. *so*] so AVCU; om. (!) L. *so muche* U; *swich a* ED.
1024. *his*] om. D. *synnwys*] *syde was U. *is*] *was* E; om. U.
1025. *þat* VC. *frekc*] *prince* C. *þe fr.*] *so* E. *þe*] *his* C; *greet* E. *faynnes* AVC; *feynhode* EDU. *þe*] *his* VECDU. *fadirs* AC. *blysse*] *worshyppe* C.
1026. *cr.*] *croompe* E *was*] *is* DU.
1027. *þe*] *his* AVECU. *fyngres*] *fistes* VECD; *fetures* U; *handis* A. *&*] *his* add. AVEC. *fustes*] *fyngirs* AVECD. *fustes & j.*] *ioyntes and handes* U.
1028. *Weryn* VDE; *Waxen* U. *letchy* V; *lithe* D; *lethy* EC; *litel* U; *lene* A. *leke*] *leef* EDU. *lorne* AV; *lefte* AC. *hade* AVEC. *here*] *þeire* V; *the* A. *strenghe* AC.
1029. *He*] so AVEDU; *Ben* L. *agayn* V. *as*] om. V. *woxen* L; *wexe* A; *waxe* CV; *wexid* D; *waxeth* U. *aȝens— woxe*] *as a crepel. al aȝens kynde* E.
1030. *&*] *But* C; om. AVEDU. *so*] *by-nommen* add. A; *by-set* add. D. *many*] *a* add. VCDU. *segge*] *man* EC. *wepide* AV; *wepte* ECDU.

þey [s]ende to þe cite ⸲ & souȝten a leche,
þat couþe keuere þe kyng, ⸲ & condi[t] delyueryn.　1032
Whan þey þe cyte hadde souȝt ⸲ with seggys aboute,
Fynde couþe þey no [freke] ⸲ þat on þe feet couþe,
Saue þe self Josophus, ⸲ þat surgyan was noble,

Josephus cures him, & he graunteþ to go ⸲ with a goode wylle.　1036
Whan he was comen to þe kyng ⸲ & þe cause wyste,
How þe segge so sodeynly ⸲ in syknesse is fallen,

Fol. 15 b. Tille he haue complet his cure ; condit he askeþ
For what burne of þe burwe ⸲ þat he brynge wolde.　1040
þe kyng was glad alle to graunte ⸲ þat þe gome wylned,

by bringing before him a man whom he hates bitterly. & he ferkiþ hym forth, ⸲ fettes ful blyue
A man to þe mody kyng ⸲ þat he moste hated,
& yn bryngeþ þe burne ⸲ to his beddes syde.　1044
Whan Tytus saw þat segge ⸲ sodeynly with eyen,
His herte in an hote yre ⸲ so hetterly riseþ,
þat þe blode bygan to [br]ed[e] ⸲ abrode in þe vaynes,

1031. þey] And AE. sende] sente AVECDU; wende (!) L. souȝt.] there add. A; hem add. C.
1032. couer A; cure EDU; hele C. condit VEC; conduyt DU; condithe A; condis L; him add. VU; þei add. D. delyueryd AVCDU; hem ȝeue E.
1033. with] the U. seggys] wyse men E; herowdis C; all add. CU. ab.] ynowe ED.
1034. can DU. frcke] so AVDU; man (!) LC. Fynde—freke] Thei non cowde fynde E. on] of VCU. þe] that A. þe f.] surgery V. knewe C.
1035. þe] hym DU. self] knyȝt E. þe s.] one V; only C. Josaphus A; Josephus VECDU. þat] om. VD. was] is U.
1036. &] om. C. grauntyd AEDCV. to go] for to comen V. with—wylle] the gome (kyng E) for to hele EDU.
1037. was c.] com EC. &] al add. EDU. cas EUDC.
1038. How] Whi AV. þe s.] þat he E. so] om. VEDU. is] was AVE. This line is omitted in C.
1039. haue] hadde AVEDU. complet] kythede A; kithe V. complet h. c.] his cure ydoon E; done his dede & cure a C. conduyt DU; condethe A. askyd ECD.
1040. For wh.] And for a V. burne] man EC. of þe b.] of town E; with inne þe cyte C.

1041. was] is DU. alle] for U. alle to gr.] and grantede AVC; all add. AVCU. þe g.] Iosephus E; wilnith D; askede AE; wolden U; desires V. þat—wylned] his askynge C.
1042. &] anon add. E. ferkede hym AV; wente E; hertely wente C. forþ] and add. AVE. fette E; fetehes U; fetchede AV; to fette C; hym add. ECU. ful] om. AVUCD. blyue] anone C; an oþer A; a bœrne D! a leche E.
1043. þe] that A. mody] sykke E; dowȝty C.
1044. yn] soone A; om. ECDU. browȝte C; bysily add. D; forth add. U; he add. A. þe] þat CU. man C. þe b.] hym euyn foorth E; sodenly add. C. bedde AU.
1045. saw] sees A. þat] þe VC. segge] manne C. saw þ. s.] that segge sawe UD; þis man sey E; so add. ED. with eghe AV; with syȝte CD; hym by E; in sight U.
1046. In his EDU. in] om. EDU. an] om. V. in an] and his A. hote y.] hete EDU. so] om. AVECU. etterly A; sodainly VECDU; for teene anon E. aryses VEU; a-vose C.
1047. þat] om. AVC. blode] al add. EU. began] wiþ þe (in þat C) hete add. VC. brede] so AVCU; blede D; spred (!) L; wurche E. abr.] om. AVCUDE. þe] his EDU.

He is cured by Josephus.

& þe synwes [to] resorte in her' self kynde.   1048
Ffeet & alle þe fetoures ⁊ as þey byfore wer',
comyn in her' owen kynd ; ⁊ & þe kyng ryseþ,
þonkeþ God of his grace ⁊ & þe goode leche
Of alle, saue þat his enemy ⁊ was yn on hym broȝt.   1052
Þan sayþ Josophus ; ⁊ " þis segge haþ þe holpyn,   *Josephus makes him forgive his enemy.*
& her' haþ be þy bote, ⁊ þoȝ þou hym bale wolde ;
þerfor graunte hym þy grace ⁊ a-ȝen his goode dede,
& be frende with þy foman ⁊ þat frendschup haþ serued ! "
Þe kyng satles with þe segge ⁊ þat hym saued hadde,   1057
& þer graunted hym grace ⁊ to go wher' he wolde ;
With Josophus he made joye ⁊ & jewels hym rauȝte,   *He will take no reward, but returns to Jerusalem.*
Besauntes, byes of gold, ⁊ broches & ryngys ;   1060
Bot alle forsakeþ þe segge : & to þe cite ȝede
With condit as he come ; ⁊ he kepiþ no more,
[And] Tytus segyþ þe toun, ⁊ þer tene is on hande,
For hard hunger & hote ⁊ þat hem is bylompyn.   1064

1048. þe] his E. synwes] colour E ; rode D ; rody U. to] so AVECDU ; om. L. restore EDU ; comforts VC. her] the AV ; his UDCE. self] owne ECD ; right U. kynde] wise V.
1049. alle] om. EDU. þe] om. ACDU. fetoures] ichone add. EUD. afore ED ; ere U.
1050. They come C. in] to CEUD ; till V. þeire V ; the A. owen] om. E. kynd] aȝen add. E. &] þenne add. C. aryseth EDU.
1051. Thonkyd DU ; He thanked C ; Thankyng E. þe] his AC.
1052. saue] but of E. þat] only V ; om. ACEDU. enemy] þat add. EDU. yn] om. UD ; so VC. on] to VCDU. was—br.] þat stood hym besyde E.
1053. sayde AVECDU ; him add. U. Ios.] þe gentill add. A ; thoo add. C ; sir add. AVC. segge] wreche C ; man E ; om. U. haþ þe h.] is þy (þe D ; thin owen U) leche EDU.
1054. her h. b.] he is C ; here bene A ; om. EDU. þy] om. ECDU. bote] of all (om. ED) þi bittirnes add. ECDU. bale] sle C. woldist VE.
1055. And therefore AC ; Forthy U ; For (!) D. þy] om. VC. aȝen] for AVE CDU. dede] will A.
1056. &] om. UD. be] om. AV. frende] fayn D. to E. foo C. deseruyd E ; shewed VU.

1057. Thanne þe C. saughtled AVU ; saughtlis D ; acordyd E. þe] þat D. segge] man E. satles—þat] sawe how þe manne C.
1058. þer] om. AEVCDU. grauntis A ; ȝaf EDU. grace] gudly A ; for add. DU. wher] thare A ; þat add. E. he w.] hym beste (good DU ; om. V) lykede AVDU.
1059. With] Of AVC. With—joye] He ioyed with Josephus EDU. jew.] iewes (!) E, rauȝte] ȝaue EC.
1060. Bothe besantes of C. byes] bedis A. byes of] of clene E.
1061. Bot] Thanne E. forsoke DUC ; lefte E. þe] that AU. þe s.] þis man E ; he thanne C. cite] he add. AE. ȝede] turnedde C.
1062. Bot with AV ; Safe with þe C. Wiþ saaf cundyt EDU ; he] thei U. as he c.] þat he hadde C. he kepte E ; kepis he AV ; kept he DU ; kept thei U ; he asked C. no more] noghts ells A.
1063. And] so AEDU. Thanne C ; om. V ; Now L. Tyt.] he add. C. besegedde C ; þan add. D. & þer C ; her V ; where E ; om. U. tene] wo E ; sorowe C. is] was C. on] in UD. is on h.] begynneth E.
1064. For] With A ; Thorow C. hard] gret E. hote] scharp E ; hete VDU. thaym A. byl.] bystadde A ; byfalle UD ; be-warpen V ; is byl.] now befalleth E. he is byl.] þey with inne hadde C.

The Jews suffer from Famine.

Many in the town die of famine.

[Nowe] of þe tene in þe toun �ötwerȝ [tor] for to telle
What moryne & meschef ⁘ for mete is byfalle,
For fourȝ dayes byfor ⁘ þey no fode hadde,
Noþer fisch ne flesch, ⁘ freke on to byte,   1068
Bred, browet ne broþe ⁘ ne beste vpon lyue,
Wyn ne water to drynke ⁘ bot wope of hemself.
Olde scheldes & schone ⁘ scharply þey eten ;
þat liflode for ladies ⁘ was luþer to chewe.   1072
Fellen doun for defaute ⁘ [f]latte to þe grounde,
Ded as a dore-nayl, ⁘ eche day many hundred ;

They behave like wild Fol. 16 a. beasts. A mother devours her own child.

Wo wakned þycke, ⁘ as wolues þey ferde ;
þe wy[ght]e waried on þe woke ⁘ alle his wombe-fille.
On Marie, a myld wyf, ⁘ for meschef of foode,   1077
Hirȝ owen barn þat ʒo barȝ. ⁘ ʒo brad on þe gledis,
Rostyþ rigge & rib ⁘ with rewful wordes,

1065. *Nowe*] so AVE ; om. CDU ; & L. *tene*] *sorowe* C ; & add. D. *in*] *of* AECDU. *wer tor*] *tym ware* A ; *tyme* (*it* add. E) *is* EC ; *is tyme* DU ; *were* (!) V : *wer hard* L. *for*] *now* D ; om. AEC. *telle*] *saye* AV.
1066. *meteles* D. *es by-tyde* A ; *þer yn groweth* EU ; *þer is growyn* D.
1067. *For*] om. DU. *fourty* ED. *beforn* V ; *a-fore* D ; *a-forne* U. *fode*] *mete* C. *fode* (*bote* D) *þei ne* (*non* E) EDU.
1068. *Nor* C. *ne*] *nor* C. *flessch ne fyssh* ED. *flesch*] *no* add. A. *on*] *for* AV. *frekc—byte*] *þat þey myʒte on byte* C ; *þat freke might bye* D ; *þat hem releue myʒte* E. This line is omitted in U.
1069. *Nother brede* C. *browet*] om. AVECDU. *ne*] *nor* CDU. *ne*] *ne no* A ; *neyþer* EDU. *beste*] *befe* D ; *ne thyng* add. EDU. *appon* A. *lyue*] *erthe* ECD. *vpon l.*] *that beres lyf* U.
1070. *ne*] *nor* C. *Wyn ne*] *Water ne* ⸱ EDU. *water*] *wyn* EDU. *to dr.*] *drunken* U. *water to dr.*] *windregges* V. *wope*] *wepyng* VCU ; *þat com* E. *wope of*] *wepe for* D. This line is omitted in A.
1071. *schetis* A ; *schepisfeete* E ; *shepefete hornes* U. *& schone*] om. E ; *full* add. A. *þei*] *þe* (!) C.
1072. *þat*] *Swich* AVC ; *was* add. V. *lift.*] *mete* E. *for*] *to* A. *luþer*] *heuy* C. *to*] *for to* A ; *vn to* C. *chewe*] a letter has been erased before *c* ; *schewe* AC. *was—chewe*] *þat somtyme were shene* VD ; *þat tyme was wol swete* E. This line is omitted in U.

1073. *Thei fyllen* ECDU ; *dede* add. A. *Fellen d.*] *And fele* V. *flatte*] so EDU ; *platte* L ; *fellen* V. *grounde*] *þe*] om. V. *grounde*] *erthe* U. *flatte—grounde*] *on þe colde erthe* C ; *ilke a daye many hundrethe* A.
1074. *As deed* ECDU. *eche*] *ilk a* U. *many*] *a* add. C. *hund.*] *thowsande* A ; om. VEDU.
1075. *The woo* A ; *Sorowe* C. *wakned*] *wakid* VEDU ; *awaked* C ; *wakynnys* A ; *so* add. A. *þycke*] *þer with* ECDU ; *for* add. E.
1076. *wyghte*] so ADU ; *wye* L ; *grete* E ; *feble* C. *werreyde* A ; *weried* U ; *eete* E ; *wyries* D. *on*] om. ECDU. *woke*] *wayke* ADU ; *smale* E ; *full* C. *alle his*] *& his* DU ; *for he his* C ; *thaire* A ; *& so her* E. *wombes* E ; *for* to add. A ; *fillis* D ; *fylde* ECU.
þey had nought in VIII daies . ones þeire womfull V.
1077. *And one* V ; *Ther was on* E ; *O saynt* A. *Marion* VEDU. *myld w.*] *mydewyf* E ; *good w.* C ; *þat* add. E. *meschef*] *defaute* VE.
1078. *barn*] *chyld* ECU. *ʒo*] om. AV ECDU. *braid* U ; *made brede* A ; *leyde vp* E ; *leyde hit* C ; *brad hit* V. *gledis*] *colys* ECDU.
1079. *She* add. C. *Rostyd* CDU ; *& roostyd bothe* E ; *Scho ruschede owte* A. *ribbe* (*rybbis* DU) *and rygge* AVDU ; *rybbe & syde* C, *with*] *wol* add. E. *rewely* EU ; *rulich* D.
Sayse : Enter thare þou owte come . and etis the rybbis add. A.

A Woman eats her own Child. 63

Sayþ : " Sone, vpon eche side ⸵ *our* sorow is a-lofte,   1080
Batail a-boute þe borwe, ⸵ *our* bodies to quelle,
Wi*th*yn hunger so hote, ⸵ þat neȝ *our* herte brestyþ ;
þerfor ȝeld þat I þe ȝaf ⸵ & aȝen tourne,
& entr' *þer* þou cam out ! " ⸵ & etyþ a schoulder'.   1084
þe smel roos of þe rost ⸵ riȝt to þe walles,
þ*at* fele fastyng folke ⸵ felde þe sauere ;   *The hungry citizens are attracted by the savour.*
Dou*n* þei daschen þe dore : ⸵ dey scholde þe berde,
þ*at* mete yn þ*is* meschef ⸵ hadde from me*n* loyned.   1088
þa*n* saiþ þat worþi wif : ⸵ " in a wode hunge*r*
Myn owen barn haue I brad ⸵ & þe bones gnawen ;
Ȝit haue I saued ȝ*ou* som." ⸵ & forþ a side feccheþ   *Hearing her confession,*
Of þe barn þ*at* ȝo bar' ⸵ & alle hir' blode chaungeþ.   1092 *they go away in tears.*
A-way þey went for wo, ⸵ wepyng echone,
& sayn : " Alas, in þ*is* lif ⸵ how longe schul we dwelle ?

1080. *Seyd* DU ; *And said* V ; *ȝhe seyde* E. *Sayþ s.*] *And sone* A ; *Dere sone sche seyde* C. *appone* A ; *on* EVCDU. *eche*] *ilk* UA ; *a* add. AC. *our*] om. ECDU. *is*] *comes* V. *a l.*] *on honde* VECUD ; *newe* A.
1081. *And sore bat.* C ; *Alle* A. *aboute*] *with owttyn* AVC. þ*c*] om. V. þ*e b.*] *forth* C. *Bat.—borwe*] *About* þ*e borow* (*town is* E) *batayle* DEU. *our b. to*] *vs all forto* U. *kylle* C ; *melle* (?) A.
1082. *And with in* A ; *is* add. AV. *hunger*] *is* add. C. *neȝ*] *nere* A ; om. ED. *our*] *myn* ED. *the* U. *hertis* AV. *bresten* V ; *breketh* C.
1083. *And there fore* AC ; *Now* EDU. ȝ*eld*] *me* add. EDU ; *to me* add C. *I* þ*e ȝ.*] þ*ou ȝafe* A.
1084. &*c.*] om. VCDU. &*e.*] *In to my body* E. *owte come* AVCDU. *etyþ*] þ*anne eete sche* C ; *eet faste of* E. *a*] *the* AD ; *his* E. *schulder*] *childe* A.
1085. *arose* VU. þ*e*] þ*at* E. *of* þ*e r.*] *sone o lofte* U. *riȝt*] *anoon* E ; *aboute* C ; om. U ; *to þe w.*] (*al* add. U) *in* (*to* add. EDU) *the strete* AVECDU.
1086. þ*at*] *Ther* DU ; & E. *fele*] *many* EC. *felde* þ*e s.*] *fastyd had longe* D. *folke*] þ*er* add. C. þ*e s.*] *it sone* EU. This line is added on the margin in A.
1087. *And downe* AE. þ*ey dasshedin* V ; *dasschedde* þ*ey* CD ; þ*ei casten* U ; *drnwyn* E. *dores* C ; *and* add. AE : *and said* add. V. *berde*] *barin* V. *scholde*

þ*e b.*] ȝ*he schulde* EU ; þ*at womman schulde* C. *dei—berde*] *hastely thay askede* A.
1088. þ*at*] *Why that* þ*at* A ; *For* E. *mete*] om. V. þ*is*] þ*at* AECDU ; om. V. *hadde*] *was* A. *fro* A. *men*] *good mete* add. V. *leyned* V. *hadde—loyned*] *frome* (*fro* U) *menne* (*hem* U) *hadde i-keppte* CDU ; *fro hem dode keepe* E.
1089. *And* þ*anne* C. *sayde* AVECD ; *saiden* (!) U. þ*at*] þ*e* VU ; *this* D. *worthiliche* A ; *wofull* C ; om. DU. þ*at w.*] om. (!) E. *ane* A ; þ*at* D ; *her* E ; om. V.
1090. *barn*] *child* EC. *brad*] *brend* E ; *roste* C. *haue I b.*] *es my brede* A. &*c*] om. U ; *j* add. A. *bones*] *body* E ; *al to* add. U. *gnawe* A.
1091. *But ȝit* E. *I*] om. E. ȝ*ou*] om. E. *forþ*] om. AVCDU. *a*] þ*e* C. *fechide* ADU ; *fette* VC. &*—feccheþ*] *to parte with ȝow* þ*is tymne* E.
1092. *barn*] *chylde* C. &*.*] þ*anne* C ; *bot* A. *alle*] *then* U ; om. D. *her* VUCD ; *thaire* A. *ble* A. *chaungede* AVD ; *turned* C.
     And fette forth of here child · a gobat red yroosted E.
1093. *Forþ* VECDU ; *And furthe* A. *went*] þ*an* add. D. *wente* þ*ay* AV. *for*] *with* A. *echone*] *full sore* ACDU ; *wol sore* E ; *sore* V.
1094. &*.*] om. U. *sayd* AVEDU. *Alas* þ*ey seyde* C. *dwelle*] *lenge* A ; *du*₁*e* EDU ; *lyfe* C.

64   *Titus will not make Terms.*

               3it beter wer' at o brayde ⁆ in batail to deye,
               þan þus in langur to lyue, ⁆ & lengþen our [p]yne."   1096

They kill all non-combatants. þan þey demeden a dom, : þat deil was to hure :
               To voiden alle by vile deþ ⁆ þat vitelys destruyed,
               Wymmen & weyke folke ⁆ þat weren of olde age,
               My3t no3t stonde in stede ⁆ bot her' stor' mardyn.   1100
               After [þay] touche of trewe, ⁆ to trete with þe lord,

They then ask for terms, but Titus will not treat with them. Bot Titus grauntep no3t for gile ⁆ þat þe gomes þenke,
For he is wise, þat is war, ⁆ or hym wo hape,
& with falsede a-fer' ⁆ is fairest to dele.   1104
To worchyn vnder' þe wal ⁆ w[a]yes þey casten,
Whan Tytus nold no trewe ⁆ to þe toun graunte,

They then mine under the ground. With mynours & masouns ⁆ myne þey bygonne,
Grobben faste [i]n þe grounde ⁆ & god 3yue vs joye !   1108

As Tytus after [on] a tyme ⁆ vmbe þe toun r[i]deþ
   Wyþ sixty speres of þe sege, ⁆ segges a fewe,

1095. 3it] It EU. beter wer] were (it add. A; vs add. D) better AVCEDU.
1096. langur] sorowe C. lyue] ly A. lengþen our] meche lasse ED; in lasse U. peyne EC; pyne AVUD; fyne L.
1097. demed þey C. þey—dem.] was ymad a cry E. dole D; sorwe E; pyte C; wel (!) V. þat d. w.] was doleful A; is doelful U.
1098. by] with D; to V; the A; om. C. vile] wild D; om. C. deþ] om. A. To—deþ] þat alle schulde voyde þe town E. vitaille V.
1099. As wommen EC. wayker U; werke VD. þat] and those A; fallen add. C. of] in ECDU. olde] gret EDU; om. AVC. age] elde AVCDU.
1100. My3t] That AVDU; þo þat E; And all swych þat C. no3t] om. ECDU; ne add. AU. stode AVECDU. in] no add. ECDU. thaire A; þe VE. mardyn] destroyed E; wasted C; dispendid D; spended U.
1101. And aftir ACD; And afterward U. And thanne E. thay] so A: to LC; om. VEDU. touchede V; tretyn EC. of] to U; a add. AVED. trewce C. to] a D. to—þe] and entrete with U; with þe grete C. lordes CDU. to—lord] whan þey sey tyme E.
1102. graunted EC; graunte D; hem add. ED; hit add. C. nat E. grauntep n.] wolde noght graunte V; thare to add. A. for gile] om. EUDC. þe] om. V.

þenke] þoghtyn VAD. þat . . . þenke] for all here queynte gynne C; þat þei þanne desyred E.
1103. or] he add. E. hym] he U. happes VU; happyn AC.
1104. &] Ay V; For ay A; Euer C; & is EDU. with] of E. on fare A; on feere V; afeerd EU; a felde D. is] om. DU. faire VC; for add. VC. melle C. is—dele] & putte it at þe wurse E.
1105. wallis AVEC; þan add. D. wayes] so AVECDU; wyes L. þey c.] for to make U.
1106. Whan] om. D. Tytus] þay ne A. wolde AVD; om. E. trewes D. vn-to A. nold—toun] to þe Iewes no trewce wolde C. grauntyd E.
1107. masouns and mynours AVECDU. to add. AVECDU. bygynne C.
1108. & gr. AVECDU. grubbed EDU; and dyggedde C. in] so A: vndir VECDU; on L. þe] om. CDU. &] there A; om. D. god] lorde V; om. C. (added in another hand). &—joye] speede what they my3te E. Septimus Passus VUC.
1109. after] om. CU. on] so AVECDU; om. L. vmbe] aboute AECDU; abouten V. cete A. rydys AVECDU; redeþ L. rode C.
1110. speres sixty EDU. sege] & add. ECDU; other add. U. segges] archers E; 3emen C; a fewe] many U.

The Jews make an unsuccessful Attack.

Alle outwith þe ost, ⁊ out of a kaue,
Vp a buschment brake ⁊ alle of briȝt hedis. 1112
Fyf hundred fiȝtyng men ⸧ ⁊ fellen hem aboute
In jepouns & jambers ⁊ Jewes þey wer',
Hadde wroȝt hem a wey ⁊ & þe wal myned,
& Titus tourneþ hem to ⁊ without tale mor'. 1116
Schaftes schedred wer' sone ⁊ & scheldes yþrelled,
[And many schalke thurghe schotte with þe scharpe ⸧ ende,]
Brunyes & briȝt wede ⁊ blody by-runne,
& many segge at þat saute ⁊ souȝte to þe grounde. 1120
Hacchen vpon hard steel ⁊ with an herty wylle,
þat fur' out flowe ⸧ ⁊ as of flynt stonys;
Of þe helm & þe hed ⁊ hewen at-tonys,
þe stompe vnder' stede feet ⁊ in þe steel leueþ. 1124
þe ȝong duk Domycian ⁊ of þe dyn herde,
And issed⸧ out of þe ost ⁊ with eȝte hundred speres,

Fol. 16 b.
and attack Titus with 500 men.

Domitian comes to his help.

1111. *And alle* A. *outwith*] *a wey fro (from* U) EDU; *with owte the Owttyn* A. *Alle—ost*] *By þe dike as he rode* V; *At þe sowth est syde* C.
1112. *Up*] *Out* U. *A busshment vp* ED. *Up—brake*] *A busshement brake oute* V; *Vppe bruschede a buschement* A. *briȝt*] *white* D. *hedis*] *helmys* ECDU.
1113. *hundr.*] *of* add. C. *men*] *folke* AED; *&* add. LCD. *hym* AECDU.
1114. *jope* C. *&*] *in* add. AC. *jamb.*] *hauberkes* V; *jambewes* CED; *iambes* U. *Iewes þ.*] *all þe Iewes* C.
1115. *That hade* ADU; *þey haddyn* VC; *That* E. *ywrought* E; *wrokyn* A. *hem*] om. AVC. *&*] *vndir* add. VU. *þe*] om. U. *wallis* AVC.
1116. *&*] *Thenne* C; *But* E. *turned* EC; *to* add. E. *him* U; *thaym* A. *to*] *tho* E. *with outtyn* AVC. *more tale* C.
1117. *And þer was schaftis* A. *schiuered* VECDU; *sondirde* A. *wer s.*] *full* A. *&*] om. V. *scheldes*] *many schelde* A; *thorow* add. C; *were* add. V. *yþr.*] *yhurled* U.
1118. *And*] om. VECDU. *many*] *a* add. VC. *schalke*] *segge* VD; *legge* C; om. E; *was* add. C. *schotte*] *was* add. E. *þe*] *wol* E. *sharpe*] so VECDU; *scharpere* A. *ende*] *arwes* E. *And—ende*] so A; om. L.
1119. *Biernes* D; *Haburgynes* EC.

wede] *iryns* A; *irne* V. *br. w.*] *hauberkes* E; *armour* C; *al* add. U; *was* add. C. *blody*] *were* add. E.
1120. *&*] om. C. *many*] *a* add. VC. *segges* U; *beryns* A; *barin* V; *man* EC. *at þ.*] *atte* U; *at a* V. *saute*] *brayde* AV; *fyȝte* C. *to*] om. E. *þe*] om. U. *souȝte—grounde*] *birssede (brusshed* V) *to (þe* add. V) *dede* AV; *fell doun dede* C.
1121. *Hacchen*] *Hewen* DU; *Thay (The* E) *hewe* AVEC. *appon* A; *vp an* D. *an*] *full* AV; *so* U; om. E. *hertely* EU; *ettire* A; *hettill* V; *byttur* C.
1122. *þat*] *the* add. AVECDU. *flowe*] so AVCDU; *flowen* (!) L. *fley out* E. *of fl. st.*] *it dooth of flyntes* E.
1123. *Of*] *Bothe* AC. *helm*] *hede* A *þe h.*] *her helmys* E. *þe*] *her* E; om. D. *heuedys* ED; *helme* A; *þay* add. AECU. *at—t.*] *to gedirs* A; *to gedre* VC.
1124. *That þe* C. *stompes* U. *þe st.*] *Thay tombill* A. *vnder*] *þe* add. V. *stedis* AE. *lafte* VE. *in—leueþ*] *and stampes one stele wedis* A. This line is omitted in D.
1125. *þe*] *that* AC; *þis* EDU. *dyn*] *noyse* C; om. E.
1126. *issed*] so U; *issued* ED; *issues* V; *dissed* (!) L; *faste hyes* A. *And—ost*] *He houede with oute þe chase* C. *eȝte*] *an* U; om. V.

SIEGE OF JERUSALEM   F

They refuse Titus's Offer of Peace.

The Jews are defeated.

Ffel on þe fals folke, ⸴ vmbe-feldes hem sone,
As bestes bretnes hem alle ⸴ & haþ his broþer holpen.   1128
Þan Titus toward his tentis ⸴ tourneþ hym sone,
Makeþ mynour[s] & men, ⸴ þe myne to stoppe;

Titus offers pence; but John and Simon, leaders of the Jews, refuse it.

After profreþ pes ⸴ for pyte þat he hadde,
Whan he wist of her' wo ⸴ þat wer' withyn stoken.   1132
Bot Jon þe jenfulle ⸴ þat þe Jewes ladde,
An oþer Symond of his assent ⸴ forsoke þe profre,
Sayn, leuer in þis lif ⸴ lengen hem wer',
Þan any renke out of Rome ⸴ [re]joycid her' sorowe.   1136
Sale in þe cite · was cesed with þanne,
Was noȝt for besauntes to bye ⸴ þat men bite myȝt,

There is no food to be bought in the city.

For a ferþyng-worþ of fode ⸴ floryns an hundred
Princes profren in þe toun ⸴ to pay in þe fuste;   1140
Bot alle was boteles bale, ⸴ f[or] who so bred hadde,
Nold a gobet haue [g]ouen · for goode vpon [erþ]e.
Wymmen falwed faste ⸴ & her' face chaungen,

1127. þey fellin V; Than thay felle A; Falles U; And felliþ D; They fellede C; and fallyn E. on] of AC; om. V. folke] abouten add. V; & add. AVE CDU. vmbe f.] felliþ D; vmby fawldis A; felden VE. þam A; doun add. E; ful add. U. vmb. h. s.] & slewe hem euerychone C.
1128. And als A. bretynede AV; he murthered C. þam A. alle] om. C. bestes . . . alle] þei hadde be beestes E. haþ] om. ADU. holpen] o altered from e L; helpede A; helpis DU. haþ—holp.] helpyd his brother E.
1129. towardes A; to EC. tent AVE DU. turnyd EAC. hym s.] be lyfe AV; a none C.
1130. made U; And makes V; & made AE; He made C. mynours] so AVECDU; mynour (!) L. þe] that AC. myne] for add. AVEDU.
1131. Efter A; Thanne A; And þan DU; thei add. E; he add. C. proferde AC; preyde E; hem add. VCU; thaym add. A; he add. D; hym of add. E. þat he h.] of his sowle E.
1132. Whan] þat add. A. of] om. A. thaire A. stoken] closede AVC; om. EDU.
1133. Iona C; Iosaphus AEDU; sone V. gynful EDU; gylefull C; gentill A; sinfull man V. þat] alle add. AV.
1134. And an oþer AC; & EDU. Symon C. of] at EDU; by C. his] om. AVC. þe] þan þat A.
1135. And sayde AV; Thei seyde ECDU; thaym were add. A. leuer] lenge DU; byde C; om. E. þis] þat AVECDU. lif] longe add. E. lengen] leuer ECDU. hem] thei U. lengen h. w.] langare to lenge A; to ligge add. E.
1136. renke] manne C; wiþt (!) E. out] om. AE. rejoycid] so D; joycid L; rewede of A; shulde reioisse of V; sholde reioyse C; renewyd EU. thaire AV.
1137. Sale] Bot seknes A. cesed] seson V. with] by AVECDU.
1138. for] a add. C. besaunt ECD; beisaunt V. man E. bite] ete C; bye (!) DU.
1139. fode] mete C. ane h.] C V.
1140. profirde AECDU. þe f.] hand E.
1141. bale] wo U. for] so AVECDU; fro L. who] he A; om. E. so] þat ACU.
1142. Ne wolde VED; Ne wolde noȝt U; Wolde not C. haue] om. U. gouen] gevynne V; gyuen ACU; ȝouen L. a—gouen] haue (om. E) ȝyue a gobat ED. goode] gold VECUD; that was add. U. appon AV; on U. erþe] so AVECDU; lyue L.
1143. Females DU. falwed] fadyd EC; full add. A. thaire AV; al the DU. faces C. chaungeth U; changede AVED; wannede C.

The Famine increases. 67

Ffeynte & fallen doun, ꞉ þat so fair' wer' ; 1144
S[ome] swallen as swyn, ꞉ som swart wexen,
Som lene on to loke, ꞉ as la[n]terne-hornes.
þe morayne was so myche, ꞉ þat no man couþe telle   There is no room to bury
Wher' to burie in þe burwe ꞉ þe bodies þat wer' ded, 1148 the dead;
Bot wenten with hem to þe walle ꞉ & walten [hem o]uere ;   they are thrown over the walls.
In-to þe depe of þe diche † ꞉ þe ded doun fallen.
Whan Titus told was þe tale, ꞉ to trewe god he vouched
þat [he] hadde profred † hem pes ꞉ & grete pite hadde ; 1152
þo praied he † Josophus to preche ꞉ þe peple [to enforme]   Titus asks Josephus to
[For] to saue hemself ꞉ & þe cite ȝelde. Fol. 17 a.
Bot Jon forsoke þe sawe, ꞉ so forto wyrche,   urge them to yield; John
With Symond, þat oþer segge, ꞉ þat þe cyte ladde. 1156 and Simon withstand him.
Myche peple for þe prechyng ꞉ at þe posterne ȝatis
Tyen out of þe toun ꞉ & Tytus bysecheþ,

1144. *Feyntyd* EU. *Feynte &*] *For fayntnes (feinte* V) *thay* AV ; *For* þe *fawte some* C. *felle* AVEC ; *feyned* U. þat] *arst* add. E ; *ere* add. D. *down*] *all* add. U. *so*] *full* A. *so—were*] *were wol fayre* E ; *fayre before weren* C.
1145. *Some*] so AE ; *Swonyng* C ; *Swollyng* U ; *Summen* V ; *swounen* L. *swollen* V ; *swellede* AEC ; *swellyn* D ; *swelling* U. *as*] *a* add. A. *swyn*] *and* add. AVEUDC. *swart*] *pale* C. *wuxen* E ; *waxen* VCD ; *were* A. *swart w.*] *waxen worthe* U.
1146. *And some* AC ; *For* U ; *Ful* D ; *was* add. A ; *were* add. VC. *onto l.*] *as a leke or* A. *as*] *a* add. A. *lanterne*] so AVECDU ; *laterne* (!) L. *horne* A.
1147. *was*] *wexe* AV. *mekill* A. þe —*mekill*] *So meche was* þe *moreyne* EUD. *coupe*] *myght* D.
1148. *burie*] *bere* A. *burwe*] *town* E ; *cyte* C. þe] om. V. *were d.*] *deyde* ED ; *there dyed* U.
1149. *with thaym* A ; om. CE. *with hem (hym* D) *went to* DU ; *drowe hem ouer* E. *wallis* AEC. *welte* A ; *warpen* V ; *waltyn* D ; *walwed* U ; *tumblede* C. *hem*] so VCDU ; þam A ; om. L ; *alle* add. A. *ouere*] so AVCDU ; *euere* (!) L. *&—ouer*] *whan they sey tyme* E.
1150. *& so in* E. *to*] om. AV. *depe of* þe] om. E. *dikis* A ; *depe* add. L. *felle* AV. þe—*fallen*] *down (adown* E). *gan they falle* ECDU.
1151. *Whan*] *& whan* þat E ; *to* add. above the line, V. *telled* A. þe] þis D.

told—tale] þe *tale tolde was* V ; *was this tale tolde* U ; *herde* þis *tale* C ; *wiste this* E. *to*] *of* ACV. *trewe*] om. ACV. *vouched*] *vowed* DU ; *witnes* A ; *tas witnesse* V ; *toke recorde* C ; *seyde* E.
1152. þat *he hadde*] so ED ; þat *he* AV ; *How* þat *he* C ; þat *hadde* L. *propfred* L. *thaym* A. &] *he* D. *grete pite*] *pete on hem* V. &—*hadde*] *it greuyd hym sore* E. This line is omitted in U.
1153. þo] *Than* AVC. *he J.*] *he he hadde J.* ꞉ L. þo—*Ios.*] *He bad Iosephus* þanne E ; *He bad Iosephus* þe *Iewe* DU. *to pr.*] om. CUDE. *preche*] *to* added above the line, V ; *&* add. A. *to enforme*] so ACUDE (*to* om. ED) ; *& hem for to lerne* add. V.
1154. *For*] so AVC ; *enforme hem* L. *For to saue*] *In sauyng of* EDU. *hem*] *thaym* A ; *hym* EU. &] om. EDU. *cite*] *towne* U ; *to* add. AE ; *vp to* add. D ; *forto* add. U.
1155. *Iosaphus* AEDU. *forsakis* A. þe *s.*] þo EDU ; om. A. *Ion*—þe] *sone folkes* þey V. *Ion*—*sawe*] *all forsoke Iosephus* C.
1156. *And Symon* AC. þat *o. s.*] *his seruaunt* ED ; *his seriaunte* AUC. þat] *all* add. AVCDU. *lede* A ; *laddyn* V.
1157. *Mekell* V ; *Bot mekill* A. þe] þat AC. *Myche—prech.*] *For al his preching (talkyng* E) *to (of* D ; om. U) þe *peple* EDU. þe] *a* E. *gate* EU.
1158. *Tyen*] *Ten* U ; *Turnes* A ; *Turned* VC ; *Ten went* E ; *Ten turnid* D. þe] om. D. *of* þe *t.*] *priuyliche* E. *beseched* ED ; *byschen* UC.

|Many leave the town and give themselves up.| To for[g]yue hem þe gult, ⁘ þat þey to god wroȝt;
& he graunteþ hem grace · & gaylers bytauȝt.　1160
Bot whan þey metten with mete, vnmyȝty þey wer'
Any fode to defye, so faynt was her' strengþe,
Fful þe gottes of gold ⁘ eche gome hadde :
Lest fomen fongen hem schold, ⁘ her' floreyns þey eten.　1164
Whan hit was broȝt vp abrode ⁘ & þe bourd aspyed,
|They are slain for the sake of their gold, which they have swallowed.| [Wiþou]ten leue of þat lord, ⁘ ledes hem slowen,
[G]oren euereche a gome, ⁘ & þe gold taken;
Ffayn[ere] of þe floreyns ⁘ [þan of] þe frekes alle.　1168
Ay wer' þe ȝates vn[ȝ]et ⁘ tille two ȝeres ende,
So longe þey [s]ouȝt hit by sege, ⁘ or þey þe [cite] hadde;
Eleuen hundred þousand Jewes ⁘ in þe mene whyle
Swalten, while þe sweng last ⁘ by swerd & by hunger.　1172
Now Titus conseil haþ take ⁘ þe toun to assayle,
To wynne hit on eche [wise] ⁘ of warwolues handes,

1159. *forgyue*] so AV; *forȝyue* LCED. *thaym* A. *god*] *Crist* V. *wroȝt*] *dyde* C.
1160. &] om. C. *he*] *Titus* A. *grauntyd* EC. *thaym* A. *hem grauntid* DU; *his* add. DU. &] *to* add. D; *to* þe add. C. *gailer* V; *hem* add. E; *he hem* C. *betook* EC.
1161. *Bot*] om. V. *with*] *the* add. A.
1162. *fode*] *mete* C. *was*] *were* AEDU. *thaire* A. *strenkþes* EDU; *strenghes* A.
1163. *For full* ADUC. *eche*] *ilk* U; *a* add. ACDU. *gome*] *manne* C. *eche g.*] þe *gomes echon* V.
1164. *Lest*] *Or* AV; *her* add. C; *thaire* add. AV. *fangen*] *haue* C; *fynd* D; *founden* U. *hem*] om. U. *schulde þam* (þem V) *fange* AV. *thaire* A; om. U. *eten*] *frette* U.
Instead of l. 1163 and 1164 E contains the two following lines:
& *her guttes yschronke . & her stomak boþe,*
þat for al þe wyde wurld . þey myȝte no mete brokke.
1165. *Bot when* A. *hit w.*] *þei were* D. *vp a*] *on* D; *out a* CU. *hit—brode*] *that jape on brode was broghte* A. &] *al* add. U. *asp.*] *knawen* A; *sene* U. *&— asp.*] *ledes hem slowen* V; þe *meyne hem slewe* C; þe *bernes of þe sege* D.
1166. *Wiþ outen*] so AU; *With out* D; *Souȝten* (!) L. *þat*] *the* AUD. *thaym* A. This line is omitted in VC.
1167. *Goren*] *Toren* L; þei *gorrede* AUD; *Ther þey gorede* C; *þey slitten* V.

a] om. VCD. *gome*] *manne* C. &] *all* add. D. *gold*] þey add. C. *tuke* AVC; *rauthen* U.
1168. *And* add. A. *Faynere*] so AV UD; *Ffayn* L. *flor.*] *golde* A. *than of*] so AVUD; & *þenne of* C. *frekes*] *Iewes* C.
1165-8. are omitted in E.
1169. *Ay*] ȝit AVE; *And* ȝette C; *Euer* D. *vnzet*] so A; *vnshette* V; *vnget* LC; *yemyd* D. *tille*] *vn-to* A. *two*] *the* AD.
1170. *For so* E. *souȝt*] so V; *by-soughte* A; *þouȝt* (!) L. *by*] *with* A. þey—*by*] *thei setten the* U; *sette þey þe* C; *laste* þe E; *set was þe* D. *or*] *tul* D. *cite*] so AVECUD; *toun* (!) L. *hadde*] *wunne* E; *wan* U.
1171. *þous.*] om. A; *of* add. V. *Iewes*] om. ECUD. *mesne* U; *same* V. *whyle*] *tym* AVCU.
1172. *Sw.*] *Deyde* EC. *whils* AU; *in tyme* E. *sweng*] *sege* AEUD; *labour* C. *by*] *with* ED. *swerd*] *thrist* U. &] *or* E. *by*] *with* ED.
1173. *Now*] with great initial letter, E. *Titus—take*] *tuke Titus to consaylle* A. *conseil h. t.*] *aȝen gooth* E. *toun*] *for* add. C.
1174. *To w. h.*] & *it to wynne* E; *And þe town to wynn* A. *eche*] *ilk* U; *all* AVC. *wise*] so AVC; *half* U; *way* D; *side* L. *on e. w.*] ȝif *he may* E; *owt* add. AE. *of*] þe add. AE. *warwolues*] *warlawes* AVD; *fals* E.

Titus attacks the Town. 69

Neuer pyte ne pees ⋮ profre hem more,
Ne gome þat he gete may ⋮ to no grace taken. 1176 *Titus attacks the town again,*
[þei] armen hem as tyt ⋮ alle for þe werr',
Tyen euen to þe toun ⋮ with trompis & pypys,
With nakerers & grete noyce ⋮ neȝen þe walles,
Þer many styf man & stour' ⋮ stondiþ alofte. 1180
Sir' Sabyn of Surrye ⋮ on a syde ȝede,
Þe ȝong duke Domycian ⋮ drow to an oþer ;
XV þousand [fiȝtynge] men ⋮ eche freke hadde,
With many maner of engyne ⋮ & mynours ynowe. 1184 *with siege-engines and mines.*
Tytus at þe toun ȝate ⋮ with ten þousand helmes
Merkeþ mynour[s] at þe wal, ⋮ wher' þey myne † scholde,
On ech side for þe assaute ⋮ setteþ engynes,
& bold-brayned men ⋮ in belfrayes heye. 1188
Was noȝt bot dyn & dyt ⋮ as alle deye scholde,
So eche lyuande lyf ⋮ layeþ on oþer' ;

1175. And neuer VECU ; Nowthir A ; And D. ne] nor CU. pees] to add. ACU. thaym A. hem to profre E.
1176. Ne] Nor C ; no add. A. gome] man E ; Iewe C. gete] take E. he g. m.] thay gete A. to no] þai sall to A. to—taken] his grace for to graunte E ; no grace shall haue C ; his grace ne wynneth UD.
1177. Þei armed VECU ; Than thay armede A ; Þan armyd D ; Þey] om. L. þam A. as] also A. as t.] ryth alle in (om. D) þat tyde ED ; ryth sone C. alle for] full bryȝte to C ; & streight to DU. alle—werre] boþe hond & foote E.
1178. Tyen] Turned V ; And tournes A ; They turned C. Tournes e.] And evyn turnyd DU ; & evyn wente E. to] towarde C.
1179. nakeres AECDU ; nacornes V. þey add. CDU. nyȝede C ; euyn (om. AU) to add. AEDU.
1180 many] a add. VC. men ADE. man VC. stour] stronge U. & st.] in stoure VC ; om. E. stondyn D ; stoodyn E.
1181. & sir V. on] till AVC ; of D. on a] in þe to (¹) E. ȝede] wente ED. This line is omitted in U.
1182. And þe C. Þe—Dom.] & Domycian þe deuk E. drow] yede V ; went D. to] till VC ; hym till A.
1183. XV] Fyve AV ; Fyfty ECDU. of add. VECDU. fiȝt.] so AVC ; om.

LEDU. men] folk DE. eche] ilk U ; ayther AV ; a add. DU. freke] of hem DE. ladde E.
1184. maners AV. of] om. EDU. engines AV ; gynnes E.
1185. And Titus AVC ; ȝede add. C. at] to ECD. toun] grete V. gate V ; ȝates AC ; yede D ; set U ; om. E. helmes] menne C ; ȝede E.
1186. Markyd DU ; He markede C. mynours] so AVCDU ; mynour L. at] to AC ; in DU. þe] om. U. wallis A. merk.—wal] & mynours toolde rediliche E. wher] þere VC. myne] so AVCDU ; mynde (!) L. schulde myne E.
1187. ech] ilke A ; a add. ACU. þe] om. VD. saut EC ; thay add. AVC. her add. C. setteþ eng.] engynes he sette E.
1188. brayned] brenyede A ; bremyede V ; armedde C. in] one A. berfrayes AC ; britages D ; full add. A. in belfr. an hyȝ in britages E.
1189. þan] was AVC. noȝt] om. AVC. þan—bot] Tho were E. dyn & d.] dole and dyn AV ; þole & dynne C ; dyngis & dyntes D ; dasshynges & dyntes E. deye] down AC ; adowne V. scholde] ȝede A.
ll. 1187—1189 are omitted in U.
1190. eche] ilke AU ; euery EC ; a add. AUD ; lyu.] in add. U. lyf] lede AV ; man EC. lasshes V ; layde AECDU. on] vp on ECDU ; appon A.

Sir Sabyn is slain on the Wall.

Fol. 17 b.

Sir Sabyn scales the wall, and is killed.

At eche kernel was cry ⁏ & quasschyng of wepne,
& many burne atte brayd ⁏ brayned to deþ. 1192
Sir Sabyn of Surrye ⁏ whyle þe saute laste,
Leyþ a ladder to þe wal ⁏ & alofte clymyþ,
Wendeþ wyȝtly þeron, ⁏ þoȝ hym wo happned,
& vp stondiþ for ston[es] ⁏ or for steel gere. 1196
Syx he slow on þe wal, ⁏ sir' Sabyn alone;
þe seueþ hitteþ on hym ⁏ an vnhende dynte,
þat þe brayn out brast ⁏ at boþ nose-þrylles,
& Sabyn ded of þe dynt ⁏ in-to þe diche falleþ. 1200

Titus bewails his death.

Þan Tytus wepyþ for wo ⁏ & warieþ þe tyme,
Syþ he þe lede haþ lost ⁏ þat he loue scholde :
" Ffor now is a duke ded ⁏ þe douȝtiest y trowe,
þat euer stede bystrode ⁏ or any steel wered." 1204
Tytus on þe same side ⁏ setteþ an engyne,
A sowe wroȝt for þe werr', ⁏ & to þe wal dryueþ,

1191. At] In V; On C. eche] ilke AU; a add. ACU. cornell C; corner VU. At eche c.] Oueral E. was] a add. D; meche add. E. &] om. V. crassynge A; cratching V; cacchyng EDUC. wapyns A. of w.] and wepyng V. 1192. &] That C. many] a add. V. bernis D; barnes E; segge AV; manne C. atte] at þat AC; at a EDU. brayd] assavte A; saute VC. to] þe add. DU. brayned to d.] soughte (fell C) to þe grownde AVC.
1193. Than sir A. whils AU. þe] þat C. assawte AD; sege U. lastes AU.
1194. Layde AVCDU; Sette E. wallis A. &—clymb.] and clymbys one lofte A; vp for to clynbe E.
1195. Wendeþ] Wane vp AV; And wenne vp C; Wynnis D; He wynnes U; & faste vp AE. wyȝtly] om. VE. þer appon A; to þe walle V; om. CE. þoȝe] þat C; þofe þat A. happed VECDU.
1196. &] þer add. CU. stood E; stondis he A. for] on þe VC; on a DE; on U. stones] so A; wall VC; ston LEDU. or for] in his AV; al yn EDU. gere] weede VED; ware U. or—gere] al arnedde in stele C.
1197. He slow sixe ECDU. walles A; anon add. E. sir S.] om. EU; hym seluen add. VEU; hym add. A. alone] add. AE.
1198. seuent AECU; VII VD. hitt AVED; hitten (!) U apon V. on h.]

hym on the hede AE. vn-mcte A; hydous A; ryȝte a sore C. an vnh. d.] wol sore as y ȝow telle E.
1199. þat] al add. U. braynes A. brast] brayd E. brayn o. br.] brayd on (to the (with thicker ink above the line) brayn D. boþ] om. DE; his add. AE. at boþ] aboute the U.
1200. And] om. C sir add. AC. S.] was add. A. þe] þat EU. ded— dynt] dyedde at þat stroke C; and add. AC. in ACV. fallyd E; felle A.
1201. weep E. wepyþ f. w.] for sorowe wepte C. warieþ] werwyth E; cursed C. þat C. tyme] stownde AVEDU.
1202. Sithen V; Sen AU; Syns C. þat VDU. lorde AV; lyf D. lorn V; forlorne A. Syþ—lost] For he sey þe knyȝt deed E. þat] euer add. AV. he] neuer U. loue] lyve DU; lese A. loue sch.] moost louyed E. he—loue] þey thus haue hym sleyne . pyte it were þey lyue C.
1203. For] & seyde E a] the A. dede a duke C. douȝt.] on erþe add. C. y tr.] of erthe DU.
1204. vmbystrade A. any] euer A. or a.] oþer V. stele] armour C.
1205. Þan add. AVECDU. þe] þat EDU. same] om. DU. sette E; setten (!) U; to add. C. an] om. D.
1206. A scwe A; Wel EDU. A— werr] Wode nyȝe he was for wrothe C. walles A. dryueþ] caste E.

Titus breaks down the Wall. 71

þat alle ouerwalte, þer he went, ⁊ & wyes an hundred	Titus breaks down the wall,
Wer ded of þat dynt ⁊ & in þe diche lyȝten. 1208	
þan Tytus heueþ vp þe honde ⁊ & heuen kyng þonkeþ,	
þat þey þe dukes deþ ⁊ han so der' bouȝte ;	
þe Jewes praien þe pees ⁊ —þis was þe paske-euene—	and refuses terms,
& þe comelich kyng ⁊ þe keyes out rauȝten. 1212	
"Nay, traytours," quoþ Tytus ⁊ now take hem ȝourselfen,	
Ffor schal no ward on ȝour wal ⁊ vs þe way lette ;	for he has made a way into the town.
We han geten vs a gate ⁊ a[g]en ȝour wille ;	
þat schal be satled sour' ⁊ on ȝour' sory kynde ! " 1216	
Or þe ȝates wer' ȝolden ⁊ þre ȝer' byfore,	Many portents had been seen three years before.
Ouer þe cyte wer' seyn ⁊ selcouþe þynges :	
A bryȝt bren[n]yng swerd ⁊ ouer þe burwe henged	
Without hond oþer helpe ⁊ saue [of] heuen one. 1220	
Armed men in þe ayer' ⁊ vpon ost-wyse,	
Ouer þe cyte wer' seyn ⁊ sundrede tymes ;	

1207. þat] hyt add. C. all] om. DU. ouer-welterde A ; ouur-drewe C. þer] where VU ; so add. V. he] scho A ; it VUD. went] hent D. þer he w.] om. C. wyes] weres V ; wyghtis D ; Iewes C. an h.] made CV.
1208. of] with C. þat] the AVC ; his D. dynt] stroke C. dykes A. lyȝten] flowe A ; felle C ; dasshid D ; dasshen U; laften V.
Instead of these two lines we read in E :
& ouer al where it hitte . were þey neuer so stroonge,
Topseyl ouer throwyd & in þe dich fyllyn.
1209. heueþ] lifte E ; holdeth C. þe] his AVECDU. handis ACU. heuen k.] all-myȝty god C ; he add. A. thankyd E.
1210. þey] he D ; om. U. þe] de (!) C. þe d.] sere Sabyncs EDU. der] now add. A. hase AD. so der (thei add. U). han (hath D) VECUD. ybough (!) E ; aboght D.
1211. þan þe E. Iewes] panne add. V. prayede AVED ; hym add. C; þat prynce add. A. þe] a U ; of AECD: for V. was] at add. A. paske] ester C. euene] tyme A. þis—euene] for so yhurt þei were E ; to passe fro pyne (the deth U) DU.
1212. And] to add. AVECDU. þe] that A. out] þey CU. rauȝten] kasten C. out r.] delyueryd E.
1213. Nay] False C. now] om. U. takes AV ; kepe E.
1214. For] There C ; om. V. wardis

A. on] of ED. ȝour] the AVCD ; þis EU. walles A. way] wallis A. the wayes vs U.
1215. For we E. geten] hoten D. a] om. ED. gate] way C ; al add. E. aȝen] agains V ; aȝens ECDU ; aȝen L ; mawgrethe A. ȝour] good add. C ; owen add. U.
1216. & þat E. be s.] satell DU ; sytte C ; ȝow reewe E ; full add. CDU. sour] sore EC ; forsothe V ; one ȝoure selfe and A. on—kynde] & al ȝoure kynde after E.
1217. ȝitt or AV ; And ore CDU. ȝolden] ȝette A ; geten C. wer ȝ.] vnshette were V ; was add. A. a-for D ; aforne U. þre ȝ. byf.] all the thre (om. AV) ȝere (ȝeris A) tynne AVC.
Thre ȝer be fore . þe town was yȝuld-yn E.
1218. þe c.] it E. wer] was A. seyn] sere add. A ; many add. U. selc.] wundurful E ; meruelous C. sightis ED.
1219. brennyng] so AVECDU ; brendyng (!) L. burue] town E ; cyte C. hanges VDU ; hange A.
1220. With owttyn AVU. hond] hold VU ; hooldyng ECD. helpe or holde A. saue] but E. of] so AECDU ; þe L ; om. V. heuen] god VEU ; hem (!) D ; is add. V. alone ECD ; ovne V.
1221. Also armedde C. appon A ; ost] wondir V. vpon o.] in (on C) þe beste ECDU. wyes (!) A.
1222. Werin (Was A) ouer the cete A. sundrede] many sundvy V ; in sundry DU ; sere certayne A ; in many dyuerse E ; at certeyne C. tyme EU.

A calf aȝen kynde ! calued in þe temple
& eued an ewe-lombe ! at [þe] offryng-tyme.   1224

A prophet had foretold the coming woe.

A wye on þe wal ! cried wonder heyȝe,
"Voys fram est & fram west ! & fram þe four wyndis,"
& sayd : "Wo, wo, wo ! worþ on ȝou boþe,
Jerusalem, þe Jewen toun, : & þe joly temple!"   1228

He now speaks again, Fol. 18 a. and is killed on the wall.

Ȝit sayþ þe wye on þe walle ! o word mor.
"Wo to þis worldly wone ! & wo to my-selue!"
& deyd, whan he don hadde, ! þrow dynt of [a] slynge,
& haplich was had away, ! how, wyst I neuere.   1232
& þan þey deuysed hem ! & vengaunce hit helde,

The Jews attribute their defeat to the murder of St. James.

& wyten her wo ! þe wronge þat þey wroȝte
Whan þey brutned in þe burwe ! þe byschup seint Jame,
Noȝt wolde acounte hit for Crist, ! þe car þat þey hadde;
Bot vp ȝeden her ȝates ! [þey] ȝelden hem alle,   1237
Without brunee & briȝt wede, ! in her bar chertes;

1223. *calf*] *al* add. D. *agaynes* AVDEU. *þe*] *thaire* A.
1224. *eued*] *had* A. *&—ewe*] *An ewe euede a* V; and *an ewe was euedd* C; and *there cuyd (yeuyd* D; *yeined* U) *an ewe* EDU. *lombe*] om. DC. *at*] *in* EU. *þe*] *so* AV ECU; om. LD. *offerande* A.
1225. *Also a* ED; *And a* U. *wye*] *wight* D; *man* EC; *cryede* add. AV. *wallis* AE. *cried*] om. AV. *wondirly* VC; *wondirfully* A; *wel* D. *heye*] *lowde* AVC. *cried w. h.*] *was weylyng (walkyng* U) *þat tyme* EU.
1226. *fro* A; *of* V. *&*] *voice* A. *fro* A; *of* V. *& fr. þe*] *voice fra (of* V) AV. *wyndes*] *halues* A. This line is omitted in ECDU.
1227. *sayd*] *cryed* E. *wo wo wo*] *wo wo* V. *wurgh* (!) E. *on*] *vppon* V; *to* EDU. *ȝou*] om. V. *worþ—boþe*] *lyȝte on ȝou all at ones* C. *And wo be to ȝow alle and wo appon ȝowe worthe* A.
1228. *ȝewes* VC. *þe I.*] *and the Iewes the* A. *Ier.—toun*] *To setle Ier.* D; *The gentil Ier.* U; *Ier. þe gentyl* E. *joly*] *fayre* E; om. A. (*In* add. C.) *þe same tyme (þat* add. A) *the towne was taken (wonnen* A) *& graunted (tane* A; *ȝolden* C) add. VAC.
1229. *sayd* VUDC. *wyȝte* CD. *walles* A ȝit—wal'e] *& ȝit ofte tyme he seyde*

E. *o*] *a-nother* C; *þis ilk* D; *thyes* U; *þese wunder* E. *wordes* EU.
1230. *worldly*] *worthy* VEDU; *wordy* C; *worthiliche* A. *won*] *place* C; *town* E. *my*] *hym* V.
1231. *&*] *He* C. *deyd*] *dede* V; *anon* add. E. *had doon* E; *had said* V. *þrow*] *with* ECDU; *þe* add. AC. *dynt*] *strook* EC. *a*] so AVUDCE; om. L.
1232. *haplich was*] *was in haste* CDU. *hapl. w. h.*] *was anon ybore* E. *away*] *but* add. E. *I*] *þey* C. *wyst I n.*] *no man wyste* EU.
1233. *&*] om. EUD. *avisid* DU. *deu. hem*] *supposyde* E; *there of* add. U; *wel* add. D. *&*] *þat* E. *hit h.*] *schulde falle* E.
ll. 1234—1236 are omitted in EDU; ll. 1233—1236 in C; ll. 1232—1236 in AV.
1237. *Bot*] *Than* A; *And* DU; om. VC. *ȝeden*] *wente* C; *held* D; *yelden* U. *Bot vp ȝ.*] *Thei dode vp* E. *her*] *the* AVECD. *ȝates*] *þanne* add. E. *anone* add. AVC. *þey*] so AVC; *&* LCUDE. *ȝolden* AVECU. *thaym* A.
1238. *With owttyn* AVCU. *bremye* (!) V; *brenyes* A; *&*] *or* AV. *br. &*] *any* CDU. *wede*] *gere* A. *briȝt w.*] *armour* C; *but* add. C. *W.—wede*] *& owt comyn naked* E. *thaire* AV. *in her b.*] *al bar in (to* D) *her* DU; *alle in her* E. *chertes*] *serkes* AC.

Ffram none tille þe merke nyȝt ⁒ neuer ne cesed,
Bot man after man ⁒ mercy bysouȝt. 1240
Tytus into þe toun · takeþ his wey : *Titus enters the town,*
Myȝt no man st[e]ken [i]n þe stret ⁒ for stynke of ded corses ;
þe peple in þe pauyment ⁒ was pite to byholde, 1243
þat wer' enfamy[n]ed for defaute ⁒ whan hem fode wanted.
Was noȝt on ladies lafte ⁒ bot þe lene bones,
þat wer' fleschy byfor' ⁒ & fayr' on to loke ;
Burges with balies ⁒ as barels or þat tyme,
No gretter þan a grehounde ⁒ to grype on þe medil. 1248
Tytus tarieþ noȝt for þat, ⁒ bot to þe temple wendiþ, *and goes to the temple.*
þat was rayled þe roof ⁒ with rebies grete,
With perles & peritotes, ⁒ alle þe place ferde
As glowande gledfur' ⁒ þat on gold st[r]ikeþ. 1252
þe dores ful of dyemauntes ⁒ dryuen wer' þicke
& made merueylous-lye ⁒ with margeri-perles ;

1239. *Fro* AECU ; þe add. AV. *none*] *morwe* ED ; *morne* U. *tille*] *to* AVEU; *in to* C. þe] om. VEDU. *merke*] *derke* C ; om. AV. *neuer*] *thay* add. AVC. *ne*] om. VC. *cesyd þey neuere* EDU.
1240. *Bot*] *ay* add. VEU ; *euur* add. CD.
1241. *And Titus* ADU ; *Than Tytus* EC ; *Titus þanne* V. *toun*] *anon* add. E. *took* E. *his*] þe AVECDU. *ryȝte* add. CU.
1242. *Ne myght* U. *no m.*] *he* DU. *stcken*] *stonde* AVC ; *stynt* DU ; *stoken* L. *in*] *so* AVCDU ; *on* L. þe] *no* D. *stretes* V ; *stede* D ; *stoure* U. *stynkyng* D. *ded*] þe CU ; om. D. *But in no sted myȝt he longe abyde* E.
1243. *in*] *one* AVCU. *pament* AVCD. *For stench of dede bodyes . þei laye so thikke* E.
1244. *was* ADU. *enfamyned*] so VU ; *enfamyed* L ; *enfameschede* A ; *famysschcd* C. *for*] þe add. C. *faute* VC. *for def.*] *and defete* U. *enf. for def.*] *with famyne defetid* D. *þam* A ; *þey* VCD ; þe U. *fode w.*] *mete lakkede* C.
þat *for hungur sturue . for wantyng of foode* E.
1245. *Was*] þer add. C. *on*] *of* A ; *the* add. ADU ; *no* add. C. *lad.*] *likham* DU. *noȝt on l.*] *no flessch on hem* E. *beleft* VU. þe] *thaire* A ; *only* E ; om. D. *lene*] *bare* EC ; *dede* D ; *hide and* V. *bones*] *chekes* A.
1246. *fleschely* A ; *fresshe* V. *wer ft.*]

fressh weryn DU ; *fressch foolk were* E ; *fayre were* C. *to fore* V ; *afore* ED ; *a forn* U. *fayr*] *fresshe* C. *on to l.*] *to beholde* VECD.
1247. *And b.* CU ; *The b.* D. *with*] *her* add. U. *baylȝes* A. *barell* V ; *beralles* (!) A. *as b.*] om. U. *or þ. t.*] *some tyme* C ; *byfor* D ; *as a-forne that* U ; *þay lukede* A ; *þat hadde* E.
1248. *Were no* V. *No—greh.*] *Were as smal as grehoundes* E ; þan add. D. *on*] *in* AVECDU. *myddis* AEDU.
1249. *Than T.* EDU. *taryed* ECDU. *for þ.*] om. EDU. *went* EDU ; ȝode C.
1250. *was*] *all* add. AV. *rayl.*] *arraied* U ; *in* add. C. þat—*roof*] *Of which þe roof al was* E. *rubyes* AVEC DU ; *full* add. A. *grete*] *ryche* C ; *arayed* E.
1251. *d.*] *with* add. AC. *petitotes* E ; *baleis* V ; *precyous stonys* A ; þat add. V. *ferde*] *sette* C ; *pight* DU ; *ouer* A. *alle—ferde*] *& many bryȝte stones* E.
1252. *As*] *The* D ; *the* add. A. *glemande* A. *glow. gled*] *glcnende as golde* V. *As glow. gl.*] *That glystered as coles in þe* C. *As—fur*] *That schyned in þe sunne* E. þat] *whan it* E ; om. C. *on*] þe add. CD. *strikeþ*] so AEDU *flikes* V ; *ryche* C ; *stikeþ* L.
1253. *ful of*] *with* CE. *were*] om. U ; *full* add. AU. *picke*] *fast* U.
1254. *& m.*] *Ynade* D ; *also* add. C ; *full* add. VD. *meru.*] *gynfully* V. *& m. m.*] *And full mervellously* A ; *meruelyche ywrought* E. *mariorye* D.

Destruction of the Temple.

<table>
<tr><td></td><td>Derst no candel be [ky]nde, ⁑ whan clerkes scholde rise,</td><td></td></tr>
<tr><td></td><td>So wer' þey lemaunde lyȝt ⁑ & as a lampe schonen.</td><td>1256</td></tr>
<tr><td></td><td>þe Romayns wayten on þe werke, ⁑ warien þe tyme,</td><td></td></tr>
<tr><td></td><td>þat euer so precious a place ⁑ scholde persche for her' synne.</td><td></td></tr>
<tr><td>He orders the treasure to be removed, and the building destroyed.</td><td>Out þe tresour to take, ⁑ Tytus commaundyþ,
Doun bete þe bilde ⁑ brenne hit in-to grounde.</td><td>1260</td></tr>
<tr><td></td><td>þer was plente in þe place ⁑ of precious stonys,</td><td></td></tr>
<tr><td></td><td>Grete gaddes of gold, ⁑ who-so grype lyste,</td><td></td></tr>
<tr><td></td><td>Platis, pecis of peys, ⁑ pulsched vessel,</td><td></td></tr>
<tr><td></td><td>Bassynes of brend gold ⁑ & oþer bryȝt ger',</td><td>1264</td></tr>
<tr><td></td><td>Pelours, masly made ⁑ of metals fele,</td><td></td></tr>
<tr><td>Fol. 18 b.</td><td>In cop[r]e craftly cast ⁑ & in clene seluere ;</td><td></td></tr>
<tr><td></td><td>Peynted [with] pur' gold ⁑ alle þe place was ouer ;</td><td></td></tr>
<tr><td></td><td>þe Romayns renten hem doun ⁑ & to Rome ledyn.</td><td>1268</td></tr>
<tr><td></td><td>Whan þey þe cyte han souȝt ⁑ vpon þe same wyse,</td><td></td></tr>
</table>

1255. þurt V ; There thurt U ; It nedyd E. be om. E. kynde] so U ; kindelled VD ; tende L ; lyȝt E. Derst—cende] Thurghe thase kanells of kynde A ; The clerkes hadde none oþur lyȝte C. clerkes sch.] þat þey dede C. whan cl. sch.] clerkes (see add. V) to AVD ; to clercs forto U. aryse E ; areyse D.
1256. So w. þ.] þat one ane A ; þat euer with D ; þat ouer U. lemyng D ; lemnande U. So—lem.] þat ay (euer C) lemed (þe add. C) VC ; & euermore ȝaue E. &] om. AVEDU. a l.] lampis þay AV. shyne V ; shynid DU ; shewed C. &—schonen] as it were a laumpe E.
l. 1255 is put after l. 1256 in AVEUDC.
1257. wayted C ; beheelde E. on] om. EDU. wallis A ; & add. AVECDU ; warien] cursyd EC. tyme] Iewes AVC.
1258. euer] om. EC. her] om. VECDU. þer.—synne] for thaire syn perische A.
1259. Than out DU. Out þe tr.] The tresour a way C. comaundyd EC.
1260. A-doun U ; And down AV ; to add. V. þe] that A. bolde U ; beldynge A. brenne—grounde] and brenne it to þe erthe V ; and a-doun brenne U ; to the bare erthe A.
& þe temple to þe ground . anon to be bete E.
Instead of l. 1260 we read in D the following two :

And ouir tilt the temple tytly at onys,
A-doun brayd þei þe bielde & bete it to ground.
1261. The (!) E. was] were A ; grete add. U. þe] that A ; om. V. in þe pl. of perlis D ; om. EU. of] & D ; many] add. V.
ll. 1260 and 1261 are omitted in C.
1262. goddes EC. lyste] myght U. who—lyste] and poleschede vesselle A.
1263. peys] pris UDE. & add. VE. vessel ypulssched EDU. This line is omitted in AC.
1264. brend] full bryghte A ; clene C. Bas. of br.] Besauntes byes of ED. oþer] mekill AV. bryȝt] ryche EC. gere] thynges E.
1265. Pelers AVE ; Pylers CDU. massylye CDU ; massally A ; massy VE. metalle ADUC ; marbul E ; full ad.. AECDU. fele] fyne ACU ; riche ED.
1266. In c.] so AV ; copre] courpese E ⁑ cuppes CDU ; In coppe (!) L. cast] coruen A ; caruedde C. & in] al of ECD ; os of U. sel.] golde C.
1267. wiþ] so AVECDU ; as L. pur g.] perre ECDU. was alle þe place ouer A. was] om. VECDU.
1268. renden C. thaym A ; it V. a-doun DU. leddyn AVECDU.
1269. had AVCD ; þey—han] þe cyte was E. appon A ; on CU ; in VDE. þe] this A. same] selfe AV.

The Romans plunder the City.

Telle couþe no tonge ⁊ þe tresours þat þei þer founden,   *They take great treasures from the city.*
Jewels for joly men, ⁊ je[mewes] riche,
Ffloreyns of [fyne] gold ⁊ no freke wanted,   1272
Riche pelour' & pane, ⁊ princes to wer',
Besantes, bies of gold, ⁊ broches & rynges,
Clene cloþes of selke ⁊ many carte-fulle,
Wele wanteþ no wye, ⁊ bot wale[þ] what hym lykeþ.   1276
Now masouns & mynours han þe molde souȝte,   *They destroy the city walls,*
With pykeyse & ponsone ⁊ persched þe walles,
Hewen þrow hard ston ⁊ hadde hem to grounde,
þat alle derkned þe diche ⁊ for doust of þe pouder'.   1280
So þey wrouȝten at þe wal ⁊ alle þe woke-tyme,
Tille alle þe cyte was serched ⁊ & souȝt al aboute,
Maden wast at [a] wappe ⁊ þer þe walle stode,
Boþe in temple & in tour ⁊ alle þe toun ouer.   1284 *and the temple.*
Nas no ston in þe stede ⁊ stondande alofte,
Morter' ne m[o]de walle ⁊ bot alle to mulle fallen—

1270. tongez A. *Cowde no tunge telle* E. *tresoure* AVECDU. þei] þe V. þer] om. AVECDU. *fande* AU; *hadde* C.
1271. men] *and* add. AECDU. *jemewes*] so ECDU; *gemmys* AV; *jewels* L. *full* add. AVU.
1272. *And flor.* AV. *of*] *full* add. A. *fyne*] so AVEDUC; *rede* L. *gold*] *ywis* add. E. *non* E. *freke*] *man* EC; *ne* add. AU.
1273. *Ne ryche* CD : *Nc* EU. *pelewes* C. &] *ne* EU; *of* D. *pane*] *palle* AVED; *for* add. AC.
1274. bies] *bedis* A. *Bes. b. of*] *Bedes of fyn* E.
1275. *Clene*] *Loonge* E. *selke*] *golde* AC. *many*] om. V. *cartes* VCU; *to* add. V.
1276. *Wele*] *Wherof* V. *wanttide* A VED. *Wele w.*] *Welthe lakkede* C. *wye*] *wight* D; *man* EC. *wele* A; *welde* DU; *chese* V; *hadde* E; *wale* L. *what h.*] *þat hem* D. *lykede* AVD. *hym l.*] *he wulde* E. *wale—lykeþ*] *toke of þe beste* C.
1277. *moneours* (!) D. *molde*] *erthe* C. þe *moolde han* EDU.
1278. *pykes* A. &] *with* add. A. *pons.*] *pecas* A; *oþer crafte* V. *pyk. & pons.*] *pounsons* (*pounces* E; *poncys* D) & *pycoyses* (*pikeis* U) EDU. *perced* AV UDE. This line is omitted in C.
1279. *Hewid* E. *þrow*] *down* A; *the*

add. AED. *hard*] om. E. *stanys* AE and add. AVEC. *hadde*] *drof* V; *hurlyd* F.U; *hurtled* D. *þam* A; om. DU. *to*] þe add. D.
1280. þat] *For* U. *derked* VDU. *derkned þe d.*] þe *diches derk were* E. *for*] *of* AV. *of þe*] *and of* AV.
1281. at] *al* D. *wallis* AE. *woke*] *wlank* DU.
1282. *alle*] om. ED. þe] *riche* add. V. *was*] *were* E; *is* DU; *so* add. AV. *yseergyd* E; *serued* V; *seruede* A; *cerclid* D; & *souȝt al*] om. AV.
1283. *Maden w.*] *They wastede clene* A. *a*] so A; þe L. *Maden—wappe*] *Ouer al þey made waast* E. *The vightes* (*wyes* U) *made al wast* DU; *All they made pleine* V. *walles* AEU. *stonden* U. ll. 1280—1283 are omitted in C.
1284. *Boþe*] om. E. *in*] þe AD; *In* þe E; om. VC. *in*] *the* AD; *in* þe E; om. VC. *tour*] *town* E; *and* add. AVE. *ouer*] *after* A. *alle—ouer*] & *in þe toures ek* E.
1285. *Thare was* AVC; *Was* EDU. *ston*] *standande* add. A. þe] *that* DUC; *no* ED. *stede*] *place* C. *stondaunt* V; *liggyng vp* E; om. A. *al.*] *lefte* AC; *on oþer* ED.
1286. *mode*] so AVE; *made* LD. *alle*] om. V. *to*] þe add. E. *mulle*] *mukke* V; *mold* DE. *fal.*] *ȝode* AE; *fellyn* V. This line is omitted in U.

Noþer tymbr' ne tre, ⸋ temple ne oþer,
Bot doun betyn & brent ⸋ into blake erþe. 1288

The site of the temple is ploughed with salt.
& whan þe temple was ouertourned, ⸋ Tytus commaundys
In plowes to putte ⸋ & alle þe place erye,
Suþ sow hit with salt, ⸋ & seide þis wordes:
"Now is þis stalwourþe stede ⸋ distroied for euere." 1292

Titus enquires from Pilate of the death of Christ.
Tytus suþ sett hym ⸋ on a sete riche,
As juge Jewes to jugge, ⸋ justise hym-self.
Criour'[s] callen hem forþ ⸋ as hy þat Crist slowen,
& beden Pilat apere ⸋ þat prouost was þanne. 1296
Pilat proffriþ hym forþ, ⸋ apered at þe barr',
& he frayneþ þe freke ⸋ alle with fair' wordis,
Whan Crist of dawe was don ⸋ & to þe deþ ȝede,
Of þe he[þ]yng þat he hadde, ⸋ & þe hard woundis,† 1300
Þan melys þe man ⸋ & þe matere tolde,
How alle þe ded was don, ⸋ whan he deþ þoled.

1287. *Neyther* ED; *in* add. D. *ne*] *nor* DU; *in* add. D. *tre*] *on* add. V. *temple ne o.*] *of town ne of temple* E.
ll. 1286 and 1287 are omitted in C.
1288. *into*] *to* ACU; *all to* VD; *the* add. AECU. *blake*] *bare* ED; *harde* C.
1289. *&*] om. AVECDU. *was*] *is* U. *ouertelte* VDU; *ouer-tytt* A; *ouer-throwe* E; *ouer-kaste* C. *comandide* AECD.
1290. *plewes* A; *for* add. A. *all*] om. C. *place*] *to* add. A. *ere* VC; *erith* U; *eryed* E.
1291. *Sithen* V; *And seth* DA; *And sen* U; *& thanne* E; *And aftur* C; *þay* add. AV. *sew* AVEUDC. *scyden* VU. *þis*] *same* add. A.
1292. *is*] om. V. *stalw. st.*] *worthy place* C. *þis stalw. st.*] *þe temple & þe town* E. *stroyede* ACDU; *is* add. V.
1293. *Sythen* T. A; *And sithenne* V; *Thanne* T. ECDU. *hym*] *self* add. DU. *sett h.*] *hym seelf sat* E; *was sett* AVC. *on*] *in* AVC. *a*] om. AU. *setill* AU; *seege* V; *cheyre* C; *full* add. ACU. *on—riche*] *as a iugge* E.
1294. *As juge*] *Os alle the* U; *Alle þe* E; *And al þe* D. *to j.*] *for to deeme* E. *As—jugge*] *To juggen þe (thase* A) *Iewes* AVC; *a* add. AV; *als* add. ACD. *just. h.*] *þat laaft were alyue* E.
1295. *Criours*] so VCDU; *Criour* (!) L; *And bedells* A; *& E. called*] AVE

CDU. *thaym* A; *hym* D. *forþ*] *afore hym* E. *as*] om. EC. *þay* AVDU; *tho* EC.
1296. *bade* VED; *that* (!) C. *bad* P. *a.*] *Pilate apperide* AU. *was prouoste* CU. *þanne*] *þat tymne* E.
1297. *profr. h. f.*] *com forth þo* E; *&* add. EC. *peerid* EC; *apperis* AVDU. *þe*] om. D.
1298. *he*] *Titus* AVEC. *fraynis þe f.*] *fraynid þe f.* D; *apposyd hym* E; *askedde hym* C. *with*] *in* UD. This line follows 1296 in D.
1299. *How when* A; *How þat* C; *How* EDU. *of*] *on* (!) DU. *of d.*] *to þe deth* C. *of—don*] *was doon on þe cros* E. *&*] *howe* add. C. *þe*] om. ADU. *deþ*] *he* add. C. *to-ȝede*] *ther vp on yslawe* E.
1300. *& of* E. *hething* VDU; *hebynges* A; *betyng* E; *rebukynge* C; *heuyng* L. *þat*] om. D. *&*] *of* add. ECDU. *þe*] *his* EC. *hard*] *depe* E.
& of þe tene þat hym tidde telle hym þe soþe add. L.
1301. *meuedde* CU; *mynnys* D. *þe*] *that* ACU. *&*] *all* add. C. *mat.*] *manere* AVDU. *taulde* (!) A; *tellis* D.
Tho answeryd Pylat . & toolde þe soþhe E.
1302. *alle*] om. D. *he*] *þat Crist* D. *whan he*] *and how that Crist* U; *the* add A. *deþ*] om. DU. *þoled*] *suffrrde* C. *deþ þ.*] *was ytake* E.

The Jews are sold into Slavery. 77

For þritty penyes in a poke ⸫ his postel hym solde,   Fol. 19 a.
So was he bargayned & bouȝt, ⸫ & as a beste quelled.   1304   Pilate tells how he was sold for 30 pence.
"Now corsed be he," quoþ þe kyng ⸫ "þat þe cate made;
He wexe marchaunte amys, ⸫ þat þe money fenged,
To sille so precyous a prince ⸫ for penyes so fewe,
[Thoghe ilke a ferthynge had bene ful florence an hundrethe.]
Bot I schal marchaundise make ⸫ in mynde of þat oþer, 1309
þat schal be heþyng to hem ⸫ or I hennes passe:
Alle þat here bodyes wol by ⸫ or bargaynes make,
By lower' pris for to passe, ⸫ þan þey þe prophete solde." 1312
He made in myddel of [þe] ost ⸫ a market to crye,—   Titus sells the Jews at 30 for a penny.
Alle þat cheffare wolde chepe ⸫ chepis to haue,
Ay for a peny of pris, ⸫ who-so pay wolde,
þrytty Jewes in a þrom ⸫ þrongen in ropis.   1316
So wer' þey bargayned & bouȝt ⸫ & broȝt out of londe,
Neuer suþ [on] þat syde ⸫ cam segge of hem after;
Ne non þat leued in her' lawe ⸫ scholde in þat londe dwelle,

1303. poke] purse AED; bagge C. apoostel EC.
1304. So] Thus C. bargande A. quelled] sleyne C. & thanne was he take . & to þe deth ydemyd E.
1305. Now] om. VECDU. Acursed EU. quoþ] seyde E. þe] that A. þe k.] Tytus EC. þe] that AEU. cate] achat V; akate DU; acade E; bargan A; countes C. made] wroght DU.
1306. wexe] was DU; a add. AECD. am.] of mysse V. þat] when he AVECD. þe] that AD; om. VE. fonged VED; fonge U; toke CA.
1308. So ACV; om. LEDU. ful] om. A; worth VC. hundrethe] M¹ V.
1309. Bot I schal] I wyll now C; a add. A. Bot—march.] A marchaundyse now (om. DU) weele y make EDU.
1310. & þat E. to] till V. thaym A; all add. U. heþyng to h.] a fowle rebuke to ȝowe C. be—hem] the Iewes reewe E. hythen A. passe] wende V.
1311. Alle] Who E. thaire A. weele here bodyes E; her wyll bodyes C. bye wole D. bargaine V; marchaundyse C; of þam add. A. or b. m.] y graunte hem þis tyme E.
1312. By] For E; To C. a add. A. low.] lasse E. forto] on to D; to U; or j A. forto p.] hem to haue E. þey] om. V. þe pr.] oure god E; our prins DU. saulde A; om. V.

1313. He m.] Thanne made he E. in] a C; the add. AED. myddes AVCD; mydde E. of] om. VC. þe] so AVECD; om. L. ost] cete A; town E; market D. a m.] om. ECD. to] a D; om. E. This line is omitted in U.
1314. wille U. Alle—chepe] That alle that at that faire wolde be A; grete add. C. chepen U; chepe C. forto U. Who wulde eny Iewes bygge . þat he come anon E.
1315. Ay] Euur CD : & haue E; om. A. of] om. U. of pr.] alone E; chaffer add. U. who so] ȝif he E. paye who so C. pay] om. U.
1316. Alwey thrytty E. in] on DU. þrom] rope C. in a þ.] om. E. in] with D. þrongen in r.] bounden to gedur C; ybounde togydre with roopes E.
1317. Thus E. thei were U; they hym D. barg. & b.] bought & soold E. broȝt] dreven V. & br.] with bale A. of] þat add. E. londe] lyfe C.
1318. And neuer AEC; þat neuer V. suþ] sithen VE; aftur C; om. A. on] so VC; in D; of AU; out of L. sede A. out—syde] there aȝen E. cam] thare add. A. segge] manne C; non E. thaym A. after] more VC. hem m.] ther kynde E. This line is omitted in U.
1319. Ne] Nor C. non] man V. leueth E; lyueth U; lyvid D. in] on AVC. thaire A; þat VDU. laye AV. schal ED; shul U.

> þat tormented trewe God ⁊ þus Titus commaundyþ. 1320
> Josophus, þe gentile clerke, ⁊ a-jorneyd was to Rome :
> þer of þis mater & mo ⁊ he made fayr' bokes.

Pilate is put in prison, and dies at Viterbo.
> & Pilat to prisoun was do, ⁊ to pyne for euere,
> At Viterbe, þer he veniaunce ⁊ & vile deþ þoled. 1324
> þe wye þat hym warded, ⁊ wente on a tyme,
> Hym-self fedyng with frut ⁊ & feffyt hym with a per',
> & forto paren his pere, he praieþ hym ȝerne
> Of a knyf, & þe kempe ⁊ kest hym a trenchour, 1328
> & with þe same he schef ⁊ hymself to þe herte,
> & so þe kaytif as his kynde ⁊ corsedlich deied.

The Romans return to Rome.
> Whan alle was demed & d[on]e, ⁊ þei drow vp tentis,
> Trossen her' tresour ⁊ & trompen vp þe sege, 1332
> Wenten syngyng away ⁊ & han her' wille forþred,
> & hom riden to Rome. ⁊ Now rede ous our' lord !

> Hic terminatur bellum judaicum apud Jerusalem.

1320. *torment* A ; *turnementyd* (!) E. *god*] *Cryst* E. *þat—god*] *Man, womman ne childe* V. *þus*] *so* D ; *and so* AE ; om. V. *comaundede* ECD.
1321. *Saue Ios.* E. *gentile*] *gynful* D. *clerke*] *Iew* EU ; om. D. *a-joynede* A. *was joyned* V.
1322. *per*] *And there* A ; & E ; *þat* V ; om. DC. *maters* AD. *more* C ; *there* add. E. *he*] om. V. *he m.*] *to make* C. *fayr*] *many* D ; om. E.
1323. *Pil.*] *in* add. V. *was do*] *putte* C ; om. V. *putt was to* (*in* D) *presone* AD ; *was* (om. U) *to prison put* EU. *pyne*] *ther* add. EC.
1324. *At*] & ED. *Vittern* A ; *Vettury* V ; *Vyan* ECDU. *he*] om. A. *þer—ven.*] *a vyl* (*fowle* C) *deeth* ECDU. & *v. d.*] & *vengeaunce he* CDU ; *for his synnes* E. *þoled*] *suffred* EC ; *tuke* A.
ll. 1825—1330 are omitted in AVEC DU.
1331. *And when* A. *these d. w.*] *these doomes were* E. *done*] *so* AVECDU ;

dempte L. *drow*] *tuke* A. *vp*] *her* add. EDU ; *thaire* add. A.
1332. *Trussed* EDU ; *They trussede* C ; *vp* add. AEDU. *thaire* AV. *trumpyd* EACDU. *þe s.*] *her segges* U.
1333. *And wents* C. *thaire wills* A. &*—forþred*] *whanne þey her wille haddyn* V ; & *lefte woo there* EDU ; & *lafte woo byhynde* C.
1334. &] om. C. *hom*] *hool* E ; om. A ; *þey* add. C. *now*] *thare* A. *rede*] *helpe* C. *now—lord*] *yblessyd be god almyȝty* E. *Amen* add. E.
§ *Destruccio Ierlm per Vaspasianum & Titum* add. V ;
Explicit la sege de Ierusalem.
R. Thornton dictus qui scripsit sit benedictus. Amen.
add. A ; *Jesu joyne* (*joye* C) *hem & vs with joye in his blysse* add. CUD. *And to welthe* (*wele* U) *hem wysse that wryten* (*reden* U) *this geste* add. CU ; *That wrote þis geest to his wele he hym wisse* add. D.

APPENDIX I

Corrections in text, ll. 1–580.

1. The poem begins on f. 1b. *Tyberyus.*
4. *jewen.*
6. *Galile* †.
21. For *ouer* read *on.*
23. *wynter* †.
24. *Or* †.
26. *gate* †.
27. *in* †.
34. F. 2a begins here.
36. *in.*
45, 81. *Sensteus.*
91. *worlich* †.
123. The *es* of *piles* is written over an erasure of the same length.
127. myracles †.
134. *dempt*e †, MS. *dempt*er.
137. suwed †.
149. *h*is.
150. MS. *jħu.*
168. *hele* †.
211. MS. *clergyf.*
225. *warpe* †.
229. xij.
243. *h*is.
256. *symple* †.
260. *Romaynes* †, *Rome* †.
277. *brynnyis.*
294. *tounnes.*
295. *vppe.*
300. MS. *jħc, rouke. ȝou* †.
309. *Josophus.*
320. *Ierusalem.*

80   *Appendix I.*

325. MS. *Thoppyn.*
328. Read [*two*]; MS. *also.*
342. xij.
345. *bischopes.*
349. *Crist* †.
358. xij.
385. *vp.*
378. *fauted* : *u* is obscured by a smudge.
408. *sprongyn.*
425. *Waspasia*[*n*].
429. *fanward.*
469. *fyne.*
484. *ne* †.
489. *k*[*ny*]ȝ*t.*
491. *come* †.
511. MS. *prolate.*
537. *beste* †.
576. *to-gedre* : this curled *r* is elsewhere left unexpanded.
577. *hem.*

Corrections in Collations to ll. 1–580.

Title : *The Sege of Ierusalem* C.
7. *oft* om. C.
21. *tarieth* D.
25. For *dai* read *an.*
35. Add þis] *that* A.
44. *of miehte* A.
45. 81. U, which distinguishes *u* from *n*, has *Seustius.*
56. This line is repeated after 60 in D.
69. Read *those* add A.
81. *Systiens* D; *Sencyus* C, *Senstyus* E, *Systenis* A.
83. For *leue* L read *lord leue* L.
96. *Oper* om. U.
105. *troche* A.
114. For *byfore*, 117, read *byfor*, 116.
133. *of* has also been altered.
139. *cheytifs* D.
146. *Thadee* U.
155. For *not* read *nat.*
156. *yknowen* DUC.

Appendix I.

168. om. C.
173. *al worpen* U.
174. *Tytus,* over þe *kyng* erased E.
186. Read *levyn* D.
204. In U this follows 1. 206. A correction is made in the margin.
213. Read *by* add. ADU.
215. The addition in D is above the line, and meant to take the place of *and*.
230. The ED reading replaces this line, and is not an addition.
238. Read *felle* A.
240. *yre* D.
254. Read *thankynges* C, *those* A.
257. *vernache,* with *h* corrected to *l* C.
258. Read *worshipfully* C.
280. *gryng* D.
281. For *shift* read *shuft* U.
282. *tolterande* A.
291. *sawders* C.
293. Read *Dỹner* C.
294. *be* om. U.
304. Omit *londes* E.
310. For *folk* read *fook* E.
318. *pound* added in margin in different hand C.
329. *paviloun* D.
335. ȝit om. E.
340. Read *nowe* U.
348. *bout* corrected in second hand to *withowte* D.
358. *eny* E.
363. Read *a corps* D.
364. *chyviteyn* D.
378. *morowe| morn* U.
379. *hem myntes* UD.
380. Read *they sent* EDC.
392. *fawcoune* C.
401. *rise) ri* + about two letters erased U.
402. Read *loue* UC. For *wynne* read ȝ*elde*.
408. For 414 read 412.
412. For *beste* read *leste* C.
413. Read *pensalls* A.
428. For *that* read *thas* A.

439. *blewen* CDE.
440. *Passus iij* C in margin.
444. *pauyce* C, *paueschis* A.
450. [An] & L; *pousand* om. ACEU. *harnays*] *harnes* C.
454. *felde*] & add. C.
466. *gogeons* U.
469. *chabokles* L.
472. *perle*] *peerles* E.
479. *folk* UC.
508. Read *of*] *on* D.
511. *prolate* L.
519. For *loued* C read *leued* C.
521. *blewe* ACD.
522. Read *vndur steel wedes* EDU.
524. *Kny3tes*] & add. C. For *kaste* read *caste*.
528. wepen C.
537. Read *telles*] U.
545-6. Transposed in A.
545. Read *shyned* C.
549. *voward* C.
551. *men*] om. D.
564. Read *on bakke* C.
568. *on a*] *oon on* C.
575. *storte*, *o* probably changed from *e*. *waxen* U.
577. Read *hem*.
578. *on* U.
579. *alone* add. D.

APPENDIX II

Vindicta Salvatoris, MS. B.M. Harl. 495, pp. 3–5.
(Some variants are added from Tischendorf, *Evangelia Apocrypha*, MSS. B.M. Roy. 9 A. xiv and Roy. 8 E. xvii (denoted by T, A, E, respectively), and the A.S. version.)

De capcione Jerusalem a Tito et Vespasiano.

In diebus imperij Tiberij Cesaris, [Herode] [1] tetrarcha, sub Poncio [Pilato] [2] Iude traditus fuit Dominus zelatus a Tiberio. In diebus illis erat quidam Titus subregulus Tiberij in regno Aquitannico in ciuitate que dicitur Burdegala. Erat enim insanus in sua nare dextera qui a cancro dilaceratam habebat in tantum ut faciem teneret vsque ad 5 oculos. Exiuit homo quidam de Judea nomine Nathan filius Nahim; erat enim Ysmaelita negocians de terra in terram, de mari in mare, de terminis in terminos orbis terrarum. Missus est enim [3] a[d] Tiberi[um] imperatore[m] [3] ad portandum ei magnam pecuniam ad vrbem Rome. Erat enim Tiberius insanus uulneratus quasi nouem 10 annis [4] a lepra. Voluit autem Nathan pergere ad Romam cum nauigio per Tyberym flumen. Inflauit ventus que dicitur auster et impulit nauigium illius et deduxit eum ad septentrionalem plagam per mare. At illi recuperantes ubi Garrona fluuium ingreditur mare exierunt ad ciuitatem que dicitur Burdegala. Et vidit Titus nauigium et 15 cognouit [5] quod transmarinis partibus uenisset. Mirati sunt omnes dicentes, "Nunquam talia vidimus." Jussit Titus uenire ad seipsum et interrogauit eum dicens, "Quisnam es?" "Et dixit ei," "Ego sum Nathan filius Nahim de gente Grecorum missus ad vrbem Romanam iubente Pilato ad portandum Tyberio imperatori pactum tributi eius 20 de Iudea. Et irruit ventus validus in mare et deduxit me in loco isto et nescio vbi sum." At illi Tytus: "Sic potuisses inuenire de aliqua re aut pigmentorum aut herbarum qui potuisset uulnus delere vlcus quod in faciem meam habeo,[6] statim ego te restituam sine dubio ante Tyberium." [6] Et iurauit illi dicens, "Viuit dominus, non possum 25

[1] *So* T.   [2] *So* TAE.   [3–3] *So* TA. MS. a tiberio imperatore.
[4] MS. *adds* uulneratus.   [5] MS. *adds* eum.
[6–6] AS. ic wolde þe to medes syllan butan ælcum twy swa gold swa sylfor swa fela swa þu woldest and eac þe to-foran Tyberie þam casere gebryngan.

83

inuenire que mihi denuncias. Set si in hijs temporibus ante fuisses in Iudea, inuenire ibi posses verum prophetam nomine Jesum Christum qui erat missus a Deo et natus ex virgine Maria vt saluaret genus humanum a peccatis eorum, qui faciebat [signa] [1] et prodigia
5 coram populo terre. Primum fecit de aqua vinum, deinde leprosos mundauit, cecos illuminauit,[2] demoniacos curauit, mortuos suscitauit, mulierem de fluxu sanguinis liberauit que per xij annos a medicis curari non potuit. De v. panibus et duobus piscibus saciavit quinque milia hominum [3]; super vndas maris siccis ambulauit pedibus et
10 talia multa mirabilia fecit quorum non est numerus. Quod cum vidissent Iudei inuidia accensi accusantes senioribus et principibus sacerdotum tradiderunt principibus propter inuideam et duxerunt eum vsque ad mortem et crucifixerunt eum et occiderunt et deponentes de lingno posuerunt in sepulcro. Hunc Deus suscitauit die tercia a
15 mortuis sicut ipse ante predixerat et manifestauit se discipulis suis in ipsa carne in qua passus est et quadraginta dies cum illis conuersatus est et videntibus illis receptus est in celum et iussit fideles suos ut baptizarentur in nomine patris et filij et spiritus sancti, Amen. Et pollicitus [est][4] illis se fore cum illis usque ad consummacionem
20 seculi. Et lxxij discipulos predicare mandauit resurreccionem suam (et [5] qui ab ante dormierant in sanctitate [6] cum ipso resurrexerunt), quia lxx et due lingue erant per mundum vel terram. Quedam uero femina nomine Veronica in terra nostra que fluxum sa[n]guinis paciebatur per xij annos nisi per ipsum curari non potuit. Et postea
25 pro amore suo uultum suum figurauit in pallio suo qui ibi omnes aduenientes infirmos hodierna die adorantes et osculantes [7] mox illos tota suauitate optata sanat a labe.[7] Et hec audiens Titus admirans dixit "Ve, ve tibi Tyberio qui uulneratus [es][8] lepra circumdatus scandale, qui tales duces misisti in terram tuam, qui occiderunt filium
30 dei, liberatorem animarum nostrarum. Verumptamen si fuissent ante faciem meam ego eos occidissem in ore gladij, et aliquos in ligno suspendissem, qui occiderunt quem oculi mei videre non fuerunt digni." Factum est autem cum hec dixisset Titus; cecidit cancrus de facie eius et restituta est caro eius sicut antea, quando pulcrior fuerat,
35 et factus est sanus. Et clamans Titus dixit, "Judex meus et rex meus,

---

[1] *So* AE.   [2] T *adds* paralyticos sanavit.
[3] T *adds* et remanserunt de fragmentis duodeam scophini.
[4] *So* A.   [5] MS. AE *add* eis.   [6] MS. A, *adds* qui.
[7-7] A. mox ditat sanitate optata. E. (infirmi) mox sanitatem optimam suscipiunt.
[8] *So* AE.

Appendix II.

ego nunquam te uidi sed quia credidi sanus factus sum. Jube me super aquas in terra natiuitatis tue venire ut faciam tibi de inimicis tuis uictoriam [1] et disperdam eos in terra ut non remaneat ex eis [min]gens [2] ad parietem. Et cum hoc dixisset ait ad Nathan. Quod signum dedit fidelibus suis credentibus in se. Ipse dixit, " Hoc iussit ut baptizarentur in aqua." Ait Titus, " Ego credo in eum qui sanum me fecit. Et tu baptiza me sicut ipse precepit et mandauit." Et iussit nathan ut baptizaretur in nomine sanctae Trinitatis.

[1] T. vindictam; AS. þæt ic mæge . . . þynne deaðˍgewrecan.
[2] *So* A.: MS. vna gens.

APPENDIX III

Higden, Polychronicon, IV. x. Rolls Series IV, pp. 426-54.
(Printed by permission of the Controller of H.M. Stationery Office.
The variants are from the 15th century English translation, MS.
Harl. 2261, printed in the Rolls Series.)

In isto conflictu peritia Romanis erat cum virtute, Judæis furor cum temeritate. Nam Vespasianus primitus, cum siccitas erat, ad urbem Jotopatem [1] accedens, omnes aquæductus obstruxit; sed Josephus interius commentum invenit, quo vestes aquis infusas
5 muris urbis suspenderet, unde paulatim vaporantibus aquis, externi crederent aquas illis non deesse ad potum, quæ sic illis abundabat ad vestimentorum lavacrum. Inde Vespasianus ictu arietis [2] murum conturbat, sed Josephus saccos paleis repletos ictibus opponens, plagam delusam emollit, nam solida melius per molliora deluduntur;
10 sed econtra Romani falces contis ligantes funes saccorum succiderunt. Josephus tamen ardenti oleo superjecto omnia machinamenta exussit; quibus reparandis instans Vespasianus in talo graviter vulneratur; quo viso tanta vis telorum ex parte Titi proruit, ut unius de sociis Josephi occipitium lapide percussum ultra tertium stadium excutere-
15 tur; fœtus etiam cujusdam mulieris gravidæ ultra dimidium stadii de alvi secreto propelleretur. Igitur rupto per Titum muro secundo,[3] inventus est Josephus inter favillas triduo dilitiscens. . . .

Vespasiano tandem ad imperium vocato, Titus filius ejus ad obsidionem Jerosolimæ dimissus, cum die quadam circa urbem
20 visendam cum sexcentis equitibus deloricatis obambularet, concluditur a tergo a Judæis exeuntibus; sed animum suum audacia exacuens, penetrato cuneo ad suos redit. Verum quia acerba odia metus plerumque comprimit, dissidentes in urbe ad tempus confœderantur. Sed et pluribus Judæorum pacem a Tito petentibus, Titus
25 dolum formidans dixit suis, "Sicut inferiorum est uti insidiis, sic fortiorum est cavere insidias, ne virtuti illudat dolus." Quassato

[1] a cite callede Ioppen. [2] with gunnes and with oþer engines.
[3] adds of Ierusalem.

Appendix III.

ergo cum ariete muro primo, consulit Titus provide pugnare, ne, si desit consilium, fortitudo temeraria videatur. In ipsa quoque victoria magis timendum est, nam superiorem cum inferiore pariter perire victi triumphus est. Quassato tandem muro secundo, Titus pacem offert; sed ex parte Judæorum Symone et Johanne [1] contradicentibus, tanta in urbe crudelitas et fames invaluit, ut cessantibus emptione et venditione ac ciborum coctura, coria scutorum manderent et purgamenta olerum parietum adhærantia, nauseantium vomitus, vetera boum stercora, exuviæ serpentum, equorum cadavera, ad cibum quærebantur; facilior apud adversarios quam apud suos pietas; patibula ponebantur in muris ne quis fugeret; foris captivitas, intus fames, utrobique formido. Cingit Titus urbem novo muro, qui quadraginta stadiis urbem gyrabat. Gyrus autem castrorum denis stadiis numerabatur, ne ullus quidem evaderet custodias ponens. Invalescente tandem fame, sepultor plerumque sepeliendum prævenit ad sepulcrum, cum tanto morientium fœtore ut urbis solo ad sepulturam non sufficiente, cadavera extra muros ad milia projicerentur. Quo viso ingemuit Titus, et se veniam obtulisse sæpius protestatur. Multi tamen ad Romanos confugerunt, quibus cum daretur cibus, aut nulla erat vis edendi aut digerendi. Quidam autem ex transfugis, dum alvum purgarent, bunones aureos egesserunt, quos ante fugam absorbuerant, ne insidiatores aliquid palam reperirent. Comperit id quidam Assyrius, et ab uno in omnes opinio manavit eripiuntur igitur transfugæ Judæi, quamvis contra jussum Titi, inciduntur ventris secreta, aurum requiritur. Monet Titus Josephum ut Judæos scripturis, exemplis, promissionibus, lacrimis ad deditionem si possit inflectat, sed nil profuit. *Josephus.* Quin etiam Johannes et Symon cum complicibus ita omnia obstruxerant ut ne quidem Judæis exitus neque Romanis aditus pateret. Domus jugiter scrutabantur si quid reperiri posset, negantes trucidabantur. Denique uxores viris, parentes filiis, cibum ex ore rapiebant; si ostium domus clauderetur, statim aliquis comedere æstimabatur, unde et domus rumpebatur; inferiores spoliabantur; ditiores pro suis pecuniis accusati quasi aut fugere aut urbem prodere vellent, necabantur. *Egesippus, libro quinto, et Josephus, libro septimo.* Tunc contigit illud factum tam horrendum quam famosum Mariæ alienigenæ, quæ fame tabescens parvulum quem genuerat alloquitur in hunc modum: " Fili mi, sæva omnia te circumstant, bellum, fames, incendium, latrones; redde vel semel matri quod ab ea sumpsisti.

---

[1] *adds* gouernoures of the Iewes.

Redi in id secretum a quo existi. Feci quandoque quod pietatis erat, faciamus modo quod fames pesuadet." Hæc dicens filium igne torruit; partem comedit, partem reservavit; sed nidor incensæ carnis seditiosos allexit, quos objurgans mulier sic affatur : " Silete;
5 non fui avara, partem vobis servando "; et ad portionem reservatam sic loquitur : " Gratus es mihi, fili mi, vitæ meæ dilatator, percussorum repressor; qui venerunt necaturi jam facti sunt convivæ. Gustate ergo quod matrem novistis gustasse, aut certe totum reliquum incorporabo. Ne pudeat vos mulierem imitari quam sic
10 epulari fecistis." Replevit illico urbem tanti sceleris nefas, et Titum in tantum commovit ut manus elevans sic affaretur : " Ad bellum hominum venimus; sed, ut video, contra beluas dimicamus. Quin etiam feræ rapaces a propria specie abstinent, etiam in summa necessitate suos fœtus fovent; sed isti proprios devorant. Ipsos ergo
15 deleamus, quorum fœda sunt omnia." *Josephus.* Erat inter Romanos Sabinus quidam genere Syrus, manu et animo promptus, perpetua laude dignus; hic quidem nigro colore, exilis habitudine, sed anima heroica in macro corpore virtute enituit. Hic primus cum undecim sociis murum ascendit, Judæos fugavit, sed lapide tandem pressus,
20 sagittas et lapides parvipendens, etiam genibus innixus et scuto protectus multos sauciavit, donec jaculis undique confossus interiret. *Egesippus.* Admotis tandem arietibus ad templum, sed parum proficientibus, valvas templi auro tectas incendunt. *Ranulphus.* Refert hic Josephus quod propter occisionem Jacobi Justi excidium
25 urbis et gentis dispersio provenerit; sed verius propter occisionem Christi, secundum illud evangelii, " Non relinquent in te lapidem super lapidem, eo quod non cognoveris tempus visitationis tuæ." Quia tamen Dominus non vult mortem peccatoris, sed magis ut convertatur, et ut ipsi Judæi de præoccupatione calumniam aut
30 excusationem non haberent, per xl^a annos expectavit per apostolorum prædicationem, ad convertendum sollicitavit, per signa stupenda eos terrere curavit. *Egesippus et Josephus, libro* 7°. Nam per annum ferme ante urbis eversionem visa est gladii ignei similitudo supra templum in aere pendere. In ipsa quoque Paschali celebritate vitula
35 in medio templi immolanda agnum peperit. Orientalis quoque porta templi solido aere plurimum gravis, viginti vix hominum labore claudi solita, per plures noctes, fractis repagulis ferreis, sponte aperiebatur vix iterum claudenda. Visi sunt etiam in nubibus acies armatæ et currus volitare per aera. In festo Pentecostes sacerdotes
40 de nocte templum ingredientes audierunt voces hujuscemodi : *Tran-*

Appendix III. 89

seamus hinc; migremus ex his sedibus. Jesus quoque Ananiæ filius, vir ruricola, quadriennio ante urbis excidium in ipsis Scenopegiæ sacrificiis templum ascendens cœpit clamare patria voce: *Vox ab Oriente, vox ab Occidente, vox a quatuor ventis; Væ! Væ! Væ! Jerosolimis et templo.* Hæc die et nocte clamabat, ita ut nec verberibus afflictus nec precibus rogatus desisteret; quin etiam coram Albino præside Romano ductus, et dire tractatus proprias injurias semper negligeret, patriæ excidium proclamaret, usque ad ultimum eversionis diem, quo murum ascendens prædicta repetiit, et dum adjungeret, *Væ etiam et mihi,* ictu fundibali obiit. *Ranulphus.* Refert Marianus, libro primo, quod templo succenso, solum templi in odium Judæorum exaratum sit. *Jeronimus in prologo super Josephum.* Post urbem eversam Titus Romam rediens adduxit secum Josephum Judæum, qui statim septem Judaicæ captivitatis libros Græce conscripsit.

NOTES

1-8. This forms one sentence, translating the opening sentence of the *Vindicta Salvatoris*, and the periods at ll. 4, 6 should be commas.

13. The omission of the subject-pronoun is very characteristic of this poem; *e.g.*, ll. 18, 279, 305, 402, (?) 497, 527, 555, 595, 638, 681, 686.

mannes : ' men(nes) ' of the other MSS. is the better reading.

14. The bee seems to have been a mediæval type of blindness; *cp.* Maidstone's *Penitential Psalms*, 253, E.E.T.S. 155, where MS. Brit. Mus. Add. 36523 reads, " I stomble as doth þe blynde be."

16. **bolled** : probably a scribal error for ' bobbed,' as in EUC; cp. *Cursor Mundi*, 16623 (MSS. Fairfax, Trinity):

" And to hym pleidyn a bobet
And bad hym sey in dede
Which of hem yaf the stroke,"

also *E.E.P.* (1862) 14, " He was ibobid an i-smitte . . . an hi spette in is face."

17-24. These two quatrains are run together. After this point the quatrains are defective, the line-groups being: 25-30, 31-4, 35-8, 39-40. The variant order in CUDE is probably due to the two lines 35, 39 both beginning with " There was no." But if ll. 39, 40, in a slightly altered form, could originally have stood after l. 30, we should then have perfect quatrains.

18. **Vmbe-casten hym with a cry** : surrounded, with the idea of hunters surrounding the quarry; cp. *Sir Gawain*, 1434:

" þay vmbekesten þe knarre and þe knot boþe,
Wyȝes, whyl pay wysten wel wythinne hem hit were."

' Cry ' may suggest the hounds, though the noun is not given in *N.E.D.* with this particular use till 1535.

32. **biker** : this word, which only occurs in L, is not instanced in *N.E.D.* Under ' bike ' Jamieson quotes Icelandic biikar, a hive. I cannot find that it occurs in Icelandic, but I am indebted to Miss Whitelock for the fact that it is found in Old Swedish as the name of a vessel taken by a bee-keeper into the wood to capture bees; *cp.* Lidén, *Om några fornsvenska lagord och lagstadganden (Arkiv för nordisk Filologi*, 1911, pp. 259 ff.). Forms of the word are also found in OS, OLG, OHG, MHG; *cp.* also OE. bēo-cere, a bee-keeper. Lidén derives the OSw. word from ' bi,' bee, and ' kar,' a vessel; he considers that it is possibly, but not necessarily, a loan from the North German area. The hard *k* in our word points to its Scandinavian origin.

23. See p. xxv.

36. **liter** : a scribal error for ' lepir,' leprosy, as in AEDUC. The error was probably assisted by confusion with ME. ' lepe ' from OE. lēap, a basket.

41. **of Grec[e]** : de gente grecorum, *i.e.* an inhabitant of a Greek colony in

Syria. The words are not in the printed text of the *Vindicta Salvatoris*, but see p. 83, l. 19, and *cp.* l. 98.

45. **Sensceus** : read 'Sensteus.' This was Cestius Gallus, president of Syria; see pp. xxii–xxiii.

47. **to** : this would be better omitted, as in ACUD.

50. Presumably he went through the Greek colonies along the northern coast of Palestine, till he reached a convenient port (? Seleucia; *cp. Acts* xiii. 4).

54. **Cloudes clateren gon** : cp. *Troy Book*, 12500–2 :

"Hit skirmyt in the skewes with a skyre low,
Thurgh the claterand clowdes clos to the heuyn,
As the welkyn shuld walt for wodenes of hete,"

also *Cleanness*, 972, "þer-of clatered þe cloudes."

55. **þe racke myd a rede wynde roos on þe myddel** : cp. *Troy Book*, 1984, " A rak and a royde wynde rose in hor saile." If 'rede' is not an error for 'royde,' OF. roide, violent, or possibly for 'reyde,' from the NF. form reide, it may derive from Boethius II, Met. vi:

"Quos notus sicco uiolentus aestu
Torret ardentes recoquens harenas."

A gloss on this may have produced the 'red wind.' This is known in the Mediterranean as a wind charged with red sand from the African coasts (see *Notes and Queries*, Second Series, Vol. IV, p. 114). The Metrum deals with the crimes of Nero,—" when Rome was burnt and senators were slain," and may well have been known to our poet, *cp.* l. 896 and p. xxi.

56. **out of þe souþ syde** : ventus que dicitur auster, p. 83, l. 12; in the printed text the wind is from the north.

60. "So that he who kept the helm fell prostrate." For the omission of the pronoun, *cp.* l. 168.

63. **scher vpon schore**: ran along by the coast; *cp.* to march upon = to border. Cp. *Pearl*, 107, " I wan to a water by schore þat schereȝ."

65. **tourres** only here and in *Troy Book* 1983 (see p. xxx) does this mean 'mountainous waves.'

70. A gives the better reading here. Cp. *Patience*, 234, 'styffe stremes & streȝt.' In each case the line is the last descriptive touch of the storm.

74. **[citezeins]**: the MS. reading, 'suþ,' would give better metre.

78. **[Hem]** should be added as the object of 'hadde yferked.'

83–4. Cp. *Parlement of the Thre Ages*, 199, 206 :

"Me were leuere one this launde lengen a while . . .
Than alle the golde and the gude that thoue gatt euer."

As the *Parlement* is of about the same date as *Winner and Waster* (see Note on ll. 489–90), this is probably an imitation on the part of our poet.

88. This combines the printed *Vindicta*, 'multis bonis erogarem te' and our poet's emendation of the allusion to Tiberius in the MS., *cp.* p. 83, l. 24.

95. **graces**: *cp.* Chaucer, *Squire's Tale*, 153–5:

"And every gras that groweth up-on rote
She shal eek knowe, and whom it wol do bote,
Al be his woundes never so depe and wyde."

98. **in our londe**: *cp.* Note on l. 41.

Notes.

104. et ere: cp. *Minor Poems of the Vernon MS.*, E.E.T.S. 98, p. 126:

> "Blessed be, ladi, þy Right Ere:
> þe holygost, he liht in þere,
> Flesch and Blod to take,"

and the Latin hymn beginning

> "Gaude Virgo mater Christi,
> Quae per aurem concepisti."

J. Vriend (*The Blessed Virgin Mary in the Medieval Drama of England*, Purmerend, 1928, pp. 150–60) devotes a chapter to this subject.

112. Neþer: this form occurs in *Havelok, Sir Degrevant*, Norfolk guild records and London charters. Luick attributes it to loss of stress; see his *Untersuchungen zur englische lautgeschichte*, pp. 183–4.

122. logge: all other MSS. read 'luke' or 'loke.' Either this represents *Luke* xvii. 12, "et cum ingrederetur quoddam castellum" (Wiclif 'castel'), or *Luke* xvii. 14, "Quos ut vidit dixit."

124. eche day: this exaggeration is perhaps due to the needs of alliteration. The printed text has 'tres mortuos suscitavit.'

129. ferr: probably caught by the scribe from l. 131; 'ferly,' as in the other MSS., gives a better reading.

133. cite: L is alone in this reading. Probably the original word was 'suite,' company; cp. *Luke* x. 1, "designavit Dominus et alios septuaginta duos." The twelve formed an inner circle, *cp.* l. 137, where again L alone reads 'cite.'

163. priuely: in spite of the form, the sense is obviously 'openly, manifestly.' Two words of opposite meaning have evidently been confused under the same spelling. Other examples may be pointed out, as *Cleanness*, 1107:

> "Displayed more pryuyly, when he hit part schulde
> þenne alle þe toles of Tolowse moȝt tyȝt hit to kerue,"

and *Richard the Redeles*, II. 174–5:

> "And brouȝte to þe brydd / and his blames rehersid
> Preuyly at þᵉ parlement / amonge all þe peple."

The adjective is also found, especially in *Richard the Redeles*, III. 324–5:

> "þei had non oþer signe / to schewe þᵉ lawe
> But a preuy pallette / her pannes to kepe,"

where the sense is 'strong, proved'; also II. 108, 'her priuy prynte,' used of the badge given broadcast by Richard to his followers; III. 14, 'her preuy age,' their manifest age; III. 111, 'a preuy poynt,' an outstanding point; similarly *Mum and the Sothsegger*, 1055, "And of other pryvy poyntz." It is also possible that the same word is found in the *Pearl* refrain, l. 12, 'Of þat pryuy perle wyth-outen spot,' and in l. 24. In the three other forms of this refrain the adjective is 'precious.' The word may have arisen from a substitution of the strong for the weak stem in the OF. pp. prové.

164. Cp. p. 84, ll. 24–7 (not in printed text), and the Latin hymn in Daniel's *Thesaurus Hymnologicus*, I, p. 341:

> "Salve sancta facies nostri redemptoris
> In qua nitet species divini splendoris,
> Impressa panniculo nivei candoris
> Dataque Veronicae signum ob amoris."

This prayer carried an indulgence of 10,000 days, granted by John XXII (Dobschutz, *Christusbilder*, p. 224).

166. ma*n*: OE. ā does not remain in this MS. The scribe has evidently taken the word to be from OE. mann. The presence of this form points to either (i) a northern original which retained OE. ā, or (ii) a West Midland original in which OE. *an* was written *on*, and has for the most part been replaced by a later scribe.

167. cloþ: the variant 'clay' in U has probably come from a northern form 'claþ.'

169. The alliteration is awkward, and the order of the words in AUDE is preferable. They were probably altered in order to bring verb and subject nearer to each other.

170. hym: *i.e.* Pilate.

177. riche: only in L; probably picked up by the scribe from l. 169.

181. MS. bayne me my bone. This can be retained, and translated "forward my petition, assist my prayer, that I may, etc." ON. beina, to promote. 'Baythe,' from ON.* beiðna, the earlier form of ON. beina, is also found. See Note on l. 327 in *Sir Gawayn*, ed. Tolkien and Gordon.

183. This should be emended to 'buske me [&] bou*n*,' as in A; cp. *Scottish Field*, 83, "He did buske and bowne him." The adjective is not found in this connection.

187. at þries: cp. 'at once.'

192–3. There is possibly some omission between these lines, as we do not hear why the barons were brought together. In the *Vindicta* he sends messengers to Vespasian, who comes to him bringing an army.

199. & heyly y a-fowe: cp. *Parlement of the Thre Ages*, 178, 'and heghely I a-vowe.'

203. taste on: probably this was originally 'fele of,' corrupted through some scribe's misunderstanding of 'folowed.'

207. For 'who' in the sidenote read 'and.'

213. There seems to have been an omission here; apparently Nero commissioned the knights to demand his tribute (cp. l. 48); the Jews refused to pay the tribute and took away the safe-conduct.

wyes: read 'w[a]yes,' as in AU. The absence of the 'trewes' made the journey hard.

215. þat: this refers to the Pope; the other MSS. read 'and.'

216. pres: '[of]' might be added, as in all other MSS.

225. [he]: MS. 'þey,' which may be right; cp. ll. 227–8.

warpe: there is no example in *N.E.D.* of this word in the sense of 'take away.'

229. emperour: the other MSS. read 'kyng,' *i.e.* Titus; this is probably correct.

232. They brought both St. Peter and Veronica into the presence of Vespasian.

233. forþ myd: read 'forþ-myd,' before.

235. Cp. *Troy Book*, 4312, "Bothe Mawhown*us* & ma*u*mette*s* myrtild in peces."

255. carieþ, hangyþ: possibly these are southern plurals of transitive verbs. A few of these are found; see p. xiv, and cp. the addition of 'hit holdeþ,' in l. 260, clearly due to a southern scribe.

258. agysen: the first example of this verb in *N.E.D.* is from Spenser. The

Notes. 95

noun 'aguise' or 'anguise' glossed in the *Catholicon Anglicum* as 'indula,' a tight-fitting garment, seems to come from F. 'anguisse,' see Godefroy. Otherwise it is not instanced till 1647.

259. **hym**: 'it' of the other MSS. is the better reading.

261. **& non ny3tes reste**: perhaps this might be translated 'and did not rest at all at night;' cp. *God's Complaint* (Wheatley MS.), 92, "Wele neiþer wo may þee noon pay."

269-72. This quatrain has the appearance of being a later addition, introduced, perhaps by the poet himself, in order to make it quite clear who were the 'dukes' of l. 267.

277. **rotlyng**: cp. *Wars of Alexander*, 943, "Sees slike a rottillyng in þe rewme."

278. **scharpe**: cp. *Joseph of Arimathie*, 513, "mony swou3ninge lay þorw schindringe of scharpe."

280. In *Morte Arthure*, 2026, a 'dragone of golde' is the standard of Lucius Iberius.

285. Cp. *Morte Arthure*, 743, "In floynes, and fercostez, and Flemesche schyppes."

286. Cp. *Morte Arthure*, 738, "Coggez and crayers."

288. **[þe brede]**: MS. Sprad. The original reading was probably 'brad'; cp. l. 599; also ll. 405, 486, 1047, where the same corruption has occurred.

289-90. From the *Troy Book*; see p. xxviii.

293. **seken**: perhaps a scribal error for 'syken,' sigh. 'Siking and sorow' is a common alliterative phrase; cp. *Troy Book*, 1515, 2680.

301. "They attacked each district."

310. This line should end with a comma. 'Cite' is in apposition to 'Ierusalem,' and 'þat' must be understood before 'sett.'

313-16. Cp. Higden, Vol. IV, p. 426, "Idcirco tanta multitudo Jerosolimis tunc erat, quia in diebus Azymorum ex mori Judæa ad templum confluxerant."

325. **Choppyn** = chapen, cover; OF. chappe, chape. The verbs 'chap' and 'chop' are interchanged in ME. in senses of 'to exchange' and 'to cut.'

328. MS. "& lyk to lyouns also." The alliteration points to this being the right reading; moreover, it is not likely that the number of lions would be stated, and the dragons left indefinite.

330. **strayned**: a scribal error for 'stayned'; cp. *Registr. Aberdon.* (Maitland Club), II. 174, "Ane grite arres bed . . . with þe kingis armes and bischoipe Willeam Elphinstone's sten3eit" (1519).

332. "A hundred crenellations round that pavilion alone."

333-6. This quatrain breaks badly in the middle.

334. **britaged**: cp. *Cleanness*, 1190, "In bigge brutage of borde, bulde on þe walles."

344. **com[e]**: Orm's frequent use of this word, in all cases, at the line-end, e.g. l. 718, 'þe Laferrd Cristess come' (*nom. s.*), points to its derivation from OE.* cōme.

345-52. Two quatrains are run together here.

360. **flocken**: probably a scribal error for 'floghen,' OE. flugon; cp. Malory, *Arthur*, I. xxvii, "They gaf hym their berdys clene flayne of."

361. **houe**: hove C, howve D; cp. Vulgate 2 *Kings* x. 4 (= 2 *Samuel* x. 4), "Tulit itaque Hanon servos David rasitque dimidiam partem barbæ eorum et præscidit vestes eorum medias usque ad nates, et dimisit eos." The word looks

like a scribal error for 'neþer gloue,' leg-covering; cp. *Allit. Alex.*, 4959, "Nymes of ȝour nethirgloue & nakens ȝoure leggis." In l. 2767 the 'neþire gloues' are made of skins.

373-80. These two stanzas divide into groups of two, three and three lines. The full stop is probably after l. 377 instead of l. 378.

375. **ne**: other MSS. 'and'; cp. *Melusine*, 144, "The moost strong and fell folke that euer I sawe ne herde speke of."

385. **standard**: cp. Caxton, *Myrrour*, II. xviii, 106, "There [in helle] deth holdeth his standard."

387. **feld**: the better reading is 'fighte,' as in ADUC. When anything pertaining to the fight was lacking among the men, they were to be, etc.

402. "Unless they yield the town."

407. **whan ouȝte runnen**: ? when any ran (out from the city); cp. l. 403. The use of 'ouȝte' is unusual, but cp. 'noȝt,' l. 419. It is also possible that 'ouȝte' = 'out' and that the bells could be run out or lowered in some way to catch the wind. This, if permissible, makes better sense.

410. **gawged**: the Cheshire dialect form 'gag out,' to project, may account for the variant readings 'gaggede, goggid.' The tower overlooked the town, but did not overhang it; cp. *Titus and Vespasian*, 2948-50:

"And berffreys to risen on hye,
þat þei myght seen into þe toun
What men dede up and doun."

411-12. Cp. 1 *Macc.* vi. 39, "Now when the sun shone upon the shields of gold and brass, the mountains glistered therewith, and shined like lamps of fire." The MS. reading in l. 411, 'batail,' may well be right; the army would be perceived from a distance of four miles by the brightness of the dragon.

413. Cp. Maundeville xxxi (p. 183, l. 11, ed. Hamelius), "And abouen the chief tour of the palays ben .ij. rounde pomeles of gold."

417. Cp. *Troy Book*, 6334-5, "The ffourthe batell in feld he fourmet to leng With Archelaus."

422. **Strogelyng**: cp. straggle, to rough-dress a grindstone; 'in' should read 'of,' as in EDUC.

427. Cp. *Joel* iii. 12; *Legenda Aurea*, ed. Graesse, p. 8, "Judex enim in vallem Josaphat descendet et bonos et malos judicabit;" also *Cursor Mundi*, l. 22969.

429. **fauward**: read 'fanward'; cp. l. 549.

442. **hamberkes**: as in l. 845, the other MSS. read 'hauberks,' which is clearly the right sense. The scribe may have confused the word with OF. hamberge, a part of a gauntlet.

448. In *King Alisaunder*, 2025-30, 2521-38 (ed. Weber, *Metrical Romances*, Vol. I), Darius fights against Alexander with elephants, each of which carries a castle with twelve knights therein.

450. **þousand**: only in L, and should be omitted; cp. note on l. 577.

469. **fyne**: read 'fyne.'

476. **Joseph**: this should certainly be Joshua, a military hero.

482. **& batayled**: probably a corruption of 'i-batayled.'

486. **ouer-sprad**: this should read 'ouer-brad'; cp. l. 599, and note on l. 288.

489-90. Cp. *Winner and Waster*, 327-8:

"Ne es nothir kaysser, ne kynge, ne knyghte þat the folowes,
Barone, ne bachelere, ne beryn that thou loueste."

Since *Winner and Waster* can be dated 1352-3 (see ed. Sir I. Gollancz, *Select Early English Poems*, III, 1920), our author is the borrower.

494. þe body : the reading of the other MSS., 'he one body,' is preferable.

497. See Note on l. 13.

505-6. " But to-day we remember a greater thing, a more general principle, namely, that," etc. But 'mynne' used impersonally regularly takes 'of' or 'on.' Perhaps 'myneþ' = 'myngeþ,' and the sense is 'but a greater thing admonishes us.'

516. st[erynne]s : perhaps the original was 'stourness' (OE. stŏr); cp. *Troy Book*, 9015, " stowrnes of strenght "; l. 10345, " stowrenes of strokes."

518. hede : this is a verb, and emendation is unnecessary.

521. to neȝe : read 'to-neȝe,' approach; cp. Wiclif, *Judith* xiv. 14, " He wente to-neȝhende to the curtin."

524. There should be a full-stop at the end of the line, and a comma after l. 525.

525. loude clarioun cry : cp. *Cleanness*, 1210, " Cler claryoun crak; " *Sir Gawayn*, 118, " nwe nakryn noyse." Possibly 'clarioun' is a genitive plural.

532. þrowolande : not otherwise recorded. The line is taken from *Troy Book*, 12496, " A thoner and a thicke rayne þrublet in the skewes," or l. 7619, " A thondir with," etc. Hence the MS. reading is probably a scribal error for 'þrowblande.' The same word is found twice in *Cleanness*, 504, 879, " þroly þrublande in þronge, þrowen ful þykke " (of the animals leaving the ark), " þus þay þrobled & þrong & þrwe vmbe his ereȝ " (of the men of Sodom upbraiding Lot). The sense seems to be 'to jostle.' Prof. R. J. Menner (*Purity*, Yale University Press, note on l. 504) connects it with 'thrumble,' to crowd together, first instanced in 1589. *N.E.D.* takes the *Troy Book* word as a variant of 'trouble,' to rage. It may be noted that A reads 'threpande,' contending.

533. [þei] : this emendation is hardly necessary; cp. Note on l. 13.

545-8. Cp. Note to ll. 411-12.

547. schyueryng : scribal error for 'schymeryng,' as in other MSS.

549. fanward : cp. 'a-fowe,' l. 199. Such spellings may be traced to a southern scribe, to whom 'fan' and 'van' represented the same sound.

552. There should be a full-stop at the end of this line, rather than after l. 551.

555. " They drew from their sheaths the things which were ground sharp (*i.e.* swords)."

557. There should be a comma at the end of the line.

558. If 'burne[s]' is interpreted as coats of mail, the MS. reading 'schedered' can be kept here.

560. Cp. *Wars of Alex.*, 4796, " As gotis out of guttars in golanand wedres."

567. rispen : not in *N.E.D.*; probably connected with 'rasp,' to belch, first recorded in 1626. Forby's *E. Anglian Glossary* has 'rasp' and 'resp.' *Prompt. Parv.* gives 'rospynge,' *eructatio.* Cp. Flem. ruispen, ruspen (Kilian).

redles : without need for taking counsel, without a doubt. *N.E.D.* gives no example of it as an adverb. Perhaps the correct reading is ' redders,' cleaners-up; cp. 'rydders,' A.

576. Cp. *Troy Book*, 10888, " Till his head with the hard yerthe hurlit full sore; " also l. 1198, " When helmes and hard stele hurlet to-gedur." In MS. Jac. 7, 27 in the Advocates' Library, Edinburgh, in a burlesque alliterative poem, there occurs the line " The hare and harthestone hurtuld to-geydur "

98   *Notes.*

(Wright, *Rel. Ant.*, I, p. 84), which appears to be a parody of a line of this type.

577. **& vnder** : CUDE give a better reading here. The hundred dromedaries mentioned in l. 450 are all dead; the only beast of war left alive is one elephant. All the other MSS. have ' dyede ' for ' doun diȝten.' The full-stop should be after l. 576 and the comma after l. 577.

578. Cp. *Troy Book*, 4764, " Was no lede opon lyfe þat a lofte stode."

579. **[ane]** : perhaps this need not have been inserted, cp. *Havelok*, 2107, " Her he spak anilepi word."

590· Cp. *Troy Book*, 3170, " Chaundelers full chefe & charbokill stones."

595. See Note on l. 13.

599. Cp. *Morte Arthure*, 1863, " The bente and þe brode felde all*e* one blode rynnys."

613–5, 617. Cp. *Troy Book*, 10462–4 :

> " þai wan in wightly, warpit to þe yates,
> Barrit hom full bigly wi*th* boltes of yerne ;
> Braid vp the brigges in a breme hast."

618. **vnfonded** : LUD vnfounded, A vnfandide. *N.E.D.* translates this word as ' not numbed or powerless,' taking it as an aphetic form of ' affound ' ; but the men whom they replaced would not have been suffering from cold.

619. **Tyeþ** : this verb occurs four times ; here, where it is trans., the other MSS. replace it by ' take ' ; in ll. 843, 1178, and generally in l. 1158, they have ' turn.' But in l. 1158 U has ' ten,' taken by DE for a numeral. The vowel may have been levelled from imp. sg. ' tēoh ' ; cp. Layamon, 17416, ' tih þe aȝan.'

622. **Quar[r]en** : MS. Quarten ; cp. *Wars of Alex.*, 2226, " Whirres owt qwarels, wappyd thrugh males " (Dublin), " Quirys out quarrels, quappid," etc. (Ashmole) ; also l. 1414, " Whirres owt quarels " (Dublin). *Troy Book*, 4743, ' Whappet in wharles,' may have been in our poet's mind, but he alliterates ' wap ' always on *w*. ' Wharr ' is a variant of ' whirr ' ; cp. *Sir Gawain*, 2203 " What ! hit wharred and whette, as water at a mulne " (made a whirring noise).

633. The text of A gives better alliteration ; ' rathe, which is found in D, does not occur elsewhere in the poem.

648. **groded** : cp. *Troy Book*, 1659, " gret vp fro þe ground vppon gray marbill," raised above the ground. Our form is a blend of ON. greiða and OE. gerādian (see *Supplement to A.S. Dict.*, Toller), not quoted in *N.E.D.* ; cp. the common ME. form ' graide.'

651. In *Medieval England*, Barnard and Davis, 1924, there is an illustration (p. 123) of the siege tower and its stairs, taken from Viollet-le-Duc's *L'Architecture Militaire*.

666. Cp. *Wars of Alex.*, " Schot*is* vp scharply at shalk*is* on þe wall*is*."

675. Cp. *Troy Book*, 1634, " a clene wall c[l]ustrit wi*th* towres " (MS. crustrit).

677–80. Cp. p. 87, ll. 12–15.

684. **coþe** : infect with disease. Though the noun is found several times in OE. and ME., the verb is only quoted in *N.E.D.* from modern dialects. In E. Anglia it means ' to faint,' and in the S.W. (Hampshire, Dorset and the Isle of Wight), ' to cause disease of the liver in sheep ' ; see *E.D.D.*

685. See p. 86, l. 3.

Notes. 99

686. **str[ande]** : cp. *Patience*, 311, " & þy struande stremeʒ of strynde3 so mony." 'Strynde' may be the correct reading here; cp. 'spryng,' EDC.

699. **claures** : the only other example of this word is 'cleafres,' *Ancren Riwle*, p. 102; cp. Dan. klavre, to clamber.

700. **kagge[d]** : probably a variant of 'catch,' to fasten, bind; cp. *Wars of Alex.*, 1521, " caggis vp (Dublin cachez vp) on cordis; " also *Troy Book*, 1077, "Cogges with cablis cachyn to londe."

725-35. Imitated from the *Troy Book*; see pp. xxvi, xxvii.

727. **r[y]s[t]en** : so A; not in *N.E.D.* The MS. form 'rusken' would mean 'to tear out violently'; see *N.E.D.*

736. Cp. *Troy Book*, 9208, " þen he turnys in his tene " (of Achilles in his bed).

745. **[grate]** : evidently some part of his armour; probably the same word as appears in *Libeaus Desconus*, ed. Kaluza (Kölbing, *Altenglische Bibliothek* V), 1675 :

" He smitte his schaft in grate
Almest him þouʒt to late
Whan he hem siʒ wiþ siʒtes,"

describing Sir Lambard when he saw two knights awaiting him. *N.E.D.* glosses this as 'collision of weapons,' but Sir Lambard is not yet within striking distance. As Kaluza says in his note, it is evidently a support or rest for the lance; *cp.* Malory, *Arthur*, VII, xvi, 237, " Thenne they putte their speres in their reystes and came to gyders." It cannot have been fixed to the crupper, but to the breastplate. For an illustration of a lance-rest so placed, see F. W. Fairholt, *Costume in England*, 1885, Vol. II, p. 271. Possibly it was so called because the lance pressed or rubbed against it. The MS. reading 'grayþed of,' in the sense of 'made of,' is very rare in ME., though *N.E.D.* gives an example from *Cursor Mundi*, l. 550, " Of þir things . . . was Adam cors to-gedir graid."

746. **colour[ede]** of his **armys** : embroidered with his armorial bearings.

753. Cp. *Morte Arthure*, 912, " His gloues gaylyche gilte, amd grauene at the hemmez; " also l. 3462.

754. **hauleþ** : *i.e.* 'haulleþ,' a fifteenth-century form of ME. hallen. The gauntlets of the gloves are pulled over the sleeves of the brinie.

765-6. The approaches to the walls were defended by barriers and chains; *cp.* Lydgate, *Siege of Thebes*, E.E.T.S., E.S. 108, ll. 2774-5 :

" Barbykans and bulwerkes newe,
Barreris, cheynys and diches wonder depe."

773-8. " If any of you were to pass the palisade I have set up, which encloses the town so strongly, and if we were only 40 against 500, and you were all giants, you would have to turn back." The reading of ADU, 'fende off,' may be the better.

778. Cp. *Troy Book*, 7861, " And þof we maitles marre, may we no fer."

782. Cp. *Parlement of the Thre Ages*, 447, " And he was dede of that dynt: the deuyll hafe that reche."

784. **owene** : this appears to mean 'accept, acknowledge,' but this meaning is not recorded in *N.E.D.* till the seventeenth century.

785-96. This is derived from an episode at the siege of Jotapata, see p. 86, ll. 2-7, and p. xxviii. It had the effect of discouraging Vespasian so that he was forced to return to active measures against the town, as related in ll. 797-800.

His speech in ll. 793–6, which is inserted by the poet, breaks the sequence of thought here.

791. " Seeing that their clothes," etc.

801–28. See p. 86, ll. 7–16, and footnote to l. 7. In both Josephus (III, vii, 19–20) and Hegesippus (III, xi, 1–2) the sacks are used against the battering-ram. Only the English translation of Higden agrees with our poem.

804. Cp. *Troy Book*, 808, " Ne neuer dere hym a dyse."

dy[n] : so ADUC; MS. dyt. ' Dit(e) ' occurs four times in *Troy Book*, ll. 1347, 5788, 8680, 11946, always in connection with ' din,' in the sense of ' noise, clamour '; *cp*. l. 248 of our poem.

819. **Jo[k]ken** : MS. Jolken; cp. *Cleanness*, 1414 ' tulket,' emended by Sir I. Gollancz and *N.E.D.* to ' tukket '; also *Pearl*, 11, ' dolked,' emended by Sir I. Gollancz to ' dokked.' It is probably a variant of ' chokked,' (?) from F. choquer; cp. *Morte Arthure*, 2956, " With a chasyng spere he chokkes hym thurghe."

826. **staf[-slyng]** : ' slyng ' was omitted by a scribe, and ' staf,' which in ME. can mean the rung of a ladder, was emended to ' stayre,' with a change of preposition, by the scribe of A. Cp. *Sir Thopas*, 117–18 :

" This geaunt at him stones caste
Out of a fel staf-slinge."

In *Titus and Vespasian*, 2946, " With stafslynges and with oþur atyre," they are used against Jerusalem.

836. **archers** : engines of war, presumably some kind of bow. The same word is found in the *Romance of the Rose*, 4191, " spryngoldes, gunnes, bows and archers," translating " perrières Et engins de maintes manières " (ed. Michel, ll. 4462–3). ' Achillers,' ' asschelers,' in A and C = ashlars, glossed in *N.E.D.* as ' stones used as missiles '; but this line is the only example quoted, and the original meaning appears to be that of a stone hewn square for building. *N.E.D.* gives ' arrow ' as a meaning of ' archer,' adducing the passage from the *Romance of the Rose* and also one from Malory (the edition printed by Stansby in 1634), " one of them with a bow and archer smote Sir Gawaine." But Caxton has " one with a bowe an archer "; the words ' of them ' are added by Wynkyn de Worde, cp. Sommer, *Le Morte Darthur*, I, p. 108 ; II, p. 52. Reference to the French original (*Merlin*, ed. Gaston Paris, II, 91) shows that when Sir Gawain was defending himself against four knights in the hall of a castle, an archer came out of a room and shot him.

For the form of our word, cp. med. L. archelharia, glossed in the Supplement to Du Cange, 1766, as " Arbalista, arcus, vel *Balista*, machina jaculatoria," from a charter of 1345. This would be a derivative of * archaria, which gives our word.

837. Cp. *Castle of Perseverance*, 1400, " With spete of spere to þee I spynne."

840. Cp. *Towneley Plays*, xiii, 414, " and dos noght bot lakys and clowse hir toose," i.e. she has nothing to do.

845. **hamberkes** : see Note on l. 442.

848. *Cp.* Chaucer, *Knight's Tale*, 1854, " Some hadden salves, and some hadden charmes."

853–4. Cp. *Troy Book*, 7554–6 :

" When the derke was don & the day sprang,
Thes kynges and knightes, kid men of arms,
Were assemblit full sone in hor sure wedis."

Notes. 101

862. tor[tere] : 'torfere and tene' is a common alliterative expression; cp. *Troy Book*, 81, "Bothe of torfer and tene þat hom tide aftur"; also l. 2033; *Morte Arthure*, 1956; *Wars of Alex.*, 3729. 'Torsom,' which might be an adjective, is not recorded elsewhere.

866. One might perhaps emend to 'to layke [on] þis lesue,' to fight on this plain (OE. lǽsw-); cp. *Troy Book*, 9997, "Thus þai laiket o þe laund" (of the fighting outside Troy).

877-8. From *Troy Book*; see p. xxvii.

880. "Approving of what Titus and the people who had made him their spokesman desired."

886. Cp. *Sir Gawain*, 1719, "Thenne watȝ hit lif vpon lift to lyþen þe houndeȝ."

887. Cp. *Parlement of the Thre Ages*, 208, 217, "And ryde to a reuere . . . to rere vp the fewles."

888. Perhaps the speech should conclude with this line, and preserve the quatrains.

893-946. See pp. xxi-xxii.

941-2. This detail seems to be the poet's own, the nearest approach to it being found in the *Chronica Majora* (Rolls Series, Vol. I, p. 110), "minutissimorum ictuum punctionibus excarnificatus." Perhaps it is a recollection of the fate of Arius the heretic, who "effudit viscera et vitam cum ipsis stercoribus" (*Polychronicon* IV, xxvii, *Rolls Series*, Vol. V, p. 150). A similar fate befell the giant of St. Michael's Mount at the hands of king Arthur; see *Morte Arthure*, 1130-1.

965. "For whom I feel the greatest good will."

974. Cp. *Parlement of the Thre Ages*, 398, "While hym the ȝatis were ȝete and ȝolden the keyes," repeated in l. 575.

976. houshed : cp. Wulfstan, *Homilies*, ed. Napier, p. 235, l. 25, "þonne hyscte he on ða godcundan lareowas," but there is no example recorded of the word in Middle English.

990. Domyssian : Domitian, as history records, took no part in the campaign. Higden has no mention of him in connection with it, but Josephus and Hegesippus give an account of his doings at Rome in the meantime.

999-1000. Titus promises, in the name of Domitian and his followers, to carry out the plan of Sabinus, as he hopes to bless himself, *i.e.* to prosper.

1009. A common alliterative simile; cp. *Piers Plowman* A, xi, 109, "Thenne was I as fayn as foul on (of TU) feir morwen"; also *Wars of Alex.*, 2264; *Mum and the Sothsegger*, 337, "And as fayn of oure voiding as foul on þe skyes."

1011. Cp. *Parlement of the Thre Ages*, 175, "My wele and my wirchip."

1016. Cp. *Troy Book*, 7184, "Ouertyrnet with tene, temple and oþer."

1023. The story of the sickness and cure of Titus is from the *Legenda Aurea*; see p. xx.

1065. [tor] : the MS. reading 'hard' points to this having been the original word, replaced by 'tyme' in the other MSS.; cp. *Troy Book*, 8717, "Hit were tore any tunge tell hit with mouthe." Possibly the reading was 'tere'; cp. *Wars of Alex.*, 4918, "It ware to tere me to tell þe tirement to-gedire."

1071. They ate the leather coverings of their shields (see p. 87, l. 7). Higden has no mention of the shoes, but the *Legenda Aurea* has "calceamenta sua et corrigias comedebant" (ed. Graesse, p. 302), and the MS. *Vindicta* has "reliquias de calciamentis veteribus."

1074. **Ded as a dore-nayl** : cp. *Parlement of the Thre Ages*, 65; *William of Palerne*, 628, 3396; *Piers Plowman* A, i, 161.

1076. **wy[ght]e** : cp. *York Plays* xviii, 219, " are was I wayke, nowe am I wight." The MS. reading ' wye ' is probably a substitution for ' wyghte ' by a scribe who took the latter for a noun instead of an adjective.

1077–96. See p. 87, l. 35—p. 88, l. 15, and *Legenda Aurea*, pp. 301–2. There is a reference to the story in *Purgatorio* xxiii, 28–30 :

" Ecco
La gente, che perdè Gerusalemme
Quando Maria nel figlio diè di becco."

1083–4. See p. xxi.

1093–4. Cp. *Legenda Aurea*, p. 302, " illi vero trementes et territi discesserunt."

1097–1100. I have found no source for this. In the MS. *Vindicta*, 11,000 slay each other that the enemy may not glory in their death.

1101–4. See p. 86, ll. 24–6.

1109–16. See p. 86, ll. 18–22. The Jews did not mine the wall, but leaped out suddenly (according to Josephus and Hegesippus) at the Women's Towers.

1118. Cp. *Troy Book*, 9432, " Bare hym þurgh the brest with a bright end."

1119–20. Cp. *Parlement of the Thre Ages*, 62–3 :

" The breris and the brakans were blody by-ronnen ;
And he assentis to þat sewte and seches hym aftire."

Though the general sense is quite different, there is a certain verbal similarity which may be an unconscious echo.

1121. **Hacchen** : other MSS. hewe(n). It is not found in *N.E.D.*, except in technical senses, and then not before 1480 ; the noun is found in the fourteenth century.

1122. Cp. *Sir Gawain*, 459, " þat þe fyr of þe flynt flaȝe fro fole houes."

1131–42. See p. 87, ll. 5–7.

1133. **Jon þe jenfulle** : John of Gischala, " dolis nulli secundus versutorum, improbitate parem nesciens " (Hegesippus IV, iv, 1 ; cp. Josephus IV, ii, 1).

1134. **Symond** : Simon the son of Gioras, " inferior quidem morum improbitate, sed forma corporis magis fretus ad omne audendum nefas " (Hegesippus, IV, xxii, 1 ; cp. Josephus IV, ix, 3). They were of the same opinion in opposing the Romans, but were constantly at civil war with each other ; see the story of the siege *passim* in Josephus. But Higden says that they had conjoined themselves ; see p. 87, l. 28.

1136. **[re]joycid** : the emendation restores the alliteration ; cp. *William of Palerne*, 4102, " Miȝte reioische þat reaume as riȝt eir bi kinde."

1142. From this point the quatrains go wrong, and are rectified by a two-line stanza, ll. 1155–6.

1151–2. Kopka pointed out that the source of these lines is in Hegesippus, but not in Josephus (p. 35). But it is also in Higden, see p. 87, l. 18.

1153. As Kopka says (p. 38), it is strange that Titus should give this commission to the leader of the defending forces. The reason is to be found in the confusion of the two sieges, see pp. xxiii–xxiv, and Appendix III.

1169. Cp. *Legenda Aurea*, p. 302, " Biennio igitur a Tito Jerusalem obsessa."

1171. Cp. *Legenda Aurea*, p. 302. All the authorities give this figure.

Notes. 103

1174. warwolues: this is not quoted by *N.E.D.* until Scott. 'Lupus Belli' was the name of a siege-engine in the *Flores Historiarum*. 'Werwolf' was only used in ME. in its literal sense. The reading 'warlawes' of AVD is tempting, but so common a word is not likely to have been corrupted. The word was probably suggested by l. 1075.

1181. Sir Sabyn of Surrye: the story of Sabinus, the procurator of Syria, is given in Josephus II, ii–v, but it is not found in Hegesippus or Higden. The Sabinus who was first on the wall (l. 1193) is described by Hegesippus as "ex Syriae viris egregius bellator" (V, xxviii = Josephus VI, i, 6), and by Higden as "Sabinus quidam genere Syrus" (see p. 88, l. 16).

1196. Cp. p. 88, l. 20, "sagittas et lapides parvipendens."

1206. sowe: this was a roofed structure used to protect men while sapping or undermining a wall. But here it seems that the poet has confused it with a battering-ram, as in Higden; *cp.* p. 88, l. 22.

1211. Cp. Higden, Vol. IV, p. 424, "Secundum Martinum et alios capta fuit in diebus Pasche." According to Josephus and Hegesippus the siege ended in the month of Elul, *i.e.* August–September.

1217–32. For the account of the signs see Higden (p. 88), Hegesippus V, xliv, 1, and Josephus VI, v, 3. Only four of the seven signs are recounted here. Two things point to Higden as the source here: (i) in describing the sword sign Higden speaks of the likeness of a fiery sword, Josephus of a star like to a sword, and also a comet, and Hegesippus of a comet in the likeness of a hanging sword; (ii) Higden omits the words, "Vox in sponsos et in sponsas, vox in universum populum," which are found in Hegesippus and Josephus, and should follow l. 1228.

1225. His name is given in all accounts as Jesus the son of Ananus. Perhaps a feeling of reverence accounts for its suppression here. Cp. *Titus and Vespasian*, 1091, "His name was hoten Ananus sone," which appears in other MSS. as 'Jhesu, Ananias sonne,' 'Jhesu a mannes sone,' and 'Jhesus þat was Godys sone.' According to the historians, he prophesied first in the Temple, then in the streets of the city, for seven years before the siege began. The story is compressed by our poet, and the only mark of lapse of time is 'ȝit,' l. 1229. Hence AV add a line after l. 1228, which was taken by the C-collator (see p. xi).

1232. This does not appear, as far as I know, in any other account, and is probably an original touch by our poet. It is omitted by AV, probably by the same reviser who added the line following l. 1228.

1233–6. See p. 88, ll. 24–6, also *Legenda Aurea*, p. 298. Eusebius (*Hist. Eccl.* II, 23) and Origen (*Contra Celsum* I, 47) attribute this statement to Josephus, but it is not there. It is probably, therefore, that it had been interpolated into the copies of Josephus used by Eusebius and Origen (McGiffert, *Church History of Eusebius*, p. 126).

1250. þat ... þe: of which; apparently the neuter form of 'þat his,' whose; *e.g. Canterbury Tales* A, 2710, "Oon That with a spere was thirled his brestboon."

rebies: ME. rŭbi>rībi, either by the WM. unrounding of ŭ (Jordan, *Mittelenglische Grammatik*, p. 205), or by reduction of iu (out of ū) to ī before a labial (Luick, *Hist. Engl. Grammatik*, p. 470). The form 'rebi,' also occurring in *Aunters of Arthur* (see *N.E.D.*), may be due to the proximity of the labial and liquid, though this change is generally confined to short vowels.

1255. **Derst**: a southern form in which the vowel is levelled from ME. pres. der, OE. dearr.

[**ky**]**nde**: this rare verb, not instanced in *N.E.D.*, though preserved in the dialects (see *E.D.D.*), has been retained in U; cp. also A. L has substituted the common word 'tende,' OE. -tendan.

1259–60. In Hegesippus V, xlii, and Josephus VI, iv, the temple is burnt down, but against Titus's wishes. The source here is the *Legenda Aurea*, p. 302, "Tandem secundo anno imperii Vespasiani Titus Jerusalem cepit et captam subvertit templumque funditus destruxit et, sicut Judaei Christum xxx denariis emerent, sic et ipse uno denario xxx Judaeos vendidit."

1271. **je[mewes]**: the earliest example of this in the sense of 'ring' in *N.E.D.* is 1497.

1283. [a]: MS. þe, probably anticipated by a scribe from 'þe walle,' or caught from 'at þe wal' above; cp. 'at a wap,' l. 514; also *Patience*, 499; *Wars of Alex.*, 3040, 4142.

1286. "Wall made with mortar or mud;" cp. *Parlement of the Thre Ages*, 433, "In manere of a mode walle that made were with hondes."

1287. **tymbr ne tre**: 'timber' in OE. could mean a house; it is just possible that this phrase means 'neither house nor tree.'

1288. Cp. *Troy Book*, 12004, "And the bildynges bete doun to the bare erthe."

1291. Cp. Abimelech's capture of Shechem, *Judges* ix, 45, "and he took the city, and slew the people that was therein, and beat down the city, and sowed it with salt;" cp. p. 89, l. 12.

1300. I have omitted the line following this in L alone, both because it upsets the quatrains, and because 'frainen' does not take a simple infinitive.

1306. **fenged**: cp. *Jacob and Josep*, l. 135, "þis chapmen fengeþ þat child." We may compare the way in which the past tense of OE. hātan was levelled into the present.

1311. **Alle þat**: if anyone; cp. the common use of 'whoso' in the same sense, as in l. 458. If anyone would buy, they were to be sold more cheaply, etc.

1321–2. See p. 89, ll. 13–15.

1324. **Viterbe**: all the other MSS. emend to the more usual Vienne. Nowhere else is Pilate connected with Viterbo; it is therefore extremely unlikely to be a scribal emendation. I can only suggest that the idea may be derived from a passage from Godfrey of Viterbo's *Pantheon* (Pertz, *Mon. Germ. Hist.* XXII, p. 310), Pars XVII. Here, writing of the Emperor Frederic Barbarossa, he says:

"Qualiter a Terdona Romam consecrandus processit
Ad vite meritum veniunt vexilla Viterbum,
Unde patens herebus fontem facit igne protervum."

This may perhaps have suggested to our poet the demoniacal manifestations connected in all the legends with his place of burial; cp. the usual medieval derivation of Vienne from 'via gehennae' (Higden, Vol. IV, p. 366). Brit. Mus. MS. Roy. 14 C, xi of the *Pantheon* formerly belonged to the Austin Priory of St. Peter at Markby, near Louth.

Viterbo itself might have an interest for English people as being the scene of the murder by Guy de Montfort of Prince Henry while the latter was receiving the sacrament in the church of San Silvestro in 1271. His body was buried in the Cistercian Abbey of Hayles, and his heart was enshrined in Westminster Abbey. Cp. *Inferno*, xii. 119-20:

"Colui fesse in grembo a Dio
Lo cuor, che 'n su Tamigi ancor si cola."

1328. **kempe** : *N.E.D.* quotes this word only in the special sense of a fighting man or champion; but cp. *Mum and the Sothsegger*, 1221, where it is used of the Truth-teller.

1331. Cp. *Moral Ode*, 268, "fordon and fordemde."

GLOSSARY

(In the Glossary and Index of Proper Names *y* is treated as if *i*.)

a, *def. art.*, 9, 13; an, 60.
a, *interj.*, 177.
abasched, 795.
abide, *inf.* withstand, 308, 428; *pr.* 3 *s.*
abideþ, stands at bay, 911.
ablode, *adj.* bloodstained, 559; OE. on blōde.
aboute, *adv.* round about, 250, 314, 406; abou[t]e, 752.
abrode, widely, 405; openly, 1165; freely, 1047; far and wide, 729; a-brod, 718.
ac, but, 213; OE. ac.
acounte, reckon, 1236.
a-down, down, 713.
adradde, afraid, 459.
a-fer, at a distance, 1104.
affray, terrify, 668.
a flot, afloat, 285; OE. on flote.
a-fowe, make a vow, 199; OF. avouer.
after, *adv.* 251; *prep.* 34; along, 482.
age, 1099.
agysen, array, 258; *see Note.*
aȝen, *adv.* again, 342, 370, 1083; *prep.* opposite, 646; in opposition to, 424; in return for, 1055; towards, 157; contrary to, 1223; a[g]en, 1215.
aȝens, *prep.* in opposition to, 775.
ay, ever, 21.
ayer, air, 1221; eyr, scent, 240.
a-jorneyd, *pp.* journeyed, 1321; OF. a-jorneier (*not in* N.É.D.).
al, *adj.* 19; alle, 26; *adv.* 60, 168; al, 12, 236.
alas, 1094.
a-lofte, 331 389, 523; in the ascendant, 1080.
alone, 905.
a-loude, 488.
also, 4, 31.
aluendel, half, 128; OE. þone healfan dæl.
am, *v.* be.
amydde, in the middle of, 925; a-myd[dis], 28.
amys, *adv.* wrongly, with evil result, 1306.

a-monge, 670, 886.
an, *v.* a, on.
&, and, 4, 8; if, 972.
angren, *inf.* torment, 701.
any, 86.
anoynted, *pp.* 698; ynoyntid, 299.
anon, 53, 521, 529.
apaied, *pp.* contented, 880.
apere, *inf.* appear, 1296, *pt.* 3 *s.* apered, 1297.
apys, monkeys, 701.
aposteles, 138; *g. pl.* apostlen, 895; *cp.* postel.
appul, globe, 326.
a-proched, 243.
arblastes, cross-bows, 667, 836; OF. arbaleste.
archers, engines of war, 836; *see Note.*
aryse, 634.
armen, *pr. pl.* 1177; *pp.* armed, 391; y-armed, 461, 483.
armes, 701.
armyng, *n.* 423.
armys, armorial bearings, 330; man of armes, warrior, 434.
armur, armour, 607.
arst, first, 161; OE. ǣrest.
arwe, slow, sluggish, 423; OE. earg.
arwes, arrows, 391.
as, 12, 14; as if, 54, 68, 530, 548.
askes, ashes, 716; ON. aska.
askeþ, *pr.* 3 *s.* 202, 502; *pt. pl.* asked, 212.
aspyed, *pp.* discovered, 1165; A.F. *aspier, OF. espier.
assayle, *inf.* 563, 652; *pr. pl.* assaylen, 798.
assembled, *pt. pl.* came together, 265; *pp.* gathered together, 384.
assent, agreement, sanction, 958, 996; of his a., on agreement with him, of his party, 1134.
assenteden, *pt. pl.* agreed, 210, 879; *refl.* assented, 903.
assyned, *pp.* assigned, 430.
at, 36, 66; atte, 71, 388; at þries, thrice, 187.
athel, noble, 46.

Glossary.

atired, *pp.* equipped, 282, 442; **atyred,** 463.
atlest, *pr.* 2 *s.* dost purpose, 379; *pr.* 3 *s.* **atles,** takes aim, 565; *pp.* **atled,** planned, 366; ON. ætla.
attyr, poison, 654; OE. ātor, āttor.
attonys, at once, 338, 1123.
a-twynne, asunder, 66, 136; **attwynne,** 737.
auntred, *pt.* 3 *s.* imperilled, 147; OF. aventurer.
availed, *pt.* 3 *s.* lowered, 249; OF. avaler.
a-vental, moveable front of helmet, 756; AF.* aventail; OF. esventail.
away, 251, 581; **awey,** 253, 419.
a-wide, widely, all round, 857.

baches, streams, 559; OE. bæcc, bæce.
bade, *v.* **bidde.**
bayne, 181, *see Note.*
bak, 359; **bake,** 290, 424.
bal, ball, 397, 828.
bale, evil, 183, 496, 593, 1054.
balies, bellies, 1247; OE. bælig.
balwe-ston, fatal stone, 822; OE. bealu, *gs.* bealwes.
balwe tre; death-bringing tree, gallows, 152.
band, *n.* 586.
baneres, banners, 483; OF. banere.
baners, banner-bearers, 440; OF. baneor.
banke, *v.* **bonke.**
baptemed, *pp.* baptized, 188; *cp.* OF. baptesmement.
bar, bare, 302, 636, 1238.
bar, *v.* ber.
barels, 671, 1247.
bargayned, *pp.* bartered, 1304.
bargaynes, *n.* 1311.
barge, bark, 75.
barn, child, 825.
barn[d], *v.* **brenne.**
baronage, body of barons, 192.
barouns, 73.
barr, bar, 1297; **barriers,** 765, 817.
barren, *pr. pl.* 614.
barst, *v.* **brestyþ.**
basoketes, 132.
bassynes, basins, 1264.
bastiles, towers, 678; F. bastille.
batail, combat, 377, 1095; army, 660, 1081.
batayled, *pt.* 3 *s.* drew up in battle array, 428; *pl.* formed themselves in array, 482.
be, bee, 14; *pl.* **bees,** 32, 34.
be, *inf.* 695; *pr.* 1 *s.* am, 79; 3 *s.* **is,** 31,

109; *pl.* **ben,** 108, 376; **beþ,** 365, 796; *pt.* 2 *s.* **was,** 198; 3 *s.* 3, 8; *pl.* 209, 555, 1028; **wer,** 73; **weren,** 114; *pr.* 2 *s. subj.* **be,** 15; *pt.* 1 *s.* **wer,** 83; 2 *s.* 90; 3 *s.* 7, 400, 694; *pl.* 776; *imp. s.* **be,** 188; *pp.* 171, 1054, *Neg. forms* : *pr.* 3 *s.* **nis,** 128; **nys,** 489; *pt.* 3 *s.* **nas,** 39.
bedde, 739; *g.s.* **beddes,** 1044.
beden, *v.* **bidde.**
bekered, *pt. pl.* fought, 817; *derivation doubtful.*
belfray, tower used in siege operations, 386; *pl.* **belfrayes,** 1188; OF. berfrei, belfrei.
belles, 406.
beltep, *pr.* 3 *s.* 749.
bemes, trumpets, 521; **bemys,** 439; OE. bēme, bīeme.
bemys, rays, 416; OE. bēam.
ben, *v.* **be.**
benden, *pt. pl.* 665, 674; *pp.* **bent,** 820.
bent, field, 308, 482, 540.
ber, barley, 130; OE. bere.
ber, *inf.* bear, 364; *pt.* 3*s.* **bar,** 1078; *pl.* 466; **beren,** 533; *pp.* **born,** 72, 100, 828; b. **down,** taken down, 963.
berde, *v.* **burde.**
berdis, beards, 360.
berne, man, 75; [**beryn**], 16; **burne,** 221; *pl.* **bernes,** 73; **burnes,** 369; OE. beorn.
besauntes, gold coins (first struck at Byzantium), 639, 1060; OF. besan.
best(e), *v.* **goode.**
beste, beast, 397.
bete, *inf.* beat, 1260; *pr.* 3 *s.* **betiþ,** 539; *pt.* 3 *s.* **bet,** 542; *pr. p.* **betynge,** 766; *pp.* **beten,** 10; **betyn,** inlaid, 468; **ybetyn,** embroidered, 414.
betyn, *inf.* kindle, 714; *pr. pl.* 729; OE. bētan.
betyng, *n.* beating, 494.
better, *v.* **goode.**
beþ, *v.* **be.**
bew, fine, 587; OF. beu.
by, village, 100; ON. bȳr, north, OE. bȳ.
by, *prep.* 47, 73; at, 914; *conj.* by the time that, 352.
bible, drink, 720; *from* bib. *vb.* + -le. *First example in* N.E.D. 1529.
bycchyd, accursed, bitter, 585; **bycchet,** 661. *Derivation unknown.*
bidde, *pr.* 1 *s.* ask, 246; command, 345; *pr.* 3 *s.* **byddis,** 794; *pt.* 3 *s.* **bade,** 229, 720; *pt. pl.* **beden,** 440, 1296; **boden,** offered, 1006; OE. bidden, bēodan.
biddyng, *n.* 365.
bide, *inf.* stop, 765.

Glossary. 109

bye, *inf.* buy, 1138; *pt.* 3 *s.* bouȝt, 496; *pr. pl. subj.* byen, 510.
byes, bracelets, 639, 1060; bies, 1274; OE. bēah.
byfelle, *pt.* 3 *s.* 233; *pp.* byfalle, 1066.
byfor, *prep.* 148; *adv.* 276.
big, strong, 451; byg, 774.
bygynne, *inf.* 643, 797; *pt.* 3 *s.* bygan, 221, 1047; *pt. pl.* bygonn, 357; bygonnen, 652; bygonne, 1107; *pp.* 114.
bigly, strongly, 428, 614.
byhold, *inf.* 228; byholde, 334; *imp. pl.* byholdeþ, 493.
byhot, *pp.* promised, 1020; OE. bihātan.
by-houyþ, *pr.* 3 *s.* it behoves, 971.
biker, hive, swarm, 32; *not in* N.E.D.; *see Note.*
bylafte, *pp.* left, continuing, 983.
bild, *pp.* built, 386; bilde, 657.
bilde, *n.* building, 1260.
byleue, *n.* faith, 202, 513.
byleue, *pr.* 1 *s.* believe, 197.
bylompyn, *pp.* befallen, 1064; OE. belimpan.
byndyng, *n.* 494.
bynyþe, *adv.* lower, 705; OE. beniðan, -neoðan.
byr, favouring wind, 290; bir, force, rush, 652; by[rre], 72; ON. byrr.
by-runne, *pp.,* blody b., covered with streams of blood, 599, 1119.
bischop, 585; *pl.* bischopes, 345.
by-seche, *inf.* 777; *pr. pl.* bysecheþ, 1158.
bystrode, *pt.* 3 *s.* 1204.
bytake, *imp. s.* commit, 989.
bytauȝt, *pt.* 3*s.* committed, 1160.
byte, *inf.* 1068; *pr.* 3 *s.* byteþ, 909; *pt.* 3 *s.* boot, 813.
biterly, 221; biterlych, 911.
bytydde, *pt.* 3 *s.* happened, 917; *pl.* bytidde, 234; *pp.* bytide, 31.
bytrayede, *pt. pl.* 350.
bitter, 246.
bytwene, *prep.* 530.
by-wente, *pt. pl.* beset, 11.
bladde, cutting edge, 542; *pl.* bladdys, 392; OE. blǣd.
blased, *pt. pl.* shone, 483.
bleche, blacking, 362; OE.* blecce.
blecken, *pr. pl.* blacken, 362; OE. *bleccan.
bled, *pp.* for-bled, covered with blood, 842.
blesse, *inf.* 1000; *pr.* 3 *s. subj.* 440; *pt.* 3 *s.* blessed, 250.
blessed, *adj.* 181, 188.
blewe(n), *v.* blowe.

blyndfelled, *pt. pl.* blindfolded, 14; OE. fiellan, fellan.
blys, 969.
blyue, quickly, 214, 755, 1042, OE. bī + līfe.
blod, 496, 540; blode, 12, 936; mood, 1092.
blody, *adv.* with blood, 599, 1119.
blonke, steed, 271; *pl.* blonkes, 521; OE. blanca.
blowe, *inf.* 728; *pr. pl.* blowen, 439, 521; *pt.* 3 *s.* blewe, 57; *pl.* blewen, 718.
blowyng, *n.* 740.
bocklyd, *pp.* buckled, 752.
boden, *v.* bidde.
bodeword, message, 969; bodeworde, 955; OE. bod + word.
body, 10, 224; *pl.* bodyes, 1311.
boffetis, blows, 14.
boke, book, 1005; *pl.* bokes, 591, 1322.
bolde, 229.
bold-brayned, 1188.
bole-fur, bale-fire, 714; ON. bāl + fȳri, OE. fȳr.
bolled, *pt.* 3 *s.* 16 (?)*scribal error for* bobbed, struck; *cp.* OF. bober, to mock.
bolned, *pt.* 3 *s.* swelled, 57; ON. bolgna.
boltes, 614.
bon, bone, 716.
bone, prayer, 181.
bone, 144 (?)*scribal error for* bode, commandment, OE. bod.
bonden, *v.* bounden.
bonke, shore, 290; banke, 73.
bonked, *pp.* enclosed by banks, 663.
boot, *v.* byte.
borden, wooden, 359.
bordes, trestle-tables, 963.
bordored, *pp.* 406.
bore, boar, 543, 781.
born, *v.* ber.
borwe, town, 306, 486; borow, 652; [burghe], 404; burwe, 369, 439; burowe, 774.
bost, *n.* boast, 297, 795.
bot, *conj.* but, 21, 90; unless, 200, 510.
bote, deliverance, 1054.
bote, boot, 813.
botnyng, healing, 246; help, 388; OE. bōt + ME. -en + -ing.
boteles, incurable, 1141.
boþe, 44, 155, 232; *g. pl.* boþere, 1003.
bouȝt, *v.* bye.
boun, *adj.* ready, 345, 405; (?)183 *see Note*; ON. būinn.
boun, *inf.* 183 (*see Note*); *pr.* 3 *s.* bounys, 741; *from* boun, *adj.*

bounden, *p. pl.* 359, 585; *pp.* 825; **bonden**, 10.
bourd, trick, 1165; OF. bourde.
bowe[l]ed, disembowelled, 942.
boweþ, *pr.* 3 *s.* goes, 765; *pl.* **bowyn**, 817.
bow-men, 665.
brad, *pt.* 3 *s.* roasted, 1078; OE. brǣdan, brēdan.
brayde, moment, 1095; **brayd**, 66; **atte b.**, in a moment, 1192; OE. gebregd.
brayde(n), *v.* **breydeþ**.
brayn, 540, 822, 1199.
brayned, *pp.* 829, 1192.
brake, *v.* **breke**.
brass, 306; **bras**, 766.
brast, *v.* **brestyþ**.
breche, breeches, 942.
bredde, *pt.* 3 *s.* bred, 32.
brede, bread, 132; **bred**, 1069, 1141.
[br]ed[e], *inf.* spread, 1047; **[brede]**, 288 (*see Note*); OE. brǣdan.
breydeþ, *pr.* 3 *s.* brandishes, 543; *pl.* **brayden**, fling, 615; *pt.* 3 *s.* **brayde**, 827; *pp.* **brouden**, twisted, interlinked, 615; **browded**, 744; OE. bregdan.
breke, *inf.* 144; *pt.* 3 *s.* **brake**, 1112; *pp.* broken, 132.
brenne, *inf.* burn, 1260; **brennen**, 714; *pt. pl.* **brente**, 302; **brenten**, 657, 716; *pr. p.* **brennande**, 397, 468, 810; **brenn[a]n[d]**, 671; **bren[n]yng**, 1219; *pp.* **brent**, 722; **brend**, burnished, 1264; **barn[d]**, 468; ON. brenna, OE. bærnan.
breste, *n.* 471.
brestyþ, *pr.* 3 *s.* bursts, breaks, 1082; *pt.* 3 *s.* **brast**, 1199; **barst**, 586; *pt. pl.* **brosten**, 20, 306, 533; *pp.* 606, 977; ON. bresta, OE. berstan.
brest-plate, 744.
bretages, *v.* **britage**.
bretful, brim-full, 386; OE. brerdfull.
bretnes, *v.* **br[it]ten**.
bridul, 781.
brigges, draw-bridges, 615.
briʒt, 334, 539; **bryʒt**, 198.
briʒtned, *pt.* 3 *s.* 545.
briʒtnesse, 411.
brynye, coat of mail, 744; **brunee**, 1238; *pl.* **brynnyis**, 277; **bruneys**, 955; ON. brynja; *cp.* **burne[s]**.
brynston, brimstone, 671; OE. brinnan + stān.
britage, wooden tower, 589; *pl.* **bretages**, 573; OF. bretesche, AF. brutesche.

britaged, *pp.* provided with a projecting wooden gallery, 334; **ibrytaged**, 409.
br[it]ten, *inf.* slay, 902; *pr.* 3 *s.* **bretnes**, 1128; *pt. pl.* **brutned**, 1235; *pp.* **britned**, 404; **brytned**, 936; OE. brytnian.
broches, 639, 1060.
brode, broad, 57, 446; **brod**, 288, 600.
broʒt, *pt. pl.* brought, 192, 231; *pp.* **y-broʒt**, 297.
broken, *v.* breke.
bronde, sword, 539.
brosed, *pp.* crushed, 829; OF. bruser.
brosten, *v.* **brestyþ**.
broþ, *n.* broth, 720; **broþe**, 1069.
broþer, 148, 936.
brouden, browded, *v.* **breydeþ**.
browet, soup, 1069; F. brouet.
browne, 716; **brown**, glittering, 542.
brunee, **bruneys**, *v.* **brynye**.
brutned, *v.* **br[it]ten**.
burde, maiden, 100; **berde**, woman, 1087; OE. byrde.
burges, citizen, 490; *pl.* 1247.
[burghe], *v.* **borwe**.
burie, *inf.* 568, 1148.
burne(s), *v.* **berne**.
burne[s], coats of mail, 558; OE. byrne; *cp.* **brynye**.
burnesched, *part. adj.* 749.
bur(o)we, *v.* **bowe**.
buschment, ambushment, 1112.
busy, 568.
buske, *inf.* prepare, 183; *pr. pl.* **busken**, set forth, hasten, 369, 739; *pt.* 3 *s.* **busked**, dressed, 741; ON. būask.

cacchen, *inf.* take, 733; *pr. pl.* 524; *pt. pl.* **cauʒten**, 584; **kayʒt**, 944; *pp.* **cauʒt**, 1026; **cacched**, driven, 724; *pr. pl. subj.* **cacche**, get, 768.
caytifes, *v.* **kaytif**.
calt, 1223.
calleþ, *pr.* 3 *s.* 85; *pp.* **called**, 209; **caled**, 34, 47; **calde**, 934; **ycalled**, 6.
calued, *pt.* 3 *s.* calved, 1223.
cam(e), *v.* **come**.
cameles, 453.
cancred, *part adj.* afflicted with cancer, 125.
candel, 1255.
canker, cancer, 30;' **cankere**, 174.
canste, *pr.* 2 *s.* knowest, 86; *pt.* 3 *s.* **couþe**, 77, 89, 801; could, 128; **couþ**, 39; *pl.* **couþe**, 473, 1034.
car, care, 38, 1236.
careynes, *v.* **karayn**.
careful, anxious, 1010.

Glossary. 111

cariep, *pr.* 3 *s.* goes, 255; ON. keyra; *cp.* ONF. carier.
carpyn, *inf.* speak, 357; *pr. pl.* carpen, 730; *pt.* 3 *s.* carped, 196; ON. karpa.
carte-fulle, *pl.* 1275.
cartes, 1002.
caste, throwing of missiles, 621.
castels, battlemented structures borne by the elephants, 424, 446, 563.
castep, *pr.* 3 *s.* 746; *pt.* 3 *s.* kest, 1328; *pl.* kast, 944; kesten, 641, 675; caste, devised, 159; casten, 1105; *pp.* cast, cast, 1266.
cate, purchase, 1305; *aph. form of* NF. acat. *this sense is not recorded in* N.E.D.
cattes, 699.
cauʒt(en), *v.* cacchen.
cause, 340, 344.
certayn, 81.
certiflet, *pp.* declared formally, 380.
cesed, *pt. pl.* ceased, 1239; *pp.* 1137.
chaf, 802.
chaynes, *v.* cheyne.
chayr, chair, 467.
charbohlis, carbuncles, 325; charbokeles, 467; OF. charbucle.
chares, chariots, 457; OF. char.
charge, *n.* 343.
charge, *pr.* 1 *s.* 96; 3 *s.* chargep, 883; *pt. pl.* charged, 364; put in charge, 732; *pp.* loaded, 457.
charme, in *c.*, in the form of an incantation, 848; *pl.* charmes, 96.
chaunce, chance, 883.
chaundelers, 590.
chaungep, *pr.* 3 *s.* 1092.
chauntementes, enchantments, 96.
chef, chief, 337.
cheffare, merchandise, 1314; OE. cēap + faru.
che[f]ly, especially, 883.
cheyne, chain, 762; *pl.* chaynes, 615.
cheke, 29, 87; *pl.* chekes, side-pieces, 469.
chek-wecche, officer who goes on his rounds to challenge the sentinels, 732.
chepe, *inf.* buy, 1314; OE. cēapian.
chepis, *pl.* bargains, 1314; OE. cēap.
chertes, *v.* scherte.
ches, *pt.* 3 *s.* chose, 139; *pl.* chossyn, 154; chosen, 731; took, 337; *pp.* choice, 457; c[h]osen, 467.
chese, cheese, 364; *pl.* cheses, 380.
cheuentayn, chieftain, 337; *d. s.* chyuentayn, 364; *pl.* cheuentayns, 325; chyuentayns, 731; OF. chevetaine.

chewe, *inf.* 1072.
chiden, *pr. pl.* 731.
child, 104.
[c]hoppyn, *pr. pl.* place as a covering, 325; *see Note.*
chosen, chossyn, *v.* ches.
churche, 139.
cyte, city, 42; cite, 133, 137 (*see Note*); *pl.* citees, 135; cytees, 295.
[citezeins], 74.
clayme, *n.* 498; *cp.* quycke clayme.
clansed, *pt.* 3 *s.* purified, made bright, 241; OE. clǣnsian.
clarioun, *n.* used *as adj.* trumpet, 525; *see Note.*
clateren, *inf.* rattle (with thunder claps), 54; *pr. pl.* fall with loud noise, 569.
claures, *pl.* claws, 699; *see Note.*
clef, cliff, 102.
clene, *adj.* clean, pure, 91, 856; *adv.* entirely, 627, 694, 827.
clenly, entirely, 174.
cler, bright, 241.
clerke, ecclesiastic, 580; clerk, learned man, 128; *pl.* clerkes, 314.
cleue, *inf.* cleave asunder, 54; *pp.* cloue, 822.
clymyp, *pr.* 3 *s.* climbs, 1194.
cloched, *pt.* 3 *s. subj.*, held as with a claw, 30; OE. clyccan.
closed, *pp.* enclosed, 453, 774; croune ... closed, 'close crown,' i.e. one arched in by crossing bands, 757.
clop, 167; clope, 224, 470; *pl.* clopys, 324.
cloudes, 54.
cloue, *v.* cleue.
clustred, *part. adj.* 675.
cogges, ships, 286; OF. cogue.
cold, 534; *n.* colde, 1026.
colke, core, 916; (?)OFris. M.L.G. kolk, a hole.
colour, 331.
colour[ede], *pp.* 746.
combred, *pp.* harassed, 898.
com[e], *n.* coming, 344, 491; *see Note.*
come, *inf.* 263; *pt.* 2 *s.* cam, 1084; 3 *s.* 551; came, 119, 563; come, 626, 1062; *pl.* 441; comen, 156; comyn, 1050; *pp.* 271; comen, 489; come, 79; *imp. pl.* comep, 767.
comelich, noble, 950; comlich, 764.
comens, common people, 314.
comfort, succour, 244.
comyng, *n.* 340.
commaundip, *pr.* 3 *s.* 263.
complet, *pp.* 1039.
complyn, compline, 608.
comsed, *pp.* begun, 635; OF. comencer.

Glossary.

conceyued, *pt.* 3 *s.* conceived, 104.
condit, conduit, 685; safe-conduct, 1039; condi[t], 1032; OF. conduit.
consayl, council, 209; conseyl, 85; scheme, 350, 724.
constables, military officers, 881.
contreys, countries, 43; contrees, 314.
coppe, cup, drinking feast, 914.
cop[r]e, copper, 1266.
corde, 363.
corners, points, 759.
corres, curs, 699.
corrours, couriers, 191; OF. coreor.
cors, body, person, 220; *pl.* corses, 681, 714, 1242.
cors, *v.* cours.
corsed, *adj.* accursed, 684, 1305; coursed, 721.
corsedlich, *adv.* wickedly, 1330.
corteys, courteous, 177.
coste, district, 191; *pl.* costes, coasts, 64.
cote, coat-armour, 746.
coþe, *inf.* to infect with disease, 684; *see Note.*
countours, counters, anything used in computing, 128.
cours, course, 191; *pl.* cors, 685.
coursed, *v.* corsed.
couþ(e), *v.* canste.
coueyte, *inf.* 340.
couenaunt, 995.
couered, *v.* keuereþ.
craft, power, 86; crafte, 186.
craftily, skilfully, 462; OE. cræftiglice.
craftly, skilfully, 1266; OE. cræft+-ly.
crayers, small vessels, 286; OF. crayer.
crammen, *pr. pl.* 682.
cramp, 1026.
crepel, cripple, 1029; OE. crypel.
cry, *n.* 18, 525; proclamation, 635.
crye, *inf.* proclaim, 1313; *pr.* 3 *s.* crieþ, cries, 719; *pt.* 3 *s.* cried, 244; *pr. p.* criande, 196.
criour[s], officers of justice, 1295.
cristalle, 102.
cristen, *adj.* Christian, 190; *pl.* 424, 835.
croys, cross, 18, 268; OF. crois.
croysen *pr. pl.* cross, 524; OF. croisier.
croked, *pt.* 3 *s.* grew crooked, 1029; *part. adj.* 125.
crosschen, *pr. pl.* crash, 534; OF. croussir.
croune, crown, 17, 299.
crouned, *part. adj.* 273.
cud, *v.* kyþeþ.
cure, *n.* 194, 1039; cur, 86.
cured, *pp.* 268.

cuþe, country, 38; kuþþe, 90; OE. cȳþþ, cȳþ.

day, 124, 426; *g.s.* daies, 676; *pl.* d. in ȝour lyue, during your life, 772; do of dawe, to slay, 184, 1299; OE. dæg, dagum.
dale, 572.
dartes, 838.
daschen, *pr. pl.* 1087; *pt. pl.* dascheden, 572; dasch[e]de, 712.
daunsyng, *n.* 851.
dawe, *v.* day.
ded, dead, 124, 200.
dede, deed, 151, 904; *pl.* dedes, 99; dedis, 149.
deden, *v.* done.
deep, *v.* depe.
defaute, lack of food, 1073, 1244.
defence, 618, 668, 867.
defende, *inf.* 312.
defensable, able to defend, 445.
defye, *inf.* digest, 1162; *derivation unknown.*
dey, *inf.* die, 691; *pt.* 3 *s.* deyed, 6, 90.
deil, *v.* doil.
de[y]s, dais, 693; OF. deis.
dele, *inf.* deal, 1104.
delyueryn, *pr. pl.* grant, 1032.
dempte, *pt.* 3 *s.* decreed, 134; *pl.* demeden, 267, 693.
departe, *inf.* separate, 230.
depe, *adj.* deep, 838; *n.* 281, 1150; deep, 52, 68.
der, dear, noble, 126, 180, 222; *adv.* dearly, 200, 296.
dered, *pt.* 3 *s.* harmed, 804; OE. derian.
dereworþ, glorious, 296.
derkned, *pt.* 3 *s.* grew dark, 1280.
derst, *pt.* 3 *s.* there needed, 1255; *see Note.*
dest, *v.* done.
destruyed, *pt. pl.* 1098; *pp.* distroied, 1292.
deþ, death, 124, 222.
deue, deaf, 126.
deuel, 782; *pl.* deueles, 184.
deuelich, horribly, 449.
deuysed, *v.* dyuyseþ.
dewe, 624.
diademe, 928.
diche, trench, 625; *pl.* diches, 681.
dide(n), *v.* done.
dyemauntes, diamonds, 1253; OF. diamant.
dyȝs, noȝt a d., not a bit, 804; OF. de, a die.
diȝten, *pt. pl.* 577 (*see Note*); *pp.* diȝt, arrayed, set, 426.

Glossary. 113

dym[m]ed, *pt. pl.* grew dim, 725; dymedyn, 531.
dyn, noise, 248.
dyner, dinner, 953.
dynnyng, noise, 851.
dynte, blow, 1198; *pl.* dyntes, 799.
disciples, 134.
distroied, *v.* destruyed.
dit, (?)noise, 248; dyt, 1189; *see Note on* l. 804.
dyuysep, *pr.* 3 *s.* observes, 485; *pt. pl. refl.* deuysed, took counsel, 1233; *pp.* contrived, provided, 756.
do, *v.* done.
dogges, 782.
doil, grief, 248; deil, 641, 712, 851; OF. deol, dol.
doylful, piteous, 159, 222.
dom, sentence, 366; dome, decision, 267.
dombe, dumb, 126.
domes-men, judges, 693.
dommyn, *pr. pl.* fill up, 681; common Teut. dam(m), *n.*; *cp.* OE. demman; *first ex. of v. in* N.E.D. 1553.
done, *inf.* do, 212; do, 134, 184; doun, 904; *pr.* 2 *s.* dest, 996; 3 *s.* doþ, 310, 985; *pl.* doun, 984; *pt.* 3 *s.* dide, 127; *pl.* diden, 319; deden, 338; *pp.* don, 179; do, 1323; doun, 853.
dongen, *pt. pl.* knocked, 676; *cp.* ON. dengja.
donked, *pp.* made wet, 624; *cp.* ON. dökk, a pool.
dore, door, 1087; *pl.* dores, 1253.
dore-nayl, 1074.
doþ, *v.* done.
douȝty, valiant, 475; douȝti, 459, 990; *sup.* douȝtiest, 1203.
doun, *adv.* down, 9, 68.
doun, *v.* done.
doust, dust, 531, 719; OE. dūst.
dragoun, 280, 389.
drawen, *inf.* 713; *pt.* 3 *s.* drowe, dragged, 940; *pl.* drowen, went, 426, 449; *refl.* 319; *pp.* drawyn, hoisted, 389.
dreden, *pr. pl.* fear, 366.
drenche, *inf.* drown, 68.
drenches, potions, 95.
dressed, *pp.* lifted up, 389; ydressed, prepared, 278.
driede, *pt.* 3 *s.* suffered, 120; OE. drēogan.
d[r]yed, *pt. pl.* dried, 789.
driȝten, the Lord, 517; OE. dryhten.
drynke, *n.* 719.
drynke, *inf.* 1070.
dryueþ, *pr.* 3 *s.* is impelled, 58; aims a blow, 1206; *pl.* dryuen, endure, 708;

pt. 3 *s.* drof, was carried, 52, 531; *pl.* dryuen, hurled, 838; *pp.* set, 1253.
dromedaries, 570; dromedarius, 449.
dromound, a very large ship, 52; AF. dromund.
dropeden, *pt. pl.* dripped, 789.
droppe, *n.* 771.
drouned, *pp.* 479.
drowe(n), *v.* drawen.
duk, duke, 1125; *g. s.* dukes, 1210; *pl.* 216, 267.
dwelle, *inf.* remain, 1094; *pt.* 3 *s.* dwelde, dwelt, 309.

eche, each, 92.
echon, each one, 456, 763.
efte, afterwards, 784.
egle, eagle, 326.
eȝte, eight, 1126.
eyen, eyes, 997, 1045.
eyȝt, eighth, 145.
eyr, *v.* ayer.
eke, also, 143.
eldres, old people, 108.
eleuen, 1171.
elleueþ, eleventh, 147; *cp.* OE. endlyfta.
ellis, besides, 958; ellys, 348.
emperie, imperial rule, 5; OF. emperie.
emperour, 1, 46.
enclosed, *pp.* shut in, 688.
encresche, *inf.* increase, 139; OF. encreiss-, AF. encress-.
ende, *n.* 67; spear-point, 1118; *see Note.*
endeles, eternal, 113.
endid, *pt.* 3 *s.* 460; ended, 920; *pl.* 721.
ene, *adv.* alone, 121; OE. ǣne.
enemy, 1052.
enfamy[n]ed, *pp.* starved, 1244.
enforme, *inf.* instruct, 1154.
engyne, engine, of warfare, 1205; *pl.* engynes, 320, 674.
enys, once, 122; OE. ǣnes.
entriþ, *pr.* 3 *s.* takes possession, 930; *first example of this sense in* N.E.D. 1523.
enuenymyd, *pp.* poisoned, 654.
[er], *conj.* before, 114; *adv.* er, formerly, 252; *sup.* erst, 920.
eraunde, 46; erand, 212.
ere, *n.* ear, 104.
erye, *inf.* plough, 1290; OE. erian.
erles, earls, 264.
ernest, 859, 930.
erst, *v.* [er].
erþe, earth, 9, 86; [erþ]e, 1142.
est, east, 1226.

SIEGE OF JERUSALEM.

I

114   Glossary.

etyþ, pr. 3 s. eats, 1084; pl. eten, 1071;
  pt. pl. 1164.
etnes, giants, 776; OE. eoten.
eued, pt. 3 s. gave birth to, 1224; OE.
  eowu, a ewe.
eure, fortune, destiny, 994; OF. eure.
euen, exactly, 146; euene, 452.
euer, adv. 113.
euereche, every, 498; e. a, 1167; OE.
  æfre ælc.
ewe-lombe, ewe-lamb, 1224.

face, 28, 175; (?)pl. 1143.
fader, father, 109; d. s. 31; g. s. 1025.
fayle, inf. be lacking, 792; pt. 3 s.
  fayled, 786; pl. fayleden, lacked,
  593.
fayn, glad, 1009.
fayndom, joy, 1025; not in N.E.D.;
  OE. fægn + dōm.
faynt, weak, 1162; feynt, 877; feyn[t],
  513.
fayntly, adv. deceitfully, 492; OF.
  feint, feigned.
fair, goodly, 194, 551; sup. fairest,
  fittest, 1104; adv. fayr, 741.
fayþ, 203, 968.
faiþles, unbelieving, 481.
fale, v. fele.
falle, inf. happen, 883; pr. 3 s.
  fallyþ, appertains, 506; pl. fallen,
  fall, 238, 373, 597; pt. 3 s. ful, 61;
  pl. felle, 942; fellen, 1073; pp.
  fallen, 610, 1286; OE. feallan.
falliþ, pr. 3 s. fells, 926; OE. fællan.
fals, 513, 551.
falsede, falsehood, 1104.
falwed, pt. pl. turned pale, 1143; OE.
  fealwian.
fanes, pennants, 287; OE. fana.
fanward, vanguard, 429, 549 (see
  Note); OF. avangarde, -warde.
farcostes, ships, 285; ON. farkostr.
faste, adv. 52, 203, 230.
fastyng, part. adj. 1086.
fauchoun, falchion, sword, 395;
  fauch[ou]n, 392.
faucoun, falcon, 310; pl. faucouns,
  888.
faute, blemish, 175.
fauted, pt. 3 s. was lacking, 387; OF.
  fauter.
fa[x], hair, 360; OE. feax.
feble, 878.
fecche, inf. fetch, 211, 770; pr. 3 s.
  feccheþ, 1091.
fedde, pt. 3 s. 130; pr. p. fedyng, 1326.
feet, v. fote.
feffyt, pt. 3 s. gave, 1326; AF. feoffer,
  OF. fieffer.

fey, dying, mortally wounded, 460,
  610, 770, 926; OE. fǣge.
feynt, v. faynt.
feynte, pr. pl. grow weak, swoon, 1144.
fel, skin, 988; pl. felles, 694.
felawys, companions, 142.
felde, field, 367, 384, pl. feldes, 412.
felde, pt. pl. perceived, 1086; felleden,
  239; OE. fēlan.
fel[d]e, pt. 3 s. felled, 595; OE.
  fiellan, fellan.
fele, many, 43, 305, 898; fale, 926;
  OE. fela, fcala.
felle(n), v. falle.
fel[l]e, fierce, 867.
felleden, v. felde.
felly, fiercely, 818.
fende, fiend, 520, 834.
fenged, v. fongen.
fer, far, 78; comp. ferr, 129, 367;
  ferre, 131, 378.
ferce, v. fers.
ferde, army, 479, 551, 595; OE. fierd,
  ferd.
ferde, pt. 3 s. behaved, was, 1251;
  impers. 530, 548; pl. 1075; OE.
  fēran.
ferde, for f. for fear, 61; OE. for,
  færed.
ferke, inf. go, 873; pr. 3 s. ferkiþ,
  1042; pp. yferked, carried (them),
  78; OE. fercian.
ferly, n. marvel, 31, 194, 233; OE.
  færlic, adj.
ferlich, terrible, 454; OE. fǣrlic.
fers, fierce, 834, 987; ferce, 867.
ferst, ridge-pole, used loosely for roof,
  831; OE. fyrst.
ferste, v. first.
ferþe, fourth, 141; OE. fēorþa.
ferþer, adv. more distantly, 272.
[ferthynge], farthing, 1308.
ferþyng-worþ, farthing's worth, 1139.
fete, v. fote.
[fethyrhames], wings, 679; OE. feðer-
  hama.
fetoures, parts of the body, 1049;
  OF. feture.
fettes, pr. 3 s. fetches, 1042; pt. pl.
  fetten, 189; OE. fetian.
feþres, feathers, 727.
fewe, 1110; comp. fewer, 23.
fif, five, 130; tyf, 129, 1113.
fifþe, 142.
fiʒt, n. fighting, 509.
fiʒten, inf. 650; pt. pl. touʒt, 535, 818.
fynde, inf. 367; pr. 1 s. 23; pt. pl.
  founden, 1270; fondyn, 394; pp.
  fond, 460.
fyne, adj. 742.

Glossary. 115

fyngres, 1027.
firmament, 548, 697.
first, 109; ferste, 429; furst, 858; OE. fyrst.
fisch, 1068; *pl.* fisches, 130.
fyue, 469; *read* fyne.
flambeþ, *pr.* 3 *s.* is violently exhaled, 239; *pr. p.* flambande, flaming, 653; OF. flamber.
flasches, pools, 571.
[f]latte, *adj.* 1073; ON. flatr.
flatte, *pt.* 3 *s.* fell flat, 61; *pl.* flatten, 808; *not found in this sense in* N.E.D., *or in any sense before the 17th century.*
flavour, odour, 239.
flee, *inf.* fly, 405; fle, 888; OE. flēogan.
fleyn, *pp.* flayed, 694; OE. flēan, *pp.* *flǣgen.
flesche, 31, 175, 702.
fleschy, plump, 1246.
fleþe, *pr.* 3 *s.* flees, 520; *pt.* 3 *s.* flow, 824; flowe, 905; *pl.* flowen, 310, 611; OE. flēon.
flynt, 530, 1122.
flocken, *v.* of flocken.
flode, 78; floode, 479.
floynes, small ships, 285; OF. flouin.
flor, floor, 831.
floryns, 1139; [florence], 1308.
flot, *v.* a flot.
flow(e)(n), *v.* fleþe.
fode, food, 770.
foyned, *pt. pl.* thrust, 818; OF. foine, a fish-spear.
fole, *v.* foul.
folis, foal's, 814.
folke, 129, 203, 387.
folowed, *pt.* 3 *s.* baptized, 203; *pl.* foulled, 189; OE. fullwian, fullian.
folweþ, *pr.* 3 *s.* follows, 490; *pt. pl.* folwed, 280, 906.
foman, 1056.
fomed, *pt.* 3 *s.* 571.
[fonde], *inf.* go, 679; OE. fandian.
fond(yn), *v.* fynde.
fongen, *inf.* take, 1164; *pt.* 3 *s.* fenged, 1306; OE. fōn, *pp.* fangen.
font, 189.
for, *cong.* 36; *prep.* 92; instead of, 154; in spite of, 19, 1196.
forbesyn, example, 395; OE. forebysen.
for-beten, *pp.* severely beaten, 842.
for[g]yue, *inf.* 1159.
for-juggyd, *part. adj.* condemned, 298.
for-justes, *pr.* 3 *s.* overcomes in jousting, 538.
forlong, furlong, 824.

formes, *pr.* 3 *s.* appoints, 417; *pp.* fourmed, made, 109.
forsakeþ, *pr.* 3 *s.* refuses, 1061; *pt.* 3 *s.* forsoke, 1155; *pl.* 1134.
for-schorne, *pt. pl.* tore to pieces, 558.
for-stoppette, *part. adj.* completely imprisoned, 575.
forþ, *adv.* 189, 426.
forþ mid, *prep.* before, 233; *cp.* forwith, forth-with.
forþred, *v.* furþer.
forþ-with, *prep.* before, 855.
forwardis, covenants, 276; OE. foreweard.
fote, foot, 742; any f. the smallest distance, 520; to f., to the ground, 727; *pl.* feet, 392, 697; fete, 219.
fouȝt, *v.* fiȝten.
foul, bird, 1009; foule, 310; *coll.* fole, fowl, 888; *pl.* foules, 727.
foulled, *v.* folowed.
founden, *v.* fynde.
four, 288.
fourche, fork of the body, 742; OF. fourche.
fourmed, *v.* formes.
fourty, 436, 775.
frayneþ, *pr.* 3 *s.* asks, 1298; fraynes, 78; OE. fregnan.
fram, from, 42, 46, 336.
freke, man, 131, 219; OE. freca.
frende, friend, 1056; *pl.* frendes, 968.
frendles, 905.
frendschup, 1056.
fresch, 283; *comp.* frescher, 858.
frytted, *part. adj.* (?)fretted, tormented, 814; OE. fretan; (?) wounded, *cp.* OF. fraite, frete, an opening or breach.
fro, from, 124.
frosletes, forcelets, coffers, 831; OF. forceret.
frounte, 650.
froward, from, 63, 598, 969.
frut, fruit, 1326.
ful, *v.* falle.
fulfille, *inf.* 276.
fulle, *n.* fill, 131.
fulle, *adj.* 671; ful, 330; *adv.* 91, 214.
fur, *v.* gledfur.
fured, *pp.* burnt, 896.
furst, *v.* first.
furþer, *inf.* promote, 982; *pp.* forþred, 1333.
fuste, first, hand, 1140; *pl.* fustes, 1027; OE. fȳst.

gaddes, bars, 1262; ON. gaddr.
gaylers, *d. pl.* jailers, 1160; *cp.* ONF. gaole (*with hard* g).
gayly, *adv.* 258.

Glossary.

gayne, *inf.* benefit, 40.
galees, galleys, 287.
galwes, crosses, 696.
gan, *pt.* 3 *s.* did, 608; *pl.* **gon**, 54.
gapande, *pr. p.* 390; ON. gapa.
garde, *pt.* 3 *s.* caused, 258; ON. görva.
garrite, siege-tower, 647; OF. garite, a watch-tower.
gate, *v.* **gete**.
gate, road, 1215; ON. gata.
gawged, *pt.* 3 *s.* looked out, 410; *cp.* gadgc, *n.* and *v.* search, gauge, scrutiny, *suppl. to Jamieson*; ONF. gauger; *see Note.*
gentyl, noble, 785; **gentile**, 1321.
ger, gear, 546, 589, 638, 665.
gete, *inf.* get, take, 1176; *pt.* 3 *s.* **gate**, 26; *pl.* [**gete**], 921; **geten**, 638; *pp.* 1215.
gilden, golden, 546; **gilde**, 326; **gild**, 558; OE. gylden.
gile, guile, treachery, 1102.
gynful, ingenious, 809; **jenfulle**, crafty, 1133; *aph. form of* OF. engin.
[**g**]**yng**, company, 280; OE. genge.
girdel, 747; *pl.* **girdeles**, 638.
girdiþ, *pr.* 3 *s.* thrusts, 566; *pt. pl.* **girden**, 552; *derivation unknown.*
glad, 195, 1041.
glade, *inf.* cheer, 37.
gledfur, glowing fire, 1252; **gled-fur**, 415; OE. gléd + fȳr.
gledis, embers, 1078.
glitered, *pt.* 3 *s.* 415.
glowande, *part. adj.* glowing, glittering, 908, 1014, 1252.
glowes, gloves, 753; OE. glóf.
gnawen, *pp.* 1090.
go, *inf.* 343; *pr.* 3 *s.* **gooþ**, 1019; *pt.* 3 *s.* ȝede, 237, 561; *pl.* 353; ȝeden, 553, 1237; *pp.* **gon**, 37, 929; OE. gān, ēode.
gobet, morsel, 1142; OF. gobet.
god, God, 84, 107; *g. s.* **goddis**, 180.
goions, pivots, 466; OF. gojon.
gold, *n.* 84, 258, 397.
golden, 287.
gome, man, 165, 922; *pl.* **gomes**, 343, 390; OE. guma.
gommes, gums, 95.
gon, *v.* **gan**, **go**.
goode, *adj.* 95, 546; *as n.*, good, 84; *sup.* **beste**, 537; *adv.* **wel**, 244, 514, 791; *comp.* **better**, 93; *sup.* **best**, 266, 965.
[**g**]**oren**, *pr. pl.* disembowel, 1167; *pt. pl.* **gored**, 941; *derivation doubtful*; (?) *cp.* OE. gār.
goste, 103.

goteres, water-channels, 560; OF. gutiere.
gottes, *v.* **guttes**.
goutes, streamlets, 560; *aph. form of* OF. esgout.
[**g**]**ouen**, *v.* ȝeuen.
grace, 892; thanks, 254.
grace, grass, herb, 40; *pl.* **graces**, 95.
gray, 620, 745, 753.
greyn, branch, part, 107; ON. grein.
granteþ, agrees, 999; **grauntep**, 1030.
gra[te], lance rest, 745; *see Note.*
grecys, stairs (of the siege-tower), 651; OF. gre, *coll. pl.* grez.
grehounde, greyhound, 1248.
grem, trouble, vexation, 274, 922; ON. gremi.
gret, gritstone, 620; OE. gréot.
grete, great, 87, 195, 854; *comp.* **gretter**, 823; *sup.* **grettist**, 647.
greued, *part. adj.* angered, 552; OF. grever.
griffouns, 552; OF. grifoun.
grym, cruel, fierce, 40, 50, 327; *adv.* 165.
grype, *inf.* seize, 1262; encircle, 1248; OE. grípan.
grobben, *pr. pl.* dig, 1108.
groded, *pp.* built, 648; ON. greiða + OE. gerādian, to prepare; *not in* N.E.D., *see Note.*
gronnand, *pr. p.* groaning, 195.
grounde, 50, 218, 929; **on g.**, on earth, 908.
grounded, *pp.* 515.
grounden, *part. adj.* 566; *pp.* **ygrounde**, 555.
growyng, *pr. p.* 40; *pp.* **growyn**, 110.
gult, guilt, 1159; OE. gylt.
guttes, 566, 941; **gottes**, 1163.
ȝaf, *v.* ȝeuen.
ȝarken, *pr. pl.* place, 646; OE. gearcian.
ȝate, gate, 1185; *pl.* ȝates, 306, 347, 417.
ȝe, ye, 767, 770; *dat.* ȝou, 1091.
ȝede(n), *v.* **go**.
ȝelde, *inf.* yield, 347, 402; *pr.* 3 *s.* ȝeldeþ, 932, 943; *pt. pl.* ȝelden, 254, 1237; *pp.* ȝolden, requited, 200, 296.
ȝemyed, *pt.* 3 *s.* governed, 60; OE. gīeman, gēman.
ȝerdes, rods, 347; OE. gierd, gerd.
ȝer[m]ande, *pr. pl.* screaming, 943; OE. gyrman, *gierman.
ȝerne, eagerly, 817, 1327; quickly, 789; OE. georne.
ȝete, *inf.* grant, 365; *pp.* ȝet, 974; OE. gēatan.
ȝeten, *pr. pl.* pour, 670; OE. gēotan.

Glossary. 117

ȝeuen, pr. pl. give, 527; pt. 1 s. ȝaf, 1083; 3 s. 22, 215, 343; pl. ȝeuen, 838; pp. 274; [g]ouen, 1142; pr. 3 s. subj. ȝyue, 892, 1108.
ȝif, if, 15, 21; OE. gif.
ȝyrys, years, 23; OE. gēar, gēr.
ȝit, yet, 131; now, 1229.
ȝyue, v. ȝeuen.
ȝo, she, 101, 104; dat. acc. hir, 105, 164.
ȝolden, v. ȝelde.
ȝong, young, 1125.
ȝou, v. ȝe.
ȝour, poss. adj. 295, 340.
ȝourselfen, yourselves, 1213.
ȝouþe, youth, 33.

habben, v. haue.
hacchen, pr. pl. hack, 1121; OF. hache, hacher; see Note.
hacchys, pl. hatches, 61.
had(de), v. haue.
hail, 598.
[halfe], side, 698; pl. halues, 798; cp. aluendel.
hamberkes, hauberks, 442, 845; see Note.
han, v. haue.
hande, 347, 444; honde, 1006; hond, 1220; pl. hondis, 13, 247; on hande, at hand, 769, 862, 1063.
hande-darte, 812.
hand whyle, instant, 168.
hangyþ, pr. 3 s. intr. hangs, 255; trans. hongiþ, 751; pp. honget, crucified, 696; OE. hangian; hōn, pp. hangen.
hape, pr. 3 s. subj. befall, 1103.
haplich, by some chance, in some way, 1232.
hapneþ, pr. 3 s. happens, 168; pt. 3 s. subj. happned, might happen, 1195.
happ, luck, 1003.
hard, adj. 576; harde, 493; hard, n. hard part, 812; adv. 510, 837; harde, 57, 539.
hardy, 651.
harme, 19; pl. harmys, 495.
harmeles, 632.
harmyng, n. 438.
harnays, armour, 436.
hart, 885.
haspeþ, pr. 3 s. buckles, 755.
haste, n. 265, 382.
hasted, pt. 3 s. 19.
hate, n. 158.
hated, pt. 3 s. 923, 1043; hatide, 7.
hatte, v. hoten.
hauleþ, pr. 3 s. draws, 754; see Note.
haue, inf. 1314; habben, 816; pr. 1 s. haue, 127; 3 s. haþ, 92, 162; pl.

han, 380, 403; haue, 512; pt. 3 s. hadde, 19, 76; pr. 3 s. subj. haue, 520, 782, 1039; pt. 3 s. had, 833; pp. hadde, 1279. Neg. forms: pt. 3 s. nadde, 171; pt. 3 s. subj. nad, 834.
hauen, harbour, 192; hauene, 72.
he, 8, 12; dat. acc. hym, 14, 18, 206, 519.
hed, head, 17, 33; pl. hedis, 1112.
hede, heed, 518; see Note.
heer, hair, 711; OE. hǣr, hěr.
hey(e), v. hyȝe.
heyȝt, v. hoten.
heyly, solemnly, 199; heylych, 973.
held(e), v. holde.
heldiþ, pr. 3 s. declines, 550; OE. hieldan, heldan.
hele, heel, 812.
hele, health, 123.
hele, inf. become whole, 168; pp. heled, healed, 174.
helle, 153.
helm, 60.
helmes, helmets, 422.
helmed, part. adj. 583.
helpe, n. 103.
helpe, inf. 39, 119; pr. 3 s. helpys, 778; pp. holpen, 1128; holpyn, 1053.
hem, v. þey.
hemmyd, pp. bordered, 753.
hem-self, 524.
hengen, inf. hang, 788; pr. 3 s. hengeþ, 395; hengyþ, 1012; pt. 3 s. henged, 1219; ON. hengja.
hennes, hence, 1310.
hente, inf. receive, 544; pt. pl. hent, seized, 711; OE. hentan.
hepe, on an h. prostrate, 60; hepe = ahepe, 598; on an hep, all together, 696.
her, poss. adj. their, 40, 234; here, 1311; hir, 1092.
her, here, 245.
her aboute, in this place, 16.
here, army, 307, 992; her, 550; OE. here.
here, inf. hear, 129, 340; hure, 1096; hur, 886; OE. hīeran, hēran, lWS. hȳran.
heried, pp. harrowed, 153; OE. hergan.
heritage, hereditary succession, 5.
hert, heart, 275; herte, 496; life, 992.
herty, hearty, 1121.
heste, promise, 1003; pl. hestes, 275; OE. hǣs.
hetterly, fiercely, 544, 1046; cp. MLG. hetter, OE. hete, n.
heþen, heathen, 307.

118   Glossary.

heþes, heaths, 885.
heþyng, scorn, 493, 1310; he[þ]yng, 1300; ON. hæðing.
heuen, heaven, 67, 111; h. kyng, King of heaven, 518.
heueþ, pr. 3 s. lifts, 1209; OE. hebban, hefþ.
hewen, pr. pl. hew, strike, 1123; pt. 3 s. how, 544; pl. hewyn, 307; hewen, 557; pp. 1279; hammered, 640, 755.
hy, v. þey.
hyde, skin, 175.
hydeles, hideless, flayed ones, 698.
hien, pr. pl. hasten, 583; hyen, 651.
hyȝe, high, 413; on hey, aloft, 228; an heye, 51.
hyȝte, height, 649.
hym, v. he.
hymsulf, reflex. himself, 151; dat. hym-self, 889; OE. sylf, self.
hir, poss. adj. her, 162.
hir, v. ȝo, her.
his, 5, 10, 17.
hit, it, 22, 159; dat. acc. 30, 62, 164.
hit self, refl. 241.
hitteþ, pr. 3 s. 1198; pt. pl. hytte, 803; pp. 825.
hyued, pt. 3 s. dwelt as in a hive, 33.
hoke, inf. depart quickly, 875.
hold, stronghold, 976.
holde, inf. 263, 1003; pr. 1 s. 991; 3 s. holdeþ, 988; pl. holden, 260; pt. pl. held, 228; helde, 1233; pp. holden, 951.
hole, whole, 660; OE. hāl.
holy, wholly, 307.
holy, adj. 103.
holpen, holpyn, v. helpe.
holwe, hollowed out, 662.
hom, home, 1334.
hond(e), hondis, v. hande.
honget, hongiþ, v. hangyþ.
hony, honey, 698.
honour, 994.
honte, v. hunten.
hors, pl. horses, 438.
hosebondes, g. s. husband's, 103.
hote, hot, 670, 878, 1064.
hoten, pp. called, 134, 138; heyȝt, promised, 973; pt. 3 s. hatte, was called, 162; OE. hātan, heht, hātte.
houshed, pp. h. on, derided, 976; OE. hyscan; not in N.E.D.; see Note.
hone, inf. tarry, 871; (?)OE.* hōfian.
houe, 361; see Note.
how, 78.
how, v. hewen.
hulte, hilt, 750; OE. hilt, ON. hjalt, Layamon heolte, helte.

[hundrethe], hundred, 1308; ON. hundrað.
hunger, 878, 1064.
hunten, inf. 885; honte, 875.
hurdiȝs, wooden structure borne by elephants, etc., 576; OF. hourdeis, a palisade.
hur(e), v. here.
hurt, n. malady, 199; pl. hurtes, wounds, 846.
hurtlen, pl. dash violently, 557; pt. 3 s. hurtled, 60; pl. 576.

I, 773, 783; y, 23, 79; dat. acc. me, 83, 93, 183.
yarmed, v. armen.
ybetyn, v. bete.
ibrytaged, v. britaged.
y-broȝt, v. broȝt.
ycalled, v. calleþ.
y-casteled, pp. provided with castle-like structures for warfare, 286.
ydressed, v. dressed.
yferked, v. ferke.
ygrounde, v. grounden.
yheled, part adj. covered, 450; OE. helian.
[ilke a], each, 1308; OE. ǣlc.
yloued, v. loue.
in, prep. 1, 2; on, 24, 1243; adv. in, 1290; yn, 283.
ynempned, v. nempne.
ynowe, adj. enough, 120, 669; ynow, 204.
ynoyntid, v. anonyted.
in-to, 85, 191, 1260; until, (?)during, 256; right up to, 759.
yre, anger, 1046.
yren, iron, 614, 842.
is, v. be.
yschot, v. schoten.
issed, pt. 3 s. issued, 1126; OF. issir.
yþes, waves, 50, 64, 282; OE. ȳþ.
yþrelled, v. þrylled.
ywroȝt, v. wyrche.

jambers, greaves, 1114; AF. jambere.
je[mewes], double rings, 1271; OF. gemel, pl. gemeaus.
jenfulle, v. gynful.
jepouns, tunics, 1114; F. jupon, gipon.
jewels, 1059, 1271.
jewyse, sentence, 349; jewes, judgement, 266; OF. juise.
[ioyned], pt. pl. betook themselves, 292.
joyn[yng], n. 538.
joyntes, pl. 1027.
jo[k]ken, pr. pl. thrust, 819; see Note.

Glossary. 119

joly, splendid, 1228; gay, spirited, 1271; *sup.* jolieste, 538.
[i]ouke, *inf.* rest, 300; OF. jouqier.
juge, *n.* judge, 1294; iuge, 82.
jugge, *inf.* 172, 1294; iugge, 266; juggen, 427.
juggement, *n.* 349.
iustice, *n.* judge, 4; iustise, 82; justise, 1294.
kagge[d], *pp.* fastened, 700; *see Note.*
kay3t, *v.* cacchen.
kaytif, wretch, 1330; *pl.* caytifes, 119, 767; cay[ti]fes, 139.
karayn, carrion, 682; *g. s.* careynes, of flesh, 118; ONF. caroine.
karl, churl, 914; ON. karl.
kast, *v.* casteþ.
kaue, cave, 1111.
keyes, 974.
kempe, man, 1328; OE. cempa; *see Note.*
kene, *adj.* 392, 482.
kenely, *adv.* boldly, 563; kenly, 621.
kepe, *inf.* keep, defend, 275, 438, 608; *pr.* 3 *s.* kepiþ, desires, 1062; *pl.* kepyn, defend, 976; *pt. pl.* kepten, took heed of, 238; defended, kept, 621, 835; *pp.* kept, 995.
kepyng, *n.* 220.
kerchef, 207.
kernels, battlements, 621; kirnels, 682; ONF. kernel, OF. crenel.
kest(en), *v.* casteþ.
keuere, *inf.* cure, 1032; *pt.* 3 *s.* keuered, 125, 207; OF. couvrer, cuevre; Lat. (re)cuperare.
keuereþ, *pr.* 3 *s.* covers, 64; *pp.* keuered, 462; couered, 470; OF. couvrir, cuevre; Lat. cooperire.
kylle, *inf.* 780; *pt. pl.* kilden, struck, 835.
kyn, *n.* alle, k. of all kinds, 525.
kynde, nature, 118, 1029, 1223, 1330; race, 299.
[ky]nde, *pp.* lit, 1255; ON. kynda; *see Note.*
kyng, 6, 38, 85.
kyngdomes, 43.
kyppid, *pt.* 3 *s.* took, 477; ON. kippa.
kirke, temple, 236; [kirke], 255; ON. kirkja.
kirnels, *v.* kernels.
kysseþ, *pr.* 3 *s.* 1010; *pl.* kyssen, 1006.
kyst, chest, ark, 477; ON. kista.
kyþeþ, *pr.* 3 *s.* declares, 964; *imp. s.* kyþe, 979; *pp.* cud, appointed, 211; OE. cȳþan.
knaue child, male child, 104.
kne-depe, 572.

knees, 238, 373.
kneleþ, *pr.* 3 *s.* 167.
knew(e)(n), *v.* knowe.
knyf, 1328.
kny3t, knight, 934; *g. s.* kny3tes, 363; *pl.* 73, 209.
kny3thod, body of knights, 856.
knyt, *pt. pl.* tied, 363; *pp.* 700.
knowe, *inf.* perceive, know, recognise, 331, 411; *pt.* 3 *s.* knewe, 43, 793; *pl.* knew, 186; knewen, 156; *imp. pl.* knoweþ, 768.
kuþþe, *v.* cuþe.

lacchetes, *pl.* loops, 748; OF. lachet.
laccheþ, *pr.* 3 *s.* takes, 1017; *pl.* lacchen, 529; *pt. pl.* lau3te, 279; *pp.* 400, 692; OE. læccan.
ladde(n), *v.* lede.
ladder, 1194.
ladies, 1072, 1245.
lafte(n), *v.* leueþ.
lay, *v.* lygge.
layeþ, *pr.* 3 *s.* strikes, 1190; *pp.* leyd, laid, 171.
layk, game, 872; ON. leikr.
layke, *inf.* play, 840, 866; ON. leika.
lampe, 1256.
langour, wretchedness, 71; langur, 1096.
la[n]terne-hornes, the horn sides of a lantern, 1146.
lasar, *adj.* diseased, 252; laser, 36; *pl. n.* lasares, lepers, 122; med. Lat. lazarus.
laschyng, *pr. p.* rushing, 304.
laste, *adj.* 149, 225, 722; *adv.* 16.
laste, *inf.* 512; *pr.* 3 *s.* lasteþ, 418; *pt.* 3 *s.* laste, 421, 542, 1193; last, 1172.
lat, *v.* lete.
lau3, *inf.* laugh, 495; *pr.* 3 *s.* law3[eþ], 794.
lau3te, *v.* laccheþ.
launces, *pl.* 529, 533.
lawe, 82, 202.
law3[eþ], *v.* lau3.
lawles, 495.
leche, physician, 39, 840; *pl.* leches, 846; OE. læce.
leched, *pt.* 3 *s.* healed, 122.
lede, man, 98, 242; *pl.* ledis, 495; ledes, 519; OE. lēod.
lede, *inf.* 1007; *pr. pl.* ledyn, 1268; *pt.* 3 *s.* ladde, 435, 1133; *pl.* ladden, 564.
leed, *n.* lead, 671.
leel, loyal, 1007; OF. leel.
lef, leaf, 961.
lefte(n), *v.* leueþ, lyften.

Glossary.

leyd, *v*. layeþ.
leke, leek, 1028.
lemaunde, *pr. p.* shining, 1256; OE. lēoma, *n.*
lendis, loins, 748; OE. lendenu, *pl.*
lene, *adj.* lean, 1146, 1245.
lenge, remain, 417, 431; **lengen**, 1135; *pp.* le[ngede], 83; OE. lengan.
lent, *pp.* 1. weren, dwelt, 354; OE. lendan.
lepen, *pr. pl.* leap, 613; **lepyn**, 529.
lered, *adj.* learned, 473; OE. lǣran.
les[e], lying, false, 866; OE. lēas.
lest, *conj.* 1164.
lestenyþ, *imp. pl.* hear, 488; O North. lysna.
lete, *pt.* 3 *s.* caused to, 713; let, 62; *imp. pl.* lat, 495; OE. lǣtan.
leteres, 81; **letres**, 956.
lette, *inf.* hinder, 1214; OE. lettan.
lettered, 692.
leue, *n.* leave, 279, 1166; OE. lēaf.
leuer, *with dat.* preferable, 83, 840, 1135; OE. lēof.
leuerockes, larks, 738; OE. lǣwerce.
leueþ, *pr.* 3 *s.* believes, 167; *pt. pl.* **leued**, 186, 898, 1319; OE. līefan, lēfan.
leueþ, *pr.* 3 *s.* remains, 1124; *pt.* 3 *s.* **lafte**, 568, 603; left, 185; **lefte**, 928; *pt. pl.* **laften**, 302; **lafte**, remained, 437; **leued**, 131; *pp.* **lafte**, left, 1245; **left**, 578; **lefte**, 595; OE. lǣfan.
lyande, *v.* **lygge**.
lycam, body, 171; OE. līchama.
lye, flame, 304; OE. līeg, lēg.
lif, life, 98; **lyue**, 772; **lyf**, person, 1190; *g. s.* **lyues**, life's, 164; vpon **lyue**, alive, 39, 75, in þis **lif**, in this condition, 1135.
liflode, food, 1072; OE. liflād.
lyften, *pr. pl.* lift, 738; *pt.* 3 *s.* **lifte**, 997; *pt. pl.* **leften**, 279; *pp.* **lifte**, 399; ON. lypta.
lygge, *inf.* lie, 869; *pr.* 3 *s.* lyþ, 29; **liþe**, 508; *pt.* 3 *s.* lay, 36; *pr. p.* **lyande**, 328.
liʒt, *n.* light, 242; OE. lēoht.
liʒt, *adj.* swift, active, 762; *comp.* **lyʒtter**, more cheerful, 252; OE. lēoht.
liʒt, *pr.* 3 *s.* falls, 872; *pt. pl.* **lyʒten**, 1208; OE. lihtan.
lykeþ, *pr.* 3 *s.* pleases, 1276; *pt.* 3 *s.* **lyked**, 62, 889.
lyknesse, 245.
lyme, limb, 512.
lympis, *pr.* 3 *s.* befalls, 866; OE. limpan.

lyne, 962.
lyoun, 762; *g. s.* **liouns**, 997; *pl.* **lyouns**, 328.
lyppe, 29.
lyste, *pt.* 3 *s.* desired, 458, 1262.
lyte, *adj.* little, 375; *adv.* 22; OE. lȳt.
litel, 705; OE. lȳtel.
liter, *scribal error for* **lepir**, leprosy, 36 (*see Note*); OF. lepre.
lyþ, **liþe**, *v.* **lygge**.
lyþy, soft, weak, 1028; OE. liðig.
lyue, *inf.* live, 1096; *pr. p.* **lyuande**, 1190.
lyuered, *pp.* clotted, formed into lumps, 29; OE. lifer, *n.*
lyue(s), *v.* **lif**.
lo, *interj.* 245.
lofte, vpon l., on high, 399, 531.
lofte, *v.* a-lofte.
logge, tent, 734; OF. loge.
logge, *scribal error for* **loke** (*see Note*), 122.
loyned, *pp.* kept back, 1088; *aph. form of* OF. aloigner, AF. aloyner.
loke, *inf.* look, 242, 1146; *pr.* 3 *s.* **lokeþ**, 543, 1018; *pl.* **loken**, examine, 846; *pr. p.* **lokande**, looking, 400.
londe, land, 83, 98, 293; *pl.* **londis**, 4; **londys**, 292.
longe, *adv.* 223, 252.
longed, *pt.* 3 *s.* pertained, 387.
lord, 71, 181; *pl.* **lordes**, 39.
lord[chipe], sovereignty, 508.
lordlynges, lordings, lords, 245, 488.
lore, doctrine, 202.
loste, *pt.* 3 *s.* 946.
lote, *n.* look, 997; ON. lāt.
loþe, *n.* evil, 872; OE. lāþ.
loude, *adj.* 248; *adv.* 196, 244.
louken, *pr. pl.* fasten, 613; OE. lūcan.
loused, *pp.* loosed, 762; ON. lauss, *adj.*
louten, *pr. pl.* bow, 956; reverence, 519; OE. lūtan.
loue, *n.* love, 164.
loue, *inf.* love, 1202; *pt. pl.* **loued**, 273; *pp.* **yloued**, 145.
loues, loaves, 130.
low, *adv.* 171; *comp. adj.* **lower**, 1312.
lumpe, 29.
luþer, wicked, 149, 946; OE. lȳþre.

made, *v.* **make**.
mahound, idol, 235; *short form of* Mahomet.
may, maiden, lady, 94; OE. mǣg.
may, *pr.* 2 *s.* 293; *pl.* **mowe**, 821, 873; *pt.* 3 *s.* **myʒt**, 223.
mayde, virgin, 101, 118.
mayle, mail-armour, 450.
mayn, strength, 507.

Glossary. 121

mayntened, *pp.* retained, 927.
mayster, master, 222; *pl.* **maistres,** 336; *as adj.* **maister,** chief, 370; OF. maistre.
maist[rie], supremacy, 507.
maieste, sovereignty, 931.
make, *inf.* 315, 370; *pr. pl.* 375; *imp. pl.* 350; *pt.* 2 *s.* **made,** 995; 3 *s.* 84; *pl.* 190, 276; *pp.* 112, 172; **maked,** 1022; **made,** appointed, 336, 582.
malady, 28.
mallen, *pr. pl.* thrust, 556; OF. maller.
mametes, idols, 235; OF. mahumet.
man, 101, 145; *pl.* **men,** 124; *g. pl.* **mannes,** 13.
man, crime, 166, ; OE. mān.
manace, *n.* threatening, 375; OF. manace.
maner, kinds of, 284.
manglouns, military engines, 799; *see Note.*
manschyp, humanity, wisdom, 777.
mansed, accursed, 154; *aph.* form of OE. āmānsod.
manye, 43; **mony,** 431.
marble, 620.
marchals, commanders, 882.
marchaundise, 1309.
marchaunt, 44; **marchaunte,** 1306.
marener, mariner, 44.
margeri-perles, 1254; OF. margerie.
market, 1313; market-place, 925.
marr, *inf.* perish, 778; *pt. pl.* **marden,** impaired, 800; **ma[r]den,** 874; **mardyn,** 1100; *pp.* **mar[red],** wounded, 604.
masouns, 1107; *g. pl.* 800.
masers, mace-bearers, soldiers equipped with maces, 882; OF. massier.
masly, massily, 1265.
matere, 1301; **mater,** 1322.
me, *v.* I.
medecyn, 94.
medil, *v.* **myddel.**
mekly, 338.
melys, *pr.* 3 *s.* speaks, 1301; OE. mǣlan.
men, *v.* **man.**
mene, *adj.* mean, intermediate, 1171; *adv.* conjointly, 112; OF. meien, meen.
mened, *pp.* lamented, 179; OE. mǣnan.
mercy, 777, 1240.
mereuail, *n.* marvel, 604.
merke, dark, 1239; ON. myrkr.
merked, *pt. pl.* grew dark, 726; *cp.* ON. myrkva.
merkeþ, *pr.* 3 *s.* places, 1186; *pl.*

merken, set, 799; *pp.* **merked,** allotted, appointed, 431; created, 112; ON. merkja; OE. mearcian.
merueylous-lye, wonderfully, 1254.
meschef, misfortune, 166, 1066; want, 1077; **myschef,** calamity, 917; OF. meschef.
meselry, leprosy, sickness, 166; OF. **mesel,** leprous; Lat. misellus, wretched.
message, 338, 370; *pl.* **messages,** 210.
messengeres, 336.
mete, food, 132, 1066.
mete, *inf.* meet, 551; *pr. pl.* **metyn,** 59; *pt. pl.* **mette,** 925.
metel, metal, 556; *pl.* **metals,** 1265.
metles, deprived of food, 778.
mettyn, *part. adj.* measured, 919; OE. metan.
my, 87, 488.
myche, *adj.* great, 44; *adv.* 145; OE. mycel.
mychel, *adj.* much, 71; OE. mycel.
myd, by, 722; beside, 50.
[mydday], 346.
myddel, midst, 55; middle, 152; **medil,** 1248.
myd-ward, middle, 431.
myȝt, power, 113, 375.
myȝt, *v.* **may.**
myld, 1077; **my[l]de,** 897.
myle, *pl.* miles, 288, 412, 919.
mynde, *n.* 505; memory, 127, 1309.
mynde, *inf.* remember, 919; m. of, 501.
myne, *n.* 1130.
myne, *inf.* 1107, 1186; *pp.* **myned,** 1115.
myneþ, *pr. impers.* we remember, 505 (*see Note*); *pt.* 3 *s.* **mynned,** related, 480; ON. minna.
mynours, 1107.
myracles, 127.
myschef, *v.* **meschef.**
my-self, 966; **my-selue,** 1230.
mo, *adj. pl.* more, 127; OE. mā, *adv.*
m[o]de, mud, 1286.
modir, mother, 897.
[modur nakyd], stark naked, 346.
mody, proud, 1043.
molde, earth, 603, 1277.
m[o]n, *pr.* 3 *s.* must, 294; ON. muɴu.
money, 1306.
mony, *v.* **manye.**
montayns, 726.
monþe, *pl.* months, 917; **monþes,** 927.
mor, *adj. s.* greater, 505; more, additional, 358, 536; *adv.* any more, 300; *sup. adj.* most, greatest, chief, 94; *adv.* **moste,** 275.
mores, *pl.* moors, 726.

moryne, mortality, 1066; 1147; AF. moryn.
morowe, morning, 383.
morter, mortar, 1286.
most(e), v. mor.
mouþe, 338, 391.
mowe, v. may.
mulle, dust, 1286; OE. myl.
multitude, 603.
murdred, pp. 897.

nad(de), v. haue.
nay, 89.
nayled, pt. 3 s. 813.
naked, 361, 939.
nakerers, players on kettle-drums, 1179; g. pl. nakerer, 852; OF. naquere + -er.
name, 47, 187; pl. names, 140.
nas, v. be.
naue, ship, 58; OF. nave.
ne, nor, 40; or, 375 (see Note).
nebbe, face, 176; OE. nebb.
necke, 752.
nedel, needle, 361; nedul, 939.
nediþ, pr. 3 s. is necessary, 501.
neȝ, adv. almost, 1082.
neȝeþ, pr. 3 s. approaches, 528; pl. neȝen, 1179; to neȝe, 521 (see Note); OE. nēah, adv.
nehyng, n. neighing, 421.
nempne, imp. s. name, 187; pp. nempned, 850; ynempned, 161.
neþer, lower, 361.
neþer, neither, 112; see Note; cp. noþer.
neuer, 35, 101 144.
newe, 797; fresh, 176.
newen, inf. renew, 182; OE. nīwian.
next, adj. nearest, 966.
nyckes, pr. 3 s. n. with nay, answers 'no,' 89.
nyȝt, night, 421; g. s. nyȝtes, 261.
nyȝt-tyme, 852.
nyȝt-wacche, 728.
nis, nys, v. be.
no, 23, 39; non, 261.
noble, 26; as. adv. 311.
noȝt, no one, 419; not, 19, 138.
noye, trouble, 27, 47 (see Note), 182, 261; aph. form of OF. anoi.
noyet, pt. 3 s. harassed, 27.
noyse, 852; noyce, 1179.
nold(e), v. wole.
nome, pt. 3 s. went, 49; pl. nomen, took, 191; OE. niman.
non, none, 89; cp. no.
nonbr, number, 454; OF. nonbre.
none, noon, 1239.

nones, for þe n., expressly, 430 (as expletive), 756.
norþ, 58.
nose, 32.
nose-þrylles, nostrils, 1119; OE. nosþyrl.
note, work, 797, 800; at þis n., under these circumstances, 501; OE. notu.
noþer, neither, 489, 1068; OE. nōhwæðer; cp. neþer.
now, 41, 97, 295.

o v. on.
odour, 240.
of, prep. 6, 11, 15; out of, 184, 335, 441, 477; since, 33, 983; by, 31; from, 504; concerning, 356, 402.
of, adv. off, 537, 694, 845, 1123.
of-fleis, pr. 3 s. flays oþ, 988; cp. flein.
of flocken, pt. pl. (?)scribal error for of floghen, tore off, 360; cp. flein; see Note.
offryng-tyme, 1224.
oft, 7, 42.
oȝt, anything, 387.
oyle, 810, 848.
olde, 1071.
o-lepy, single, 579; OE. ān-liepig, -lēpig.
olyfaunt, elephant, 579; pl. olyfauntes, 423, 445; OF. olifant.
on, prep. 8, 13, 21, 49, 397, 565; an, 46, 51; on, in, 12, 29, 55, 945; into, 553; an, in, 347; adv. on, 227, 539, 766(1).
on, one, 67; one, 100; o, 66, 106.
one, adv. alone, 248, 332, 498.
open, 830; v. wide.
or, 86, 95.
or, ere, before, 173, 223, 346, 368, 768; our, 24; ON. ār.
ordeyned, pp. ordered, 848.
orible, terrible, 565.
orisoun, prayer, 848.
ornen, v. runne.
oste, army, 729; ost, 1111.
ost-wyse, army-fashion, 1221.
oþer, adj. other, 42, 68; pl. 345; oþer half wynter, one and a half years, 951.
oþer, or, 75, 95; cp. OE. oððe.
ouȝte, 407; see Note.
our, 98, 505; of us, 1003.
ous, v. we.
out, 37, 45; OE. ūt.
out, in existence, 92; OE. ūte.
out-wale, outcast, 140; ON. val, choice.
outwith, outside, 1111.

Glossary. 123

ouer, *prep.* 42, 50, 51; *adv.* 1267.
ouer-brad, *pp.* overspread, 599; OE. ofer brǣdan.
ouer-lokeþ, *pr.* 3 *s.* peruses, 962.
ouer-sprad, *pp. scribal error for* ouerbrad, spread over, 486.
ouertourned, *pp.* overthrown, 1016, 1289.
ouerwalte, *pt.* 3 *s.* overthrew, 1207; OE. -wæltan.
owen,; *pl. pr.* owe, 968; *pt.* 3 *s.* owede, owned, 217.
owene, *pr.* 1 *s. subj.*; acknowledge, 784.
owne, 518.

paas, passage, chapter, 500; OF. pas.
pay, *inf.* 318.
paynted, *pp.* 329.
pale, palisade, 677, 773; OF. pal.
paled, *pp.* surrounded by a palisade, 329; OF. paler.
paleys, palace, 901; palice, 237; OF. palais.
pallen, made of pall, rich cloth, 322; pal[l]e[n], 743; OE. pællen.
pane, cloth, 1273; OF. pan.
panne, brain-pan, 823; OE. panne.
pardoun, an indulgence, 215.
paren, *inf.* peel, 1327; OF. parer.
p[ar]il[sye], paralysis, 123.
partyis, divisions, quarters, 393.
paske, Passover, 157, 316; OF. pasque.
paske-euene, eve of the Passover, 1211.
passe, *inf.* 680; *pr.* 1 *s.* 352; 3 *s.* passyþ, proceeds, 112; *pt.* 3 *s.* passed, escaped, 318; passed, 215, 236; *pl.* 227; *pp.* 76, 153; *pr.* 3 *s. subj.* passe, 368.
passioun, 500.
paueloun, tent, 329; *pl.* pauelouns, 322.
pauyes, *pl.* shields, 444; OF. pavais.
pauyment, street, 1243.
peces, pecis, *v.* pese.
paynted, *pp.* 163, 1267.
peis, weight, 1263; OF. peis.
pelour, fur, 1273; OF. pelure.
pelours, *v.* pyler.
pendauntes, *g. s.* pendant's, 511.
penyes, *pl.* 318, 1303.
penseles, small pennons, 413; AF. pencel; OF. penoncel.
peple, 435; pople, 230.
pere, pear, 1327; per, 1326.
peryles, *pl.* dangers, 76.
peritotes, chrysolites, 1251; OF. peritot.
perle, 472; *pl.* perles, 759, 1251.

persche, *inf.* perish, 1258; *pp.* persched, torn to pieces, 703.
persched, *pp.* pierced, 1278; persched, 607; ONF. perchier.
persones, *pl.* 106.
pes, peace, 1131.
pesan, a piece of armour protecting the upper part of the chest and neck, 511; OF. pizane, *from* Pisa.
pese, piece, 823; *pl.* peces, 235, 702; pecis, pieces of plate, 1263.
pyble, pebble, 823.
picche, *n.* pitch, 670.
picchen, *pr. pl.* drop, 616; *pt. pl.* piȝten, set, 322; *pp.* piȝt, 393, 464; pyȝt, 9, 413.
piked, *pp.* pointed, 910; OE. pīc, *n.*
pykeyse, pickaxe, 1278; OF. picois.
pile, *coll.* the pointed lower ends of the uprights of the portcullis, 616.
pyler, pillar, 9; *pl.* pileres, 464; pelours, 1265.
pyne, punishment, torment,. 24, 1323; [p]yne, 1096.
pyne, *inf.* torture, 499; *pp.* pyned, 8, 123, 703; OE. pīnian.
pypyng, *n.* 253.
pipis, *pl.* 851; pypys, 525, 1178.
pite, pity, 499; pyte, 1131.
place, 444 (? *scribal error for* palace)_*, 227; in o. p., of one rank, co-equal, 106.
play, joy, pleasure, 253.
[p]l[ay]ande, *pr. p.* boiling, 670.
playn, flat, 9; *adv.* plainly, 163.
plate, 471; *pl.* platis, 1263.
platte, *pt.* 3 *s.* fell flat, 218; OF. plat, *adj.*
plente, plenty, 1261.
plowes, *pl.* ploughs, 1290.
plunge, *inf.* 787.
poynt, 910; jot, 163, 607; *pl.* poyntes, points, 393; opportunities, 779.
poke, bag, 1303; ONF. poque.
pomel, pommel, knob on the hilt, 750; round ornament on the top of a tower, 413; OF. pomel.
ponsone, a pointed tool, 1278; OF. ponçon.
pope, 201, 230.
pople, *v.* peple.
pore, poor, 138, 906.
poreil, poor people, 313; porayle, 901; OF. povraille.
port, 292.
portecolis, portcullis, 616.
postel, apostle, 1303; *cp.* aposteles.
posterne, private door, 906; *as adj.* side, 1157.
postes, *pl.* 648.

powder, 718; pouder, 1280.
prayeþ, pr. 3 s. 859; praieþ, 1019; pt. 3 s. praied, 1153.
preche, inf. 135, 148, 1153; pt. 3 s. preched, 201.
precious, 1258; preciose, 472.
preysed, part. adj. 99.
prelates, chief priests, 157.
pres, n. crowd, 216, 227.
presen, pr. pl. crowd forth, hasten, 890; pt. pl. preset, 444; pressed, 901; presed, in, assailed, 24.
presented, pt. pl. 232.
prestes, priests, 316.
preueþ, pr. 3 s. proves, 500; pp. preued, 99; manifest, 106, OF. prover, preuve.
pokes, dagger's, 910; cp. M.Du poke, MLG. pōk. Not in N.E.D. in this sense.
prime, the first of the canonical hours, 703; pryme, 368.
prince, 3; pl. princes, 24, 148.
printe, picture, 237.
pris, price, 1312; of p., noble, 15.
pris, adj. noble, 607; OF. de pris.
prisoun, 1323.
priuely, 163; see Note.
procession, 216.
proffriþ, pr. 3 s. 1297; profreþ, 1131; pp. profred, 1152.
profre, n. proffer, 1134.
prophecie, imp. s. 15.
prophete, 15, 99, 1312.
prouost, provost, 3, 160.
prudely, proudly, 759.
prute, proud, 138; 1OE. prūt.
psalmys, 474.
pulled, pt. pl. 711.
pulsched, part. adj. polished, 471, 1263.
pur, pure, 750; very, 759.
pured, noble, 472.
purged, part, adj. refined, 750.
putte, inf. 1290; pr. 3 s. putteþ, 743; pl. put, 378; pt. 3 s. 243; putte, 123; pp. put, 8.

quaynte, elaborate, 331.
quarels, square-headed cross-bow bolts, 653; qu[a]rels, 622; OF. quarel.
quar[r]en, pr. pl. hurl, 622; see Note.
quart[ote]s, cross-bows, 622; OF. quartot, not in N.E.D.
quasschyng, n. breaking, 1191; OF. quasser.
quelle, inf. slay, 514, 900; pt. 3 s. quelde, 914; pp. quelled, 894.
querel, complaint, accusation, 503; pl. querels, 497.
quyk, living, 497, 694, 900.

quycke clayme, pr. 1 s. renounce, 497; quik clayme, 503; OF. quiteclamer, -claime.
quyrboyle, cuir-bouilli, softened leather, 11.
quoþ, pt. 3 s. said, 93.
[queþer], however, 503; cp. wheþer.

racches, hunting dogs, 886; OE. ræcc.
racke, storm, 55; cp. ON. reka, to drive; Norw. Swed. dial. rak, wreckage.
radde, v. redeþ.
ragged, 65.
raȝte(n), v. rauȝte.
rayled, pp. adorned, 1250; OF. reiller.
rayn, 12, 532.
raysen, pr. pl. 323.
ran, v. runne.
rapis, pr. 3 s. goes swiftly, 65; pr. p. rapande, 954; ON. hrapa.
rauȝte, pt. 3 s. gave, 1059; pl. 934; rauȝten, 956, 1212; raȝte, dealt, 14; raȝten, reached, caught, 807; OE. rǣcan.
rawe, adj. 702.
rebel, n. 504.
rebies, rubies, 1250; see Note.
recche, pr. 3 s. subj. cares, 782; OE. reccan.
receyue, inf. 993; pt. 3 s. receyued, 226.
rede, n. counsel, resolve, 403.
rede, red, 12; re[d]e, 478.
rede, 55; see Note.
redeþ, pr. 3 s. reads, 500; pl. declare, 960; pt. 3 s. radde, read, 478; pl. redden, 591; pr. 3 s. subj. rede guide, 1334.
redy, ready, 407.
redles, adv. without a doubt, 567; see Note.
redly, straightway, 88; OE. hrædlīce.
regnance, supreme rule, 506; not in N.E.D.
reyned, pt. 3 s. reigned, 169.
[re]ioycid, pt. 3 s. subj. might enjoy, 1136; see Note.
rekene, inf. reckon, 128.
relyk, 260.
renk, man, 606; renke, 839; pl. renkes, 954; ON. rekkr, OE. rinc.
rennande, v. runne.
renten, pt. pl. tore, 702, 1268; rent, 807.
rer, inf. raise, 887; pt. 3 s. rered, 124.
rereward, rear-guard, 562.
resen, v. rise.
resorte, inf. return, 1048.
resoun, 506; a reasonable account, 504.

Glossary. 125

reste, n. 261.
resten, pr. pl. 630; pp. rest, 605.
rest[ing], n. setting, 839.
reuer, river-bank, 887.
reuerence, n. 226.
rewarde, inf. 88.
rewful, lamentable, terrible, 1079.
rewþe, mischief, 899; r[ut]h, distress, 303.
rib, n. 1079.
rybaunde, pp. set round like a ribbon, 758; *this sense not in* N.E.D.
rich, steam, 790; OE. rēc.
riche, rich, noble, 3, 169; adv. 463.
ride, inf. 403, 993; pr. 3 s. rideþ, 562, 580; r[i]deþ, 1109; pt. pl. riden, 1334.
rigge, back, 1079; OE. hrycg.
riȝt, adv. very, 664.
ryng, n. 606; pl. rynges, 766, 1274; ryngys, 1060.
rynge, inf. 407.
rise, inf. result, 401; arise, 913; riseþ, rises, 963; pt. 3 s. roos, 55, 1085; pl. resen, 899; risen, raised, 933.
rispen, pr. pl. break, 567; *see Note*.
r[y]s[t]en, pr. pl. shake out, 727; ON. hrista; *not in* N.E.D.
ryue, abundant, 791; OE. rȳfe.
robbyng, n. rubbing, 277.
roddes, pl. 805.
rode, rood, 8.
rolle, n. 477; pl. rolles, 591.
roof, 1250.
roos, v. rise.
ropis, ropes, 323, 807.
r[o]ppis, entrails, 567; OE. rop.
roryng, n. crying aloud, 303.
rost, n. roast, 1085.
rostyþ, pr. 3 s. roasts, 1079.
rotlyng, n. commotion, 277; cp. MDu., MLG. rotelen.
rounde, adj. 758.
route, troop, 562.
rowe, rough, rugged, 886; OE. rūh, rūg.
runne, pr. pl. 560, 805; pt. 3 s. ran, 12, 478; pl. runnen, (?)407; ornen, 540; pr. p. rennande, 226.
r[ut]h, v. rewþe.

sackes, pl. 806; sakkes, 802.
sacrifice, n. 315.
sadde, resolute, valiant, 815.
sadly, resolutely, 321, 353.
say, inf. 96; seyn, 864; pr. 3 s. seiþ, 488; pl. sayen, 339; pt. 3 s. seide, 79; saide, 86, 196; sayde, 89; pl. 15; imp. pl. sayþ, 345, 365.
say, v. se.

sail, n. 66; sayl, 51.
sake, 300, 935.
sakkes, v. sackes.
sakles, innocent, 7; OE. saclēas.
sale, n. 1137.
salt, n. 1291; adj. [salte], 51.
salue, remedy, 92; OE. sealf.
same, 379.
samen, in s. together, 552; OE. *samen, somen.
saphyres, 760.
satles, pr. 3 s. is reconciled, 1057; pp. satled, be s. on, be turned against, press heavily on, 379, 1216; OE. setlan, *sætlan; cp. sahtlian.
saut, assault, 643, 833; aph. form of OF. asaut.
saue, except, 103, 1035.
sauere, n. smell, 1086.
sauy, inf. safeguard, 972.
saw, v. se.
sawe, speech, 879; request, 1155; pl. sawes, teachings, 135.
sawters, psalters, 474; AF. sauter, OF. sautier.
scaped, pt. 3 s. subj. should escape, 419; aph. form of ONF. escaper.
schacked, v. schoken.
schadewes, pl. 737.
schaftes, lances, 1117.
schal, pr. 1 s. 88, 183; 2 s. schalt, 993; 3 s. schal, 1216; pl. schul, 783, 1094; pt. 3 s. scholde, 69, 1202.
[schalke], man, 1118; OE. scealc.
schame, vpon, s. wyse, shamefully, 372.
schapiþ, pr. 3 s. turns out, 994.
scharpe, adj. 699; adv. 555; n. coll. swords, 278.
scharply, 666; eagerly, 1071.
scheden, pr. pl. divide, 737; OE. scēadan.
schedered, pt. pl. shattered, 558; pp. schedred, 1117; cp. schidwod.
schef, pt. 3 s. thrust, 1329; OE. scūfan.
scheldes, pl. shields, 278.
schende, pp. reproached, 372; OE. scendan.
schene, fair, 100, 666; OE. sciēne, scēne.
scher, pt. 3 s. ran swiftly, 63; OE. sceran.
scherte, shirt, 348; pl. chertys, 1238; OE. scyrte.
schepes, pl. 555.
schewe, inf. 194, 436; speak, 783; pr. pl. scheweþ, appoint, 863 (*see* N.E.D. show vb. 24); pt. 3 s. schewed, decreed, 998; spoke, 341.
schewyng, n. displaying, 278.

schidwod, timber to be split up into planks, etc., 554; OE. scīd.
schillande, *part. adj.* resounding, 527; OE.* sciellan, lWS., scyllan.
schynande, *v.* schonen.
schynyng, *n.* 547.
schip, 63; sschip, 67; *pl.* schippis, 281.
schir, bright, 737; schyr, 672; OE. scīr.
schyueryng, *n. scribal error for* schymeryng, 547.
schodered, 558, *read* schedered.
schoken, *pt. pl.* brandished, 555; *pp.* schacked, gone, 315; OE. scacan.
scholde, *v.* schal.
schonen, *pt. pl.* shone, 412, 1256; *pr. p.* schynande, glowing, 672.
schore, *n.* 63.
schoten, *pr. pl.* shoot, 672; *pt.* 3 *s.* schot, 63; *pl.* schoten, 666; *pp.* [schotte], 1118; yschot, 281.
schoulder, 1084; *pl.* scholdres, 554.
schout, *n.* 527.
schred, *pp.* rigged, 281; OE. scrȳdan.
schrynken, *pr. pl.* 527.
schroud, apparel, 558.
schul, *v.* schal.
scorned, *pp.* 372.
scourgis, *pl.* 10.
se, sea, 42, 56, 288.
se, *inf.* see, 256, 401; *pt.* 1 *s.* sey, 180; 3 *s.* saw, 1045; say, 581; *pl.* sey, 1030; seyen, 899; se[y]en, 763; *pp.* sen, 821; seyn, 1218, 1222; sein, 986.
secunde, 110.
sede, seed, 110.
sege, siege, 321, 335, 418; besieging party, 949, 1110, 1332.
segge, man, 680; OE. secg.
segyþ, *pr.* 3 *s.* besieges, 1063; *aph. form of* OF. asegier.
seide, seyn, seiþ, *v.* say.
seyen, sein, sey(n), *v.* se.
[seygnour], lord, 80.
seint, saint, 218.
seised, *pp.* taken, 833; seysed, in possession, 2.
seke, *inf.* 367; seken, 293 (*see Note*); *pt.* 3 *s.* souȝt, went, 42, 541, 704; *pl.* souȝte, 291; souȝten, sought, 1031; *pp.* souȝt, searched, 1033, 1269; souȝte, explored, 1277; fallen, 1120.
selcouþ, marvellous, 74; selcouþe, 1218; *pl. n.* selcouþes, marvels, 821; OE. seldan + cūþ.
self, *adj.* same, 115, 1035; her s. kynde, their own nature, 1048.
selke, *v.* silk.

selly, marvellously, 806; OE. sellīce.
seluere, silver, 258, 406; OE. seolfor.
sembled, *pt. pl.* assembled, 854; OF. sembler.
semelich, goodly, 981; semeliche, 137; ON. sǿmiligr.
sen, *v.* se.
senatours, 265, 896; *g. pl.* 958.
sende, *inf.* 88, 210; *pr.* 3 *s.* sendeþ, 206; *pt.* 3 *s.* sende, 135; sent, 45, 170; *pp.* 80, 117; sende, 380.
sendel, a rich silken material, 414; OF. cendal.
septre, 945.
serche, *inf.* inquire, 339; *pp.* serched, searched, 1282.
sercle, circle, 420.
sergis, candles, 468; OF. cerge.
seriant, officer, 81; OF. serjant.
serue, *inf.* serve, 517; *pt. pl.* serued, 834; *pp.* deserved, 1056.
sete, seat, 1293.
seten, *v.* sitte.
setlyng, *n.* settlement, 401.
setteþ, *pr.* 3 *s.* 51; *pt.* 3 *s.* sette, 56; *pl.* 321; setten, 301; *pp.* sette, 335, 397; sett, 311, 760.
seuen, seven, 945.
[seuenty], 133.
seueþ, seventh, 143, 1198; OE. seofoþa.
sib, akin, 272, 966; OE. sibb.
syde, 56, 1181; region, 1318; *pl.* sides, sides, 11, 703.
sygne, ensign, 279.
siȝt, sight, 180; syȝt, 74.
sike, sick, 207.
siker, trusty, 342, 434; OE. sicor.
syknesse, 1024; syknes, 35.
silk, *n.* 323; selke, 414, 1275; OE. sioloc, seoloc.
sille, *inf.* sell, 1307; *pt.* 3 *s.* solde, 150; lOE. syllan.
symple, common people, 256.
synful, 170.
synge, *inf.* 473; *pr. p.* syngyng, 1333.
synne, *n.* 7.
synwes, sinews, 1048; synwys, 1024.
sir, 2, 79; sire, lord, 35.
sitte, *inf.* 690; *pr.* 3 *s.* sitteþ, 87; *pt. pl.* seten, 474.
syþ, *conj.* since, 1202; *adv.* suþ, afterwards, 13; also, 334; OE. siþþan. lOE. syþþan.
siþes, scythes, 806.
six, 917; sixe, 420.
sixte, sixth, 143; OE. sixta.
sixtene, 418.
sixty, 1110.
skeweþ, *pr.* 3 *s.* grows dark, 53; *cp.*

Glossary. 127

skew, *n.* sky, cloud; Corn. dial. skew, a drizzling rain, a driving mist.
skyes, clouds, skies, 532, 725.
slepiþ, *pr.* 3 *s.* 734.
slynge, 1231.
slowe, *pt.* 3 *s.* slew, 151; *pl.* slowen, 18, 268; slow, 710.
smel, *n.* 1085.
so, 30, 59.
soferayn, supreme, 986.
softe, *inf.* alleviate, 87.
softyng, *n.* allayment, 92.
solas, pleasure, 889.
solde, *v.* sille.
som, some, 1091; *pl.* somme, 711.
somme, sum; by s., in all, 418.
sommere-tyme, 704.
sonder, in s., asunder, 807.
sondes-man, messenger, 193; sondisman, 80; *pl.* sondismen, 342, 353; OE. sand, sond.
sone, son, 41, 110.
sone, *adv.* straightway, 56, 85, 999; soon, 156; *as adj.* early in time, 115.
sonne, sun, 384.
soper, supper, 256, 849.
sore, *n.* 87; *pl.* sores, 40.
sore, *adj.* 541; *comp.* sorer, 35; *adv.* sore, 844.
sory, wretched, 1216.
sorow, *n.* 151, 710; sorowe, 182.
soþe, truth, 206.
soudeynly, suddenly, 1024.
soudiours, soldiers, 430, 996; soudeours, 291.
souȝt(e)(n), *v.* seke.
soule, 520.
sour, bitterly, 1216.
souþ, 56.
sow, *inf.* 1291.
sowe, a siege-engine, 1206; OE. sugu; *see Note.*
space, time, 22.
spakly, quickly, 553; *comp.* spakloker, 784; ON. spakliga.
spar, *inf.* spare, refrain, 637.
speche, 377, 488, 964.
spedde, *pt.* 3 *s.* availed, 22.
speke, *inf.* 784; specke, 860; *pr.* 3 *s.* spekeþ, 911; *pl.* 970.
speres, 553, 566; spearmen, 1110.
spilide, *pt. pl.* slew, 22; *pp.* spilt, 637.
spoyle, *inf.* despoil, 637.
sponnen, *pt. pl.* sp. out, sent forth a stream (of missiles), 837.
sprad, *pp. scribal error for* brad, spread, 405; OE. brǣdan.
sprynges, *pr.* 3 *s.* takes its origin, 102; *pt. pl.* sprongyn, sprang, 408; *pp.* spr[o]ngen, dawned, 853.
spryngoldes, missiles thrown by catapults, 837; AF. springalde.
sprotes, splinters, 553; OE. sprota.
stadded, *pt. pl.* placed, 588; *cp.* ON. steðja, staddr.
staf, 915; *pl.* stauys, 359.
staf-[slyng], a sling the cords or strings of which are attached to the end of a staff, 826.
stage, platform, 332.
stalwourþe, strong, 1292; OE. stǣlwierþe, -wyrþe.
stampen, *pr. pl.* 522.
standard, 588; erection serving as head-quarters, 385.
standeþ, *v.* stonde.
stap, *inf.* step, 601; OE. stæppan.
st[a]rke, strong, 70.
stauys, *v.* staf.
stede, place, 223, 332; stonde in s. be of use, 1100.
stedis, horses, 421, 522; stedes, 572; (?)*g. pl.* stede, 1124.
steem, exhalation, 683; OE. stēam.
stele, steel, 422, 453; steil, 522; steel gere, weapons of war, 1196.
st[erynne]s, sternness, 516.
stertis, *pr. pl.* st. on st[r]ay, straggle out, 780.
steuenes, voices, 738; OE. stefn.
steweþ, *pr.* 3 *s.* restrains, 841; ?OE. *steowan, WG. *stawwjan; *cp.* MLG. stöuwen, stauwen.
stif, strong, 522, 761; styf, 13.
stynk, *n.* 683; stynke, 1242.
stynkande, *part. adj.* 687.
stynt, *inf.* cease, 874; stynte, 223; *pr.* 3 *s.* stynteþ, 841; OE. styntan.
stire, *inf.* stimulate, incite, 182; OE. styrian.
stiropys, *pl.* 523.
stipe, strong, 523; OE. stīþ.
stockes, logs, 687.
stode, *v.* stonde.
stof, stuff, 284.
stoked, *pt. pl.* stuck, placed, 13; *pp.* covered, filled, 330; stoken, imprisoned, 1132; *cp.* OE. stician.
stole, stool, 13.
stompe, stump, trunk, 1124.
ston, stone, 352, 530; *pl.* stones, 780; jewels, 472.
stonde, *inf.* stand, 352; *pr.* 3 *s.* standeþ, 578; *pt.* 3 *s.* stode, 223, 588; *pr. p.* stondyng, 332; stond-[y]n[g], 1015.
stoppe, *inf.* 1130; *pr. pl.* stoppen, 686, 847.
store, *n.* 284; stor, 874, 1100.

storyj, history, 826; *pl.* **storijs**, 475; paintings representing historical stories, 330.
stormes, *pl.* 70.
storte-blynde, stark blind, 575; *cp.* start-naked, *from* OE. steort.
stounde, short time, 37; OE. stund.
stour, battle, 516, 841; AF. estur, OF. estour.
stour, *adj.* stern, 385, 1180; OE. stŏr.
st[r]ay, *v.* stertis.
strayned, *pp.* scribal error for **stayned**, painted, 330; *see Note.*
str[ande], current, 686; *northern variant of* eME. strŭnde.
streem, 686; *pl.* **stremys**, currents, waters, 1021.
streʒt, *adv.* straight, 915.
streyʒt, *pt.* 3 *s.* erected, 385; OE. streccan.
strengþ, 516; **streyngþe**, 287.
strengþe, *inf.* strengthen, 284.
strete, street, 12; **stret**, 1242.
strideþ, *pr.* 3 *s.* 761; *pl.* **striden**, 523.
strif, warfare, 874.
strike, *inf.* 310, 683; *pr.* 3 *s.* **strikeþ**, 823; goes, 761.
strogelyng, *n.* polishing, 422; *see Note.*
stroyed, *pp.* destroyed, 274; *aph. form of* OF. destruire.
stroke, *n.* 803.
stronge, 677.
stuffyng, *verb. n.* lining, 422.
suche, 172.
stuny, *inf.* stun, 870; *aph. form of* astony, OF. estoner.
sundrede, *part. adj.* sundry, 1222; OE. sundrian.
surgyan, surgeon, 1035; AF. surgien, OF. cirurgien.
suþ, *v.* syþ.
suwed, *pt. pl.* 133, 137.
swallen, *pt. pl.* swelled, 1145; OE. swellan.
swalten, *v.* swelt.
swar, word, 536; OE. -swaru.
swart, black, 1145.
swelt, *inf.* die, 536; *pt. pl.* **swalten**, 1172; OE. sweltan.
swelwe, *inf.* swallow, 390; OE. swelgan.
swem, *n.* swoon, 528; ON. svimi.
sweng, *n.* fighting, 317, 1172; OE. sweng.
swer, neck, 363; OE. swēora.
swer, *inf.* swear, 1005.
swerd, sword, 317, 1172.
swetter, sweeter, 240; OE. swētra, swettra.
swykel, crafty, 317.
swyn, *pl.* swine, 1145.

swyþe, quickly, forthwith, 227, 323, 570; OE. swīðe.
swowande, *pr. p.* swooning, 536; OE. geswōgen, *pp.*
tabernacle, 463.
tabourris, drums, 526.
tachen, *pr. pl.* make attack, 655; *aph. form of* OF. atachier.
tail, *n.* 437; **taille**, 398.
taysen, *pr. pl.* aim, 655; OF. teser, teise.
take, *inf.* 118, 266; **taken**, 1176; *pr.* 1 *s.* take, grant, 220; *pt.* 3 *s.* toke, took, 429, 907; *pl.* token, 77, 305; *pp.* take, 403, 1023; tak, 861.
takled, *pp.* equipped, 282.
tale, 355, 913; telling, 863, 988; without t. mor, without more ado, 358, 1116.
talkyng, *n.* 865.
tal-sail, (?)tall, big sail, 289.
talterande, *part. adj.* rolling, 282; OE. tealtrian; *not in* N.E.D.
tarie, *inf.* 1001; *pr.* 3 *s.* **tarieþ**, 1249; *pt.* 3 *s.* taried, 21.
teldes, dwellings, 305; OE. teld.
telle, *inf.* 48, 178; *pr. pl.* **tellen**, 108; *imp. s.* telle, 93; *pl.* **telliþ**, 368; *pt. pl.* tolde, recited, 474.
temple, 234, 832.
ten, 122, 146.
tene, *n.* trouble, 736; OE. tēona.
tenful, troublous, difficult, 234, 868; harassing, 410; **tenfulle**, 213.
tente, 333, 689; *pl.* **tentis**, 324, 437.
teris, *pl.* tears, 226.
teþ, teeth, 909.
[**thurghe**], *v.* þrow.
tide, tide, 289.
tyde, *inf.* befall, 93; *pr.* 3 *s.* **tydiþ**, 1003; tides, 862, *pt.* 3 *s.* **tydde**, 25; *pp.* tid, 374.
tydyng, news, 1023.
tyen, *pr. pl.* go, turn, 843, 1158, 1178; **tyeþ**, drag, 619; OE. tēon; *see Note.*
tyʒten, *pt. pl.* hoisted, 289; OE. tyhtan.
til, 12, 25; **title**, 120, 540.
tilte, *pt.* 3 *s.* fell, 832.
tymbr, material for building, 1287; *see Note.*
tymbris, timbrels, 526; OF. timbre.
tyme, 1, 21.
[**tynt**], *pp.* lost, 262; ON. tȳna.
tyre, attire, 376; *aph. form of* OF. atirer, *vb.*
tyt, quickly, 93; **tit**, 355; as **tyt**, as quickly as possible, 630, 1177; ON. titt.

Glossary. 129

to, *prep.* 20, 24; *adv.* forward, 537, 613; [to], 1006.
to-brestep, *pr.* 3 *s.* breaks asunder, 66; *pt.* 3 *s.* to-breste, 152; ON. bresta.
to-brused, *pp.* mangled, 722; OE. to-brȳsan.
to-cleuen, *pr. pl.* split asunder, 554; *pt.* 3 *s.* to-clef, 916; OE. to-clēofan.
to-crased, *pt. pl.* broke to pieces, 236; *aph. form of* OF. acraser.
to-day, 505, 517.
to-drawe, *pp.* drawn asunder, 695.
to-gedr, 557.
to-gedres, 30, 106, 921; to-gedris, 529.
toggep, *pr.* 3 *s.* pulls, 909.
to-hewen, *pp.* hewn to pieces, 1004.
toke(n), *v.* take.
tokne, token, 185, 723.
tolde, *v.* telle.
tolles, *pr.* 3 *s.* t. of, brings down, 537; OE. *tollian; *cp.* AF. toller, to carry off.
to morow, 346; to morowe, 368.
to-mortled, *pt. pl.* crumbled, 235; *cp.* ME. mirtlen, WM. to-murten, LG. murten.
ton, toes, 840.
tonelande, *pr. p.* thundering, 526; OF. tonniller; *not in* N.E.D.
tonge, tongue, 1270; language, 77.
tonnes, casks, chests, 619; OE. tunne.
topsail, upside down, 706.
[tor], difficult, tedious, 1065; ON. OE. tor.
torche-liȝt, 846.
toret, little tower, 312, 456; *pl.* torettes, 333.
tor[tere], difficulty, 862; ON. torfæri.
torke[is], Turkish, 324.
tormented, *pt. pl.* 1320; *pp.* tourmented, 706.
torn[ei]en, *pr. pl.* take part in tournaments, 891.
touche, *n.* (?) *scribal error for* trothe, 105.
touche, *pt pl.* speak, 1101; *pt.* 3 *s.* touched, touched, 101, 224; *pp.* 105.
toun, 305, 312; *pl.* tounnes, 294.
tour, tower, 305, 451; *pl.* tourres, 619.
toured, *adj.* towered, 868.
toured, *pp.* (?) surrounded, 333; *aph. form of* OF. atourer; *not in* N.E.D.
tourmented, *v.* tormented.
tourne, *inf.* 21, 398; *pr.* 3 *s.* tournep, 537, 581; *pt.* 3 *s.* tourned, converted, 203; *pp.* stripped, 376.
tourres, mountainous waves, 65; (?)O. Welsh twrr, a heap, pile.
toward, *prep.* 49, 64, 454.

SIEGE OF JERUSALEM.

towe, tough; wonder, t. made, made great difficulties, 355; OE. tōh, tōg.
trayled, *pt.* 3 *s.* 398.
traytours, 1213.
trauail, *n.* labour, 270.
tre, wood, 456, 907, 1287; cross, 706.
trey, trouble, 723; OE. trega.
trenchour, knife, 1328.
tresoun, treachery, 723.
tresour, treasure, 1012, 1259.
trete, treaty, 402; OF. trait.
trete, *inf.* treat, 502, 1101.
treup, loyalty, 1012.
trewe, truce, 502, 1101; *pl.* (*with sg. meaning*) trewes, 402; (?)safe-conduct, 212, 213; OE. trēow.
trewe, true, 1.
tribute, *n.* 48, 213, 502.
triffiyn, *pr. pl.* dally, 891.
trinyte, 105, 187.
triste, *pr.* 1 *s.* trust, 967; 3 *s.* tristip, 882; *pl.* tristen, 515. (?)OE. *trȳsta (*cp.* Björkmann, *Scand. Loan-Words,* p. 285).
trompen, *pr. pl.*, tr. vp., call up by a trumpet, 1332.
trompis, *pl.* trumpets, 1178.
tronchoun, staff, 907.
trossen, *pr. pl.* truss, pack, 1332; OF. trusser.
trowe, *pr.* 1 *s.* believe, 1203; OE. trēowan, trūwian.
twey, two, 133, 269, 701; OE. twēgen.
twelf, 369; twelfe, 467; twelue, 132, 137.
twenti, 445.
twynne, *v.* a-twynne.
two, 130.
þan, than, 35.
þanked, *v.* þonkeþ.
þanne, in addition, 333.
þat, *rel. pr.* 7, 22, 24, 47; him that, 782; those that, 555; that which, 568.
þat, *dem. adj.* 3; þat on, the one, 67, 269; þat oþer, the other, 68; *pl.* þo, 267; *pron.* 97.
þat, *conj.* 6; so that, 398, 939.
þe, the, 1.
þe, *v.* þou.
þey, they, 15, 48; hy, 136, 1295; *dat. acc.* hem, 20, 24, 183.
þey, *v.* þoȝ.
þeyes, thighs, 700; OE. þēoh.
þen, then, 695.
þenke, *v.* þynkeþ.
þer, there, 39; where, 90.
þer a-boute, around it, 398.
þer-aȝens, towards them, 215.
þer-by, 467.
þer fro, therefrom, 239.

K

130   Glossary.

þer-yn, 715.
þer myd, in addition, 188.
þer of, 205 ; of which, 393.
þer-ouer, 746.
þer to, 10.
þy, 171, 1054.
þicke, adj. crowded, dense, 449, 532;
    þykke, 320 ; adv. þicke, densely,
    abundantly, 597, 744, 1253 ; þycke,
    1075.
þinges, pl. 427 ; þynges, 234.
þynkeþ, pr. 3 s. thinks, 736 ; pl.
    þenke, expect, 1102.
þis, 35 ; pl. 39, 140, 173, 380.
þy-self, 379.
þo, then, 449 ; OE. þā.
þo, v. þat.
þoȝ, though, 1195 ; þou, 592 ; þey,
    7, 22 ; OE. þēah, ON. *þōh, *þoh.
þoȝt, pt. it seemed, 74 ; þouȝte, 592.
þoled, pt. 3 s. suffered, 35, 1302 ;
    þolede, 38 ; OE. þolian.
þonder, thunder, 532.
þonkeþ, pr. 3 s. thanks, 1051, 1209 ;
    pt. 3 s. þanked, 195.
þornen, g. pl. of thorns, 17.
þou, thou, 15, 86 ; dat. acc. þe, 16, 88, 93.
þou, v. þoȝ.
þouȝte, v. þoȝt.
þousand, 129, 418.
þrange, strait, 17 ; ON. þrǫngr.
þraste, pp. thrust, 17 ; OE. þrǣstan.
þre, three, 106, 931.
þrewen, pt. pl. shot, 820 ; ?pp. þrow
    yn, intertwined, 70 ; OE. þrāwan.
þridde, third, 111, 433 ; OE. þridda.
þrye, thrice, 250 ; OE. þrīga.
þries, thrice, 187.
þrylled, pt. pl. fell through, 831 ;
    pp. yþrelled, pierced, 1117 ; OE.
    þyrlian.
þritly, thirty, 1303 ; þrytty, 1316 ; OE.
    þritig.
þryuande, part. adj. excellent, 433.
þrom, crowd, 1316 ; cp. OE. þrymm.
þrongen, pp. squeezed together, 1316 ;
    OE. þringan.
þrow, through, 8, 99, 484 ; þroȝ, 236 ;
    [thurghe], 1118.
þrow yn, v. þrewen.
þrowolande, pr. p. jostling, 532 ; see
    Note.
þus, 376.

vmbe, prep. about, 65, 631 ; adv. 329 ;
    OE. ymbe, ON. umb.
vmbe-casten, pt. pl. surrounded, 18.
vmbe-feldes, pr. 3 s. surrounds, 1127 ;
    pt. 3 s. vmbe-felde, embraced, 219 ;
    OE. fealdan.

vnarmen, pr. pl. 630.
[vn]arwely, swiftly, 654 ; OE. unearg-
    līc, adj.
vnbaptized, pp. 155.
vnbuxum, unwilling, 365.
vnclene, 30.
vnclosed, pt. 3 s. 224.
vncouþ, unknown, 64.
vnder, prep. 3, 61, 522.
vndertoke, pt. pl. 270.
vnfonded, untried, 618 ; OE. fandian.
vn[ȝ]et, unyielded, 1169 ; OE. gēatan.
vnhende, rude, 1198 ; OE. gehende.
vnknowen, 119.
vnlappeþ, pr. 3 s. unfolds, 961.
vnlele, disloyal, 149 ; OF. leel.
vnmarred, 101.
vn-meke, cruel, 28.
vn-mete, huge, 799 ; OE. unmǣte.
vnmyȝty, powerless, 1161.
vn-mylt, harsh, 556 ; OE. unmilde.
vnpersched, undestroyed, 76.
vnquemed, pp. troubled, 900 ; OE.
    cwēman.
vnradly, scribal error for vnrydely,
    violently, 65 ; OE. ungerȳde.
[vnrevyn], unwounded, 606 ; ON. rīfa.
vn-take, untaken, 1013.
vp, adv. 57, 1237 ; vppe, at hand, 295.
vpon, prep. 9, 86 ; in, 33, 265 ; along-
    side, 63.
vs, v. we.
vseþ, pr. 3 s. uses, 94.
vs-selue, ourselves, 872.

vale, 426.
veil, 162 ; vail, 231, 259 ; vaile, 249.
veynys, veins, 20 ; vaynes, 1047.
vengaunce, 1233 ; veniaunce, 1324.
venge, inf. avenge, 20, 184 ; vengen, 937.
veronycle, vernicle, 257 ; OF. veronicle.
vessel, coll. vessels, 1263.
vile, 1098, 1324.
vyleny, wickedness, 20.
visage, 162.
viser, visor, moveable front part of the
    helmet, 756.
vitelys, victuals, 1098.
voiden, inf. remove, 1098.
voys, voice, 1226.
vouched, pt. 3 s. affirmed, 1151.

wacche, n. 631, 884 ; wecche, 382 ;
    OE. wæcce.
way, 49 ; wey, 337 ; pl. w[a]yes, 1105.
waytes, watchmen, 728.
waiteþ, pr. 3 s. looks, searchingly, 857 ;
    pl. wayten, 1257 ; keep watch, 891 ;
    waytes, watch, 779 ; imp. pl. wayteþ,
    769.

Glossary. 131

wakened, *pt.* 3 *s.* was stirred up, 1075.
wale, noble, 1021 ; ON. val, *n.* choice.
wale[þ], *pr.* 3 *s.* chooses, 1276; *pp.*
waled, 884 ; *cp.* ON. velja.
walle, 382 ; **wal,** 1105 ; *pl.* **wallis,** 486 ;
    walles, 351, 419.
walten, *inf.* hurl, 351 ; **walte,** be
    overturned, 69 ; *pt. pl.* **walten,** threw
    themselves, 709 ; threw, 1149 ; *pp.*
    thrown down, 830 ; turned 706 ;
    OE. gewæltan, *wk.* ; *wealtan, *st.*
    (OHG. walzen), *pp.* gewælteno.
waltreþ, *pr.* 3 *s.* tosses about, 735 ; *freq.
    of* **walten.**
walwyþ, *pr.* 3 *s.* rolls about, 735 ; *pr.
    p.* **wal[w]ynde,** swinging, 465 ; OE.
    wealwian.
wanned, *pt.* 3 *s.* grew dark, 53.
wanteþ, *pr.* 3 *s.* is lacking, 163 ; *pt.* 3 *s.*
    w[ant]ed, 628 ; **wanted,** 1244;
    lacked, 1272.
wappe, blow ; **at [a] w.,** all at once,
    1283 ; **wap,** 514 ; blast, 408 ;
    derivation unknown.
war, aware, 205, 217, 801 ; OE. wær.
ward, n. watch, 419 ; defence, 1214.
warded, *pt.* 3 *s.* guarded, 1325.
wariande, *pr. p.* cursing, 673 ; OE.
    wiergan, wærgan.
waried, *v.* **werry.**
warned, *pt.* 3 *s.* 382.
warpiþ, *pr.* 3 *s.* utters, 779 ; *pt.* 3 *s.*
    warpe, (?)took away, 225 ; OE.
    weorpan, *cp.* ON. varpa, *wk.*
warwolues, war wolves', 1174 ; *see
    Note.*
was, *v.* **be.**
waschen, *pr. pl.* 847.
waspys, 205, 251 ; *g. pl.* **waspen,** 32 ;
    waspene, 34.
wasschyng, *n.* 791.
wast, destruction, 1283.
water, 51, 53 ; *pl.* **wa[ters],** 478.
waterles, deprived of water, 771.
water-waschen, *pp.* washed with water,
    788.
wawes, waves, 69 ; OE. wagian, *vb.*
we, 365 ; *dat. acc.* **vs,** 108, 367, 496 ;
    ous, 1334.
webbes, fabrics, 322.
wecche, *v.* **wacche.**
wede, garment, cloth, 217 ; apparel,
    422.
wede, *p. pl. subj.* go mad, 771 ; *pr. p.*
    wedande, raging, 381.
wedour, adverse state of the atmosphere, 59, 62 ; OE. weder.
wey, *v.* **way.**
weyke, weak, 1099 ; ON. veikr.
wel, *v.* **goode,**

weldeþ, *pr. pl.* possess, 1011 ; OE.
    -wieldan, -weldan.
wele, prosperity, 1011 ; wealth, 1276.
wem, injury, 628 ; **[weme],** 876 ; OE.
    wemman, *vb.*
wemlese, spotless, 197.
wemmyd, *pp.* blemished, 176.
wende, *inf.* go, 229, 267 ; *pr.* 3 *s.*
    wendeþ, 1195 ; turns, 781 ; *pt.* 3 *s.*
    wende, went, 69 ; *pl.* **wenten,** 251 ;
    pp. **went,** 918.
wenen, *pr. pl.* think, 514 ; *pt. pl.*
    wenden, 791.
wenes, waggons, 1002 ; OE. wægen,
    wæn.
wepe, *inf.* 221 ; *pr. p.* **wepande,** 1018.
wepyng, *n.* 247.
wepne, *coll.* weapons, 386, 457.
wer, *inf.* wear, 1273 ; *pt.* 3 *s.* **wered,**
    1204 ; OE. werian.
wer(en), *v.* **be.**
wery, weary. 844.
werian, *pr. pl.* defend, 669 ; OE.
    werian.
werk, *n.* work, 844 ; **werke,** 986, 12957 ;
    worke, 178, 676 ; *pl.* **werkes,** 158.
werr, war, 394, 538.
werreþ, *pr.* 3 *s.* makes war, 950 ;
    pt. 3 *s.* **werred,** 190, 399 ; *pl.* 856.
werry, *inf.* make war, 918 ; *pt.* 3 *s.*
    waried, 1076 ; OF. werreier.
west, 1226.
wete, *n.* wet, 787.
wexe, *pt.* 3 *s.* became, 1306 ; **wexed,**
    241 ; **woxe,** 1029 ; *pl.* **wexen,** 575,
    1145 ; **woxen,** 559 ; OE. weaxan.
whan, when, 6.
what, *rel. pron.* 134 ; *adj.* 94 ; whatever, 1040.
wheþer, *conj.* 95 ; *cp.* **[qweþer].**
which, chest, ark, 465 ; OE. hwicce.
whiche, *adj.* 16.
why, 171.
whiȝt, man, 348 ; OE. wiht.
whyȝtly, *v.* **wyȝtly.**
whyle, *n.* time, 261 ; *adv.* formerly, 27 ;
    conj. while, 3 ; **while,** 98.
whyppes, *pl.* 11.
white, 11, 348, 465.
who, *rel. pron.* 266, *dat. acc.* **whom,** 197.
who so, whoever, if anyone, 458, 500.
wicked, dangerous, 664.
wide, *adj.* 642, 649 ; *adv.* **wyde,** 390 ;
    wide open, lying at full length, 830.
wye, man, 204, 628 ; *pl.* **wyes,** 269,
    341 ; OE. wiga.
wyes, *scribal error for* **wayes,** 213.
wif, wife, 897 ; woman, 91 ; **wyf,** 1077.
wy[ght]e, strong, 1076 ; ON. vīgt,
    neut.

Glossary

wy3tly, bravely, 1195 ; why3tly, 617.
wilde, 69.
wile, stratagem, 793 ; wyle, 786 ; *pl.*
 wyles, 664, 669.
wille, *n.* 339.
willeþ, *v.* wole.
wilneþ, *pr.* 3 *s.* desires, 503 ; *pt.* 3 *s.*
 wylned, 1041 ; OE. wilnian.
wymmen, *v.* womman.
wynde, 55, 408, 717 ; *pl.* wyndes, 70 ;
 wyndis, 1226.
wyndiþ, *pr.* 3 *s.* turns, 735 ; *pp.*
 wounden, hoisted by a windlass, 283.
wyne, 121 ; wyn, 283, 847.
wynges, *pl.* 405.
wynne, *inf.* 404, 688 ; *pr. pl.* 771 ;
 wynnen, go, 617 ; wy[nn]en, 612 ;
 pt. pl. wonnen, won, 306 ; *pp.* 396 ;
 wonne, come, 173.
wynter, *pl.* years, 23, 951.
wyrche, *inf.* work, make, 183, 1155 ;
 wirche, 871 ; worche, 980 ; worchyn,
 1105 ; *pr. pl.* worchen, 996 ; *pt.* 1 *s.*
 wro3t, 178 ; 3 *s.* 120, 121 ; *pl.* 24,
 47 ; *pp.* 649 ; wro3te, 327 ; ywro3t,
 462.
wyse, manner, 385.
wite, *inf.* know, 458 ; *pt.* 3 *s.* wist,
 1132.
wyten, *pr. pl.* impute to, 1234.
with, 10, 13 ; in, 52 ; with þanne, by
 then, 1137.
with-drowen, *pt. pl.* withdrew, 625.
with-yn, *prep.* 301 ; with-ynne, 612.
without, *prep.* 103, 175 ; besides, 443.
withtake, *inf.* keep back, 48.
witt, wisdom, 980.
wlonfulle, ? = wlonkfulle, proud, 394.
[w]lonk, proud, 294 ; OE. wlanc, wlonc.
wo, *n.* 120, 247.
wode, mad, 381, 781, ; OE. wōd.
woke, weak, 1076 ; OE. wāc.
woke-tyme, space of a week, 1281 ;
 OE. wucu.
wolco[n], sky, 53 ; OE. wolcen.
wole, *pr.* 1 *s.* will, 97 ; wol, 1001 ;

pl. 782 ; wolle, desire, 632 ; willeþ,
 377 ; *pt.* 1 *s.* wolde, 965 ; 2 *s.* 1054 ;
 3 *s.* 71 ; required, 5 ; *pl.* would, 48,
 340 ; *pt. pl. subj.* 21, 54, 68. *Neg.
 forms* : *pt.* 1 *s.* nold, 1013 ; 3 *s.*
 1106, 1142 ; nolde, 144.
wolle, wool, 787, 847.
wolues, wolves, 1075.
wombe-fille, bellyfull ; alle his w.,
 without restraint, 1076 ; *cp.* ON.
 handfyllr.
womman, 91, 217 ; *pl.* wymmen, 830.
wonder, *adj.* marvellous, 458, 786 ;
 adv. 355, 677.
wonderlich, *adv.* marvellously, 649, 811.
wondres, *pl.* marvels, 120, 204.
wone, place, 792, 869, 1230 ; ON. vān.
wonne(n), *v.* wynne.
wope, weeping, tears, 1070 ; OE. wōp.
worche(n), worchyn, *v.* wyrche.
word, 121, 341 ; *pl.* wordes, 173.
worke, *v.* werk.
world, 114 ; worlde, 140.
worldly, earthly, 1230.
worlich, honourable, 91 ; worliche,
 161 ; OE. weorðlic.
worschip, *n.* honour, 980 ; worschup,
 982.
wors, 866 ; *sup.* worst, 869.
worþe, *inf.* be, become, 62, 950 ;
 pr. 3 *s. subj.* 770 ; worþ, 1227 ; OE.
 weorðan.
worþy, *adj.* 178, 197 ; worþi, 1089.
wounde, *n.* 816 ; *pl.* woundes, 493 ;
 woundis, 246.
wounded, *pp.* 165, 811, 844.
wounden, *v.* wyndiþ.
woxe(n), *v.* wexe.
wrake, destruction, 581 ; OE. wracu.
wrecche, wretch, 170, 869 ; *pl.*
 wrecchys, 298.
wrecken, avenge, 816 ; OE. wrecan.
wri3tes, workmen, 677.
wryngyng, *n.* 247.
wro3t(e), *v.* wyrche.
wroþe, angry, 371 ; wroþ, 381.

INDEX OF PROPER NAMES

Andreu, 147.
Barnabe, 155.
Bertholomewe, 144.
Bethleem, 100, 198, 297.
Burdewes, *g. s.* 72, 192.
Cayphers, 356, 470, 477, 580, 690, 715, 721; *g. s.* Cayphases, 700.
Cesar, 170; Sesar, 2, 7; *g. s.* Cesaris, 293.
Crist, 6, 90, 153, *etc.*; *g. s.* Cristes, 224.
David, 475.
Domycian, 1125, 1182; Domyssian, 990.
Gabba, Galba, 922, 929.
Galace, Galatia, 37.
Galile, 6.
Gascoyne, 26.
Gyan, Guienne, 26.
Grec[e], 41.
Grekys, *adj.* Greek, 50.
Ʒewen, *read* Jewen.
Herodes, 5.
Jacob, St. James the Less, 141.
Jaf, Jaffa, 292.
Jame, St. James the Less, 1235.
James, St. James the Greater, 141.
Ierico, 298.
Jerusalem, 298, 309, 320, 1228.
Jesu, *g. s.* 300.
Jesu Crist, 150, 349, 350, 427.
Jewe, 300, 476; *pl.* Jewes, 46, 150, 309, *etc.*; Jewys, 266; *g. pl.* Jewen, 4, 82, 1228.
Jon, St. John the Apostle, 141.
Jon, John of Gischala, 1133, 1155.
Joseph, 476.
Josophat, 427.
Josophus, 309, 786, 801, 809, 1035, 1053, 1059, 1153, 1321.
Judas, 150.
Judas, Judas Maccabeus, 476.
Judeus, *g. s.* Judæa's, 4; Judeis, 292.
Marie, 1077.
Mathie, Matthias, 154.
Mathu, 145.
Moyses, *g. s.* 480, 582.

Nathan, 49, 61, 89, 97, 187, 208, 262; N[a]than, 41; *g. s.* Nathannys, 58.
Neymes, *g. s.* Naum's 41, 208.
Nero, 47, 49, 80, 182, 208, 261, 501, 893; *g. s.* Neroes, 27.
Othis, Otho, 926, 930.
Othis L[ucy]us, 923; *see p.* xxi.
Peter, 141, 201, 218, 232; Petr, 895; *g. s.* Petrus, 148.
Pharao, 479.
Phelip, 142.
Pylat, 3, 8; Pilat, 160, 172, 1296, 1297, 1323.
Poule, Paul, 155, 895.
Prouynce, Provence, 435.
Romayns, 403, 605, 790, 805, 899, 1257, 1268; Romaynes, 260.
Rome, 2, 25, 36, 45, *etc.*
Sabyn, Sabinus of Syria, 434, 561, 967, 971, 981, 999, 1181, 1193, 1197, 1200.
Sabyns, *g. s.* of Sabinus, brother of Vespasian, 935, 940.
Sathanas, 932.
Senek, Seneca, 896.
Sensteus, Cestius, 45, 81.
Sesar, *v.* Cesar.
Symond, Simon Zelotes, 143.
Symond, Simon son of Gioras, 1134, 1156.
Syon, 311; S[yon], 295.
Surrie, Syria, 301, 434, 938, 967, 971; Surrye, 1181; Surye, 45; Surre, 79; Suree, 293.
Tadde, Thaddeus, 146.
Tyberyus, *g. s.* 1.
Tybre, 944.
Titus, 77, 93, 185, *etc.*; Tytus, 25, 594, 989, *etc.*
Tomas, 146.
Veronyk, 162, 231, 257, 259.
Vitel, Vitellius, 934, 937.
Viterbe, 1324.
Waspasian, Vespasian, 34, 205, 231, 257, *etc.*

The manufacturer's authorised representative in the EU for product safety is Oxford University Press España S.A. of El Parque Empresarial San Fernando de Henares, Avenida de Castilla, 2 - 28830 Madrid (www.oup.es/en or product.safety@oup.com). OUP España S.A. also acts as importer into Spain of products made by the manufacturer.
Printed and bound by CPI Group (UK) Ltd, Croydon, CR0 4YY

22/04/2026

02094916-0009